THE SMALL GROUP

HOWARD L. NIXON II
The University of Vermont

THE SMALL GROUP

Prentice-Hall, Inc., Englewood Cliffs, New Jersey 07632

Library of Congress Cataloging in Publication Data

Nixon, Howard L.
    The small group.

    Bibliography.
    Includes index.
    1. Small groups.   2. Social groups.
3. Sociology.   I. Title.
HM133.N58   301.18'5   78-13207
ISBN 0-13-814244-0

Prentice-Hall Series in Sociology
Neil J. Smelser, Editor

©1979 by Prentice-Hall, Inc., Englewood Cliffs, N.J. 07632

Editorial/production supervision and interior design: Jeanne Hoeting
Cover design: Richard LoMonaco
Manufacturing buyer: Nancy Myers

Printed in the United States of America

10 9 8 7 6 5 4 3 2

Prentice-Hall International, Inc., *London*
Prentice-Hall of Australia Pty. Limited, *Sydney*
Prentice-Hall of Canada, Ltd., *Toronto*
Prentice-Hall of India Private Limited, *New Delhi*
Prentice-Hall of Japan, Inc., *Tokyo*
Prentice-Hall of Southeast Asia Pte. Ltd., *Singapore*
Whitehall Books Limited, *Wellington, New Zealand*

Dedicated to Sara and Matthew

Contents

PART II

SOCIAL PATTERNS AND PROBLEMS OF SMALL GROUPS, 63

6
STATUS RELATIONS AND REWARD ALLOCATION IN SMALL GROUPS, 231

7
GROUP TASK PERFORMANCE, 287

Preface and Acknowledgments

This book developed from the frustration I felt each year when I faced a decision about what reading to assign for my intermediate to advanced level undergraduate course on the sociology of small groups. Admittedly, there were a number of fine books available that at least partially met my needs. However, none seemed to be exactly what I wanted as the main text for my course. In particular, I was looking for a book having a combination of the following features: (1) broad—though not exhaustive nor encyclopedic—coverage of the small group field; (2) an explicitly sociological perspective that focused on the small group as a discrete social entity with its own distinctive social structures and processes; (3) an overview of major theoretical perspectives and research methods used to produce sociological knowledge about small groups over the past few decades; (4) coverage of traditional and recent literature; and (5) a focus on social problems in small groups. In writing this book, my primary aim was to include at least these basic features.

This text is intended mainly for undergraduates (and perhaps even beginning graduate students) in sociology, social psychology, and communication. It should be useful for those in the fields of education, business administration, political science, and human services, where understanding group behavior seems especially important. Since this book is supposed to serve a diverse audience, I have made a concerted effort to treat a wide range of provocative and interesting patterns, issues, and problems of small groups of various sorts. To provide the conceptual tools needed to make sense of these patterns, issues and problems, basic concepts are defined and distinguished as precisely and clearly as possible. Abstract and difficult theoretical and methodological issues are not avoided, because it seems important to make the reader aware of them in trying to present an accurate picture of what we know about the small group as a sociological phenomenon. However, these issues are not the central focus of this text, so those wanting to pursue them further will have to go elsewhere. To assist those readers who have had their curiosity aroused but not satisfied by the coverage of these or other topics in this book, I have been generous with bibliographic references. To add clarity and concrete relevance to the discussion, I have tried to provide numerous examples and illustrations of important ideas. I have also tried to write in a straightforward manner, using sociological jargon when it is needed but, I hope, not more than it is needed. In general, then, I have attempted to make this book readable without sacrificing the rigor needed to make it sociologically sound. Needless to say, the ultimate judge of whether I arrived at the correct formula of readability and rigor will be the reader.

Although I am the sole author of this book, I cannot claim to have written it alone. Certainly, the faults and shortcomings are all my own, but credit for whatever this book contributes to the small-group literature must be shared. I was first encouraged to take a serious scholarly interest in small groups by my undergraduate professors in the Social Relations Department at Lehigh University, including especially Bob Jones and Bob Williamson. In graduate school at the University of Pittsburgh, my small-group interests were given additional nurturing by professors such as Oto Bartos, Martin Greenberg, Lin Freeman, and Tom Fararo. My many conversations about teaching and studying small groups with Lynn England, a former fellow graduate student at Pitt and now a fellow sociologist, have contributed considerably to the shaping of this writing project. I could not have begun the actual writing at the University of Vermont without the financial support provided by a Faculty Summer Fellowship, and Gordon Lewis, Frank Sampson, and Bob Stanfield wrote the recommendations needed to convince the fellowship committee that my work was worth supporting. At Prentice-Hall, my general editor Ed Stanford, his extremely capable assistant, Irene Fraga, my production editor Jeanne Hoeting, and my copy editor Eileen Thompson, deserve special mention for their competent, sensitive, and fair handling of my project from the time it first crossed their desks to the time of its publication. It got to their desks as a result of the efforts of their man in the field, Terry Heagney. Special thanks are due Neil J. Smelser, my series editor. In the editorial process, the reviewers, Paul Crosbie, John W. Kinch, and Mark Lefton, who read my manuscript at various stages of its development were most helpful. Even the harshest ones had something worthwhile to contribute, and I only hope I was able to translate their criticisms and suggestions into a better book than what they originally read. In this regard, the review comments by Paul Crosbie should be singled out. Not only did they encourage me to rethink the original conceptual framework and organization I had proposed for the book, but they also suggested how I might add to the clarity and precision of quite a few of the specific ideas I presented. Of course, Paul Crosbie also was one of the people, along with A. Paul Hare, George Caspar Homans, Robert F. Bales, Robert T. Golembiewski, Marvin E. Shaw, Walter Buckley, Kurt Lewin, and

Joseph Berger, Bernard P. Cohen, Elizabeth G. Cohen, Morris Zelditch, Jr., and their colleagues in the "Stanford tradition," who provided me with a great deal of assistance through their published works. For a full sense of my intellectual debts, my long list of bibliographic references should be carefully examined.

My final acknowledgments are by no means the last in importance. They are to two very special people. I do not think I could have remained committed to this project without the constant encouragement of my wife, Sara, who some-how managed to endure patiently and with good humor the many readings of rough draft versions of paragraphs and sections I foisted on her. As for my son Matthew, he always seemed to crawl into my study at just the right times, to rescue me from the frustration of inarticulateness or lack of manual dexterity at the typewriter, with the joyful antics of an infant becoming a toddler.

HLN II

I

Sociology
and the Study
of Small Groups

1

The Small Group
As a Sociological Phenomenon

INTRODUCTION

On December 3, 1977, the Ohio State University varsity basketball team visited Burlington, Vermont for a game against the University of Vermont team. Local sportswriters in Burlington described the Ohio State team as young, explosive, and extremely talented. It was supposed to be a powerhouse in the making, with all six of its freshmen ranked among the top 100 high-school players in the nation the year before. In fact, Ohio State had been quite impressive in winning its first three games of the 1977-78 season, with its very highly regarded 6'11" freshman center averaging 26 points and 10 rebounds in those games.

Vermont was also undefeated in its first two contests of the new season, but even its most loyal supporters seemed to dismiss the team's chances of victory against its more talented and quicker opponent. Furthermore, many basketball fans in the area wondered why Vermont scheduled teams like Ohio State that were clearly "out of their league" and could humiliate them on the court. Of course, Vermont won the game, 77-76. When asked which individual or individuals on the Vermont team mainly had been responsible for this victory, the losing Ohio State coach commented, "I can't single out any individual because this was certainly a team victory."

While it may be easy to see an inspirational quality in this story, it may not be quite so easy to see its relevance to the sociology of small groups. Viewing a basketball team as a small group, though, may begin to bring the relevance of this story into focus. As a small group, a basketball team combines the individual skills, feelings, beliefs, and actions of group members into patterns of group interaction and collective effort that often differ from the types of behavior we would expect from the group members if we looked at them merely as a collection of individuals. For example, most would not have predicted the Vermont victory just by looking at the individual abilities of the Vermont players in relation to those of the Ohio State players. On the other hand, the reverse often happens, too. Groups with outstanding individuals may perform miserably, or much worse than we might have expected from looking at the membership of the group.

In this latter regard, consider the case of the men who made up President Kennedy's inner circle of advisers and helped formulate the decision to support the Bay of Pigs invasion of Cuba in 1961. We might reasonably ask how intelligent people, in positions of high responsibility, could arrive at such a disastrous and seemingly unintelligent decision. This question was addressed by Janis (1972), who concluded that the Kennedy Administration's top policy makers were victims of "groupthink"; that is, this policy group had become so tightly knit and friendly that its members were reluctant to engage in the tough, critical appraisal of policy alternatives that was necessary, but might have disrupted the group's esprit de corps or its normal patterns of interaction.

In clarifying the meaning of "groupthink," Janis wanted to draw attention to the idea that its source was not to be found in the individual nor in the organizational setting, but in small group interaction. He proposed that:

> . . . Beyond all the familiar sources of human error is a powerful source of defective judgment that arises in cohesive groups—a concurrence-seeking tendency which fosters overoptimism, lack of vigilance, and sloganistic thinking about the weakness and immorality of out-groups. This tendency can take its toll even when the decision makers are conscientious statesmen trying to make the best possible decisions for their country and for all mankind.
>
> I do not mean to imply that all cohesive groups suffer from groupthink, though all may display its symptoms from time to time. Nor should we infer from the term groupthink that group decisions are typically inefficient or harmful. On the contrary, a group whose members have properly defined roles, with traditions and standard operating procedures that facilitate critical inquiry, is probably capable of making better decisions than any individual in the group who works on the problem alone. And yet the advantages of having decisions made by groups are often lost because of psychological pressures that arise when the members work closely together, share the same values, and above all face a crisis situation in which everyone is subjected to stresses that generate a strong need for affiliation. . . . (Janis, 1972:13).

We will say more later in this book about the behavior of small groups. For now, the cases of a successful basketball team performance and policy groups victimized by "groupthink" enable us to dramatize some important ideas about the small group as a sociological phenomenon. First, they demonstrate that small groups can exist for different purposes and their interaction can have very different consequences. Second, they show that groups can have a character of their own, distinct from the personalities or qualities of their individual members. And third, they reveal that this "group character" can have a significant impact on how individual group members feel, think, and act, both individually and collectively.

In treating the small group as a sociological phenomenon, we will draw special attention to this "group character"; we will be especially interested in the collective values, norms, and patterns of interaction created by people coming together as small groups. We do not want to imply that individual personalities, pathologies, awareness, motives, beliefs, emotions, and actions are unimportant in trying to understand what happens in small groups and elsewhere in society. Rather, because of our background, training, and interests, we will rely most heavily on a sociological perspective, as opposed to a psychological one, to examine and analyze small groups in this book.

Thus, while recognizing the contributions of psychologists and other social scientists to our understanding of behavior in small groups, our basic aim is to show the relevance and value of the sociological perspective for understanding small group interaction. We attempt to achieve this aim by focusing on theoretical and empirical approaches used by sociologists in the study of small groups, on major sociological findings concerning various basic aspects of small group behavior, and on applications of sociological knowledge to social problems in small groups. That is, we attempt to examine how sociologists look at small groups, what sociologists know about small groups, and how the application of what sociologists know can enable us to understand and deal with problems, conflicts, and challenges that we confront as members of small groups.

All of us are members of small groups of various kinds, including families, peer groups, and formal and informal work groups. Therefore, the issues, assumptions, and findings discussed in later chapters should have at least general relevance to all of us at one time or another. The *specific* relevance of this book will probably be most clearly seen in the discussions in these chapters of research concerning a variety of concrete small group problems and issues, ranging from group disharmony to social deviance, dilemmas of leadership and group decision-making, and inequity in the distribution of rewards. In all these discussions, we make a special effort to indicate the sociological sources, meanings, and implications of these group problems and issues. In the next section we will consider in more depth what it means to treat these and other small group phenomena from a sociological perspective; that is, what it means to treat the small group as a sociological phenomenon. This theme is carried through the various parts of this book and gives all of them a common focus.

SMALL GROUPS FROM A SOCIOLOGICAL PERSPECTIVE

It is a standard practice of sociologists to begin their discussions with definitions of key terms, and this book will not depart from that general pattern. This practice may seem a dull, perfunctory exercise that unduly taxes the patience and interest of nonsociologists, but, in fact, it is necessary in most sociological discussions, including even highly sophisticated ones because of the lack of popular understanding of the meaning of basic sociological concepts and the lack of agreement among sociologists about the precise meaning of many concepts. Thus, this book will present definitions of key ideas for the purposes of clarity and precision, to avoid ambiguity or confusion about the meaning or boundaries of ideas, arguments, and findings.

Logic suggests that we begin by defining the most basic concept to be confronted in this book, which is, of course, the concept of the small group. From a sociologist's perspective, a small group is not simply any small collection of people. Though gatherings of five or six or fewer people at a bus stop, in a business meeting, or in a corner at a cocktail party are obviously quite small, their size alone is not a sufficient basis for sociologists to treat them as small groups. Such collections of people must possess additional distinctive qualities to be called *small groups*. There are numerous conceptions of the nature of these qualities.[1] However, Crosbie (1975:2) seems to have captured the essence of these sociological conceptions in defining the small group as ". . . a collection of people who meet more or less regularly in face-to-face interaction, who possess a common identity or exclusiveness of purpose, and who share a set of standards governing their activities." Thus, whether or not a particular collection of people constitutes a small group in sociological terms is determined by the collection's possession of the kinds of qualities specified by Crosbie, not by the number of people in it.

When a set of regularly interacting people possesses a common identity or purpose and shared behavioral expectations or norms, it tends to engage in the kinds of relatively stable patterns of interaction that sociologists call *social structure*. For example, when a husband and wife regularly consult with each other and share in the important decisions for their family, their typical manner of interaction about family decisions represents a particular structure of family authority relations. Authority is one of the types of social structures we are interested in examining in relation to small groups. The fact that social structural arrangements are the basic subject matter of sociology should help clarify why sociologists have developed the kind of distinctive conception of small groups found in Crosbie's definition. Sociologists tend to define small groups in a way that focuses attention on the forms of social behavior that are of fundamental interest and importance in sociology. Small-group investigators who are sociologists pursue as their basic aim an understanding of the social causes and consequences of the emergence, nature, and transformation of small group structures. Related to this focus is a concern with the relationship of small groups to the formal and informal social structures of other small groups and of

---

[1] For example, see Olmsted (1959:2), Verba (1961:11–16), Golembiewski (1962:Ch. II), Hare (1962:9–10), and Mills (1967:2) for a representative sampling of sociological definitions of the small group.

larger and more complex social systems like bureaucracies, social movements, communities, or perhaps even whole societies.

Small-group specialists in sociology and other social-science fields generally have confined their attention to the internal structures and processes or patterns of change of small groups. For example, two recent collections of readings in the small-group area edited by sociologists are called *Interpersonal Behavior in Small Groups* (Ofshe, 1973) and *Interaction in Small Groups* (Crosbie, 1975). However, it is unusual for sociologists to view the individual social units, social systems, or levels of society as if they existed independently of one another, or in social vacuums. Certainly, whenever sociologists study small groups in "natural" settings—i.e., outside the laboratory—whether to learn about internal group structures and dynamics in general or about a specific kind of small group such as a family, a delinquent gang, or an industrial work crew, they focus at least implicitly on the relationship of the small group to its social environment. Their close examination of small groups in such settings tends to reveal the imprint of the small group on the society around it or society's imprint on it. Furthermore, as Crosbie (1975:2) has pointed out, many social patterns that are viewed as societal events "are actually the aggregated products of individual events that either occur in or are directly influenced by small group associations." Examples of such "societal events" which tend to reflect or be mediated by interaction patterns at the small group level are divorce, crime, delinquency, industrial production, educational achievement, and suicide.

This book aims to give more explicit and direct attention to small groups in society than is commonly found in general overviews of the small group field by explicitly considering the relationship between small groups and their social environments and by examining research focused on concrete small group behavior and problems with societal implications.

THE SIGNIFICANCE OF NUMBERS FOR SMALL GROUPS

It is not exactly clear at what point a collection of people becomes too large to merit being called a small group. However, it appears that social units possessing the qualities proposed by Crosbie to designate small groups tend to range from two to twenty members. In general, small groups are not larger than about twenty. Increased size tends to limit the possibility that a given set of people will be able to interact regularly in a direct and meaningful face-to-face manner, *and* develop and maintain a shared identity or sense of collective purpose, *and* develop and maintain a consensus about norms for their behavior as group members (see Hare, 1962: Ch. 8: Wilson, 1971; 54–64). In this context, it should be easy to understand why small-group sociologists use the adjective "small" in referring to social groups, and why their study of social groups is the study of *small* social groups.

The fact that changes in group size can substantially alter the quality of social relationships among group members has been well appreciated by sociologists who have studied small groups. For example, Simmel (1950:87) observed that

> . . . a group upon reaching a certain size must develop forms and organs which serve its maintenance and promotion, but which a smaller group does not need. On the other hand, . . . smaller groups have qualities, including types of interaction among their members, which inevitably disappear when the groups grow larger.

These qualitative changes in the nature of social relationships in groups are not merely a result of the fact that the number of people in the group has changed. It appears that the effects of size on the structure of interaction in groups tend to be mediated by some other prominent variables, and the potential number of social relationships seems to be especially prominent among these mediating factors.

Increases in group size tend to bring about disproportionate increases in the number of possible relationships in a group. The impact of increased size on the number of possible relationships is suggested by the following formula: $y = x(x - 1)/2$, where y = number of simple, two-way (or dyadic) relationships and x = number of people.[2] This formula implies that one distinct dyadic relationship is possible between two people, fifteen distinct dyadic relationships are possible among six people, and *190* distinct dyadic relationships are possible among twenty people. These figures clearly demonstrate the disproportionate increases in the potential complexity of the network of interpersonal links among group members that are created by small increments in group size. Of course, if we attempted to calculate the effect of increased numbers on the potential complexity of relationships between subgroups and between an individual and a subgroup, as well as between individuals, the figures would be even more impressive (see Hare, 1962:228-229). However, the figures presented here should be impressive enough to convey the importance of the number of possible social relationships as a mediating variable.

Other variables that seem to have an important mediating effect on the relationship between group size and the structure of interaction in groups include the complexity of the division of labor or amount of social-role differentiation, the amount of formal administrative coordination, and the amount of formal control (Wilson, 1971:54-65). Increased group size generally seems to produce increased differentiation, formal administrative coordination, and formal control, along with disproportionate increases in the potential number of social relationships in a group. These effects of group size, either individually or in combination, help us understand the significance of numbers in limiting the

---

[2]This formula was initially suggested by the work of Bossard (1945), and it was cited and discussed by Wilson (1971:58, 60).

development or persistence of the basic sociological characteristics of small groups.[3] Simmel's (1950:122-169) classic discussion of dyads (two-person groups) and triads (three-person groups) helps us understand how even the smallest possible change in the number of group members can have a profound impact on the nature of group life.

FROM DYADS TO TRIADS AND LARGER GROUPS

The dyad, which for obvious reasons is the simplest of all social groups, differs from larger groups in its relationship to each of its two members. In particular, unlike any other group, a dyad can be destroyed by the loss of a single member. "This dependence of the dyad upon its two individual members causes the thought of its existence to be accompanied by the thought of its termination much more closely and impressively than in any other group, where every member knows that even after his retirement or death, the group can continue to exist" (Simmel, 1950:123-124). This recognition places a unique responsibility on both members to remain constantly involved with each other when they are together; and it is a characteristic of the dyad as a small group that its members are together on a regular basis. This need for regular close interaction imposed by the size of the dyad can have functional or dysfunctional consequences for it and its members.

The unique need for closeness within the dyad can be beneficial in that it makes possible a special level of intimacy that cannot be duplicated in larger groups. The attainment of such intimacy can be a source of stability for the group and of emotional gratification and support for its members. In comparing the dyad to the triad, Simmel (1950:135-136) made the following relevant comments:

> . . . No matter how close a triad may be, there is always the occasion on which two of the three members regard the third as an intruder. The reason may be the mere fact that he shares in certain moods which can unfold in all their intensity and tenderness only when two can meet without distraction: the sensitive union of two is always irritated by the spectator.

The size of the dyad can also be a cause of pressure and tension that make the existence of the dyad precarious. For example, the feeling of exclusive dependence on one another that may develop in a dyad ultimately can produce a destructive form of jealousy when dyad members confront outsiders. In addition, the special closeness needed to sustain a dyad severely restricts privacy and places group members under constant pressure to account for their actions and feelings. There is nowhere to escape in a dyad, which explains why relations in

---

[3] See Hare (1976:Ch. 10), for a recent review of relevant literature concerning the group size factor.

a dyad can become very tense, and why the life of the dyad is uniquely vulnerable to destruction by the disenchantment, caprice, or hostility of a single member.

It should be apparent that dyads have distinctive features not found in larger groups. Even the introduction of one additional person to a dyad dramatically transforms the character of group relations. The addition of a third person in triads results in three general kinds of typical group formations that could not develop in dyads and could only be multiplied, but not altered in basic structure, in larger groups. The three cases are: (a) nonpartisans and mediators, (b) "the tertius gaudens," or, "the third party who enjoys" (at the expense of the other two), and (c) "divide et impera," or, divide and rule (see Simmel, 1950: 145-169).

In regard to third parties as mediators, in the most significant of dyads, monogamous marriages, the child as the third party often performs the function of binding the whole group together, specifically by tying the parents to one another. This function could be performed in two ways. First, the existence of the child could directly initiate or reinforce the union of parents, by increasing their mutual love or at least the love of one for the other. Second, the relation of each parent to the child could produce a new and *indirect* bond between parents. In the latter case, the child represents a common object of love for both parents and may cause them to interact more frequently, and possibly, more intimately. In this context, Simmel offered the interesting suggestion that unhappily married couples may *not* want children because they sense that a child would close a circle within which they would be nearer to each other, both externally and psychologically, than they want to be. Of course, it is also possible that unhappily married couples, or individual spouses in unhappy marriages, who see themselves drifting away from their marital partner, will view a child as a means of restoring lost bonds of affection or perhaps even of salvaging their marriage. The history and amount of cleavage in a marriage should have much to do with how marital partners view the addition of a child to their group and with how this child influences the solidarity of the family unit.

Simmel saw third parties who serve as nonpartisan mediators in triads as acting in two different ways. On the one hand, the nonpartisan may produce agreement between two conflicting parties by bringing together the unconnected or quarreling elements and then withdrawing. On the other hand, the third party may act as an arbiter who balances the contradictory claims of the antagonistic elements and eliminates what is incompatible in that antagonistic relationship.

In the former case, the mediator's success depends on the opposing parties' desire to achieve reconciliation and the mediator's ability to eliminate misunderstandings and to make effective appeals to the good will of the contending parties. By serving as a nonpartisan, objective, third party in negotiations, this person forces the parties to the conflict to confront their differences and present their arguments in more objective terms. This tone of objectivity can defuse the emotionalism that often stands in the way of negotiated settlements for conflicting members of a dyad. It can also reduce antagonism, a crucial transformation in the attempt to unite conflicting parties or resolve their differences. "It is the function of the mediator to bring this reduction about, to represent it, as it were, in himself; or to form a transformation point where, no matter in what form the conflict enters from one side, it is transmitted to the other only in an objective form; a point where all is retained which would merely intensify the conflict in the absence of mediation" (Simmel, p. 148)

When a third party acts as a mediator, the ultimate decision lies exclusively in the hands of the conflicting parties themselves. But when a third party acts as an arbitrator, they relinquish the final decision. Thus, the appeal to arbitration reflects more subjective confidence in the impartiality and judgment of third parties than any other form of decision. In such cases, one would expect third parties to possess a considerable amount of respect, personal influence, and authority.

Third parties in triads can play important unifying roles as indirect or direct mediators or as arbitrators. However, such roles are not without certain perils. The nonpartisan third-party role can become severely complicated when it derives from equal commitment to both sides of a conflict, rather than from strict neutrality or detachment. Graduate teaching assistants sometimes find themselves in this situation when they are caught in the middle of a dispute between students in their course and the instructor in charge of it. The nonpartisan third-party role can become terribly emotion-laden when it derives from equal closeness to the conflicting parties, rather than from equal distance. Family conflicts often seem to produce this kind of situation, where one family member feels compelled by love to settle a dispute between two others but finds intervention especially painful because of that love.

Third parties do not restrict their efforts to pursuing group unity or other group purposes. The third party may try to use the interaction between the other two members of the group as a means to his own ends rather than as a means to group ends. According to Simmel, this tendency occurs in two general forms in triads: the case of "the tertius gaudens" and the case of "divide et impera." The former situation is one in which an existing or emerging conflict between two group members is exploited by a third party. For example, a clever child may try to get what he or she wants by taking advantage of a disagreement between parents. Or, a person may step into a conflict between a friend and his wife or girl friend, seemingly with the most altruistic of motives, but in fact, with the hope of redirecting the woman's affection from his friend to himself.

The divide and rule situation is a special case of the "tertius gaudens" situation. It is distinguished by the fact that the third party intentionally produces the conflict in order to gain a dominating position. The case of a coach who attempts to gain greater control over a clique of two players by making them rivals for the same position illustrates this particular pattern. As in the other patterns of group formation associated with triads, this one first becomes possible in triads but can also occur in groups of larger size.

Simmel offers considerable insight into the crucial importance of numbers at the most elementary levels of group life. He clearly indicates how dramatically the patterns of interaction in groups can be changed by the addition of a single person to a group, especially if that group is a dyad. His insights help clarify why researchers have found that dyads tend to have high rates of showing tension, consistently avoid disagreement and antagonism, and have high rates of asking for opinion, but avoid giving opinion (Bales and Borgatta, 1955). They also help us understand why the potential instability of dyads might lead their members to assume asymmetric roles, with each member specializing in different activities, presumably to avoid conflict and strain to the relationship. In the latter regard, Strodtbeck (1951) found that husband-wife pairs in three cultures tended to assume asymmetric roles with respect to each other, with one generally being more active and influential than the other.

Simmel indicates that the addition of another person to a dyad may introduce more stability, at least if that third person performs a *positive* direct or indirect mediating function. Because there are three group members, triads, unlike dyads, are not threatened by the possibility of deadlock (which is a potential problem for all small groups with an even number of members) or by the presence of a single disenchanted, capricious, or hostile member. However, the majority resolution of group conflicts which is possible in triads (and larger groups with an odd number of members) can cause considerable dissatisfaction for the member who is consistently on the losing side of issues. In this regard, Hare (1962:242) has shown the considerable power of a coalition of two in a triad to force a decision in particular disagreements. Hare suggests that members may change coalitions from one disagreement to another to prevent one member's being permanently excluded. Along with the possibilities of oppression and exclusion of one member by a stable coalition of the other two, it is also possible that the *third party* in the triad may play a deviously or overtly disruptive role in the group, as in the cases of "the tertius gaudens" and "divide et impera."

The advantages and disadvantages, or functions and dysfunctions, of various group sizes raise a question about whether there is some optimum size for small groups. An adequate answer would probably contain many qualifications for different types of groups. Indeed, it may be that an answer can be given only in relation to a particular set of values. Certainly, it would seem more appropriate to try to answer this question at the end, rather than beginning, of this book. Despite all this hedging, though, there is something more definite that we can say in response to this question. There has been research which has found that at least in terms of member satisfaction and for groups involved in discussion, five may be the optimum group size (see Hare, 1962:243). Below this size, members complain that the group is too small, although the potential rate of participation of each member increases. This reaction may be a result of the possible strains associated with face-to-face interaction in two-, three-, and four-person groups and of the odd and even effects. Above the size of five, members complain that the group is too large, perhaps because it restricts participation. Five-member groups combine the following stabilizing and satisfying characteristics:

1. a strict deadlock is not possible with an odd number of members;
2. the group tends to split into a majority of three and a minority of two, so that being in a minority does not isolate the individual but allows him or her sources of gratification; and
3. the group appears to be large enough for the members to shift roles easily and for any individual to withdraw from an awkward position without necessarily having resolved the issue (Hare 1962:243–244).

By now, the significance of numbers for the nature of social relationships in small groups should be quite evident. However, it must be remembered that group size, alone or in conjunction with other factors which mediate its effects, does not always provide an adequate explanation of basic differences in the character of different groups. In order to understand these differences, it is necessary to recognize that there are different types of groups existing for different purposes and in different social settings. They perform different functions for their members and the society of which they are a part, and they pursue different kinds of goals in different ways. One basic type of small group having substantial influence on its members and the society around it is the primary group.

THE PRIMARY GROUP

In the opening words of his comprehensive examination of the primary group, Dunphy tried to provide a relatively concrete and familiar expression of both the nature and importance of primary groups in social life. He said:

> Over our lifetime, we spend much of our time in small groups. We are born into a family. As we grow older we venture out from our family into the play groups of childhood and later into the cliques and crowds of adolescence. We marry and establish a new family group of our own and participate in the work groups and leisure groups of adulthood. Out of the associations formed in these groups, we fashion and have fashioned in us a changing and developing conception of self; we learn ways of behaving appropriate to varied social situations, and we acquire a set of social values and attitudes that allow us to respond to the structure and pressures of the larger society about us (Dunphy, 1972:3).

Although it is likely that the special kind of small group that Dunphy described has existed since the first two human beings interacted regularly with each other, the term "primary group" that refers to it did not become part of sociological jargon until 1909 when Cooley published *Social Organization.* Furthermore, it has only been during the past few decades that small group investigators have begun to refine Cooley's original conception of this type of group to make it more explicit and precise. In this original conception, Cooley (1909: 23) defined primary groups in the following way:

> By primary groups I mean those characterized by intimate face-to-face association and cooperation. They are primary in several senses, but chiefly in that they are fundamental in forming the social nature and ideals of the individual. The result of intimate association, psychologically, is a certain fusion of individualities in a common whole, so that one's very self, for many purposes at least is the common life and purpose of the group. Perhaps the simplest way of describing this wholeness is by saying that it is a "we;" it involves the sort of sympathy and mutual identification for which "we" is the natural expression.

Cooley uses the term "primary group" to refer to groups playing a fundamental role in socialization and having a "we" feeling. Certainly, the primary group characteristics he identified are found easily in the concrete groups—such as families and friendship groups—generally treated by him and other sociologists as primary groups. However, by failing to be more elaborate or explicit, Cooley provided a rather fuzzy basis for understanding how primary groups differ from other kinds. As Davis (1948:290) pointed out, "It is generally agreed that *all* groups tend in some degree to possess consensus—to engender a 'we' feeling in their members. This was implied by Cooley himself in his . . . discussion of the necessary extension of 'primary ideals' to larger groups. Without the 'we' feeling (no group can retain its) cohesion."

Davis (1948:290–307) tried to resolve the ambiguity in Cooley's definition. He described the distinctive interrelated qualities of social relationships typically found in concrete primary groups and proposed three "physical" conditions (or group properties) that might be critically important for primary-group formation. Davis argued that the basic primary-group qualities are most likely to emerge when small-group size is combined with the conditions of close physical proximity of group members and relationships among members that persist for a long period of time. He assumed primary groups were distinguished by interpersonal relationships of a personal, informal, spontaneous, sentimental, and inclusive nature. Furthermore, he characterized the members of such groups as possessing similar values, goals, and attitudes, and as pursuing their mutual friendship and welfare as a basic end.

Davis and other sociologists after Cooley have used the term "secondary group" to refer to all groups or larger collectivities in which primary relationships are not predominant. Thus, secondary groups (with "group" being used somewhat loosely here) have been characterized by impersonality; formality; nonspontaneity; cold, rational calculation; narrowly circumscribed roles; dissimilar values, goals, and attitudes of group members; and relationships viewed as means rather than ends in themselves. Secondary relations and "groups" tend to arise under conditions that are the opposite of those spawning primary relations and groups: that is, large "group" size, limited opportunities for face-to-face contact, and fleeting interpersonal contacts.

Just as we tend to associate the notion of the primary group with the intimacy of family life, we tend to associate the notion of the secondary group with the cold impersonality and formality of large-scale modern bureaucracies and urban communities. However, a close examination of both examples reveals that neither type of concrete "group" fully embodies the distinctive qualities of the type of collection of people it is supposed to represent. In fact, this is almost always the case. Pure examples of primary or secondary groups are rarely found in actual social life. Furthermore, as Davis pointed out, "The groups embodying most completely the characteristics of primary relationships are those that are freest from any connection with social organization . . . . The truth is that every society is of necessity inimical to the full expression of primary association" (p. 299).

Even if society must limit the full expression of primary association to make social order possible, society still relies on the partial expression of it. Human history suggests that social chaos results when society fails to exercise some control over its members and their interaction. People appear extremely unlikely to get along with each other and to do what is necessary for their mutual benefit or survival without some form of mutual obligation, normative constraint, and stable status expectations. However, these qualities of secondary association can be effective in producing social order and in inducing the performance of basic societal functions only when the expression of primary association is used in the exercise of authority and social control. In particular, human behavior in any group, organizational, community, or institutional setting in a society can be effectively constrained to follow orderly patterns only if the people in these various social settings are effectively socialized. The process of socialization can be fully effective only when it occurs in concrete groups like families that emphasize the physical conditions and qualities of primary association.

According to Davis (1948:300), interaction with others in an organized and meaningful way, which is the essence of socialization, can occur only in stable and familiar group settings where people feel secure and can relate to others intimately and personally. Thus, it is not by accident that primary groups such as families, childhood-play groups, neighborhood circles, school and business cliques, and college fraternities play an essential role in our social development, nor that groups possessing the basic qualities of primary association and involved in socialization have been organized as part of the basic institutional structure of society. The family most readily comes to mind in this regard. Thus, concrete primary groups blend the qualities of primary association with the constraints, obligations, and controls of secondary association.

Even though primary groups (*and* secondary groups) do not exist in a pure state, we still can refer to them as essentially primary (or secondary) in nature because of the conditions of their formation and the predominance of primary over secondary qualities of association (or vice versa). It should be clear, then, that the concept of the primary group is an abstraction, or "ideal type" in sociological jargon (Davis, 1948:305, 307); in this sense, we classify real groups as primary or secondary on the basis of their degree of approximation to the qualities we have associated with one or the other concept. We expect that primary-group qualities will be nurtured by small-group size and by sustained, frequent face-to-face contacts between group members, and that these qualities may develop unintentionally or despite the original intentions of group members. However, we also know that groups developing or existing under such conditions may be quite different from the ideal-typical conception of primary groups.

Unfortunately, it is not very difficult to think of families, work groups, athletic teams, juries, civic groups, or governing boards that have been severely split by interpersonal hostility among their members; and this hostility is often exacerbated by the very conditions of smallness, closeness, and continuation that should nurture the opposite kind of association. These examples clearly imply that there may be other factors, including externally imposed pressures, demands, or constraints on group members and an intense commitment to group tasks and goals among members, that can deflect a group from actually becoming a primary group or remaining one. In deciding whether a particular small group is a primary group, it might be helpful to think of Dunphy's (1972) definition of a primary group, which tends to be a distillation of prior sociological conceptions.

> (It is) a small group which persists long enough to develop strong emotional attachments between members, at least a set of rudimentary, functionally differentiated roles, and a subculture of its own which includes both an image of the group as an entity and an informal normative system which controls group-relevant action of members (p. 5).

THE REDISCOVERY OF THE PRIMARY GROUP

If a group conforms to Dunphy's definition of the primary group, we can be reasonably sure that it will have a substantial impact on the social development, beliefs, and actions of its members; for such groups are, as we have already suggested, where socialization takes place. Although sociologists have generally recognized the essential importance of primary groups in socialization and in the maintenance of social and personal solidarity, they have not always fully appreciated the vitality of primary groups. Nineteenth-century European social theorists tended to view the primary group as a "vestigial remnant" of traditional society and as one that was being steadily eroded by the impact of the industrial revolution. The focus of nineteenth-century social thought tended to concentrate mostly on the large-scale structures of society and on the transition from traditional "Gemeinschaft" social organization based on intimate, cohesive, communal or primary association to modern "Gesellschaft" social organization based on impersonal, individualistic, rational, secondary association.[4] This perspective parallels to some extent the focus in twentieth century American sociology on "mass society" and the "eclipse of community."[5]

The nineteenth-century social theorists especially tended to underestimate the vitality of primary groups in the face of Gesellschaft processes of industrialization, urbanization, and bureaucratization. This necessitated a "rediscovery" of primary groups in modern societies. This rediscovery refers to a realization by twentieth-century social scientists that primary groups could be found in important new forms, other than traditional family, play, or neighborhood groups, in secondary structures that were previously seen as destroying or replacing primary association.[6] For example, primary groups and relations have been discovered to have a considerable amount of importance in factories (see Roethlisberger and Dickson, 1939), on the street corner of the large city (see Whyte, 1943), in modern armies (see Shils, 1950) and corporations (see Dalton, 1959: especially 57-65), in correctional institutions (see Street, 1965) and schools (see Trow et al., 1950), as a mediator between the individual and the mass media (see Katz and Lazarsfeld, 1955), and in politics (see Verba, 1961).

An interesting and important aspect of the rediscovery process, which was observed by Verba (1961:18), is that many researchers who have uncovered significant findings about primary group influence were themselves surprised by their findings. For example, as Katz and Lazarsfeld (1955:36) noted, "Just as in the study of mass communications and voting intentions where the research blueprint gave no inkling of the possible relevance of interpersonal relations, so here, in the case of the mass production factory . . . nothing less than a *discovery* that the 'model' was wrong could have revealed that primary relationships were in operation and were *relevant to productivity.*"

In response to the realization that primary groups could exist in a variety of forms, Dunphy (1972:5) identified four general classes of groups that met his defining criteria for primary groups:

1. families;
2. free association peer groups of childhood, adolescence, and adulthood—including delinquent gangs and some small, cohesive political elites ("cabals");

[4] See Toennies (in Parsons et al., 1961), for a more extensive treatment of the Gemeinschaft and Gesellschaft concepts.
[5] The superficiality of social affiliations in modern industrial and urban societies has been examined by Riesman, Glazer, and Denney (1950) in *The Lonely Crowd.* The ostensible decline of communal or primary relations in modern communities has been treated by such sociologists as Nisbet (1953), Stein (1960), and Vidich and Bensman (1960). The dehumanization of twentieth-century man has been chillingly treated in the counter-utopian novels of Aldous Huxley (*Brave New World*) and George Orwell (*1984*).
[6] The rediscovery of the primary group has been discussed more extensively by Shils (1951), Verba (1961:17–22), and Dunphy (1972:10–35).

3. informal groups existing in organizational settings such as classroom groups, factory work groups, small military units, and "house churches;" and
4. resocialization groups such as therapy groups, rehabilitation groups, and self-analytic groups.

PRIMARY AND TASK GROUPS

Dunphy's general types encompass a broad range of specific types of small groups. They suggest the rich assortment of experiences possible in primary groups, as well as the diversity of social settings in which they exist, the variety of social influences that they have on their members, and the kinds of different purposes that they serve. However, Dunphy's classification scheme does not cover the full range of small groups in general. The primary-secondary group dichotomy implies that small groups, as defined here, tend to be primary groups; but there also are small groups which, at times, are or are supposed to be more like secondary groups than primary ones. A prominent example of such groups is the *task group,* which is a small group that has been formed by its members to pursue some specific task or set of tasks or that has been assigned a specific task or set of tasks by a person or persons having formal authority over it.

The problem in understanding the distinction between small groups that are primary groups and those that are task-performing ones is that some individual groups seem to illustrate both types. For example, groups such as construction-work crews, consumer groups, political campaign organizations, committees, civic groups, and athletic teams, are supposed to achieve specific goals through efficient and effective task performance. But at times they seem to be more concerned with fraternizing or having fun than with getting their work done. Similarly, some families strictly regiment their lives together to achieve specific goals, such as a political campaign victory for one of its members or the success of the family business. And some groups of friends and neighbors organize to lobby against new superhighways or oil refineries in their community or in favor of the construction of new parks and recreational centers in their neighborhood. These examples should underscore the importance of exercising care in labeling specific, concrete small groups as primary or task-performing.

To understand the nature of particular small groups, one must recognize that primary groups are small groups that *generally* exhibit more primary than secondary qualities, and task groups are small groups that explicitly are oriented to task performance and that *over time* tend to exhibit more secondary qualities than primary groups. One must recognize also that the interpersonal orientations of members of specific concrete groups may alternate between primary and secondary emphases and between nontask and task activities at different points in time, especially in groups that tend to be viewed as task-performing ones. In this book, the primary group and the task group will represent the two major categories of small groups we will examine.

By using the concept of a task group to refer to small groups with more secondary qualities than other kinds of small groups, we will avoid the ambiguity and inclusiveness of the catch-all "secondary-group" term, while still being able to talk about secondary association. Rather than referring to task groups as secondary groups, *per se,* it seems more appropriate to locate them with respect to other kinds of small groups on a continuum running from "pure" primary groups to "pure" secondary groups. Closest to the primary group end, we would expect to find families, peer groups, and informal groups in organizations. Then we would expect to find resocialization groups, which are more explicitly oriented than other types of primary groups to the attainment of socialization as a goal of group activities, but which tend to have a more diffuse orientation to task performance than task groups. Farthest from the primary group end, we would expect to find task-performing groups oriented to tasks other than socialization.

Steiner's (1974:2) statements clarify the distinction between primary and task groups and its relationship to group success:

> . . . People who assemble for the purpose of enjoying one another's company act quite differently from those whose aim is to learn about themselves or their society. Both of these kinds of groups differ dramatically from those that are created for the purpose of making policy decisions or turning out a product. When the aim (of a group) is to have fun, to learn, or to experience a therapeutic effect, the proper measure of the group's success is its impact on the members themselves. The important consideration is what members do to one another, how each contributes to the enjoyment, knowledge, or peace of mind of the others. But when the purpose is to perform a task, group success is a matter of influencing the outside environment or of plotting a course of action that will have such an influence. Task-performing groups attempt to build houses, win ball games, sell groceries, or devise a strategy for preventing war . . . The acknowledged function of such groups is to provide products or services that are valued by some segment of society. . . .

SUMMARY AND A GLANCE AHEAD

It should be evident by now that much of what we do, say, feel, and believe occurs in, or bears the imprint of, small groups. As members of small groups, (1) we learn who we are and how we are expected to act; (2) we experience joy and frustration, love and hate, success and failure; (3) we formulate dreams, plans, and tactics and try to make them real; (4) we make and defy decisions and issue and carry out orders; (5) we enforce rules and break them; (6) we earn rewards and suffer penalties; and (7) we pursue the frivolous and the serious, play and work, games and "real life." Small groups may be too small to duplicate the complexity of social structure and structural links found in larger social systems. As discrete social systems that are small enough to be studied intensively, we can learn from them important insights about the social patterns characterizing

larger social systems. Furthermore, small groups are important objects of sociological inquiry because it is often difficult to achieve an adequate understanding
of basic social structures and processes in organizations, communities, and
societies apart from an understanding of the social influence of small groups and
what happens in them. Applying sociological perspectives and findings in trying
to understand the nature and influence of small groups is important because
human behavior in small groups or at any other level of society cannot be adequately explained strictly in terms of the minds, emotions, or actions of individual personalities. It must be viewed in terms of patterns of social rules, roles, and
relationships.

If the importance of the sociology of small groups is not yet obvious, we
hope that subsequent chapters will eliminate lingering ambiguity or doubts.
These chapters are not meant to be a totally exhaustive review of small group
research.[7] Instead, they are a general overview of basic sociological perspectives,
findings, and applications concerning small groups. They are to convey a sense of
the importance of small-group influence in our lives. To achieve this aim, they
place special emphasis on research with applications to specific social problems
and issues occurring in a variety of concrete small groups. We realize that this
book cannot be all things for all people. However, we still hope that it will stim-
ulate small-group sociologists at the same time that it communicates the meaning
and importance of small groups to its main target audience of people who are
not social scientists but who want to learn more about small groups and may
already have some background in a social-science field.

There are obvious pitfalls involved in trying to discuss applications of
sociological knowledge primarily for an audience of non-social scientists.[8] The
main pitfalls may be the dangers of oversimplification and misrepresentation.
Thus, even at the risk of a loss of interest or patience, we present the definitions,
measures, and qualifications needed to understand the actual or full meaning of
research findings and generalizations. We avoid unnecessarily abstruse or esoteric
theoretical and methodological points, so that there is no need to begin closing
this book and putting it back on the shelf just yet. In fact, the value of defining
terms should have been suggested by the previous discussion in this chapter of
the special and various meanings sociologists have attached to the small- and
primary-group notions. We hope the discussion on the ensuing pages generally
will be interesting, relevant, and clear enough so that efforts to be sociologically
precise and systematic will be regarded as necessary for understanding its full
meaning and implications. Indeed, we hope that these efforts are not seen as
departures, but as integral parts of the discussion of even the most topical small-
group problems and issues.

This first chapter is the first half of Part One of this book. The two
chapters of Part One show how sociologists look at and study small groups. In

---

[7]Good examples of this kind of book are by Golembiewski (1962) and by Hare (1962,
1976).
[8]Golembiewski (1962) discusses these problems in his "Introduction."

focusing on the small group as a sociological phenomenon, the first chapter suggested what it means to look at small groups through a sociological eye, and it gave special attention to how sociologists define the concept of a small group and how the size of a group may affect the development, nature, and persistence of patterns of group interaction. In addition, it tried to indicate the range and importance of our small-group experiences by focusing on primary and task groups, which are viewed here as the two most basic forms of small groups. The second chapter concerns some of the most prominent, general theoretical approaches that have been used to study sociological aspects of small groups over the past several decades, as well as the basic methods that small-group researchers use to collect sociologically interesting data. It gives special attention to social-system perspectives because in this book we are mainly interested in looking at small groups as whole social units and social-system perspectives tend to allow us more than other major theoretical perspectives to see and interpret basic social patterns and problems of small groups in the context of the group as a whole.

The imprint of the social-system perspectives appears throughout the five chapters of Part Two. These five chapters present an overview of current knowledge about the small group as a sociological phenomenon. Part Two begins with the third chapter, which concerns patterns and problems of communication, group integration, and interpersonal relations in small groups. "Communication," *per se*, can be seen as one of the fundamental defining characteristics of small groups in general, having relevance to all aspects of group functioning. Thus, it seemed fitting to begin the review and discussion of small-group assumptions and findings by focusing on the form and flow of the patterns of communication or interaction linking group members. The third chapter also deals with the bonds or linkages holding groups together, the attachments of members to the group as a whole, and the attachments of members to each other within the group, in its focus on group integration and interpersonal relations.

The remaining four chapters of Part Two review and discuss assumptions and findings about a variety of other basic sociological dimensions of small groups. Under the general topic of social control, the fourth chapter deals with the normative structure of groups, the creation and maintenance of patterns of group conformity, and the control of deviance. The fifth chapter concerns patterns and problems of leadership, interpersonal power, and rebellion in small groups. The sixth chapter treats a number of different aspects of status relations and reward allocation in small groups. The final chapter focuses on group task performance in terms of such things as the factors associated with successful performance and the nature of task-group behavior in larger organizational settings.

A single systematically formulated social-system model or theory was *not* used throughout these chapters to explain small group behavior, although it might have provided a better integration of the assorted assumptions and findings presented in the chapters of Part Two. Because we were mainly concerned with providing a broad, though not exhaustive or encyclopedic, coverage of the small group field, we have tried to avoid the restrictions and theoretical weaknesses that might have resulted from relying on a single model or theory. The difficulty of staying consistently within the conceptual boundaries of a single social-system perspective, whether new, refined, or existing, should become more evident after considering some of the most prominent social-system models of the small group in the second chapter. In view of the purposes we had in mind for this text, the payoff from trying to do this seemed quite dubious. However, this is not to say that use of an eclectic collection of social-system ideas for defining and analyzing basic social patterns and problems of small groups served no integrative purpose in this book. In fact, one of the basic insights to be gained from a social-system perspective of any kind is that the various sociological aspects of small groups, ranging from patterns of interpersonal attraction to conformity, authority, and status relations, are interrelated. To the extent this is true and the use of even an eclectic social-system perspective demonstrates this fact, the social-system ideas and interpretations spread throughout Part Two will create a web that at least loosely integrates its different sections and chapters. Of course, the most fundamental basis for coherence in Part Two is the persisting theme of the small group as a sociological phenomenon. Each new section can be seen as revealing another sociological dimension of the small group, and all of these dimensions collectively constitute what we referred to at the beginning of this chapter as the "character" or overall social structure of a group. We hope the ensuing chapters will clearly demonstrate that it is interesting, as well as important, to try to understand the small group as a sociological phenomenon.

2

Small Group
Perspectives and Methods

INTRODUCTION

In the first chapter, we pointed out that we will rely on a sociological concept of the small group as a social system. This concept draws our attention to such aspects of small-group interaction as:

1. how and how often particular group members interact with each other;
2. how much group members value membership in their group;
3. how committed they are to their group's goals;
4. how they get along with each other;
5. the degree of conformity or deviance in the group;
6. how authority and power are wielded in small groups;
7. the nature of status relations among group members;
8. how rewards are distributed in small groups;
9. how group members work together;
10. the degree of task success attained by people when they work as members of a small group.

Although this is only a general list of the types of things we will consider concerning small groups in this book, it should be evident that an overview of the small-group literature could easily yield an overwhelming array of facts concerning small-group interaction. A *theoretical perspective* such as the social-system approach attempts to provide some meaningful organization of these facts by showing how and why they are related to one another. This means that looking at small groups from a social-system perspective makes it possible to see such things as the attraction of group members to each other, their status and authority relations, and their success in achieving group goals as interrelated aspects of their mutual interaction as members of a small group, rather than as unconnected or isolated fragments of social behavior.

23

Without some sort of theory, indeed we would be overwhelmed with all these facts and they would have no apparent relationship to each other. Theory, whether represented by a social-system perspective or some other one, is an essential element of sociology as a social *science*[1] because it enables us to organize, interpret, and give meaning to the multitude of social facts constituting social reality. However, as essential as the assumptions, questions, explanations, and predictions derived from theories are to our understanding of the small group from a sociological perspective, the sociology of small groups cannot rely only on theories. It must also rely on systematic sociological *research methods* to collect the sociological facts about small groups that confirm or refute the ideas contained in theories.

Some small-group studies by social scientists seem to suggest that theory and research can be treated independently and that one problem is of substantially greater importance than the other. But neither statement truly applies to genuine scientific work. The most elegantly refined theories contribute little to scientific knowledge unless they give us an accurate picture of social reality, accurate explanations of the reasons for social behavior, or accurate predictions of future social behavior. Similarly, the most clever and sophisticated research procedures have limited scientific value unless they are developed on the basis of precise and systematic theories and they generate data that can be interpreted on the basis of such theories. Thus, the growth of scientific knowledge about small groups must proceed from an interdependent, symbiotic relationship between theory and research, where each depends on and nurtures the other. Only when the pursuit of small-group knowledge is based on this kind of relationship between theory and research can the basic scientific goals of accurate description, explanation, and prediction of small group behavior be maximally attained.

Shaw (1976:21–22) has succinctly stated the heart of this matter:

> Probably no one would deny that theorizing and empirical research are interrelated processes and that both are needed for the complete analysis of group behavior. Empiricism provides the evidence necessary for the construction of a meaningful theory. Theory, in turn, organizes and extends known data and thus serves as a framework for further empirical work. Theory often suggests new directions for future research that otherwise might be overlooked. New empirical evidence either strengthens the theory, if consistent with it, or forces rejection or modification if not. Thus, scientific knowledge escalates through successive increments from both theory and research. The important choice, then, is not between

---

[1] Further insight into the nature of the scientific perspective is given by Shepherd (1964: Ch. 2), who has contrasted "the scientific attitude" with "the attitude of everyday life." The scientific attitude was characterized by a greater emphasis on general versus personal perspectives, a posture of doubt, and objective typifications of aspects of reality. Olsen (1968:Ch. 2) has also provided concise overviews of the nature of the scientific process, the scientific method, scientific requirements for the social sciences, and scientific limitations of them.

theoretical and empirical approaches, but between kinds of theories and between kinds of empirical methods.

In the remainder of this chapter, we will consider a variety of prominent theories and empirical or research methods that have been used to study small groups over the past several decades. Since we will rely mainly on a conception of the small group as a social system, we will give the greatest attention to the most prominent social-system perspectives that have been applied to small groups. In considering each of these perspectives and methods, and perhaps especially the social-system approaches, keep in mind its limitations as well as its advantages regarding the types of insights it allows us to derive about social patterns and problems of small-group interaction.

SMALL-GROUP THEORETICAL APPROACHES

THEORIES, MODELS, AND FRAMEWORKS: AIMS AND LIMITATIONS OF SMALL GROUP THEORIES

Popular usage of the term "theory" often obscures the more technical, scientific meaning of it. Frequently, when people seem to be idly speculating about something, we dismiss their comments by saying they are "only a theory." Since it is only in terms of theoretical concepts, propositions or assumptions, and systems that scientists can know, explain, and predict things about the world, it is unlikely they would refer to theories in such a pejorative or casual sense. Nevertheless, it is often difficult to understand the nature of the term "theory" by looking at how *social* scientists use it, since their use of it varies.

Social scientists with a more rigorous interpretation tend to view a theory as a system of "logically consistent and interrelated concepts and propositions that outline relationships among various aspects or properties of the phenomena being studied" (Olsen, 1968:11). The nature of a theory according to this definition can be illustrated by a possible theory about group-task effectiveness containing assumptions or propositions about three basic *variables,* which are factors whose value can vary. These factors are the amount of group-task effectiveness, the amount of group cohesiveness, and the amount of group goal commitment. This theory aims to explain why some groups are more effective than others, which will allow us to explain and predict different levels of effectiveness of different groups.

In this theory, we will assume or hypothesize that more cohesive groups (i.e., in which members value group membership more highly) tend to perform group tasks more effectively than less cohesive ones. If our research concerning various types of task groups confirms this hypothesis about the relationship between cohesiveness and effectiveness, we are left with the question of why this relationship exists. Turning to our theory once again, we might assume that more cohesive groups tend to be more effective because greater cohesiveness produces greater commitment to group goal attainment among group members, which in turn makes the group as a whole more effective in its task performance. We will propose later in this book that the attainment of effective group task performance is actually more complicated and has more causes or reasons than we have assumed in this theory. Nevertheless, this simple example, despite its limitations, should help clarify the basic components of theories and how they might be used to understand small-group interaction.

There are a variety of less rigorous interpretations of the nature of a theory. There are also some that are more rigorous and sophisticated. But less rigorous interpretations tend to be more prevalent. The most common of the less rigorous interpretations refer to loosely connected sets of propositions, hypotheses, or arguments meant to describe or explain social behavior; individual propositions or hypotheses that are presented by themselves or in isolation from other potentially relevant ones and tend to serve mainly descriptive purposes; analogies between social phenomena such as small groups and other kinds of phenomena such as human bodies or various sorts of machines; or even schemes of classification of different aspects of social life as in the case of a scheme for classifying different types of small groups. All of these interpretations designate components of the theory construction process and therefore are "theoretical;" but none by itself designates a theory in the most rigorous sense of the term.

Perhaps the most important reason for varied interpretations of the meaning of theory among social scientists is that no theoretical approach in social science has been particularly successful in generating consistently and highly accurate predictions, which are the ultimate goal of theory construction in any scientific field. Certainly this is true in the small-group area, a fact that should be kept in mind throughout our later discussion of small-group literature. We do not imply that efforts have not yet been made to develop rigorous theories at the small group level,[2] or that sociologists do not know anything worthwhile or important about the social structures and processes of small groups. However, small-group sociologists do have substantially greater difficulty predicting when or under what conditions a particular coalition will form or a particular marriage will dissolve than a physical scientist has predicting the rise and fall of tides, or solar eclipses. Since social scientists have not yet developed a universal or highly consensual, theoretical paradigm for studying small groups,[3] we find a varied assortment of theoretical approaches or perspectives at different levels of abstraction and generality in the small-group area. This variety has also resulted from the different perspectives of psychologically and sociologically oriented small group investigators.

[2] Some excellent examples of attempts at rigorous formal theory construction in the small-group area are given in Berger et al. (1962) and in the two volumes of *Sociological Theories in Progress* edited by Berger, Zelditch, and Anderson (1966, 1972).
[3] Kuhn (1970) offers an interesting and insightful discussion of the nature and importance of theoretical and research paradigms in science and how they change, and of the difficulties experienced by social scientists in trying to develop paradigms in their individual disciplines.

The most prominent and influential of the general theoretical orientations to small groups are probably more appropriately seen as loosely connected, theoretical frameworks or as theoretical models rather than as theories *per se.* These theoretical approaches tend to lack the precision usually attributed to fully developed scientific theories. They may be less precise in their definitions of concepts, the measures we can derive from them, their specification of assumptions and predictions and the conditions to which they are meant to apply, or the assessments they allow of their validity. We may better understand these and other limitations of small-group theoretical approaches if we consider, somewhat more explicitly, the distinction between models and theories. In addition, our consideration of this distinction should show that despite their shortcomings, models can make valuable contributions to the pursuit of scientific knowledge about small groups.

As one would expect from the varying interpretations of the nature of a theory, social scientists are not in complete agreement about the meaning and use of models.[4] Generally speaking, though, they tend to agree that models are at least abstract and simplified representations of concrete phenomena that are used to organize our understanding of the phenomena in a meaningful way and to indicate worthwhile areas for further research.[5] Some social scientists might attribute more of the characteristics of theories to models. However, most would probably agree that models are more than simple analogies, but less than scientific theories.

Models are heuristic devices meant to facilitate the entire scientific process, from concept formation to research design. They are rarely developed to represent the full complexity or substance of concrete phenomena. Instead, they are intended as selective and simplified representations of the *most salient* features of the phenomenon under study, and as such, they can guide theory and research in fruitful directions. For example, there are "organismic" models of small groups that draw attention to basic similarities between biological organisms, such as individual human beings, and small groups; and on the basis of this kind of analogy, they emphasize the essential functions and interdependence of the constituent elements of small groups, as well as the basic survival needs of groups as integrated systems. Although models make valuable contributions to theory construction and research, they are not substitutes for either of them.

Caplow (1964:90-91) has summarized the main features of the nature and use of models in the following way:

> The study of a model should not be confused with the study of the real world. . . . The model contains only what we put into it. The real world contains more than we can ever get out of it. No model is an exact replica of its subject, but a useful model identifies and simplifies strategic vari-

---

[4] See Dunphy (1972:81-83) for a brief discussion of this point, and Brodbeck (1959) for a more general treatment.
[5] This definition was distilled from ones by Olsen (1968:227) and by Dunphy (1972:82).

ables so as to produce a fairly good—never a perfect—fit between effects in the arena of observation and effects obtained by manipulating symbols (in the model). The tests of an analytic model are its internal consistency, the amount of simplification achieved, and whether it can be used to predict real events.

On the one hand, then, models cannot completely describe, directly explain, or predict with substantial accuracy the occurrence of particular small-group patterns. But on the other hand, they can have considerable scientific use in guiding the direction of theory and research. Try to keep in mind these possible limitations and contributions as we turn our attention in the next section to some of the major theoretical models and frameworks that have been used in small group analysis.

MAJOR THEORETICAL MODELS AND FRAMEWORKS

As noted earlier in this chapter, a number of different kinds of theoretical approaches have been used to study small groups. Some have focused on particular and basic facets of group behavior, as in the cases of Moreno's sociometric approach concerning affective or socio-emotional relations among group members (Olmsted, 1959:95-99), and Steiner's (1972, 1974) recently formulated theoretical perspective concerning group productivity. Others have focused on the relationship of individual motives, personality characteristics, or adjustment to group settings. These have included Cattell's (1948) "group syntality" approach concerning "group personality traits" and the psychological needs served by group membership, and psychoanalytic approaches, such as Schutz's (1958) "fundamental interpersonal relations orientation" (or "FIRO"), which treats patterns of interpersonal relations with respect to individual needs for togetherness, control, and affection. The social exchange perspectives of Thibaut and Kelley (1959) and of Homans (1961, 1974) attempt to explain and predict behavior in informal and small-group settings on the basis of general propositions from behavioral psychology and elementary economics.

Approaches focusing more on the structure and functioning of whole groups than on individual and interpersonal behavior in them have most prominently included group-dynamics and social-system models. The group dynamics (or "field theory") approach was initially formulated by Lewin (1951). It reflects both the influence of Gestalt psychology, in its focus on groups as whole entities, and the influence of physics, in its treatment of groups as fields of interdependent forces pushing and pulling groups and their members in various directions. Social-system models have had various forms, but probably the best known have been developed by Bales (1950) and by Homans (1950). Whereas the starting point for Bales' formulation of his "interaction process analysis" approach was the task group, Homans' system model was inspired mostly by his interest in informal and primary-group relations. Bales' model focuses attention on four basic and interrelated social structural dimensions of small groups, concerning access to resources, control over people, status, and group solidarity. Homans' model focuses on the interdependent network of relationships among activities, sentiments, interaction, and norms in small groups.

We should add here that along with Parsons and Shils (1951), Bales was mainly responsible for the concept of a social system and its functional prerequisites that continues to have a major impact on sociological theorizing.[6] This fact is important because undoubtedly Bales is much more famous for the system of observational categories derived from his theoretical model, than for the model itself. Since social-system models such as those developed by Bales, Homans, Parsons, and Shils have strongly influenced our treatment of small groups in this book as well as in the small-groups field in general, we will discuss the main features and research implications of these models in more detail in this chapter. However, before beginning this discussion, we will present some additional summary comments about the field theory and social-exchange perspectives. These latter perspectives merit some added attention because they also have had an especially strong impact on sociologically oriented, small-group research.

The Field Theory Approach

Kurt Lewin probably has had a greater impact on modern small-group research than any other single person. Certainly no other individual has had a greater influence on psychologically oriented small-group researchers. After he emigrated from Nazi Germany, Lewin and his co-workers set up research centers at the University of Iowa and Massachusetts Institute of Technology, and later at the University of Michigan. Collectively, these centers produced a plethora of experimental studies concerning small-group dynamics.[7] Lewin's direct influence on these studies was felt most during the late 1930s to the early 1950s. His influence was due mainly to three factors: (a) *his phenomenological position,* whose emphasis on the importance of what people subjectively perceive as reality, rather than on what observers view as "objective reality," was rare in psychology in the 1930s and 1940s; (b) *his ingenuity in employing the laboratory* for research; and (c) *his theoretical perspective,* which he tried to represent mathematically by using topology, a type of nonquantitative geometry (Shepherd, 1964:24). It is the nature of his theoretical perspective, which reflects his phenomenological position, that most interests us here.

Lewin's field "theory" conceives of groups in terms of their orientation

---

[6] Bales was in close contact with Parsons and Shils when he wrote *Interaction Process Analysis . . .*, and he was influenced by their conceptual scheme in *Toward a General Theory of Action* (Parsons and Shils, 1951).

[7] The research inspired by Lewin just at the Research Center for Group Dynamics at the University of Michigan is suggested by *Institute for Social Research, 1946-1956* (Ann Arbor: University of Michigan), cited in Olmsted (1959:153).

toward goals. A group is seen as occupying a position in its subjectively salient environment or "life space." Within this life space, a group (or group member) *locomotes,* or changes its position, toward regions with *positive valences* (attraction) and away from regions with *negative valences* (repulsion). The direction of movement (*vector*) during this goal-seeking activity reflects the existence of the opposing *power fields* and *group forces* which can change this direction of movement. Locomotion toward goals could involve overcoming or circumventing barriers in the life space, or altering goals of the life space itself.

Shepherd (1964:26) has argued that cohesion may reasonably be viewed as the key concept of field theory of small groups. This emphasis significantly departs from field theory of individuals, where life space (*psychological field*) is the key concept. By *cohesion,* or *cohesiveness,* group-dynamics researchers have usually meant "the total field of forces which act on members to remain in the group." This concept typically has been defined for research purposes as " . . . the average for all members of the resultant force toward remaining in the group. . ." (Festinger, Schachter, and Back, 1950:164–165). This conception of cohesiveness has been a main focus of a substantial amount of small-group research guided by the group dynamics, or field theory, approach. According to Shepherd (1964:26–27), some of the major hypotheses of field theorists that have been examined in research include the following:

1. Cohesion is directly related to agreement on goals, agreement on norms, extent of democratic and stable leadership, agreement on shared understandings, and similarity in background (age, experience, ethnic identification, and the like).
2. Cohesion is directly related to productivity, satisfaction, conformity (and influence), and cooperative interaction patterns.

In a later chapter, we will consider the results of research concerning hypotheses like these, along with some important shortcomings of defining "cohesiveness" in the typical manner of field theorists. We hope, though, that by considering these hypotheses, the reader can gain a sense of some major directions of small-group research influenced by basic concepts of field theory. But despite the extensiveness of this research and the amount it has contributed to what we know about small groups, it also has demonstrated some significant limitations of field "theory" as a vehicle for producing scientific knowledge about groups. Both the contributions and limitations of the field-theory approach, with respect to the scientific process, have been summarized by Olmsted (1959:116–117):

> . . . (T)he fact that it is possible to see behavior in terms of certain categories does not insure that these categories will be the most fruitful ones to employ. The history of scientific inquiry is strewn with the wreckage of once fashionable but ultimately inadequate categories and conceptual

models. . . . What is required (to make a science) . . . is a knowledge of what to look for and an understanding of how the variables selected for observation constitute the framework of a functioning whole. . . . Grim pursuit of a few handy variables on the one hand, or essentially wistful talk about "total fields" on the other, do not quite measure up to this implacable demand.

In sum, the achievements of Group Dynamics (or field theory) include its concern for carefully formulated hypotheses, the large amount of interest it has aroused in group behavior, and its findings which spell out in detail some relationships which we might otherwise have only suspected. Its limitations . . . lie in the inadequacy and probable inappropriateness of its working-level concepts (including *locomotion, valence, vector, power field,* and *group forces*) and in its failure to pay attention to what non-Lewinian thinking might have to suggest as to major problems or variables in group life—especially with reference to the dimensions of role differentiation.

While sharing Olmsted's general views on the contributions and limitations of field theory for small-group studies, Dunphy (1972) added three, more specific, interpretations of its contributions to the development of a model of the (primary) group as a whole. Perhaps it would be most appropriate to conclude this discussion of field theory on this positive note. From Dunphy's perspective, the main value of the field theory approach can be seen in:

1. (its) stress on some variables of tested value, particularly variables of a . . . holistic kind, such as cohesiveness;
2. (its) stress on the importance of examining the relationship of the group to its environment; and
3. (its) emphasis on two central facets of all group life, namely goal orientation and group integration (p. 85),

The Social-Exchange Approach

Social-exchange models offer a very different conception than the field perspective of the nature and causes of group behavior. The field perspective is rich in the imagery of physics, in suggesting a picture of groups struggling to stick together while contending with various positive and negative forces in their environment that could affect their progress toward goal attainment. The social-exchange perspective is rich in imagery derived mainly from animal psychology and elementary economics. Social-exchange theorists tend to focus on group behavior at the level of individual members. The behavior of these individuals is seen as motivated by the desire to maximize self-interest and as following the same general propositions used by Skinner (especially 1938, 1953) to analyze the behavior of pigeons and rats. That is, social exchange theorists analyze human behavior in terms of the pursuit of rewarding experiences and the avoidance of painful ones; and they analyze group behavior in terms of the adjustments self-seeking individuals make in trying to deal with the problems of sustained interaction and social interdependence (Shaw, 1976:25-26).

The work of Thibaut and Kelley (1959) and of Homans (1961, 1974) provide the best known examples of general applications of social-exchange theory to informal and small-group behavior. Although somewhat different in terminology, the basic arguments derived from these two frameworks to explain social behavior tend to be quite similar. However, Homans tended to be more explicitly and extensively committed to explaining the emergence and persistence of social structures with his exchange perspective; and his work tends to be better known among sociologists than that of Thibaut and Kelley. For these related reasons, we will concentrate mostly on Homans' ideas in discussing social exchange theory.

It may not be particularly flattering to view our behavior in terms of basic propositions of animal psychology or as a result of unrelievedly self-interested motives. Nevertheless, Homans has been quite explicit about the appropriateness of treating human behavior in just such terms. In the former regard, he has said:

> . . . (the research of behavioral psychology) has largely been given over to the behavior of higher animals other than man, but its critics are quite mistaken when they imply that only pigeons and rats support the findings of behavioral psychology. . . . (M)an is also a higher animal and research on man's behavior supports the findings too. (For a good example, see Bandura, 1969.) The same general propositions hold good of the behavior of all the higher animals, though they have more complicated implications for the behavior of man than they do for that of the others, by reason of his exceptional intelligence and his use of language (Homans, 1974:12).

In regard to the profit-seeking implications of his argument he has said:

> Let not a reader reject our argument out of hand because he does not care for its horrid profit-seeking implications. Let him ask himself whether he and mankind have ever been able to advance any general explanation why men change or fail to change their behavior other than that, in their circumstances, they would, as they see it, be better off doing something else or that they are doing well enough already. . . . He may ease his conscience by remembering that if hedonists believe men take profits only in materialistic values, we are not hedonists here. If men's values are altruistic, they can take a profit in altruism too. In fact, some of the greatest profiteers we know are altruists (Homans, 1974:47).

Homans also has made explicit the psychological roots of his exchange perspective.

> . . . though much emerges in social behavior, and is emerging all the time, which goes beyond anything we can observe in the behavior of isolated

individuals, . . . nothing emerges that cannot be explained by propositions about the individuals as individuals, together with the given condition that they happen to be interacting. The characteristics of social groups and societies are the resultants . . . of the interaction between individuals over time—and they are no more than that . . .[8] (Homans, 1974:12).

Homans' social-exchange framework implies that people initiate social interaction with the expectation that the interaction will provide something of value for them. This "something of (positive) value" is called a *reward* and could be money, or advice, or approval, or love, or whatever else has positive value for a person. Since social interaction brings together two or more people simultaneously in pursuit of rewards, each must have something of value to give the others in order to get something of value in return. Thus, the implication of the social-exchange framework is that to get something of value from someone, one must give something of value to that someone; that is, you cannot reasonably expect to get something for nothing in this world.

What we give up in social exchange, whether in terms of time, energy, or resources, are our *costs*. Presumably, as rational profit-seekers, we will pursue those social relationships that provide us with the greatest available excess of rewards over costs, or, the greatest available profits. Homans' general explanatory framework implies that a given exchange between people will be more attractive to those involved in it and more likely to be repeated, the more often (up to a certain threshold level of satiation) it is a source of mutual rewards and the more valuable those rewards are. Of course, groups can only emerge when patterns of interaction are repeated over time, and norms develop to obligate people to continue them. This perspective assumes that the patterns of exchange of rewards and costs will be the basic determinant of the development of the needed "norms of reciprocity" and subsequent group structures. Needless to say, the basic concepts used by Homans to analyze the social structures of groups—including interaction, status, esteem, authority, and fair exchange—are all tied to his reward-cost, exchange framework.

In the years since Homans first presented his social-exchange theory, it has become widely accepted among sociologists and social psychologists.[9] A

---

[8]By taking such a perspective, Homans explicitly challenged those who followed in the tradition of Durkheim (1927) and believed that social groups and larger social units were greater than the sum of their parts, and imposed constraints on their members beyond those which members individually imposed on each other. Homans (1974:12) stated his challenge in the following way: "Whereas Durkheim argued (1927, p. 125) that sociology was not a corollary of psychology, that its propositions could not be derived from those of psychology, we take here what is in effect the opposite position and confess ourselves to be what has been called—and it is a horrid phrase—a psychological reductionist."

[9]To support this contention, Crosbie (1972) reported Oromaner's (1968) finding that in the years following the publication of Homans' *Social Behavior: Its Elementary Forms* in 1961, its author became one of the most cited sociologists in introductory sociology texts. Of course, his popularity also can be attributed to the earlier publication of *The Human Group* (1950), which presented the social-system model Homans later abandoned when he developed his exchange theory.

great deal of the popularity of this framework is probably due to its apparent ability to explain so much of human behavior and, hence, so many results of sociological research, especially those concerning informal and small-group interaction. Perhaps Homans himself gives one of the most interesting examples of how his theoretical perspective is used to explain patterns of interaction in such settings in the now classic case of *status inconsistency*. This case involves *cash posters* and *ledger clerks* in an accounting office, and was researched by Homans and explained by exchange theory in *Social Behavior: Its Elementary Forms* (1961, 1974).

Status inconsistency refers to a situation where group members individually have different rankings on status characteristics that the group as a whole considers important. For example, a particular committee of business executives might consider very valuable characteristics the possession of extensive business experience, a high-ranking position in their company, and being male. A given member of that committee would exhibit status inconsistency by having only a few years of business experience (a lower ranking on this characteristic), being female (also a lower ranking), and occupying a top position in the company (a higher ranking).

In the case of cash posters and ledger clerks, Homans looked at a special kind of status inconsistency called *distributive injustice,* involving the relationship of rewards to other kinds of status characteristics. Homans tied this notion of distributive injustice (or justice) to his exchange framework in the following way:

> . . . distributive injustice occurs when a person does not get the amount of reward he expected to get in comparison with the reward some other person gets. He expects to get more reward than the other when his contributions—what he gives in social exchange—and his investments—his background characteristics—rank higher than the other's, equal reward when his contributions and investments are equal to the other's, etc. Though many men in many societies implicitly accept this general rule, they may still disagree as to whether the distribution of rewards is just in particular circumstances, because they do not admit the same dimensions of reward, contribution, and investment as relevant . . . (1974:268).

Homans used the distributive injustice notion to help explain a source of tension in the relations among clerical workers in the office he studied. In this office, with about sixty workers, ledger clerks represented the largest group. Homans (1974:especially 242-248) was concerned with the relations between ledger clerks and cash posters, all of whom were women. He found that within this office, ledger clerks occupied a higher status level than cash posters, because the ledger clerks had a more difficult and responsible job and generally were older and had more experience in the company. However, he found also that cash posters and ledger clerks received the same weekly pay, although the normal line of promotion in the accounting division was from cash poster to ledger clerk. Thus, it is not surprising that despite their general enjoyment of their jobs, the ledger clerks expressed to researcher Homans a sense of unfairness about their pay, which was a complaint they had also expressed to their supervisors and union representatives.

The interesting aspect of this case is that the ledger clerks did not feel badly paid—but rather, *unfairly* paid—in comparison with the cash posters, who were seen as having less responsible jobs. The ledger clerks expected superior rewards from management in exchange for the greater contributions and investments they brought to their work and the greater costs (e.g., greater responsibility) incurred in carrying it out. Because the rule of fair exchange was violated for the ledger clerks, they felt unjustly treated and complained about their pay to supervisors and the union.

General morale in the accounting division of this company remained fairly high, despite management's failure to respond to the ledger clerks' complaints. Although this particular case did not constitute a seriously divisive status conflict, it offers an excellent illustration of the use of Homans' social-exchange theory for analysis of small-group problems such as status inconsistency and distributive injustice, which are of general sociological interest. We will examine these problems again in a later chapter. Homans' own analysis is much more extensive than what has been presented here, but this brief presentation should suggest the nature and possibilities of social-exchange analysis, at least in Homans' terms.

Although Homans has used his social exchange theory to explain a broad range of elementary social behavior, widespread acceptance and use of his theory by small-group investigators may not be entirely justified at this time. For one thing, it has been used mostly to explain research findings not explicitly generated to test social-exchange theory. This does not mean that direct tests of social-exchange theory done in the future may not produce repeated support for its basic propositions and conclusions. In fact, one such test recently conducted by Crosbie (1972), produced at least qualified support for three hypotheses concerning compliance in a power exchange that were derived from Homans' general propositions concerning frequency, value, and accumulation of rewards. Nevertheless, the limited amount of direct confirmation of this theory suggests the need to exercise some caution for the time being in applying it.

One of the basic reasons for conducting direct tests of Homans' theory is to determine the actual range of its applicability. As Buckley (1967:112) has observed:

> When we look closely at Homans' development of exchange theory we see that, quite early in the game, he leaves far behind the kinds of laws that explain pigeon behavior. Otherwise he could never have arrived at such concepts as social approval, norms of justice, esteem, and so forth. He agrees that pigeons do not use symbols and men do, but he seems not to want to

go the rest of the way to agree that men, and not pigeons, have selves and self-awareness, and will thereby suffer for long periods all kinds of deprivation, negative reinforcements, and even death for mere symbols and self-esteem. Perhaps we can discuss such behavior in terms of "conditioning" and profit-seeking. We cannot object to the usefulness of such concepts *per se,* under certain conditions. But to make them applicable to all and any kind of behavior whatsoever, no matter how "altruistic" or "egoistic," is to engage in tautology or truism. . . .

Tautologies are the kinds of statements that lead us in circles and cannot be proven wrong, simply because of the way we define our terms. One is flirting with tautology by labeling as "profit-seeking" the apparently altruistic behavior of a person who risks his life to save a drowning person and leaves the scene before gaining any public recognition for his effort. We might readily agree with Homans that the rescuer would be a profit-*taker* in this case if his heroic act caused him to think more highly of himself. However, it seems more dubious to assume that such acts are generally *motivated* by profit-*seeking.* The problem is trying to *prove* whether behavior in these sorts of situations is motivated more by the desire to serve oneself or others. Of course, *defining* all behavior as profit-seeking precludes the possibility of finding behavior not of this type; this is the kind of problem that might confront us by accepting Homans too literally or without qualification.

The Small Group as a Social System

Although our discussion of the small-group literature in the coming chapters repeatedly will show the influence of the field and social-exchange perspectives, it will primarily show the imprint of social-system models. We have chosen this heavy reliance on social-system models because, as noted earlier, more than these other prominent perspectives, this type of theoretical approach tends to allow us to see and interpret basic social patterns and problems of small groups in the context of the group as a whole. This type of focus has been common in small-group sociology. In fact, Olsen (1968) has proposed that social-system models have been the most widely used analytical models in contemporary sociology in general. Although a number of different versions of this type of model have been developed, all of these versions tend to be based on the kind of general conception of a social-system Olsen has presented. This general conception refers to a form of social organization having "a distinctive total unity beyond its component parts, that is distinguished from its environment by a clearly defined boundary, and whose subunits are at least partially interrelated within relatively stable patterns of social order" (Olsen, 1968:228–229). In somewhat simpler terms, a small group as a social system is a bounded network of interrelated activities that constitutes a discrete social entity.[10] Before we

[10]This is similar to the simplified definition presented by Olsen (1968:229) and based on Hall and Fagen (1956).

consider specific formulations of social-system models of the small group, we will give further attention to some of the most important social-system ideas that tend to be characteristic of such models.

The distinctive character of the system perspective in general has been described in colorful terms by Miller (1955:515). He has suggested what a system is not, as well as what it is:

> The opposing lines of two football teams in scrimmage, independent of their backs, would not ordinarily be considered together as a system. If the Headless Horseman of Washington Irving had not been fictional, he could not have held his head in his arm and yet behaved like an intact system. All the blondes in the United States are themselves not a system unless they are organized by some sort of communication, like the Redheaded League of A. Conan Doyle. In simple, naive, common-sense terms, then, a real system is all of a thing. Even though it is possible to construct a conceptual system which includes grandpa's moustache, Chinese haiku poetry, and the Brooklyn Bridge, this would not correspond to a real system of general systems theory, because these things are not surrounded by a single boundary, are not continuous in space-time, and do not have recognizable functional interrelationships.

Thus, even though social-system models *as models* do not represent all of the elements or the full complexity of concrete social entities such as small groups, they must correspond to at least some of the crucial features of real social systems to be useful as analytical tools. A major feature of system models, and one especially valuable for our sociological purposes here, is their emphasis on the totality of basic units of analysis. This emphasis means that our basic unit of analysis in this book, the small group, is viewed as a social whole. This social whole is seen as possessing properties or structures of its own that emerge from the interaction of group members or their existence as a collectivity. These properties or structures have no meaning except in relation to the group as a whole. For example, it makes no sense to refer to group size or authority and status structures as characteristics of individual group members or individual instances of interaction between members, since these factors characterize whole groups. From this perspective, then, we assume social behavior occurring in small groups is most meaningfully interpreted with respect to groups as whole social entities.

The interrelatedness of small groups as social systems implies that whatever happens to one part of the group has at least an indirect influence on the other parts of the group and on the group as a whole. This means, for example, that when two members of a family fight with each other in a way that departs from the family's norms concerning interpersonal hostility, we can expect their deviance to have an impact on the way other family members relate to them, and perhaps even, to each other, as well as an impact on the shared expectations of the entire family about how interpersonal hostility should be handled in the future. Thus, a social-system model forces us to look beyond the ostensible isolation or autonomy of individual social acts or aspects of group behavior to how all the basic elements of the group are tied to each other and to the whole group.

The different versions of social-system models used by sociologists have focused attention on a variety of basic features of small groups as social systems.[11] However, one basic feature that seems to be treated in one form or another in all social-system models—whether based on a mechanical, organic, organismic, or some other kind of system analogy—is *equilibrium*. In its simplest conception, equilibrium refers to the tendency of a system to establish a state of balance between its elements and their interrelations and to maintain that state within a very limited range of deviation. This conception suggests the image of a group with relatively fixed patterns of interaction and social structural arrangements in general. As one might suspect, many social-system theorists have found this static conception of equilibrium too simplistic to be useful in analyzing real social systems such as small groups.

Some of the more biologically oriented system modelers have used the concept of *homeostasis* to capture the more dynamic aspects of the maintenance of equilibrium in basically *unstable* social systems. In justifying his use of this elaborated conception of equilibrium (to apply to biological systems), Cannon (1939:20,24) said that:

> When we consider the extreme instability of our bodily structure, its readiness for disturbance by the slightest application of external forces . . . its persistence through many decades seems almost miraculous. The wonder increases when we realize that the system is open, engaging in free exchange with the outer world, and that the structure itself is not permanent, but is being continuously built up again by processes of repair. . . .
>
> The constant conditions which are maintained in the body might be termed *"equilibria."* That word, however, has come to have fairly exact meaning as applied to relatively simple physico-chemical states, enclosed systems, where known forces are balanced. The coordinated physiological processes which maintain most of the steady states in the organism are so complex and so peculiar to human beings . . . that I have suggested a special designation for these states, *homeostasis*. The word does not imply something set and immobile, a stagnation. It means a condition—a condition which may vary, but which is relatively constant.

Although the homeostasis concept is a clear improvement over simpler, more static, and more mechanistic equilibrium notions, social-system theorists such as Buckley have still found it inadequate for analyzing actual social sys-

[11]For more detailed treatments of these different versions of social system models, see Buckley (1967:Ch. 2) and Mills (1967:Ch. 1). The ensuing set of comments about social system models owes much to Buckley's discussion.

tems. This concept draws attention to disruptive forces that constantly threaten the stability of a system's structure and create *temporary* lapses into *disequilibrium,* which are ultimately *corrected* to protect the crucial features and *the same* overall stability and unity of the system. In this sense, the maintenance of equilibrium in social systems is similar to temperature regulation in animals or in buildings where a thermostat controls the source of heat. However, according to Buckley, "In dealing with the sociocultural system, . . . we jump to a new system level and need yet a new term to express not only the *structure-maintaining* feature, but also the *structure-elaborating* and *changing* feature of the inherently unstable system, i.e., a concept of morphogenesis" (1967:14–15).

The morphogenesis notion allows us to see the maintenance of a group's equilibrium as the protection of the basic character of a group and the fulfillment of its crucial survival needs or *functional prerequisites* in the context of regular changes in particular group structures, group growth, and creation of new group equilibria. In a more concrete sense, better than other equilibrium notions this concept allows us to understand how groups such as the Boston Celtics professional basketball team could make personnel changes, alter some of the ways team members interact both on and off the court, and get older over the years while continuing to maintain the same distinctive style of "team play" and the same high level of competitive success. Thus, it helps us to see more clearly that the more things change in some ways, the more they remain the same in other, more fundamental ways.

A social-system model is most useful for sociological analysis of small groups when it assumes the kind of sophisticated dynamic perspective implied by the morphogenesis concept, and when it focuses on the capacity of groups not only to react to disruptions but also to shape their own growth, or demise. Probably one of the most insightful and useful discussions of the equilibrium problem in small groups was offered by Homans. His comments about *practical equilibrium* conditions are especially valuable because they have general implications for the study of small groups as social systems. Parenthetically, one might detect some irony in the fact that Homans offered these comments at a time when he was in the process of abandoning (or going beyond?) his own social-system model developed in the *Human Group* (1950) in favor of the social-exchange theory he presented in *Social Behavior: Its Elementary Forms* (1961). He said:

> Practical equilibrium is not a condition in which no change of behavior occurs. . . . But (the changes occurring in groups in practical equilibrium) are regular and recurrent: no new kind of change seems to occur. The behavior of a group is in practical equilibrium in the sense that one day's work is much like another's. . . .
>
> We speak of *"practical equilibrium"* instead of plain *"equilibrium"* in order to avoid the almost mystical arguments that have encrusted the latter word in social science. We make no assumption here that the behavior

of a man or a group tends toward equilibrium. . . . Nor do we assume that if a change from practical equilibrium does occur, behavior necessarily reacts so as to reduce or get rid of it. There is no homeostasis here: no belief that a group acts like (a) . . . body shaking off an infection. . . . For us, . . . specific effects must follow from specific causes, but more than that we do not ask of the behavior of any group; there is no more *must* about it. Practical equilibrium, then, is not a state toward which all creation moves; it is rather a state that behavior, no doubt temporarily and precariously, sometimes achieves. It is not something we assume; it is something that within the limits of our methods we observe. It is not something we use to explain the other features of social behavior; it is rather something that, when it does occur, is itself to be explained by these other features (Homans, 1961:113-114).

What are these "other features of social behavior" to which social-system models draw our attention? Beyond equilibrium, they are things such as functional needs, structural differentiation, patterns of interpersonal sentiment, conformity, leadership, and status relations. They are the kinds of things that generally interest sociologists when they study social entities such as small groups; and they will therefore be basic topics of consideration in later chapters of this book. In the next few sections, we will consider more fully how the key social system ideas for small-group analysis have emerged and evolved in the work of major social-system theorists.

PARSONS' MODEL. Although the social-system models of Bales and Homans have an important place in the development of sociological theory, especially in the small-group area, the social-system model of Talcott Parsons is most frequently mentioned when sociologists discuss functional analysis of social systems.[12] Since Parsons applied his model more broadly to whole societies, which partially accounts for the pervasiveness of his influence in sociology, we will deal first with his general functional approach to social systems. Then we will turn to the social-system perspectives of Bales, Homans, and some others, which have been applied more specifically to small groups.

Parsons has been a prolific source of theoretical ideas about the structure and functioning of societies; his work has prompted a great deal of criticism, as well as discussion. Fortunately, we do not need to grasp the full scope or intricate details of the nature and criticism of Parsons' work to understand its contributions to the construction of a model for small-group analysis. This kind of treatment of the Parsonsian framework is more appropriately found in more

[12]Gouldner (1971:168) has written: "Intellectually viable or not and socially relevant or not, it is Parsons who, more than any other contemporary social theorist, has influenced and captured the attention of academic sociologists, and not only in the United States but throughout the world. It is Parsons who has provided the focus of theoretical discussion for three decades now, for those opposing him no less than for his adherents."

general discussions of sociological theory.[13] In this section, we will restrict our attention to those parts of Parsons' work emphasizing important, general, and basic sociological aspects of social systems. In particular, we will make a broad, and brief, sweep of those basic concepts in Parsons' work that appear or are developed in other social-system models more specifically formulated for small-group analysis.

Parsons' theoretical framework evolved from a focus on individuals to one on social systems as whole entities. Parsons shifted his orientation from a focus on the moral values providing internal stimuli to social behavior at the individual level, in order to concentrate more on the functioning and survival of whole social systems. It is this latter focus that is relevant to us here.

Parsons' work has consistently shown his strong concern about social order, reflected in his conception of a *system:*

> The most general and fundamental property of a system is the interdependence of parts or variables. Interdependence consists in the existence of determinate relationships among the parts or variables as contrasted with randomness of variability. In other words, interdependence is *order* in the relationship among the components which enter into a system (Parsons and Shils, 1951:107).

Later in the same work, Parsons offered a somewhat different conception of order. "Order—peaceful coexistence under conditions of scarcity—is one of the very first of the functional imperatives of *social systems*" (Parsons and Shils, 1951:180). Buckley pointed out that these different meanings of "order," which refer to "neutral causal relations" in the former case and "normative, or evaluative relations" in the latter, are a source of many of the problems in interpreting Parsons' framework. However, despite these differing meanings, it is possible to identify a major implication of his *general* concern about order in social systems. This is his image of these systems as self-maintaining, homeostatic entities with basic functional requirements that must be met regularly for system survival.

Gouldner (1971:211-212) has contended that Parsons, "more than any other modern social theorist, has persuasively communicated a sense of the reality of a social *system,* of the boundaried oneness and coherent wholeness of patterns of social interaction. . . ." Thus, from Parsons' perspective, we see social systems as discrete organisms with their own needs for coherence and survival, which go beyond the needs of their individual members. Parsons, the functionalist and social-system theorist, draws attention to how social systems are able to maintain a stable equilibrium—or "order" in both of his senses of this term—by

---

[13]Gouldner has offered an excellent and lengthy discussion and critique of "the world of Talcott Parsons" in *The Coming Crisis of Western Sociology* (1971). Many have criticized Parsons' work for its unnecessarily ponderous verbiage. Especially prominent among such criticisms is Mills' (1950:Ch. 2) brief, but trenchant one.

inducing members to want to do what is required and expected of them and by restraining and controlling the behavior of those challenging the system's needs and expectations. According to Gouldner:

> . . . Much of Parsons' system analysis . . . resolves itself into questions either about the nature of system interdependence or about the nature of system-stabilizing forces, boundary-maintaining or equilibrating mechanisms (1971:210–211).

> . . . In short, emphasis is on how the system preserves itself; a system has no inherent strains, only situational discrepancies or "disturbing" factors of marginal significance (1971:231).

Parsons' reliance on biological and mechanical equilibrium imagery[14] and his "conservative" bias toward stability and order seem to impose significant limitations upon the use of his social-system framework for analyzing real social systems such as families, peer groups, or delinquent gangs. Nevertheless, we can still draw from his work in constructing a useful model for small-group analysis if we treat the conditions implied by his basic concepts, such as interdependence, order, the fulfillment of functional needs, and system survival, as problematic rather than assured. In other words, by using Parsons' basic concepts without assuming the absence of inherent strains, tensions, or disruptive tendencies in systems, it is possible to develop a conception of the small group as a social system that can help us understand the structure and functioning of real small groups. Bales' theoretical work is an excellent example of how one can build on Parsons' conceptual framework to construct such a model.

BALES' MODEL. As suggested earlier in this chapter, Bales' "interaction process analysis" tends to be better known as an observational rather than theoretical approach. In fact, the observational categories of his research method were systematically derived from his model of small groups as social systems. This model, which has incorporated the Parsonian emphasis on functional prerequisites and the maintenance of equilibrium,[15] has had a continuing impact on how small groups are viewed by sociologists.

Bales and Parsons use a similar conception of the functional problems of social systems (Parsons, Bales, and Shils, 1953:63–109). Both focus on problems concerning: (a) *integration,* or, how the parts of a system fit together as a whole; (b) *pattern maintenance,* or, how the major patterns of culture and interaction in a system are maintained; (c) *goal attainment,* or, how a system organizes and controls the pursuit of its tasks and goals; and (d) *adaptation,* or, how a system

[14] See Buckley (1967:30–31), for an explicit discussion of this weakness in Parsons' framework.

[15] It should be recalled from footnote (6) in this chapter that Bales was in close contact with Parsons and Shils and was influenced by their theoretical perspective in *Toward a General Theory of Action* (1951), when he was developing his small group theoretical approach.

relates to its environment. Beyond this common focus on functional problems, it is much more difficult to identify similarities between Bales' and Parsons' system perspectives.

While Bales and Parsons agree that a social system must adequately meet all its basic functional needs to remain coherent and viable, they disagree sharply about how these needs are normally met. This disagreement represents a major distinction between their perspectives. Bales' perspective is more dynamic, emphasizing tension and rivalry, which Bales sees as necessarily linked to the attempted resolution of different kinds of functional problems. Bales described the nature of the assumed antagonism between different system needs in the following terms:

> . . . Even in cases of successful solution of the sub-problems we assume that there is a "wear and tear" involved . . . which demands periodic activity oriented more or less directly to the problem of distributing the rewards accruing from productive activity back to individual members of the system and re-establishing their feeling of solidarity or integration with it. In particular we believe that the necessities of control or modification of activity in order to control the outer situation productively (are) likely to *put the existing integration of the system under strain, no matter how successful* the attack on the situational problem may eventually be (Bales, 1950:61).

Accordingly, social systems such as small groups become stabilized by developing a social structure, which Bales viewed as "a system of solutions to the functional problems of interaction which become institutionalized in order to reduce the tensions growing out of uncertainty and unpredictability in the actions of others." Bales identified four dimensions of role differentiation as the basic components of a group's social structure and defined these dimensions in terms of: (a) access to resources or property relations; (b) control over persons or authority; (c) status ranking or social stratification; and (d) group solidarity (1950:73).[16] Bales' conception of the state of precarious balance existing between these different aspects of social structure clearly reflects the dynamic nature of his social-system model of small-group functioning. He described this state of "dynamic equilibrium" in the following way:

> . . . The social system in its organization, we postulate, tends to swing or falter indeterminately back and forth between these two theoretical poles: optimum adaptation to the outer situation at the cost of internal malintegration, or optimum internal integration at the cost of maladaptation to the outer situation (Bales, 1950:157).

---

[16] See Olmsted (1959:119–121), for a brief review of the meaning of each of these aspects of social structure identified by Bales.

Bales' argument that groups, particularly problem-solving ones, *in equilibrium* swing back and forth between antithetical task, or instrumental, and socio-emotional, or expressive, orientations may need some qualification. Even so, his perspective is valuable for its identification of basic functional problems and aspects of social structure of small groups and of the possible tension between different types of problems and roles. Another model aiding us in identifying basic aspects of small groups as social systems was presented by Homans (1950).

HOMANS' MODEL. Earlier in this chapter, we considered Homans' concept of "practical equilibrium," which goes beyond Bales' "dynamic equilibrium" concept in that it emphasizes the possibility of changing states of equilibrium and group growth and elaboration of its structures. Homans assumed that when a group, as a social system, was in equilibrium, a change in one of its main elements (of activities, interaction, sentiments, or norms) would produce a change in the others to restore the original state of balance, or equilibrium, among these elements. However, Homans also assumed that groups were *not* characterized by inevitable or *natural* equilibrating tendencies. Denying the homeostatic idea of equilibrium, he argued that the maintenance of a given pattern of interrelations among the basic elements of a social system was a relatively temporary condition, whereas system change and the establishment of new equilibria were normal occurrences. Thus, Homans' model tends to be more dynamic than the one formulated by Bales, since Homans placed more emphasis on the structure-elaborating, or *morphogenetic,* possibilities of social systems.

We have noted that Homans identified activities, interaction, sentiments, and norms as the most fundamental parts of social systems. He saw *activities* as the things people do by virtue of group membership that do not involve reciprocal exchange or interaction with other people. Examples could include such diverse things as eating, writing, reading, walking, or flying a kite. He defined *interaction* as reciprocal exchange or mutual stimulation between different individuals. Homans illustrated this concept with the case of two men at opposite ends of a saw, sawing a log. In this case, sawing is an *activity,* but the fact that a push by one man is followed by a push by the other means that the men are *interacting*—or reacting to each other—while they are sawing. More typically, interaction involves words or some other form of symbolic communication. Homans conceptualized *sentiments* as internal states of a person (e.g. happy or sad feelings, conservative or liberal attitudes, and beliefs of various sorts) that can be inferred from what people say and do and how they interact. He viewed *norms* as ideas members of a social system have about how people should act under given circumstances. Norms are rules for proper conduct that people are expected to accept and follow.

Homans focused on these basic elements of social behavior, along with concepts of role differentiation, authority, status ranking, and practical equilibrium, to construct his social-system model of human groups. In this model, he sees groups as having two major aspects, an *external* one and an *internal* one.

The *external system* of a group represents its way of reacting to what Bales called the *adaptive* problem or the relationship of the group to its social and physical environments. This system consists of the patterns of interrelations among activities, interaction, sentiments, and norms imposed on a group by external forces such as a larger group or organization, a supervisor, or the physical environment, as in the case of a mountain climbing team (Homans, 1950: 90–94). The *internal system* consists of the remaining patterns of linkage among activities, interaction, sentiments, and norms that are not conditioned by the environment, but are spontaneously elaborated and standardized by group members.

According to Homans, the relative dominance of the external or internal system may vary. For example, the basic character of relations among the members of a young family may be mostly influenced by their own demands and wishes or it may be very strongly influenced by demands or wishes of external forces such as parents or employers. The concept of *autonomy* refers to cases where groups are relatively free to develop their own character. No group, though, is entirely free of environmental influences.

Unlike Parsons and Bales, Homans did not treat the emergence of structures and problems in a social system as a response to its functional needs. Instead, he viewed their emergence as a consequence of social forces tied to the basic elements of a system and the way they are balanced or unbalanced at any given time.

While Homans may have been justified in rejecting the literal implications of functionalism, it may still be useful to retain functionalist language in constructing a small-group model. One need not infer from the use of such language as "functional prerequisites" and "functional problems" that a group has survived because it has fully resolved all its basic functional needs or that it has a life, a mind, or needs apart from those of the individual human beings who relate to each other as its members. Presumably, then, one can use the functionalist perspective for heuristic purposes, without becoming mired in the teleologic and anthropomorphic fallacies often attributed to its proponents by its critics (see, e.g., Buckley, 1967:29). Furthermore, it is believed that the use of functionalist language, along with the social system perspective in general, will emphasize the importance of looking at a group as a whole that has a special character that cannot be understood simply by summing the actions or attributes of its individual members. This special character is presumed to include a recurring set of collective problems, or *functional needs,* that arise when people interact as group members and a related set of social structures and processes created by group members to respond to these problems. Homans' concept of *practical equilibrium* becomes especially relevant when we try to understand the condition of balance among these basic elements of groups.

OTHER MODELS. An examination of other models of social systems and small groups reveals that Parsons, Bales, and Homans have identified, at least in general terms, most of the basic concepts needed to understand small groups and how they function. By briefly considering some representative examples of this other work, it becomes easier to appreciate the value for small-group analysis of the conceptual frameworks of Parsons, Bales, and Homans; it also becomes easier to see their influence on the way sociologists have viewed small groups. For example, Mayer (1975:8) suggested that mathematical models of social structure in informal groups, as systems of social relationships, have focused mainly on three general types of problems. These problems concern: (a) structural solidarity, or the structural bases of a group's cohesion and cleavage; (b) structural equilibrium, or the stability of the network of relationships among group members; and (c) structural hierarchy, or the system of inequality in a group. Although these problems may receive fuller or more systematic attention in the work of specific math modelers, it should be evident even from the cursory review in this chapter that they are treated in one or more of the frameworks of Parsons, Bales, and Homans.

Many of the conceptual frameworks developed for analyzing small-group interaction include Bales' general distinction between task and socio-emotional activities. Olmsted (1959:138–143) and Hare (1976:Ch.1) offer two prominent examples of such perspectives. However, in addition to Bales' distinction, Olmsted distinguished between *social structure,* or the *inner* situation in groups involving relationships among members, and *culture* or the *outer* situation involving relationships between group ideas and values. Hare, on the other hand, treated the task and socio-emotional behavior as the major manifestations of the content of group behavior. Content was differentiated from form in his analysis, with *content* referring to the deeper substance of what is going on in a group and *form* to a less specific reflection of the outward appearance of a group's structure. Hare described the major categories of the form of group behavior as the communication network and the rate of interaction among members.

A valuable contribution by Hare (1973; 1976:12–15) to the functional analysis of small groups as social systems is his effort to give more concrete meaning to the major categories of functional problems initially proposed by Parsons and by Bales: that is, the problems of adaptation, goal attainment, integration, and latent pattern maintenance and tension management (or simply pattern maintenance). He presented the substance of this effort in the following way, drawing a basic distinction between acts positively oriented toward a particular functional problem and those negatively oriented (Hare, 1976:14):

Pattern Maintenance Acts:
+   Seeks or provides basic categories or ultimate values
        Asks for or seeks to define:
                basic purpose or identity of group
                fundamental meaning of "all this"
                general orientation
                basic obligations

- Seeks to deny, take away, or inhibit the development and recognition of values

Integration Acts:

+ Seeks or provides solidarity or norms (as primary mechanisms of conflict management)
            Asks for or seeks to define:
                how the group can get along better, promote harmony or decrease conflict
                what the specific norms governing relations should be
– Seeks to deny, inhibit, or prevent the formation of norms and movement toward group solidarity

Goal Attainment Acts:

+ Seeks or provides relatively specific direction, goal-definition, or problem solutions relevant to the group's goals
            Asks for or seeks to define:
                relatively specific group goals (be careful to distinguish goals from values and norms)
                decisions which, in effect, are attainment of group goals
– Seeks to prevent or inhibit movement toward group's goals

Adaptation Acts:

+ Seeks or provides facilities for goal attainment
            Asks for or seeks to define:
                ways to get or increase (especially to generalize) resources, relevant information, or facts
– Seeks to deny, inhibit, or prevent the provision of facilities and relevant information

USES AND LIMITATIONS OF SOCIAL SYSTEM MODELS. Although Hare's conception of the basic content of actions related to major functional problems of small groups as social systems is fairly general, it should help clarify what social-system theorists mean by highly abstract concepts such as *functional problems, functional imperatives,* or *functional needs.* We can see from his work that system theorists with a functional orientation want us to focus on group members' efforts to grapple with problems or pressures concerning such things as their collective identity, purposes and goals, mutual obligations, solidarity, feelings toward each other, manner of making decisions, resource allocation, and group goal attainment. Unfortunately, though, despite Hare's attempt at clarification, it still does not seem possible to classify the important social structures, processes, and problems of small groups we will examine in this book precisely in the way the social system models described in this chapter propose we should. Nevertheless, with Hare's interpretation in mind, it *is* possible to see more clearly how we can use the abstract functional and system concepts of these models to discuss small-group research.

Even if we cannot fit individual types of social patterns and problems of small groups neatly into the functional categories of the social-system models we have described, we can enhance our understanding of them by relating them to the functional orientation in general and to other key social-system ideas associated with this type of orientation. For example, it is possible to relate structures or processes of group cohesion, interpersonal sentiments, and rivalry or conflict to the functional problem of integration. The establishment of group norms and the maintenance of social control could be seen as relevant both to integration and pattern maintenance. While more difficult to classify, status relations could also be tied to both of these functional problems insofar as they reflect group members' values or sense of importance about different positions in the group and group members' feelings of respect or disesteem for each other. When status relations concern the rewards people receive for their contributions to group performance, status relations seem to become relevant to the group goal-attainment function as well. Leadership, interpersonal power, and coalition formation also seem relevant to group goal attainment, and the mobilization and use of group resources such as the talents of group members, facilities, and information to achieve group goals seem to be related both to goal attainment and adaptation, especially insofar as the group is brought into contact with its social or physical environment. As we suggested earlier in the book, communication or interaction is perhaps the most fundamental group structure, cutting across all aspects of group functioning.

We do not want to stretch the functional framework too far. However, we hope it is evident that this framework provides a meaningful interpretation of the things people do as members of small groups. The meaning of group members' behavior is the group function or functions their actions serve or disrupt. We might assume that when small groups successfully resolve the kinds of functional problems given some concrete definition by Hare, the outcome is relatively stable patterns or structures of group interaction. Similarly, we might assume that when group interaction is dominated by the *negative* actions suggested by Hare, most likely the consequences are disruptive, and they may create pressures toward change or breakdown of one or more group structures.

The use of functional and social-system imagery allows us to see the relationship of group structures, processes, and problems to major functions group members regularly confront in their efforts to remain together and act as a coherent small group. This sort of imagery implies a crucial notion we want to stress here, that an especially meaningful interpretation of behavior in small groups is provided by looking at this behavior in the context of the group as a whole and the distinctive character and properties of the whole group. Functional and social-system imagery show how group behavior is part of a network of interrelated functions of the group as a whole. A group's success in dealing with integrative problems ultimately has a bearing on its resolution of its other major functional problems, and thus, the varied forms of interaction we find in small groups have a potential relationship to each other through their common relationship to one or more of these major functional problems. We can use the notion of *equilibrium* to describe the often precarious balancing act found at any given time in a small group as its members grapple simultaneously and with some success with the full range of functional problems they face.

The use of a social-system perspective here is not meant to imply that total interdependence among the parts of a group exists always or at any time or that a group can maintain its integrity in its environment without much effort. There may be times, for example, during group formation, deterioration, or change in general, when there is only a loose connection among certain or all parts of the group or when a group's boundaries or sense of its identity are rather vague. Despite these conditions, a given set of people still may have some sense of its identity as a group, have at least a minimal set of shared standards or expectations for behavior, and interact fairly frequently in a face-to-face manner. If these essential conditions exist, according to our definition a set of people will be a small group; and thus, it will warrant our investigation as one, despite or perhaps because of its difficulty in maintaining itself or our difficulty in defining the nature of or connection among its main elements.

The use of functional concepts here is not meant to imply that groups always do what is needed to remain coherent and viable or that whatever happens in a group contributes to its stability and persistence. Small groups, like all other social systems, frequently must deal with strains, tensions, and threats to whatever kind of equilibrium they have been able to establish. A group may be quite durable and even relatively stable in its overall structure while still having to cope with a variety of social problems caused by difficulties in handling basic functional issues. Or, a group may break down or dissolve as a result of such difficulties. In the latter case, we know that marriages fail at an alarmingly high rate in our society, but in view of the pressures of job, finances, and child rearing, one might argue it is a miracle so many marriages endure. We know, for example, that former President Nixon's family has endured, in fact, apparently become closer, despite the severe external pressures associated with Watergate and its aftermath, and that the marriages of congressmen and senators have persisted despite public disclosures of affairs with secretaries and "ladies of the evening." Although the nature of group relationships may have been altered in such cases, the important if not fascinating fact is that the groups themselves were not destroyed by the rather severe pressures they faced. Predicting whether groups will survive or dissolve under such pressures requires an understanding of how they *typically* function and respond to functional strains and tensions. An important measure of the utility of social system and functional ideas is the extent they contribute to our understanding of how and why small groups cope or fail to cope with conditions of substantial stress, strain, or tension, since we would expect at least the potential for these pressures to be present in groups all the time.

SOCIAL STRUCTURE AND SOCIAL PROCESS: A DYNAMIC EMPHASIS

It has been suggested that the stability of social structures in groups is not inevitable or inherent. Indeed, since it seems that many groups can be characterized by a steady flow of at least mild strains, tensions, and disruptions, it should be easy to understand why the persistence of particular social structural conditions is always somewhat problematic. It seems necessary to emphasize that given social structures are constantly being challenged by social processes, forces that disrupt the regular and expected patterns of group interaction. In this sense, then, it is *social process, rather than social structure,* that may deserve special attention in the forthcoming chapters. However the reader interprets the findings of these chapters, he or she should keep in mind this dynamic conception of small groups.

Emphasis on a dynamic perspective does not mean that the *social-structure* concept is meaningless or merely a heuristic device. Rather, it implies that when we talk about various types of group structures, we want to make clear that they *may* be undergoing numerous small or subtle changes, while still retaining the same overall outlines of their basic patterns during a particular period of observation. We may overlook the changes because they concern details of these patterns or because a change in one direction is followed by another back in the prior direction. However, a steady succession of minor changes in group structures could lead not only to a change in the details of a particular pattern of interaction, but also to a major transformation of the structure over an extended period of time. For example, parents who initially establish relatively rigid or authoritarian patterns of authority with respect to their children may, as the children grow older, give in little by little, to their demands for more participation in the decisions affecting them. Gradually, these minor concessions could build to produce a fundamental change in the way decisions are made and carried out in this family, from an authoritarian to a democratic structure of authority.

This kind of change is what is implied by Buckley's *morphogenesis* notion, and it is important to understand its potential implications for any kind of group, even if the group seems quite static at first glance. *Social structure* probably is best understood in terms of the group's potential for elaboration and the precarious state of its stability. Thus, in addition to *morphogenesis,* Homans' *practical equilibrium* idea, and perhaps even Bales' concept of *dynamic equilibrium,* should also be kept in mind. From this perspective, one can more readily appreciate the regularity of change that may accompany the persistence of *general* features of group interaction. Changes are seen as regular and recurrent, but no new ones seem to occur. As Homans suggested, "One day's work is much like another's (despite the essentially dynamic nature of group functioning)." By keeping in mind these dynamic perspectives, it should be possible to avoid whatever static or *conservative* biases seem to be implied by functional views of small groups as social systems.

SMALL-GROUP RESEARCH APPROACHES

There are three basic approaches used by sociologists to collect data: surveys (including interviews and self-administered questionnaires), field studies (including both experimental and nonexperimental types), and laboratory experiments.[17] Although all three basic approaches have been used to some extent in small-group research, laboratory experimentation has been used much more frequently than the other approaches, to gather small-group data. Since the laboratory approach has several potential advantages over the other approaches as a means of generating scientific knowledge about small groups, it is easy to understand its appeal. However, it also has some potentially serious limitations. To understand the relative value of this approach, in comparison with other possible small-group methods, it is necessary to consider both its potential advantages and limitations, against those of the other major small-group methods.

LABORATORY EXPERIMENTATION

In the ideal experiment, the investigator creates an environment in which all *extraneous* variables are controlled, and the relations between the *independent* and *dependent* variables of the investigator's theory are systematically manipulated and observed (Crosbie, 1975:6).[18] *Extraneous variables* are ones about which the investigator has not explicitly theorized. *Dependent variables* are factors whose value is expected (theoretically) to change as a result of manipulated changes in the *independent variables* (or, experimental stimuli). Researchers go into the laboratory to carry out their experiments because manipulation of variables and control over the environment are most easily and fully attained in such a setting. If researchers are able to reproduce in the laboratory the actual group structures and processes relevant to their theoretical perspectives, they may be able to derive the following advantages from their laboratory approach (Golembiewski, 1962:46):

1. a more selective approach to specific group factors than is normally available when studying groups in natural settings;
2. the direct testing of hypothetical relations through the manipulation of variables, and the replication of results in a large number of similar experimental settings, that would be difficult to do in natural settings;
3. the use of various statistical techniques whose application requires more than a small number of similar cases;
4. the use of *control groups* (matched with *experimental groups* but not subjected to the experimental manipulation) which allows greater assurance that any results obtained are due to the experimental manipulations (independent variables) rather than to extraneous factors, whose effects are usually difficult to interpret.

These are impressive potential advantages for scientific research. Unfortunately, though, the laboratory approach also can create problems for small-

---

[17] Brief introductory discussions of sociological methodology are by Blalock (1970) and Leik (1972). Books offering more extensive coverage of basic research methods in social science are by Simon (1969) and Denzin (1970). A book explicitly focusing on small group data collection techniques, with particular reference to political science, is by Madron (1969).

[18] See Festinger (1953) about laboratory experiments.

group researchers, which may offset these possible advantages. Probably the most serious of these problems concerns the issue of *realism*. This is not to say, as people sometimes seem to infer, that experimental subjects are not real people engaging in real behavior in even the most artificially contrived laboratory settings. Rather, this problem concerns the possibility that the kinds of ostensible groups created by experimenters in the laboratory may not reproduce the real groups or group factors to which small-group theories are generally supposed to apply.

Small-group laboratory experimenters typically have relied on small *ad hoc* collectivities with no history of, or prospect for, long-term interaction and have treated them as small "groups." In doing so, they have cast doubt on the generalizability of their findings to collectivities outside the laboratory—in the "real world"—that qualify as small groups in the sociological sense specified in the first chapter of this book. Homans (1974:117) expresses the nature of these doubts:

> . . . Should the findings of the laboratory differ from the experiences of real life, the reason lies in no fundamental intellectual contradiction but in the fact that the two were established under different given conditions. But we are far from agreeing that the laboratory findings do always differ from those of real life. Much depends on what side of real life we have in mind. By its inherent characteristics, (laboratory research) is more apt to demonstrate how persons behave when they have met for the first time and have only just begun to influence one another than how they behave when their mutual influence has done its worst (or best) and they have settled down to more or less repetitive and well-established relationships. To understand the latter we need field studies of real groups.

Although Homans took his own advice, relatively few other small-group investigators have followed his lead or that of other field researchers. Whether because they have appreciated the methodological advantages suggested earlier, or the greater economy and convenience usually afforded by this approach, small-group researchers have tended to study small (and typically *ad hoc*) "groups" in the laboratory (Golembiewski, 1962:47-48). Much of this laboratory experimentation has been conducted since World War II; a great deal of it reflects the influence and productivity of Lewin (1947a, 1947b) and his followers in the field theory, or group dynamics, tradition.

The chapters of Part Two of this book will provide a detailed look at some important and interesting examples of small-group laboratory methods, along with other major types of small-group research. However, among the more sociologically oriented small-group investigators, Bales' (1950) systematic development and use of a category system for observing and coding basic dimensions of social interaction, which he called *interaction process analysis,* have provided the inspiration and tools for a large number of laboratory experimental studies. Bales' own work suggests the variety of aspects of small-group inter-action that can be studied on the basis of his empirical approach. For example, along with colleagues, he used interaction process analysis in the laboratory to study phases in group problem solving, (Bales and Strodtbeck, 1951), channels of communication in small groups, (Bales et al., 1951), alternating instrumental and socio-emotional, or secondary and primary, emphases in the group goal attainment process, (Bales and Strodtbeck, 1951), and role differentiation in small decision-making groups (Bales and Slater, 1955).

Unfortunately, for the purposes of generalization, most of the experimental research in this sociological tradition, like the group dynamics tradition, has relied on small *ad hoc* collectivities such as the ones suggested by Homans' comments. Of course, this does not imply that such laboratory research has not been the source of considerable insight and knowledge about real small groups. However, since small-group investigators, especially sociologically oriented ones, are ostensibly interested in producing knowledge about how small groups and their members function in society, it seems surprising that more have not been encouraged by the imaginative work of Homans and others to study real, or "experienced," small groups outside the laboratory in field or natural settings. Of course, some have, and we will now give more attention to the types of small-group research conducted outside the laboratory.

OTHER SMALL GROUP RESEARCH METHODS

Field Experiments

Field experiments generally involve an exposure of experienced, or natural, small groups to experimental manipulations in the settings where they normally function. They represent an important compromise between laboratory experiments and nonexperimental studies. Through laboratory experimentation, one may benefit from superior manipulation, control, convenience, and economy in trying to produce scientific knowledge about small groups; but one may also be faced with severe limitations in trying to reproduce, and generalize to, the real small groups or group factors that are of theoretical relevance. Non-experimental field research has the advantage of realism, but this advantage may be offset by the absence of control and manipulation, which restricts the capacity to use findings for systematic and precise explanation and prediction. Field experiments occupy something like a middle ground between both the advantages and limitations of laboratory experiments and nonexperimental field research. Imaginative examples of how field experimental techniques can be used in small-group research are provided by Coch and French (1948), who studied resistance to change in work procedures among groups of workers in a factory; by Miller and Bugelski (1948), who studied group frustration and the expression of prejudice toward minorities at a boys' summer camp; and by the Sherifs

(1953), who also used the natural setting of a boys' summer camp in their research concerning group harmony and intergroup hostility.[19]

Nonexperimental Approaches

Despite the many potential advantages of laboratory or field experimental approaches in small-group research, other, nonexperimental approaches have sometimes been used. The choice of these other approaches may occur for a number of reasons. For example, researchers may feel they cannot create in a laboratory the group conditions they want to study, and they may be unable to get permission to introduce experimental manipulations into the field setting of interest. Researchers may also feel that their research aims would be better met by a nonexperimental design. This could be the case if the research is intended as an exploratory study, aimed at generating rather than testing hypotheses, or if it is meant as a descriptive study, aimed at providing rich, detailed information about the structure and functioning of particular groups. Or, perhaps a researcher may feel that the use of experimental manipulations would be excessively costly, difficult, or offensive.

Small-group investigators who have not used experimental approaches generally have relied on two major methods of data collection: nonparticipant and participant observation. In addition, they have based some small-group studies on survey methodology, which is a major research approach in other areas of sociology; Wolfe's (1959) study of power and authority in the family is a good illustration of the application of this approach in small-group research. However, small-group researchers have much preferred direct observation to other empirical approaches that depend exclusively on verbal responses, such as survey methods, or on indirect observation through the use of materials such as public documents. Of course, unlike sociologists studying larger social collectivities, small-group sociologists have been able to use, without too much difficulty, various systematic means of direct observation in their research, because the social units of interest to them have been small enough to allow such an approach.

NONPARTICIPANT OBSERVATION. Nonexperimental field studies seldom provide more than descriptions of small groups in natural settings, whether or not the investigator is an active participant in the group or groups being observed. The best of the nonexperimental field studies have made important contributions to our knowledge about small groups, despite the limitations on hypothesis and theory testing, explanation, and prediction imposed by the lack of control and manipulation. One of the best examples of a nonexperimental small-group field study done by a detached or nonparticipant observer is Homans' (1953, 1954) case study of cash posters and ledger clerks. The findings of this investigation were later used by Homans to demonstrate the explanatory

[19]The nature of field experiments with groups has been discussed by French (1953); Sherif (1954) has treated the integration of field work with the laboratory in small group research.

power of exchange theory; we have already encountered some of these findings earlier in this chapter in that context. However, Homans initially reported his results to illustrate and qualify some basic hypotheses about sociometric choices, interaction patterns, status relations, and subgroups in small groups. In this original presentation, his work showed the method, procedures, and interpretive power of a careful and systematic case study. For these reasons, it is a model of small-group sociological research of this type. In addition, it offers a rich source of interesting hypotheses and illustrative materials for further small-group research. Furthermore, as Shepherd (1964:113) suggested, despite its own limitations as a predictive study, its general method could be used for prediction (of at least a modest sort) if the researcher went beyond Homans' focus on a single case.

PARTICIPANT OBSERVATION.   Somewhat less systematically, but still carefully, done nonexperimental field studies by participant observers have also provided interesting and important small-group data. These studies have been conducted both by investigators who have revealed their identity and intentions as researchers and by those who have not. An excellent example of the former is Whyte's (1943) intensive study focusing on a lower-class urban street-corner gang of young men, which he called "The Nortons" or "Doc's boys." For about two years, Whyte immersed himself in the environment and social life of the people he was observing, to provide vivid details and keen insights about the social patterns of street-corner gangs and about lower-class urban culture and social organization. Whyte's detailed and insightful sociological account is a tribute both to his method and to his own skills of observation and analysis.

It is doubtful that the amount and depth of information included in Whyte's account could have been produced by more detached and "objective" methods *or* by less skillful participant observers. Probably the same thing could be said, perhaps even with greater emphasis, about Festinger, Riecken, and Schachter's (1956) study of a doomsday group and Caudill's (1958) study of life as a mental patient in a private psychiatric ward. These are particularly distinctive illustrations of participant observation because the researchers kept their research roles concealed while they involved themselves and gathered data in the group settings of interest to them. The covert nature of these attempts to learn about groups may be brought about by the groups' secretive nature and rigid barriers to outside penetration, as in the case of the doomsday group, which was waiting to be saved before the impending destruction of the world and was extremely intolerant of nonbelievers. Or, it may be brought about simply by the investigator's feeling that a full and accurate understanding of a particular type of group setting cannot be achieved by other, more open means.

While there is no question that this covert approach has resulted in some fascinating sociological descriptions of group behavior, it also should be stressed that it is a very radical means of data collection and can be accompanied by some rather severe restrictions and problems. One fairly obvious problem concerns the dilemma of gathering accurate and sociologically interesting data in a relatively systematic manner *without being noticed* by group members. In this regard, members of Festinger's research team occasionally had to resort to trips to the bathroom to make notes when they were afraid they would forget something important. But, as Dunphy (1972) pointed out, this kind of research role may have some serious disadvantages beyond the problems of systamatic data collection.

> . . . The researcher's freedom to observe the group from the point of view of an outsider often becomes very limited as the study progresses. His membership role tends to bias his observations of the relationship between the . . . group and the larger social system. Maintaining an "objective" viewpoint can place considerable strain on the observer by severely limiting his own self-expression and yet, the more he attempts to express himself as a group member, the more he runs the risk of "over-identification" with the point of view of those in the group. In addition, the social scientist usually emerges from his disguise when the study is completed, often revealing his identity through publication. He can expect at this point to be regarded by the group as a spy or traitor, especially if his association has been secretive. Having been accepted as a *bona fide* member of the group, he should hardly be surprised by reactions of outrage when his deception is revealed. He must also be prepared to cope with the ethical issues when it comes to reporting material he has gathered in this guise. The invasion of privacy is becoming not only a social but a legal issue, and as this trend increases, the possibility of using the role of complete participant may diminish substantially. Therefore this role is only appropriate in a minority of research situations, should be used sparingly, and with a clear recognition of the ethical issues involved as well as the limitations it places on the application of systematic quantitative measures (p. 145).

SOME FINAL CAVEATS AND COMMENTS ABOUT SMALL GROUP METHODS

The Problem of Deception in Small Group Research

Dunphy's warnings about deception apply in general terms not only to covert participant observation, which is, in fact, used rather sparingly in small group research, but also to experimentation, which is used more than any other small-group data collection method. Although the experimenter's role as a researcher tends to be quite evident during an investigation, his research objectives and manipulations frequently are not. Indeed, deception of some sort is commonly used in experiments to mislead subjects about the nature of their research participation, in an effort to enhance the validity of experimental manipulations. The practice of deception, in both experimental and nonexperimental settings, has often raised ethical and legal questions about the legitimacy of studying people without their informed consent, especially when the results could cause them physical, psychological, or social harm. Dunphy has suggested the nature of such questions as they apply to covert participant observation. Research by Milgram (e.g., 1963, 1973) on obedience indicates the kinds of ethical and legal issues that could be raised by deception in experimentation.

Milgram led his subjects to believe they were participating in a study of the effects of punishment on memory. Naive subjects were given the role of "teacher" and were instructed by the experimenter to punish each successive incorrect answer of the "learner," an accomplice of the experimenter, with an electrical shock level 15 volts more than the prior one—and ranging up to 450 volts! In reality, the shocks were fake. Nevertheless, the naive subjects took the situation seriously, and believed that the shocks were real and the learner's expressions of pain and demands to be released were real too. Incredibly, 26 of the 40 subjects in this experimental situation continued administering shocks up to the maximum 450-volt level, and none defied the experimenter and discontinued participation before 300 volts, at which point the learner began pounding on the wall of the room in which he was bound to the electric chair. These rather chilling results may be at least slightly tempered by the fact that even the 26 totally obedient subjects tended to follow with great reluctance and personal agony the experimenter's instructions to continue shocking the ostensibly suffering learner.

Milgram's research may be a source of important insights about the occurrence of the apparently mindless and heartless killing of innocent people in places like Nazi Germany and My Lai. However, one may wonder whether even the most important knowledge about our behavior should be obtained under such research conditions. For not only is there the question of the legitimacy of subjecting people to such emotional agony during the course of the experiment; there is also the question of whether people can ever be effectively and fully "debriefed" in such cases, once they have realized the full meaning of what they have done. This particular investigation, which has created considerable controversy among social scientists (and non-social scientists), brings into sharp focus the issue of the justifiable limits of the pursuit of scientific knowledge. This is an issue having no simple resolution, either in the realm of scientific ethics or in law.

Distorting Influences in Small Group Research

Milgram's experiments have created a great deal of controversy at least in part because he was so successful in inducing his experimental stimuli. However, much more frequently the experimental manipulations of laboratory experimenters are not taken seriously enough. College students have been a major source of experimental subjects; increasingly in recent years, they have become canny, suspicious, or wary about deceptions to which they might be exposed in the laboratory. As a result, it has been difficult to get them to respond in a natural and motivated fashion to experimental manipulations, which, in turn, has meant that experimenters have often been faced with a large amount of random or otherwise difficult to explain behavior. The scope of this problem will increase to the extent clever or controversial experimental deceptions become part of popular knowledge.

Although some small-group research techniques tend to have more inherent problems than others in generating reliable and valid data, all those based on direct and open observation share a common potential problem. This problem concerns the "Hawthorne effect," and recognition of it has made social researchers more sensitive to the possible impact their presence as observers in a research setting can have on their findings. The Hawthorne effect generally refers to the positive influence of research involvement on the people being observed, when they know they are being observed. It was discovered in a series of field experiments conducted during the late 1920s and early 1930s at the Western Electric Company's Hawthorne plant in Chicago, by a team of researchers from the company and from the Harvard Graduate School of Business Administration (Roethlisberger and Dickson, 1939).[20] Along with the discovery of the Hawthorne effect, this study produced a number of landmark results concerning the influence of primary groups on worker productivity in industrial organizations.

The Hawthorne effect was found in experiments concerning lighting and productivity and in subsequent ones carried out in the "Relay Assembly Room," a special observation room in the factory. In the earlier experiments, researchers adjusted the lighting to see how different levels of illumination affected worker output. They found that productivity increased not only when lighting became brighter, but also when it became dimmer—almost up to the point where workers could barely see. These unexpected and puzzling results, which defied prevailing "scientific management" assumptions[21] about the impact of physical working conditions on worker output, prompted the Relay Assembly Room experiments.

In this test room, six women who had been randomly selected from among the workers in their department, were closely watched for two years as they reacted to a succession of manipulated changes in their working conditions and pay incentives. The aim was to determine the most efficient and productive conditions of work at the factory. As in the earlier illumination experiments, it was found that *whatever* experimental stimuli were introduced to affect the women's rate of producing electrical relays for telephones, their productivity increased. It did not matter whether their lighting was made better *or* worse, their rest pauses were increased *or* decreased, their work days and work weeks

---

[20] This research team was directed by Harvard's Elton Mayo; and his chief field investigator was Fritz Roethlisberger, who collaborated with William Dickson, the head of the company's research organization, in the research and in writing the most extensive report of the results, *Management and the Worker* (1939).

[21] See Taylor (1911), for an example of this type of management approach.

were lengthened *or* shortened, or their pay was by salary *or* piece rate; the women's output steadily improved over the two years they were under observation.

Once again, as in the initial illumination research, the investigators were puzzled by what they found. Eventually, though, they were able to make sense of their anomalous findings by interpreting them in terms of the increased attention they and company officials had given the test-room employees, and the opportunity they had provided for the development of primary-group interaction among these employees. Apparently, these workers had felt rewarded by the increased attention and the opportunity for primary-group contacts; as a result, they responded favorably to whatever manipulations were introduced into their work situation.

The discovery of the Hawthorne effect alerted social researchers to the potentially distorting (positive *or* negative) effects their presence could have on the people they were observing. This has become an especially salient potential problem for small-group observers, since the small size of the group settings where they conduct their research can bring them into close contact with their subjects. In an attempt to eliminate this effect, small-group observers have watched experimental group interaction from behind one-way mirrors in the laboratory, recorded the conversations of people in laboratory and field settings with hidden listening devices, and employed a number of other "unobtrusive" techniques to measure group behavior.[22] Unfortunately, though, the use of such techniques has sometimes raised the kinds of ethical issues discussed earlier in regard to covert participant observation. The dilemma posed by the possibility of the Hawthorne effect, or any similar distorting influence, is therefore a tough one, since the effort to solve this kind of problem can create other ones, including the invasion of privacy and abuse of subjects in other ways.

It may seem remarkable after just having considered the various kinds of obstacles and disadvantages that can plague small-group researchers of all sorts, but there have actually been many excellent small-group studies that have collectively produced a wealth of sociological knowledge about small groups. We have provided a preliminary glimpse at the findings of some of these studies in this discussion of research methods. In the ensuing chapters, we will examine this research and its bearing on basic patterns and problems of small groups, much more extensively and in greater depth.

SUMMARY

The discussion in this chapter has ranged from the nature and aims of scientific theory and research in general to the nature of major small-group theoretical and research approaches. More specifically in regard to theory, we have considered varying interpretations of the notion of "theory" among social scientists, the tendency of small-group investigators to employ theoretical models rather than

---

[22] See Webb *et al.* (1966), for a treatment of a variety of unobtrusive procedures.

rigorous theories for analytical purposes, and the aims, benefits, and limitations of this type of theoretical approach. We have also examined the main features and research implications of the field, social exchange, and social system perspectives, which have been the most prominent approaches to small group analysis in recent decades. Since in this book we will be relying mainly on social-system ideas to discuss small-group research we gave special attention to key social-system ideas and to the theorists such as Parsons, Bales, Homans, and Buckley who have been largely responsible for them.

In regard to research methods, the advantages, disadvantages, and problems of the most commonly used small-group method, laboratory experimentation, have been treated along with those of the other major small-group research approaches, which include field experimentation, nonparticipant observation, and overt and covert forms of participant observation. We paid special attention to methodological limitations, ethical problems, and observational biases that could undermine the utility or applicability of each of these approaches. We hope these kinds of comments, along with those concerning the limitations of existing small group theoretical perspectives, will be remembered as we consider the small-group literature.

To appreciate the full meaning and implications of the findings and issues examined in the coming chapters, it is worthwhile to keep in mind the most important aspects of small groups that have been discussed so far in this book. In particular, it should be recognized that a small group can be treated as a whole social unit having distinct boundaries and a network of interdependent relations linking its main components, whether they are construed as social structures, processes, relationships, functional needs, or group members. Furthermore, we want to emphasize a dynamic perspective for viewing small groups. This means that change and possibly even deviance, can be seen as normal—not aberrant—in small group functioning, and that small groups have the capacity for "morphogenesis" or the elaboration of structures and the creation of new equilibria.

Probably the most appropriate perspective for looking at social structure and the condition of balance among the basic patterns of social behavior in small groups is Homans' *practical equilibrium* idea. This idea implies, in a sense, that "the more things change (or seem to change), the more they remain the same." We know that groups do not always remain the same, even in overall structure, but it is important to realize that even when they do, we cannot necessarily assume that no changes have taken place. The notion that the maintenance of a given condition of equilibrium is precarious and probably quite temporary is a most important insight to take from Bales, Buckley, Homans, and others emphasizing the dynamic character of social systems such as small groups.

The value of knowing the kinds of things we have discussed so far and those we will discuss later in this book seems best summarized by Bales. He noted that the goal of small group theory and research is to enable a person

" . . . to read the signs that appear in the behavior (his own as well as others)—to diagnose accurately what is going on, predict where it is going, and how it will change if he takes a given action—all of this soon enough for him to intervene and try to change the course of events if he deems it desirable" (Bales, 1959:296). This book is an attempt to show how far small-group sociology has come in the pursuit of this goal.

II

Social Patterns
and Problems
of Small Groups

3

Communication, Group Integration, and Interpersonal Relations in Small Groups

INTRODUCTION

This chapter is the first of the five chapters of Part Two dealing with important and interesting concepts, assumptions, and findings concerning basic dimensions of the small group as a sociological phenomenon. It focuses on communication, group integration, and interpersonal relations. These seem appropriate topics to begin with, since, according to our definition of the small group, people can only form small groups when they communicate or interact regularly with each other. Group integration refers to the forces or relations binding people together as a small group and interpersonal relations concern how people communicate or interact with one another as group members. Shortly, we will offer more precise definitions of the structures and processes related to the communication, group integration, and interpersonal relations concepts than we have so far suggested. However, we hope it is already clear that these are fundamentally important concepts for understanding how groups form and hold together and how group members interact.

Problems of communication, group integration, and interpersonal relations often seem to cause the greatest or most obvious distress among people in small groups. Since these problems involve how often and how well people interact and how they feel about belonging to the group, it is usually fairly easy for people to recognize when these problems are not being handled well. Especially in primary groups, where close interpersonal relationships are, or are supposed to be, predominant, the impact of mismanaged problems of these kinds can be quite sorely felt by individual group members and by the group as a whole. We all know from personal experience that inadequate or ineffective communication, group apathy, rivalries, hostilities, and rejection can be devastating when we are supposed to be intimately involved with other people or must interact regularly with them in a face-to-face manner. We hope that by reading what is presented here about these sorts of group problems, you will find these problems less confusing and frustrating, and perhaps even less likely to happen in the groups in which you are a member.

There is no pretense of exhaustiveness in this or the other chapters of Part Two in the coverage of small-group literature or dimensions. Instead, the main purpose of these chapters is to convey the meaning of basic sociological concepts related to group interaction, and to present a representative sampling of interesting and important sociological findings concerning basic dimensions of the small group as a sociological phenomenon. The ideas used to examine small groups in Part Two mainly will be drawn from social-system and functional perspectives. In each chapter of this part of the book, special emphasis will be given to some studies about the ways group members collectively create or resolve strains, tensions, or problems having significant implications for their lives together in a given group. These are the kinds of strains, tensions, or problems that could confront any of us at some time in our group experiences, and some of these problems could trouble us deeply. Thus, examination of these selected studies is explicitly intended to have practical applications to what actually happens to us and concerns us as members of small groups.

COMMUNICATION IN SMALL GROUPS

GENERAL ASSUMPTIONS AND FINDINGS

Golembiewski (1962:90) proposed that the most obvious necessity of small-group life may be communication. Experimental research suggests this necessity derives from two general classes of *forces* (Festinger, 1954). One class concerns the presumed need of a group as a whole to resolve the basic set of persisting functional problems it faces as a social system. The second concerns the presumed needs of individual group members to achieve a clear sense of where they stand in comparison with other group members regarding their beliefs and abilities, and to establish a state of balance or consistency among members' beliefs.

The Sources and Nature of Communication in Small Groups

According to Golembiewski, the combined effect of these needs is the inducement of a relatively stable communication structure, which constitutes a patterning of how and at what rate group members interact with each other. This structure tends to show patterns of differential use of the various possible communication channels between group members as they relate to each other in pursuit of their common purposes. Thus, the communication structure of a group is a vehicle for achieving both differentiation and unity in groups. On the one hand, this means that people in a group tend to interact more frequently with some members than with others, and that they interact in different ways and for different purposes with different members. On the other hand, it means that the overall patterning of communication in a group may be oriented to the basic functional needs, purposes, or goals of the group as a whole. Although the development of stable patterns of communication in groups is not inevitable, there is a tendency for them to develop fairly quickly in most groups, even those created in the laboratory for limited and short-term purposes.

Communication Research: The Organization, Content, and Effectiveness of Communication

Small-group studies of communication structures generally have focused on the organization of communication channels, the content of communication, or the problem-solving effectiveness of different types of communication structures (Crosbie, 1975:258). Studies of the first type have usually been concerned with the nature of patterning in the relative frequency of communication contacts among group members. Crosbie's (1975:258-262, 267) review of studies of this sort suggested to him that the shape of emerging communication structures in groups tends to be closely associated with the development of status and leadership structures.

Research by Larsen and Hill (1958), involving two large groups of boys at a summer camp with more and less stable status-leadership structures, respectively, illustrates Crosbie's point. Their research indicates that while groups are developing their status and leadership structures, their members tend to direct their communication downward to gain status recognition. It also suggests that once these structures have become stabilized, and the need to gain recognition presumably has diminished, members tend to direct communication upward, reflecting a desire among lower status members either for vicarious experience or enhancement of upward mobility chances. This latter tendency toward upward communication has been a consistent finding of studies of the organization of communication structures of small, informal groups. Along with it, a tendency for higher status members to direct most of their communication to status equals has consistently been found (Crosbie, 1975:259).

Apparently, the tendency for people to direct communication upward in the status and leadership hierarchies is confined mainly to small, informal groups (with stable structures). It seems that as collectivities become larger and more formal, there is an increasing tendency for people to limit their communication *within* status-leadership levels (Simpson, 1959; Blau and Scott, 1962; Collins and Guetzkow, 1964). The reasons for these different patterns of communication may be, as Crosbie (1975:259-260) has proposed, the generally greater (and more rigid) status-leadership differences among people in such collectivities and the bigger risks (of status, leadership, *and* popularity) tied to communication with superiors in them.

Generally, laboratory studies of communication in task-oriented groups have focused on a number of different communication networks (or "nets") manufactured by experimenters for their research. Some prominent examples of these nets for five-person groups [which derive initially from the work of Bavelas (1950) and of Leavitt (1951)] are portrayed below:[1]

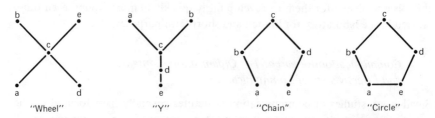

FIGURE 1.   Types of Communication Nets in Five-Person Groups. Reprinted by permission of the American Psychological Association and Leavitt (1951)

A major concept in studies of communication nets like the ones portrayed is *centrality*, which refers to the sum of channels needed to get, by the shortest route, between every pair of positions in a communication net. For Leavitt (1951), the four patterns of communication we have presented were extremes in centrality (especially in the cases of the highly centralized "wheel" and the highly decentralized "circle"). In his framework, the most central position in a network was the one closest to all the others, as in the case of position c in the wheel, Y, and "chain" nets.

Equipped with these conceptions of *communication nets* and *centrality,* it is possible to understand some of the most basic sociological findings tying the organization of communication channels to their content[2] and effectiveness.[3] The main thrust of these findings has been summarized by Hare (1962:290):

> Proximity in the communication network tends to increase intermember attraction. However, if there is no opportunity for "feedback" between members who are close to each other, hostility may appear and efficiency in problem-solving declines. In a comparison of five-man groups in circle, chain, Y, and wheel networks, Leavitt found that the circle, at one extreme, was active, leaderless, unorganized, erratic, and yet enjoyed by its

[1] Letters designate member positions and lines designate open or available communication channels between them. See Shaw (1964), for a more recent and extensive discussion of communication networks.

[2] Crosbie (1975:62) has suggested "there are probably more measures of communication content than of any other aspect of small-group behavior . . . and the simple proliferation of measures may account for many of the inconsistent results." The operational scheme for measuring communication content most familiar to small group investigators is Bales' Interaction Process Analysis; and its broadest distinction is between socio-emotional or affective and task or instrumental communication.

[3] The main focus of studies of small-group communication has been the relative task effectiveness and efficiency of different types of communication nets (Crosbie, 1975:265).

members. The wheel, at the other extreme, was less active, had a distinct leader, was organized, less erratic, and yet unsatisfying to most of its members.

Hare's comments suggest the possible dilemma faced by groups with highly centralized (wheel-like) or highly decentralized (circle-like) communication nets when they try to resolve both group emotional or primary and task needs. We would predict from a social-system perspective that to meet both kinds of needs effectively over time, a group might have to establish a shifting equilibrium between centralized and decentralized communication nets, or a stable equilibrium between these kinds of nets. Research by Cohen and Bennis (1962), concerning change in communication patterns, suggests a somewhat different kind of equilibrium for groups initially establishing circle and wheel nets.

In Cohen and Bennis' study, one set of groups worked with a wheel, and then shifted to a completely open network; a second set worked with an open network in both phases of the investigation. The first set of groups tended to resist changing to a more open and enjoyable communication structure, while the second set tended to retain their open structure rather than change to one that was more centralized and efficient (Mills, 1967:65). These results indicate the apparently powerful grip of the initial state of equilibrium established in a group. They also suggest that groups do not necessarily organize networks of communication or emphasize the kinds of roles or activities most likely to help them function best to meet the full range of their functional needs.

Unfortunately, Cohen and Bennis' research does not tell us the conditions under which groups establish the kinds of interaction patterns and content emphases needed to maximize fulfillment of all their basic functional needs. Nor does it reveal the kind of equilibrium associated with such conditions. More research is needed to answer these questions in a definitive way. However, it should be evident from Hare's brief summary of communication findings that a group's communication structure can have marked effects upon the kinds of things that will interest us later in this chapter. These include, in particular, patterns and problems of group and interpersonal attachments and of feelings members have about the group and each other. In the next section, we will give special attention to two studies that concentrate on problems of group communication, while relating communication to group integration and interpersonal relations. Thus, the discussion of these studies not only provides the basis for a richer appreciation of the meaning and implications of communication structures and problems in small groups; it also provides a nice connection between communication and the other major topics of this chapter. Since these studies focus on groups that are explicitly task-oriented, their relevance to other functions, such as group goal attainment, treated in later chapters, should also be apparent.

COMMUNICATION PROBLEMS IN SMALL GROUPS:
A SELECTIVE FOCUS ON RESEARCH

For all the major topics in the substantive chapters of this book, we will supplement the discussion of general assumptions and findings with a special emphasis on a few selected pieces of research about relevant and salient group problems. We hope to make the discussion of these selected studies more meaningful by focusing on research about groups or group problems to which most of us can relate directly or indirectly on the basis of our personal knowledge, interests, experiences, or concerns. Since communication pervades all aspects of group life, it was difficult to choose particular studies for special attention. The two we chose seemed to merit special recognition because they show the tensions that can be associated with basic aspects of group communication when groups are pursuing important collective goals.

We already have mentioned possible tensions surrounding group problem-solving efforts when groups with highly centralized or decentralized communication nets try to maximize group enjoyment and task effectiveness at the same time. The group members most likely to be highly satisfied with their relations to other members *and* the productivity of their group are those in the centralized positions in centralized nets. As members of such task-oriented groups, the conditions under which we might maximize our personal satisfaction within them is not a small matter to most of us. However, there are other issues, concerning group integration and communication, that are of more immediate and direct concern to us here because they affect the group as a whole. Among these issues are the relationship between communication feedback and sustained group goal-striving, which was considered by Emerson (1966), and the relationship between barriers in the communication process and group integration, which was examined by Back, Bunker, and Dunnagan (1972). These two issues will be the main focus of the remainder of this discussion of communication.

Communication Feedback
and Sustained Commitment to Group Goals

Many of us have been in groups (e.g. sports teams, juries, medical research teams, industrial or construction work crews, business conference groups, negotiation teams, or school classes) faced with seemingly insurmountable group goals. But few of us have faced a group goal as awesome and demanding of sustained group integration and task performance of the highest order as the conquest of Mount Everest. Emerson's research into the attainment of this goal is focused explicitly on an American team of climbers who made an ascent of Mount Everest in 1963. It tries to show the relationship between the nature of communication feedback characterizing this group and the group's success in its attempted ascent.

In general, we associate uncertainty with strain, tension, or disruption we would ordinarily be anxious to eliminate. In fact, people generally try to establish a system of roles and regular patterns of behavior to try to reduce such uncertainty and these potential effects. In an interesting reversal of this perspective, Emerson has tried to show that the creation of uncertainty about the outcome of group goal-attainment efforts through selective communication feedback can enhance sustained group morale and commitment to its goals. This means that the deliberate maintenance of uncertainty of this sort may keep group members nervous, anxious, *and challenged* enough to exert maximum effort in the pursuit of the group goal.

Emerson viewed sustained group goal-striving as a self-maintaining system, at least partially independent of environmental effects. He assumed that in group goal-attainment efforts such as the conquest of Everest, which required high task coordination and collective assessment of the environment, communication feedback was most beneficial for the group when the feedback selectively transmitted information maximizing and maintaining uncertainty about the success of the group's performance. On the basis of his longitudinal case study of the Mount Everest expedition, in which he himself participated, Emerson was able to produce evidence to support certain points in his theory. In particular, he found that:

1. Communication tended to counter the prevailing information in the environment, and feedback was predominantly negative, especially under conditions of high motivation.
2. In assessments of likely goal outcome, uncertainty appeared to be sustained *possibly* as a result of such communication.
3. Energy mobilized in goal-striving appeared to be increased under conditions of uncertainty.

In general, Emerson's research supports the argument that prolonged uncertainty about the outcome of group goal-attainment efforts, nurtured by selective, and perhaps misleading, information feedback by group leaders to members, can maximize and maintain group morale or goal-oriented motivation and goal attainment itself. Thus, Emerson has shown that a potential source of group tension may be an important aid, rather than impediment, for members of at least certain kinds of groups. However, since his research was an uncontrolled field study, we should use extreme caution in generalizing from its results. In addition, even if these results can be replicated for similar kinds of groups, one wonders about the range of task-oriented groups to which his results might apply.

Certainly, there must be many kinds of groups for which sustained uncertainty about goal outcome would severely threaten group morale, cohesiveness, and group integration in general. Past research in the field and in the laboratory has suggested that group task effectiveness and group morale or motivation tend to be hindered when group goals or the paths to them, as opposed to the goal *outcomes,* are uncertain or unclear (Shaw, 1976:323–324, 333). Combining the results of this research with Emerson's results, one might infer that the conditions characterizing groups able not only to tolerate sustained goal outcome uncertainty but to use it as a spur to goal attainment would be high, initial group integration, clearly defined goals and goal paths, and a high level of group ability. Of course, this is pure guesswork, requiring much additional research to be validated. Because Emerson's research has prompted such speculation and offered a number of potentially provocative insights about the effects of group communication feedback on sustained group goal-striving, the value of giving it careful consideration and trying to replicate it systematically in a variety of group settings should be evident.[4]

Implications of Communication Barriers in Discussion Groups for Group Integration, Interpersonal Relations, and Group Efficiency

Even if group members can tolerate ambiguity about the outcome of their goal-striving, it appears they cannot accept interaction with other members who use language with abusive, threatening, or otherwise discomforting connotations for them. This is a main finding of research by Back, Bunker, and Dunnagan, who looked at the effects of the use of key words on group efficiency, group integration, and interpersonal relations in group interaction involving professionals in the areas of science and theology. The subjects of this research were members of a discussion group dealing with important and mutually interesting issues of science and society. These scientists and theologians had been meeting monthly for three years.

Although this discussion group had a fixed membership recruited by invitation, there was a rather high turnover in the specific individuals who were members at any given time. It may be that such high turnover—a possible indication of weak group cohesion—as well as the interpersonal friction found among members with different backgrounds, generally can be expected whenever these differences are emphasized and translated into clashing interpretations of the meaning of interaction content. After all, Back and his colleagues found that even in a group of highly educated people such as scientists and theologians, differences in background created communication barriers that may have seriously undermined the group's efficiency, group integration, and patterns of interpersonal relations.

One can imagine the kinds of communication difficulties that could have disrupted relations between the theologians and scientists. The words used by scientists in a casual or technical way may have been considered too sacred or profane to be used at all by theologians. It should be fairly easy to picture the potential occurrence of similar kinds of communication difficulties in groups of males and females, of management personnel and workers, of blacks and whites, of rich and poor, of Marxists and capitalists, of officers and enlisted men, or of

[4]Emerson intended to extend his study and conduct it under more controlled conditions.

parents and children. Of course, the list could go on and on; but the same general point may apply to all these cases, if Back, Bunker, and Dunnagan's argument can be generalized validly. People may not understand or like what they hear in conversations with other group members because they attribute different connotations to key terms in these exchanges. These communication difficulties may be the result *of* different backgrounds and socialization experiences; they may result *in* a deterioration of various aspects of a group's integration and patterns of interpersonal relations, along with a disruption of efforts to meet other basic functional needs of the group.

In view of the pervasiveness and fundamental importance of regular, face-to-face interaction in groups, it should be apparent why such breakdowns in communication have the potential for considerable group disruption. Perhaps by recognizing their origins, their disruptive effects can be minimized. Of course, as Back and his colleagues noted, the mere detection of the communication problem itself may be quite difficult, which makes its successful resolution appear even more difficult.

Despite the potentially disintegrative effects of heterogeneous membership on groups, it should not be concluded that heterogeneous composition will inevitably lead to group disintegration, even when it causes uncertainty, strain, or tension. In fact, to some degree, all groups are heterogeneous. To understand more fully the ways it can affect group integration, we will have to look beyond Back, Bunker, and Dunnagan to other research concerning group composition and group integration, which we will consider later in this chapter.

COHESIVENESS AND GROUP INTEGRATION

UNDERSTANDING THE MEANING
OF GROUP INTEGRATION AND RELATED CONCEPTS

Hare's (1976:14) interpretation of the content of acts related to the function of integration suggests that group solidarity, group harmony, and the manner in which group members get along with each other are all aspects of the integrative dimension of small groups. Among sociologists and other small-group investigators in the social sciences, the term *cohesiveness*—or *cohesion*—is frequently used to refer to these various aspects of integration. This implies that both cohesiveness and integration encompass the common bonds and sentiments holding together the group as a whole as well as relationships among individual members within the group. Unfortunately, though, defining and using the cohesiveness and integration notions in such a broad or inclusive sense can be misleading in small-group analysis[5] because it may obscure the distinction just mentioned between integration as it applies to the group as a whole, or *group* integration,

[5]After considering the generality of its conceptual definition and the various operationalizations of it, Albert (1953) asked whether we needed the concept of *group cohesiveness* at all.

and integrative elements of interpersonal relations. This distinction is important to maintain because the various forms of *group* integration are not only different in content or substance from integration on an *interpersonal* level, but they may also be different in their sources and implications for group behavior.

In view of its importance, we have tried as much as possible to treat group integration separately from interpersonal relations. In addition, we have tried to use *cohesiveness* in a way that helps maintain this distinction. First, we will present the meaning of cohesiveness we employ in this book. We hope that by clarifying the meaning of this term and how it differs from other aspects of integration at both the group and interpersonal levels, we will help the reader gain a better understanding of the key concepts needed to discuss integrative patterns and problems in this chapter. A clear understanding of the meaning of cohesiveness is especially important here because it will be the aspect of group integration receiving the most attention in this chapter and throughout the remainder of this book.

Cohesiveness

Golembiewski (1962:149) has written, "Theoretically, cohesiveness is the essential small group characteristic. This 'stick togetherness,' or member attraction at once characterizes a small group and differentiates it from other social units." It would be easier to appreciate the importance of cohesiveness implied by this statement if there were agreement among small-group investigators about the conceptual and operational, or concrete, meanings of this idea. Unfortunately, no such agreement exists. As a result, it often is difficult to compare cohesiveness findings produced by different investigators or distinguish antecedents, correlates, and consequences of cohesiveness from those of similar, but still distinct, aspects of group integration.

Golembiewski identified three general classes of conceptual meanings that have been attached to *cohesiveness:* (a) the attraction of a group for its members; (b) the coordination of the efforts of group members; and (c) the level of motivation of group members to do a task with zeal and efficiency, or what is often called *group morale.* Most researchers who use this term today accept some version of definition (a). However, despite widespread agreement about the *general* conceptual meaning of cohesiveness, there still exists disagreement and ambiguity regarding its specific conceptual meaning, as well as a variety of quite different operational measures of it.

The first prominent definition of cohesiveness focusing on the attraction of a group for its members was formulated by Festinger, Schachter, and Back. They defined cohesiveness conceptually as "the total field of forces which acts on members to remain in the group . . . and . . . (operationally) as the average for all the members of the resultant force toward remaining in the group" (1950: 164-165). Even though this definitional work made an important early contribution to the modern study of cohesiveness by somewhat restricting its meaning, it seems to have some significant deficiencies regarding precision, explicitness, and correspondence between the conceptual and operational definitions.[6] Despite these deficiencies, though, a very similar version of this early definition continues to play a prominent role in guiding cohesiveness studies. Festinger (1950:274) defined cohesiveness as "the resultant of all the forces acting on the members to remain in the group;" this definition has been the most widely used conceptualization among cohesiveness researchers. While its greater emphasis on the resultant character of cohesiveness makes this definition somewhat clearer than the one Festinger formulated with Schachter and Back, nevertheless it has been the source of a number of conceptual and operational difficulties for those relying on it in their research. Research by Peterson and Martens (1973) offers a good illustration of such difficulties.

Peterson and Martens' research focused on the relationship between group cohesiveness and group success of basketball teams. Although they indicated their difficulty and that of others in trying to operationalize the full array of forces on members to remain in the group, they still tended to rely on Festinger's conceptual definition to guide their operationalization. They perceived the problem not as one of conceptual ambiguity, broadness, or inexplicitness, but rather as one of insufficient scope in measurement. Thus, they did not try to refine or restrict the conceptual definition. Instead, they developed a set of operational measures that they hoped would assess as many of the "forces acting on members . . . " as possible.

Peterson and Martens were influenced by Gross and Martin's (1952) criticism of the validity of "arbitrary" operational measures of cohesiveness expressing it in terms of only one component of the conceptual definition, or only one component of the "field of forces." Gross and Martin suggested it was most desirable to have each member directly assess his group's cohesiveness, and to derive a measure of the total "field of (cohesiveness) forces" perceived by individual group members. Taking off from Gross and Martin's arguments and from the diversity of prior operational definitions of cohesiveness, Peterson and Martens (1973:65) developed nine different operational indicators falling into three different categories to measure the cohesiveness of basketball teams:

1. *Direct individual* assessments of:
   a. the value of team membership,
   b. how strong a sense of belonging a person felt toward his team,
   c. how much a person enjoyed playing basketball with his teammates.
2. *Direct team* assessments of:
   a. the level of teamwork,
   b. how closely knit the team was.
3. *Sociometric* measures of:
   a. the perceived degree of interpersonal attraction,
   b. the perceived contribution of each member based on his ability,
   c. the perceived contribution of each member to team satisfaction,
   d. the perceived influence or power of each member.

[6] See Golembiewski (1962:151–152), for a fuller treatment of these apparent deficiencies.

Although Peterson and Martens' attempt to-measure cohesiveness directly and with multiple items can be construed as fruitful, their use of a broad assortment of measures deriving from a rather diffuse and somewhat unclear conception of cohesiveness makes their approach theoretically dubious. Indeed, Golembiewski's (1962:153, 155) suggestion that many studies of cohesiveness have been based on "a 'rubber concept' with which anything and everything might be predicted" seems to apply here to some extent. In Peterson and Martens' case, it is likely that some or at least one of their ostensible cohesiveness measures will have some predictive use regarding sociologically interesting phenomena. However, it is not clear that all of the operationalizations are valid measures of the same concept of cohesiveness, even one so broadly defined as Festinger's.

Golembiewski's conceptualization of cohesiveness was an improvement over earlier ones because it explicitly emphasized a more readily measurable phenomenon, member attraction-to-group, *and* it restricted attention to cohesiveness as a resultant factor. He defined cohesiveness as a group property that was "a function of the individual members' *resultant* attraction-to-group, or wish to remain in the group" (1962:152). He provided further clarification when he separated potential *sources* of cohesiveness (e.g., personal attractiveness of group members, task attractiveness, and prestige of group membership) from cohesiveness itself. This conception of cohesiveness seems to capture in clear and readily interpretable terms, the basic meaning intended for this concept by most who have used it in recent years.[7]

Cohesiveness and Other Aspects of Group Integration

It is easy to confuse the meaning of cohesiveness with the meanings of other possible aspects of group integration such as structural integration and functional integration because all these terms broadly refer to the "glue" holding groups together and all can be construed as group properties. However, in order to avoid misinterpreting these terms, it is necessary to indicate their different meanings. Since cohesiveness refers to attraction of *members* to a group as a whole, cohesiveness cannot be viewed as an *emergent* social structural property of groups or one that is created during group interaction and only exists because of it, in the same sense as structural or functional integration. Instead, it is more appropriately viewed as a kind of *synthetic* or aggregative property of the sum of the feelings of attraction to the group of each of the individual group members.

Structural and functional integration are more justifiably seen as emergent group properties in the sense that they develop or have meaning as a result

[7]For example, see Enoch and McLemore (1967). These investigators reviewed a number of conceptual and operational issues concerning the meaning of *group cohesion;* on the basis of this review, they derived a definition of it as "the relative attraction, both intrinsic and instrumental, of a small group for its individual members" (p. 180). Though it may represent a further refinement of Golembiewski's definition, it is still quite similar in its basic meaning.

of group interaction and do not characterize individual people who belong to the group. These two forms of integration can be distinguished if one defines *structural integration* as the strength of linkages between positions and roles in a group (such as mother, father, and child in a family) and between the different social structures (such as communication, leadership, and status) of a group, and if one defines *functional integration* as the strength of linkages between the specialized functional pursuits (such as defining values, creating solidarity, making decisions, and striving for group goals) of group members. The meanings of these two concepts will overlap to the extent that emerging social structures of groups are seen as patterned responses to persisting functional needs of groups. In view of this possible overlap, we might combine these two concepts and refer to *structural-functional integration* and distinguish it from two other basic forms of group integration identified by Feldman (1968) as *normative integration* and *interpersonal integration*.[8]

Cohesiveness and Interpersonal Integration

Normative integration, which concerns the amount of consensus among group members about proper group behavior, much less frequently than interpersonal integration has been identified or confused with the other forms of integration mentioned before. Generally speaking, small group investigators have tended to conceptualize or operationalize cohesiveness as if it meant the mutual attraction of group members, and that has often complicated the theoretical interpretation of cohesiveness *and* interpersonal attraction findings. Even though it is possible to identify cases where group members have positive feelings about belonging to their group, but not about each other, cohesiveness and interpersonal attraction often have been treated as equivalent in small-group literature.[9]

The need to distinguish between cohesiveness and interpersonal sentiments at both conceptual and operational levels is suggested by Peterson and Martens' (1973: 72) finding that direct questions about member relations to the group as a whole did not significantly correlate to a sociometric question or vice versa. Other research has produced similar findings (e.g., Eisman, 1959; Ramuz-Nienhuis and Van Bergen, 1960). Thus, in the present framework, we want to maintain clear distinctions not only among cohesiveness, structural-functional integration, and normative integration, but also between these factors and interpersonal integration. The social structure in groups most relevant to interpersonal integration is the *sociometric* structure, which consists of the patterning of sentiment relations in groups, or the regular patterns of expression of likes and dislikes among group members (Crosbie, 1975:115-124).

---

[8] These types of distinctions among forms or bases of group integration are presented, in a somewhat more elaborated fashion, by Akers (1970) in his typology of *group cohesion* (which translates into *group integration* in our framework).
[9] Indeed, Lott and Lott's (1965) massive review of *cohesiveness* literature from 1950–1962 was titled "Group Cohesiveness as Interpersonal Attraction . . ."

Group Emotion

Though there are a number of other possible distinctions among aspects of integration, we will only consider one more. It is the factor of *group emotion.* Although it can be loosely applied to other aspects of integration such as cohesiveness and interpersonal sentiments, this concept goes beyond these factors when it refers to the configuration of feelings among group members *and* their collective emotional responses to group events (Mills, 1967:58). In this sense, it can refer to such factors as *group morale*—or a group's emotional approach to task performance—and the general level of satisfaction or frustration group members feel about their life together in their group. These are somewhat different dimensions of the integrative aspect of groups than the ones mentioned previously in this section; thus, they deserve to be separated from these other dimensions.

The term *group emotion* has had special meaning (in its general sense) for those who have been interested in studying or developing enduring patterns of mutually rewarding or satisfying socio-emotional relations among group members through *T*-groups, sensitivity training groups, encounter groups, therapy groups, or other, similar kinds of "experiential groups."[10] In the final section of this chapter, we will examine the nature and aims of these groups with respect to group emotion and group growth. However, before getting to that topic, we will consider assumptions and findings concerning such aspects of integration as cohesiveness, subgroup formation, and interpersonal attraction.

GENERAL ASSUMPTIONS AND FINDINGS

Cohesiveness: Sources and Consequences

Because there has been a lack of agreement among small-group investigators about how to conceptualize and measure cohesiveness, we find *cohesiveness* assumptions and findings covering various aspects of group and interpersonal integration. However, it should be recalled that we have tried to separate the meaning of cohesiveness from the meanings of these other aspects by treating it as a *synthetic* group property reflecting overall member attraction to a group as a whole. The assumptions and findings about cohesiveness presented here are based on this conception of it and not on any of the other meanings that have been attached to it.

The fact that cohesiveness is such a basic group property makes it difficult to summarize briefly the full range of sociological assumptions and findings about it. Thus, we will try to focus on a representative sample of the most basic ones. In the most general terms, the more effective groups are in serving the

[10]The meaning and nature of "experiential groups" of various sorts are discussed by Shaw (1976:Ch. 10).

functions that could attract people to them, the more cohesive they will be. Golembiewski (1962:164) outlined four very basic functions of this sort:

1. The group may serve as an agency through which members obtain and evaluate information about their environment.
2. The group may create some aspects of reality that are relevant for the individual and may control some aspects of the physical and social environment that are of consequence to individual members.
3. The group may fill a need for affiliation and affect.
4. The group may function as a defense against the extra-group environment.

In this same context, Golembiewski (1962:164) also identified an "elemental law of small-group physics" regarding cohesiveness: "The greater a group's cohesiveness, . . . the greater the force holding the group together, and the greater the force necessary to pull the group apart."

Research has suggested that higher levels of group cohesiveness tend to imply greater group control over the attitudes and actions of group members, more commitment and conformity to group norms, and greater acceptance of group values (Back, 1951; Schachter, 1951; Schachter *et al.,* 1951; Seashore, 1954; Deutsch, 1959; Wyer, 1966). In his classic experimental study of "deviation, rejection, and communication," Schachter (1951) found that those who resisted or deviated from group standards tended to be rejected more by other group members in high cohesive than low cohesive groups, with the relevance or importance of group activities held constant. In addition, communications directed toward deviants to bring them in line tended to be *initially* more frequent, and *eventually,* less frequent, in high cohesive than low cohesive groups. Golembiewski (1962:165) interpreted this finding as implying more strenuous attempts to preserve the integration and integrity of the group by members of more cohesive ones, first by attempted conversion of the deviant and then by strong rejection once conforming group members conclude that the deviant's conversion is unlikely.

In general, studies have shown that the amount of interaction is greater in more cohesive groups (e.g., French, 1941; Back, 1951; Lott and Lott, 1961); that members of highly cohesive groups tend to be friendlier, more cooperative, and more inclined toward behavior enhancing group integration than members of groups low in cohesion (Back, 1951; Shaw and Shaw, 1962); and that member satisfaction with the group and its products tends to be greater in more highly cohesive groups (Marquis, Guetzkow, and Heyns, 1951; Van Zelst, 1952; Gross, 1954; Exline, 1957).[11] Though these generalizations are not unequivocal, they tend to represent the main thrust of cohesiveness findings in these areas. The findings concerning cohesiveness and group goal attainment seem to be

[11] See Shaw (1976:197–209, 233–234), for a recent review of cohesiveness findings and hypotheses.

much more inconsistent. However, it may be that the main differences in these results can be explained by how they were produced, as Shaw (1976:234) has suggested.

Laboratory studies have shown that more cohesive groups perform at only slightly higher levels than, or the same levels as, less cohesive ones, while field and field-experimental studies have shown a more marked superiority in goal attainment of more cohesive groups over less cohesive ones. According to Shaw, we may be justified in accepting the latter as a better indication of the actual pattern in small groups, because groups created in the laboratory may not always accept the goal imposed on them by the experimenter. Support for the generalization that more cohesive task groups tend to work harder and be more productive has been generated by research in military settings (Goodacre, 1951; Hemphill and Sechrest, 1952; Strupp and Hausman, 1953), in industrial settings (Van Zelst, 1952), and in the classroom (Shaw and Shaw, 1962), among other places.

Although these results may seem quite expected on the basis of our prior comments about the general impact of cohesiveness on group behavior, they do not imply that a higher level of cohesiveness will always mean a higher level of task productivity. More cohesive groups might produce a *lower* amount of output because they have set a lower standard for production than their less cohesive counterparts (Seashore, 1954). The important point to remember in this regard is that whatever the goal set by group members, whether it is high task productivity or low task productivity, enjoyable socio-emotional relations or efficient and effective task performance, members of more cohesive groups tend to be more successful in goal-attainment efforts than members of less cohesive groups. The relationships among cohesiveness, other aspects of group integration, interpersonal integration, and group task success will be explored in greater depth with respect to sports teams in the discussion of group task performance in a later chapter.

Clique Formation and Group Integration

An aspect of the structural composition of groups that can have an important bearing on cohesiveness, structural-functional integration, and interpersonal integration is clique formation. By *clique*, we generally mean a subset or subgroup of members of a group "whose average liking for each other is greater than their average liking for the other members" (Davis, 1966:86), and "who somewhat consistently support each other and commonly oppose outsiders in conflicts running across problem areas" (Carlson, 1960:329). There may be a natural tendency to view clique formation as a threat to the structural-functional integration of a group and perhaps to its overall cohesiveness and interpersonal integration as well. But circumstances exist when cliques could contribute positively to the integration of a group as a whole. If the patterns of interaction and activities, and the norms and goals of cliques are well-integrated with those of the group in which they have formed, the integration of the larger group can be reinforced by the existence of cliques. In addition, cliques may have positive effects on overall group integration by allowing group members to avoid or temporarily escape pressures in the larger group and by providing opportunities to reconfirm the larger group's values and to strengthen identification with it (Stogdill, 1959; Carlson, 1960).

Although a balanced view of the effects of cliques is desirable, one should not be misled about the general effects of clique formation by these positive comments. While the effects *may* be positive, they may also be negative. Carlson (1960) proposed that cliques tend to produce group disintegration and prompt intragroup conflict when goals or goal orientations of different subgroups, or of subgroups and the larger group, differ, and when there are differences between perceptions or interpretations of events in group interaction.

Cliques can also encourage the development of norms or patterns of inter-action, activity, or sentiment that clash with those in other subgroups or in the group as a whole, and this conflict can nurture uncertainty about role behavior and consequent disorganization and ineffectiveness in the larger group context (Stogdill, 1959). Furthermore, Carlson (1960) observed that prior research by French (1941) had shown that cleavage into opposing factions made unorganized groups more likely than organized ones to fail in efforts to deal with group problems. More specifically, in comparing the problem-solving behavior of eight organized groups (athletic teams) with eight unorganized "groups" (Harvard undergraduates who had no prior contact with each other), French found distinct differences in task approaches and in levels of structural-functional integration and task effectiveness. In the organized groups, where roles and norms were more clearly defined, frustration led to aggression and open hostility, *but* the groups remained relatively interdependent in feelings and in task performance. In the unorganized "groups," frustration tended to cause sub-group formation, which substantially decreased the task effectiveness of the group as a whole.

Whatever the consequences of cliques for the groups in which they form or for group members, they tend to be a normal part of adolescent development in most communities in the United States and in similar countries. Dunphy (1963) studied the social structure of urban, adolescent peer groups in Sydney, Australia and was able to identify a pattern of stages of group development in adolescence. Figure 2 shows the pattern he found. An important aspect of cliques in most adolescent "crowds"[12] is their tendency to practice social exclusion with respect

[12] Dunphy (1963) viewed the "crowd" as an association of cliques and as the largest of the social units formed by adolescents. He distinguished cliques from crowds by the smaller size and greater cohesiveness of cliques and by the different functions performed by them. He saw crowds mainly as centers of larger and more organized social activities, such as dances, while cliques as primarily "for talking." On the average, the crowds Dunphy looked at had about twenty members, while the cliques had about six members.

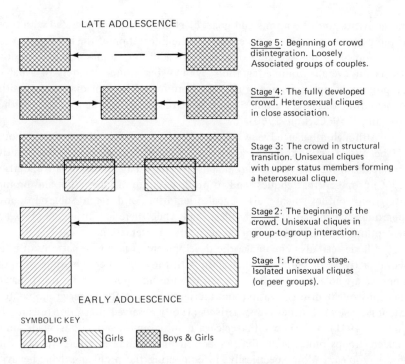

FIGURE 2. Stages of Group Development in Adolescence (Dunphy, 1963:236)

to nonmembers, an aspect that has been emphasized by some in their basic conception of adolescent cliques (e.g., Hurlock, 1949:448).

As one might suspect, the tendency for groups to split into subgroups such as cliques increases with group size (Hare, 1962:132). This tendency and related ones have been studied in some depth by Homans (1950), Lazarsfeld and Merton (1954), and Lipset, Trow, and Coleman (1956). In recognizing their contributions to our understanding of clique formation, Davis (1966:86) said:

> . . . Homans emphasizes the importance of differential rates of interaction in clique formation, a major theme of *The Human Group* being that differentials in social interaction determined by work (the external system) lead to differentials in liking, other sentiments, and activities so that "the activities of a subgroup may become increasingly differentiated from those of other subgroups up to some limit imposed by the controls of the larger group to which all the subgroups belong" (1950:136). Our impression is that the research literature over a variety of studies tends to support the claim that in day-to-day social life, differences in rates of interaction are the major factor behind subgroup formation . . . . For groups with undifferentiated patterns of interaction, Lazarsfeld and Merton and the authors

82

of *Union Democracy* (Lipset, Trow, and Coleman) have stressed the importance of "value homophily" and "similarity."[13]

Davis' ensuing analysis suggested that the splitting of a group into cliques is associated with heterogeneity of the social characteristics of group members. This means heterogeneous group composition can undermine group integration not only by disrupting communication, as we earlier observed, but also by promoting the formation of cliques that could emphasize and exacerbate differences among group members. Since cliques are built on the similarity of some group members and their differences from others and are characterized by high levels of interaction and mutual attraction among their members, cliques can have a strong influence on them. Whether that influence is functional or dysfunctional for the larger group, or beneficial or detrimental for the clique members, depends on the values, norms, goals, and activities of the clique. This point is underscored by the first study highlighted in the next section concerning research about social problems connected with group integration.

PROBLEMS OF GROUP INTEGRATION: A SELECTIVE FOCUS ON RESEARCH

Cohesiveness of Adolescent Drinking Groups

It has already been suggested in regard to Dunphy's (1963) research that clique membership tends to be a normal part of adolescent development. One of the ways cliques can shape adolescent experiences is shown by Alexander and Campbell (1968).[14] They collected data concerning alcohol usage and friendship choices of male seniors in thirty North Carolina high schools, and they examined factors influencing the cohesiveness of adolescent drinking groups. Their data showed that behavioral consensus, particularly regarding drinking, within triads of friends, or cliques, increased as the number of affective bonds increased.

On the basis of their results, Alexander and Campbell proposed that adolescent drinking could be viewed as a function of the pressure of peers in cliques and the attitude of parents about such behavior. They argued that in cases where parents were opposed to their son's drinking, peer pressure favoring drinking would have to be greater than parental pressure against it for a boy to start drinking. Peer pressures of this sort were assumed to increase in strength with increases in the number of drinking friends, in the closeness of friends, and in the cohesiveness of cliques of these friends and himself. Cautiously, one might

---

[13] On the basis of literature such as that which he cited in these comments, Davis (1966: 85-91) systematically presented and discussed a series of definitions and propositions about clique formation.

[14] See Alexander (1964), for a related article about consensus and mutual attraction in adolescent cliques.

conclude from this research that if parents do not want their adolescent son to drink, their desires will be respected to the extent that the cohesiveness, solidarity, and quality of their family ties are superior to those of relationships between their son and his friends or acquaintances who drink. From this perspective, one can see why parents try to influence the friendship choices of their children. Of course, their ability to do this is likely to depend on how well family members get along and how important family membership is to all of them, parents as well as children. When group integration of a family is high, parents will probably have much less worry about the "undesirable" influence of their children's cliques and peers than when family integration is low, and they will probably have much less need to "interfere" in their children's lives.

Alexander and Campbell's research is interesting because it touches a responsive chord in most of us, since the questions of alcohol usage, or perhaps, drug usage these days, and the "right" kinds of friends are potentially explosive issues for most families. Their research is also sociologically interesting in the present context because it focuses on the interrelationship of clique formation and influence, cohesiveness, and interpersonal integration, and on the effects on group members of the relative levels of integration of different groups to which they belong. There is one other study, by Wheaton (1974), dealing somewhat more narrowly with problems of group integration, that we also want to consider.

Cohesiveness and Interpersonal Conflict in Dyads

Wheaton collected questionnaire data from over 100 dyads of female roommates to discover the relationship between cohesiveness and interpersonal conflict in dyads. More specifically, Wheaton wanted to identify different types and sources of conflict that would illustrate how conflict could have both positive and negative effects on group cohesiveness. In this context, two types of conflict were examined: *principled,* concerning clashes over basic principles having moralistic or normative overtones, and *communal,* concerning clashes where agreement exists on general principles, but not at more specific or concrete levels. Cohesiveness was viewed as a reflection of interpersonal attraction as well as group attraction and identification. The results of this study indicated principled conflict has a negative effect on cohesiveness and communal conflict has a positive one.

The communal conflict finding may be more striking because it seems more inconsistent with our intuitive understanding of how conflict, *of any sort,* affects group cohesiveness, or more generally, integration. Wheaton was able to give a plausible interpretation of these conflict findings by looking at different phases of group development. Presumably, in the early stages of group activity, group solidarity is beginning to develop and is, therefore, relatively precarious. There is a search for basic group goals and purposes, a struggle by various factions in the group about what goals and standards to adopt, and a polarization of group versus individual rights and duties. Thus, the early phase of group development is a period when conflict is most likely to be of a *principled nature;* the more serious and divisive this type of conflict, the less likely there will be strong ties of group and interpersonal solidarity to hold the group together.

It can be assumed that a group will not attain much more than a very limited amount of group and interpersonal solidarity unless at least some consensus exists about basic group principles, such things as why they are a group, what is important to them as a group, and how they should behave in group interaction. It might be recalled that these are the types of things Hare associated with the latent pattern maintenance function. However, according to Wheaton, once such consensus has been reached, conflict, which will then be of a *communal nature,* will tend to draw attention to, and reaffirm, the basis of the relationship between members of dyads and presumably, larger groups too. In other words, if there are common basic principles for group members, they can engage in conflicts of a more concrete or specific sort (for example, about how they should act under certain circumstances or how they should approach certain group goals or problems) without upsetting how they feel about each other or their group. In fact, on the basis of Wheaton's results, we could expect such conflicts to reinforce group integration by reminding group members of the fundamental and important principles about which they *agree* and which tie them together.

This interpretation brings to mind the concept of *fair fighting* some marriage counselors have advocated and the media have popularized. This concept seems to imply that conflicts are normal in interpersonal relationships and that the free expression of them will be more conducive to healthy and stable group relationships than suppression of them, *as long as* these conflicts do not strike at the basic foundations of group consensus and solidarity or draw in issues outside the boundaries of tolerable disagreement, such as those about which people are personally quite sensitive. Unfortunately, the divisive pressures on many marriages and similar types of primary groups tend to be felt so intensely and to cause such despair that restriction of conflicts to potentially fruitful forms is either impossible or very difficult; or perhaps the thought of restrictions never even enters the minds of those involved. In these groups, conflicts can only succeed in reconstructing or reaffirming the consensus on which the groups were founded to the extent consensus still exists.

Wheaton's study is an example of research relying on measures of *cohesiveness* based on both interpersonal and group-attraction items. While this approach may not have made a difference in Wheaton's results because the groups were dyads, it is always possible that it can lead to a misinterpretation of the actual patterns of group and interpersonal integration in the groups under investigation. Earlier in the chapter, evidence was cited showing that direct (group-level) and indirect (sociometric or interpersonal choice) measures of cohesiveness may not be related for at least some types of groups. This finding means that ostensible cohesiveness results must be viewed carefully or suspiciously when based wholly or partially on interpersonal choice measures, and that many of the research findings supposedly concerning cohesiveness are actually more directly related to interpersonal attraction and integration.

INTERPERSONAL ATTRACTION AND INTEGRATION

GENERAL ASSUMPTIONS AND FINDINGS

Whether it has been incorrectly called *cohesiveness* or correctly called *interpersonal attraction,* this interpersonal aspect of group integration has received substantial attention from small-group researchers.[15] In this section, we will examine general assumptions and findings about antecedents and consequences of this factor. Then, after looking more closely at some studies dealing with group problems related to these assumptions and findings, we will concentrate on sociological aspects of intimacy in small groups.

Interpersonal Sentiments,
Sociometric Research, and Sociograms

Studies of group structures of interpersonal sentiment follow in a tradition of sociometric research initially inspired by Moreno and his colleagues, who developed the sociometric test (Moreno, 1934, 1943; Jennings, 1950). Moreno was interested in changing social arrangements in working groups so that they reflected more accurately the feelings and wishes of members (Mills, 1967:4). In pursuing his aim, he asked group members to report to him their feelings about other group members, indicating those whom they liked, and disliked, those with whom they wanted to work, and those with whom they did not want to work. In this way, Moreno was able to determine the basic patterning of sentiments in group relations and to see what kinds of changes might be needed. Furthermore, on the basis of responses to questions of this nature, he could develop a sociogram, or map of the sociometric structure of a group (see Figure 3). Moreno's general sociometric approach has been used extensively in small-group research, and at times somewhat misguidedly by those wanting to assess cohesiveness directly.[16]

Sociograms allow us to represent a number of interesting sociological aspects of groups based on the patterning of sentiment relations. For example, using the symbolic key for Figure 3, we can see by links of reciprocal solid

---

[15]To illustrate this point, Lott and Lott's (1965) survey of literature concerning "group cohesiveness as interpersonal attraction" covering mostly 1950–1962 has nearly 300 bibliographic references.
[16]For a discussion of the various types of sociometric questions, how they have been used, and how data derived from them have been analyzed, see Lindzey and Borgatta (1954).

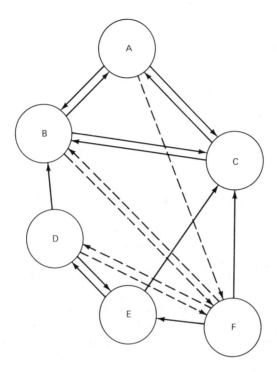

FIGURE 3. Illustration of the Sociometric Structure of a Group Represented by a Sociogram

Symbolic Key: Circled letters designate group members. Solid arrows designate the direction of positive attraction or liking, and broken arrows designate the direction of negative attraction or disliking. The absence of an arrow between any two group members represents a tendency toward neutral sentiment, neither marked liking nor disliking. This illustration comes from Crosbie (1975:116).

arrows that in the group portrayed, there are two friendship cliques, *A-B-C* and *D-E.* We can also notice that *C* is a "sociometric star" by virtue of being well liked by all other group members but one, *D,* who has neutral feelings about *C.* Member *F* appears to be a "social isolate," since this person is not well liked by anyone, but is disliked by three others, *A, B,* and *D.* Since there are no reciprocal broken arrows between the friendship cliques, one can infer there are no structural cleavages based on subgroup rivalry or hostility.

Antecedents of Interpersonal Sentiment Patterns

REWARDINGNESS AND INTERPERSONAL SENTIMENTS. Several interesting and important factors have been shown to be associated with sentiment patterns in small groups. According to Crosbie (1975:116), research has suggested that the factors of reciprocal need fulfillment or *rewardingness,* propinquity or the physical proximity of people to each other, and attitude similarity are among the most important antecedents or determinants of interpersonal attraction. The factor of rewardingness seems to appear most prominently in explanations of interpersonal attraction by exchange theorists, but other interpretations of the sources of interpersonal attraction and attachments also view it as an important factor (e.g., Berscheid and Walster, 1969; Byrne, 1969). The exchange interpretation assumes that people become attracted to others who provide them with rewards or satisfy their needs.

Crosbie (1975:117) has pointed out that the tendency to seek rewards is conditioned substantially by the perceived likelihood we will obtain those rewards. Therefore, we may be attracted to someone with the capacity to reward us, but we may not attempt to associate or form a friendship with this person if we do not think he or she will reward us personally. Furthermore, even when we decide to approach a person who is attractive to us, we must feel this person reciprocates our liking before we form a mutual friendship. According to Crosbie, research indicates that once a person expresses his or her liking for us, we will tend to reciprocate. However, he has noted that some evidence from a field study on dating by Berscheid and Walster (1969) indicated that no relationship existed between how much a man liked his date and how much she liked him. Thus, it appears that although attraction is reciprocated, it is not always reciprocated in degree. As Crosbie has suggested, " . . . the simple fact that (a person) likes us may not be enough to warrant a strong friendship attachment" (p. 117).

In general, it seems that rewardingness alone is not sufficient to produce reciprocal feelings of liking and an interpersonal relationship based on such feelings. In fact, it may be that the importance of rewardingness in producing interpersonal attraction and attachment is limited by the effect of satiation. A friendship based only on rewardingness may begin losing its hold on the people involved if the continuous giving of rewards, whether in the form of approval, or acceptance, or help, or emotional support, or financial or material gifts, tends to lessen the value of those rewards over time. Perhaps, as Aronson (1972) has suggested, close relationships need the injection of costs once in a while, preferably in the form of an honest expression of complaints or grievances, to prevent them from stagnating or becoming satiated with rewards. We will have more to say about intimate or close relationships later in this chapter.

PROPINQUITY, SIMILARITY OF BELIEFS, AND INTERPERSONAL SENTIMENTS. The effect of propinquity on interpersonal sentiments tends to be mediated by the occurrence of interaction resulting from it. In a study of clerical workers in a large corporation, Gullahorn (1952) found that distance was the most important condition affecting the rate of interaction between any two workers, and that there was a tendency for those who interacted frequently to develop "sentiments of friendship."[17] General support for this interpretation has been produced in a number of other types of group settings, ranging from sororities (Willerman and Swanson, 1952), to a married veteran university housing project (Festinger, 1953b), an elementary school (Heber and Heber, 1957), a summer camp (Sherif and Sherif, 1953; Sherif, White, and Harvey, 1955), and the military (Kipnis, 1957; Zander and Havelin, 1960).

One of the more socially meaningful and encouraging results of studies of interpersonal contact and sentiments is the finding that negative sentiments of prejudice by whites towards blacks could be reduced by increased contact between people of these two races. This finding was produced in settings as different as a meat packing plant (Palmore, 1955), a housing project (Deutsch and Collins, 1958), and a university classroom (Mann, 1959). Unfortunately, though, other research has shown that reducing prejudice and creating positive interpersonal sentiments are more complicated tasks than simply getting people who are prejudiced toward, or dislike, each other to meet and interact. By recalling earlier comments in this chapter about communication and clique formation, it should become apparent that people must be, or perceive themselves as being, similar to others in certain salient respects for them to want to initiate or continue interaction or to be able to develop patterns of smooth, harmonious interaction and positive interpersonal sentiments. In other words, in a group context, we would expect interaction to promote liking—or lessen prejudice and disliking—when there is homogeneity, rather than heterogeneity, regarding socially salient characteristics of group members.

The importance of perceived similarity in attitude or belief systems for reduction of racial prejudice and promotion of interpersonal attraction across racial lines was a major result of an experimental study by Stein, Hardyck, and Smith (1965). Their study involved the feelings of attraction of white ninth graders toward descriptions of other teenagers who were portrayed as white or black and as similar or dissimilar in attitudes and values to the experimental subjects. Their research implies that perceived similarity in beliefs and interests will be more important than differences in race or other similar kinds of social characteristics in determining how well people get along and how they feel about each other. Of course, as Stein and his colleagues have suggested, people who are different racially or in other respects must be able to interact under conditions where similarity in salient beliefs or interests exists and can become obvious if interaction is to reduce prejudice and enhance interpersonal attraction.

The tendency for interaction to promote more positive interpersonal sentiments also is likely to be limited by circumstances where people feel "forced" to interact and the interaction occurs in an atmosphere of rivalry or insecurity con-

---

[17]Much of the following discussion of research on interpersonal attraction in this section is based on Lott and Lott's (1965) comprehensive survey of literature on this topic.

cerning prestige, power, or economic status. Homans (1974:64) has clearly illustrated the nature of this qualification in the following way:

> . . . One important case in which (this tendency) does not hold good is the one in which . . . two men are not, as we say, "free" to decrease interaction with one another even though they dislike one another. For example, two men may be working for the same company and required by the company to collaborate with one another, yet they know that they are rivals for promotion. Since if either one gets promoted, he by that fact denies reward to the other, each is, by the aggression-approval proposition, apt to inspire some degree of hostility in the other. In this case, their frequent required interaction is not likely to increase their liking for one another but rather the reverse. They are not "free" to cut off interaction because . . . each is independently rewarded by employment in the company and so is unwilling to leave it, even though each hurts the other.

The implication of this qualification of the general assumption of the positive interrelationship of similarity, interaction, and liking may be contrary to what humane and liberal people would like to believe, but research suggests it is more than just a logical derivation from Homans' exchange theory. For example, Festinger's (1953b) study of social life in a housing project found that residents, who felt "forced" to live there because of a housing shortage, had generally negative attitudes toward their community and neighbors. In addition, Gundlach's (1956) study of members of a left-wing union with a strong commitment to fair employment practices showed that anti-union feelings could spill over into feelings about other union members. In particular, Gundlach found white women in a subgroup with high education and high social aims who were in contact with black people of similar education and aims were *most* hostile and derogatory toward blacks, while also being most anti-union. The other white union members, by contrast, tended to show far *less* prejudice than that reported for samples of the general population.

What has been said so far about antecedents of interpersonal attraction should strongly reinforce the impression that the achievement of interpersonal harmony in groups can be a complicated process, with several possible stumbling blocks along its path. However, we know many groups are successful in establishing patterns of positive interpersonal sentiments among their members. Prior research indicates feelings about a group as a whole can affect the nature of its sociometric structure, implying that the conditions associated with cohesiveness can contribute to more positive interpersonal sentiments. Combining this insight with the assumptions and findings discussed so far about cohesiveness and about interpersonal sentiment, we can derive a general picture of the conditions most conducive to a positive sociometric structure in groups. In general, it seems when group members are able to display similarity in *salient* beliefs, interests, and social characteristics and interact regularly and closely in a secure, cooperative, and mutually rewarding atmosphere, their group will tend to be highly cohesive and they will tend to have positive feelings about each other.

Consequences of Interpersonal Sentiment Patterns

In comparison with the findings about antecedents of interpersonal attraction, those concerning consequences have tended to be much less "clear-cut and definitive" (Lott and Lott, 1965:299). The consequences of greatest interest to us are sociological ones concerning such things as uniformity of behavior and beliefs, communication, and task performance. Among these factors, the findings regarding the first one have been most consistent, with interpersonal attraction generally found to have a positive effect on uniformity of behavior and beliefs (Lott and Lott, 1965:292-296). It appears that people who like each other generally try to reduce the perceived differences in their behavior and beliefs as much as possible, perhaps to achieve either consciously or unconsciously, some balance in interpersonal and group interaction. Thus, perceptions of similarity may draw people into friendly interaction, and the resulting positive interpersonal sentiments may, in turn, reinforce the original perceptions of similarity and create pressures to establish new kinds of agreement regarding socially salient issues, which may contribute to a condition of equilibrium in group interaction.

Though intuitively we might expect liking to produce higher rates of interaction than disliking, the actual relationship between interpersonal attraction and communication seems more complex than this. In their review of relevant literature, Lott and Lott (1965:292) observed:

> The hypothesis that persons communicate more with liked than with disliked persons has been supported by a number of investigations but the results of other studies have indicated that in situations where opinions differ, and where there is pressure toward uniformity, individuals tend to increase their communication to deviates. In some of these latter investigations measures have indicated that the deviates are disliked or rejected while in others this must be assumed.

Apparently, the impact of interpersonal attraction on group performance is also a somewhat complicated one. In this regard, Lott and Lott (1965:298) concluded:

> Findings relevant to (this) relationship . . . are contradictory. It seems likely that in a task situation other variables such as the demands of the situation itself (instructions or job specifications), the standards of performance preferred by liked co-workers, and the degree to which sociability may interfere with the required behavior for a particular job, may be highly significant.

When we look more closely at the relationship between cohesiveness and group task performance in a later chapter, we will also consider in more depth how interpersonal attraction affects task performance.

PROBLEMS OF INTERPERSONAL INTEGRATION IN SMALL GROUPS: A SELECTIVE FOCUS ON RESEARCH

In the prior section's general literature review, evidence was cited concerning problems of race relations in groups. This evidence suggested racial differences among group members produces the most tension in their interpersonal relations when these members have unfavorable feelings about their group as a whole or their membership in it, and when they differ on socially salient attitudes or other beliefs. In this section, we will examine studies concerning other kinds of interpersonal problems in groups. In particular, we will give special attention to studies about interpersonal rivalry and conflict, rejection and scapegoating, and relations with a newcomer in a group.

Intergroup Rivalry and Conflict, and Friendship Within and Across Groups

In a series of classic field experimental studies involving groups of boys in a summer camp, Sherif and his colleagues showed that an *increase* in hostility toward some out-group is usually associated with an *increase* in affection for members of the in-group (e.g., Sherif and Sherif, 1953; Sherif, White, and Harvey, 1955; Sherif, 1956).[18] For this research, careful selection procedures were used to produce a sample of eleven- and twelve-year-old boys who were all healthy, social well-adjusted, a bit above average in intelligence, and from stable, white, Protestant, middle-class families. The selected boys spent three weeks in an isolated summer camp, thinking they were there strictly for recreational (not experimental) purposes. In other words, the boys thought the researchers were a regular camp staff and the boys' three weeks with them a normal summer camp experience. In this context, Sherif's research team initially observed the natural evolution of friendships and a coherent informal group among all the boys and later manipulated group membership and intergroup relations to determine the effects of such manipulations on interpersonal attraction within and across groups.

After friendships had been allowed to form in the large group, the researchers divided the boys into two groups, with those who had chosen each other as "best friends" separated into different groups wherever possible. Despite the initial pain of separation from their new buddies, a pain eased by

---

[18]Hare (1962:132–138) offers a good, brief summary of this research. Our discussion of the Sherif experiments owes much to Hare's summary.

permitting each group to go immediately on its own hike and camp-out, both groups quickly developed informal social structures and an "esprit de corps." In addition, after these two groups became organized and developed their identities, the friendship choices shifted to become overwhelmingly in favor of those *within* their group. Homans (1974:178) interpreted this shift as an indication that "increased interaction between some persons had increased liking between them, and decreased interaction between others (including former 'best friends') had decreased their liking."

The part of the Sherif team's research having greatest interest to us here, beyond this aspect regarding shifts in friendship choices, concerns group rivalry. Sherif's research team was guided by the hypothesis that when one group can achieve its aims only at the expense of another group, the members of each group will become hostile to the other, even though the members of both groups are well adjusted. The researchers used a tournament of games such as baseball, touch football, and a tug-of-war to create rivalry and tension between the two groups they studied. Although a spirit of good sportsmanship prevailed at the outset of the tournament, it soon disappeared as the tournament progressed. Members of each group began to call rival group members "stinkers," "sneaks," and "cheaters." These bad feelings spilled over into the boys' desire to associate with members of the rival group. In fact, the deterioration of social relationships between rival group members was so bad in the 1949 camp that the boys no longer wanted to associate with members of the rival group who had been chosen as "best friends" at the beginning of camp. Not surprisingly, a large proportion of the boys in each group gave negative ratings to all the rival group members. In one setting called the "Robbers Cave" camp, "name calling, scuffles, and raids (became) the rule of the day," according to the researchers (Sherif, 1956). However, while antagonisms *between* groups became more intense, solidarity, morale, and cooperativeness *within* each group also became stronger.

Having created intense intergroup tensions, perhaps more intense than they had anticipated or wanted, the researchers faced the problem of bringing the conflicting groups back into harmony. They initially tested the theory that pleasant social contacts between rival groups would lessen the antagonism. In the 1954 camp, Sherif and his colleagues brought together members of the rival "Rattlers" and "Eagles" for social events such as going to the movies and eating in the same dining room. However, rather than reducing conflict, these occasions provided opportunities to rival group members for further name calling and scuffles. The researchers then examined the effects on intergroup friction of situations threatening both groups and requiring their joint cooperation. The research team assumed that just as competition created friction, working in such a common endeavor could reduce that friction. They believed that a crucial element in the restoration of harmony was the existence of "superordinate" goals that had a strong appeal to both groups and could not be achieved without cooperation between groups. To test their assumption, they created a series of emergency situations such as a breakdown in the water supply and of a truck on its way to town for their food. Although joint efforts between the groups did not *immediately* eliminate intergroup antagonisms, the series of cooperative acts *gradually* reduced friction and tension between the groups. Eventually, members of the two groups again began to feel friendly toward each other. Divisive in-group and out-group feelings began to break down as many of the boys shifted from choosing best friends almost exclusively in their own group to choosing boys in the other group as well. Following the cooperative pursuit of superordinate goals, the new ratings of the boys in the other group became largely favorable.

Sherif and his colleagues' research offers a number of valuable insights about interpersonal feelings and relations in and between groups. Perhaps the most valuable ones are that interpersonal integration and cohesiveness of a group may be gained at the expense of harmony in intergroup relations *and* that attempted improvement of intergroup harmony could result in a reduction of interpersonal integration and cohesiveness within each of the interacting groups. Thus, the implications are that rivalry is not without possible benefits for groups and cooperation is not without certain costs. It seems, though, the "benefits" a group gains from intensified rivalry with others must be weighed very carefully against "costs" in intergroup relations when those costs may include destructive forms of hatred and hostility toward people who just happen to be members of a different group. Certainly, this research offers a good lesson for adults who incite athletic teams of youngsters into "mortal combat" aimed at "killing" the opposing team of "enemies" by any means possible. It implies not only that such incitement may be taken seriously, but also that it may be difficult to reverse the resulting intergroup tensions and conflict as the hold of a group and its goals on its members becomes stronger.

Scapegoating and Interpersonal Conflict in Families

In another study of group conflict, this time within a group, and of functional and dysfunctional aspects of interpersonal problems of groups, Vogel and Bell (1960) looked at scapegoating in families. In particular, Vogel and Bell did an intensive study of matched sets of nine "disturbed" families, each with an emotionally disturbed child, and nine "well" families, without a clinically displayed disturbed child. A major finding of their investigation was that in the disturbed families, the disturbed child tended to be used as a scapegoat to help resolve parental conflicts, while in the well families, children tended not to serve as scapegoats. Vogel and Bell were especially interested in the functional and dysfunctional aspects of scapegoating for the disturbed families.

According to these researchers, the induction of the disturbed child into the scapegoat role was a gradual, subtle, and largely unconscious process during which the disturbed child internalized the role of "problem (or deviant) child" conveyed by parents and reinforced by their inconsistent expectations and authority. Once the scapegoating pattern was established, with the disturbed child regularly serving as a "problem" to deflect potential tensions from the parental relationship, a relatively stable equilibrium tended to exist in the family, even though it was always a somewhat delicate one balanced by frequent instances of rationalization by parents. In this equilibrium, parents minimized contact with each other and minimized expressions of sentiment, especially hostility, that were strongly felt for each other, making it possible for them to achieve a relatively "peaceful—albeit *potentially* explosive—coexistence."

Scapegoating allows the disturbed family to maintain its structural-functional integration with parents performing their normal obligations in their community so that their family does not become a community burden. While these could be construed as functions of scapegoating, we can also identify dysfunctions arising from the same scapegoating tendency. The major dysfunction is the continued impairment of the emotional health of the child, which also places additional pressures and burdens on the parents. Thus, the problems of the child that are emphasized in creating the scapegoat role and that help relieve certain parental tensions, are not in themselves resolved; consequently, they are a continuing source of potential family tension and disruption. Though an uneasy equilibrium is established in such families, it is certainly not a pleasant one. By using their child as a scapegoat, parents in disturbed families merely avoid surface manifestations of problems in their own relationship. By suppressing these problems, they make life with each other and their child tolerable, but not enjoyable.

Intense Interpersonal Disliking and Group Integration

In his study of ninety cabin groups at four summer camps for children, Feldman (1969) examined a process, the intense interpersonal disliking of a single group member, he believed to possess the same essential dynamic qualities of the more complex interpersonal rejection and scapegoating processes. Feldman found this process to occur relatively infrequently, in only 10 percent of the groups he studied, and to be unaffected by major sociological factors such as sex of group members, their age, group size, or social class. Furthermore, he discovered that groups with an intensely disliked member tended to have significantly lower levels of functional and interpersonal integration than groups lacking such members, thus implying that this kind of process has mainly *dys*functional rather than functional consequences for group integration. While this finding stands in marked contrast to what Vogel and Bell reported, Feldman added a qualification that could explain the apparent contradiction. He suggested that:

> . . . Although (his) data severely question the (special) integrative efficacy attributed to processes such as intense interpersonal disliking, they do not permit complete rejection of the hypothesis that such pro-

cesses serve an integrative function for small groups. It can be posited, for instance, that intense interpersonal disliking and related social processes primarily are associated with enhanced group integration only when small groups are faced with the threat of extreme or, perhaps, total disintegration . . . (1969:412).

It may be that families constantly faced with potentially traumatizing and stigmatizing effects of raising an emotionally disturbed child are this type of small group.

Group and Interpersonal Integration and the Newcomer

Another possible source of tension and difficulty in groups that involves integration and group relations with an individual member concerns the entry of a newcomer. This process was investigated by Mills and his colleagues (Mills *et al.,* 1970), who did a laboratory study of the expansion of triads into groups of four. In their experiment, the original group consisted of two role players trained by the investigators and one "naive" subject. After interacting with each other on a group problem-solving task, this original group took a break, and then began work again with a new member. The experimenters' main goal was to determine how variations in the original group's sociometric structure and in its acceptance of a given member, in particular, the naive subject, affected the newcomer's relationship with this member.

Initially, the experimenters were interested in the effects of combinations of personal acceptance or rejection of a member in the original triad and of different amounts of interpersonal or emotional integration of the triad. They manipulated the acceptance and sociometric structure variables to create four basic group patterns. In one, the "all positive," there was complete acceptance among the three original group members and "full" emotional integration. In another, the "all negative," there was rejection of the naive subject in a context of mutual disagreement and antipathy among all group members and of "malintegration." In the two others, there were acceptance and rejection, respectively, in a context of "partial integration." In one partially integrated pattern, the naive subject was accepted in a subgroup, clique, or *coalition* against the third; in the other, he was out of the subgroup and therefore rejected. Ultimately, the researchers had to revise their initial conception of the group structural factor to provide a more meaningful interpretation of their results. Instead of looking at amount of emotional integration—full, partial, and weak—as they had first intended, they considered the effects of heterogeneity (partial integration) and homogeneity (all positive and all negative) of emotional ties. After finding the amount of integration had no effect on how the old and new members got along, they discovered that the heterogeneous sociometric structure, with positive *and* negative emotional ties, combined with personal acceptance to maximize the probability of a congenial, mutually supportive relationship between the old and new members. Thus, the pattern most conducive to the development of a positive relationship was the one where a subgroup existed in the original group and the subject was part of it. In this case, the newcomer was welcomed into the subgroup, leaving the fourth member of the expanded group as a rejected isolate. It should be added that none of the independent variables, heterogeneity, personal acceptance, nor amount of integration, was found to have a statistically significant effect on mutual liking between the old and new members.

Perhaps the most important implication of Mills and his colleagues' study is that once patterns of sentiment relations and subgrouping have been established in triads, these patterns tend to be preserved with minimal modification when these groups add a fourth member. This study suggests a general principle of group expansion: "Given a clear group organization and the addition of a new member, a set of forces operates which tends to preserve, with the minimum alteration, the essentials of the state of organization before the addition" (Mills *et al.,* 1970:163). This homeostatic principle of group equilibrium implies that in well integrated groups, newcomers are accepted and easily assimilated; in weakly integrated groups, newcomers are rejected and poorly assimilated; and in groups with subgrouping, the old socio-emotional and power balances tend to be sustained after the newcomer joins the group, with former social and political rejects continuing to play the same role. Although we cannot be sure how far these generalizations apply beyond the laboratory problem-solving groups studied by Mills and his colleagues, we know at least one definite exception.

From comments in the first chapter about differences between dyads and triads, it should be evident that basic transformations in group structures generally can be expected when dyads expand to triads. Thus, even if Mills' expansion principle applies to many types of groups larger than dyads, it generally cannot operate in the same way for dyads, since subgroups such as cliques and coalitions that emerge in larger groups cannot exist in dyads and since the quality of the relationship between two members in dyads, unlike larger groups, is always identical with the nature of the group as a whole. Undoubtedly, there are numerous other types of group expansion not conforming to this principle. Nevertheless, Mills and his co-researchers at least provide food for thought for those of us who hope or fear that the addition of a new member to our group—whether it is a family or an industrial work crew, a therapy group or a school committee—will dramatically alter its socio-emotional character.

INTIMACY IN SMALL GROUPS: A MORE DETAILED FOCUS ON INTERPERSONAL SENTIMENTS

A discussion of patterns of sentiments in groups would seem incomplete without a closer look at intimate relations, and at least a brief consideration of experiential groups such as sensitivity training groups. The examination in the first chapter of the main features of primary groups indicated how the notion of intimacy in groups can be approached sociologically. In this section, we will try to go beyond those first comments and consider this important aspect of integration from a more detailed sociological perspective. After doing so, we will shift the focus to the growth of intimacy and group emotion in general through various sorts of experiential group experiences.

In the preface of his book about intimate relations, Davis (1973) noted that:

> There has been a spate of books recently designed to change the way people relate to one another . . . These books have been moralistic and melioristic on the one hand, or cynical and strategical on the other. The former tell the reader how to fix the *mechanism* of his intimate relations: "If only he would stop playing games with his intimate, be more honest, bring his feelings out into the open, touch his intimate more . . ." The latter tell the reader how to win the *game* of his intimate relations: "If only he would learn to use skillfully the various tactics (strategic increases of affection, strategic withdrawals of affection, etc.) necessary to seduce the other player into yielding to his goals (sex, marriage, etc.) . . ."

Davis eschewed both these approaches and tried to present a sociological discussion of major qualities and complications of intimate relations typifying the stages of emergence, stabilization, change, and deterioration. More specifically, he focused on the intimate or close and personal behaviors essentially characterizing *intimates,* whom he defined as relatively equal-status pairs of interacting people who reciprocate numerous intimate behaviors. Though this definition excluded the intimate behaviors of unequal pairs like mothers and children, it still allowed the identification of four of the most basic types of intimate two-person primary groups: friends, lovers, spouses, and siblings. Davis also contrasted intimates with nonintimates, defining the latter as pairs of interacting people who do *not* reciprocate numerous intimate behaviors. He identified four basic types of nonintimates: strangers, secondary role relations, acquaintances, and enemies. The dynamic nature of these various types of relationships can been seen in Davis' conception of *sociable mobility,* portrayed in Figure 4, which shows the general likelihood assumed by Davis of movements between the various kinds of intimate and nonintimate relationships he conceptualized. The solid lines indicate frequent movements; broken lines represent relatively infrequent movements.

Creating Interpersonal Integration
and Intimacy of Small Groups

Probably the most important contribution of Davis' study is the set of basic concepts and ideas he presented to clarify how individuals construct and communicate an intimate relation, the nature of that relation itself, and its varia-

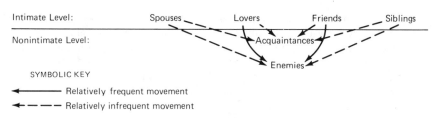

FIGURE 4. Sociable Mobility Flow Charts (Davis, 1973: xx)

tion, stresses, and strains in different social contexts. In the present chapter, the concepts in this set having greatest relevance are those Davis identified as major binding or integrative forces transforming isolated individuals into cohesive and otherwise well integrated primary groups. He identified six of these forces and described them in the following way:

1. facilitation of the potential of independent individuals to form a closer association through such means as: (a) identifying *qualifiers* (such as status symbols, personality, or physical attractiveness) justifying closer or further encounters, (b) determining whether the other person is *cleared* for more encounters and a relationship, (c) finding an *opener* to engage the other's attention, (d) discovering an *integrating topic* that is mutually interesting, (e) projecting a *come-on self* to induce the other to continue the present encounter and seek future ones, and (f) scheduling a *second encounter* (Ch. 1, "Pickups");
2. the routinization of an interacting pair's cycle of coming togethers and going aparts (Ch. 2, "Let's Get Together");
3. the continual verbal and nonverbal statements indicating members of an interacting pair are intimates (Ch. 3, "Tell Me You Love Me");
4. the potentially damaging secret knowledge of each other's weaknesses that both acquire (Ch. 4, "Getting to Know You");
5. the favors each intimate derives from the other that facilitate transactions with the environment (Ch. 5, "Do Me a Favor");
6. the blurring of individual identities and fusing of them into a single integral whole (Ch. 6, "Couples").

99

Intimacy and Group Integration:
Maintaining Intimate Groups and Relationships

Once an intimate relationship has fully developed, we can expect the persistence of its characteristically high levels of cohesiveness, and interpersonal and structural-functional integration, to be affected by the same kinds of general factors discussed earlier in this chapter as sources of group integration. These factors include the maintenance of close and regular contacts, similarity, and a feeling of being rewarded by the relationship. Levinger and Snoek (1972:10) have said about the stability of such relations:

> . . . continuing (them) may require more than the openness and empathy of two warmly positive individuals. To endure, interpersonal relationships require maintenance just as do physical systems. Consequently, a considerable proportion of action between interdependent persons is required merely to maintain the system itself. Maintenance activities are needed to work through conflict, to enhance positive feelings, and to perform chores associated with living together . . . .
>
> To survive the distractions of alternative relationships and the pressures generated by changing circumstances in a pair's environment, stable relationships seem to require some form of contractual commitment. Stability in (an intimate group) is likely to be supported by barriers around it that prevent the partners from evading their commitment to each other . . . . In certain formal relationships, society helps reinforce informal volition by providing legal sanction at a crucial point in time—as in the marriage ceremony.

Levinger and Snoek applied a concept similar to Davis' notion of the integrative force of fusion of intimates' selves to make an important distinction [suggested by Kurth (1970)] between levels of intimacy, or *mutuality* (of interpersonal attraction), as they called it. The concept concerns the depth of interpersonal involvement of people in a relationship. It allowed them to distinguish between *friendship,* implying "an intimate interpersonal relationship involving each (member) as a personal entity," and a *friendly relation,* implying "an outgrowth of a formal relationship . . . prevalent in our society today" (Kurth, 1970:136). Thus, in a friendship as in other intimate groups, there is a high degree of intersection between the lives of members, and a considerable amount of sharing of experiences, beliefs, interests, and activities.

The intimate relations of families, marriages, courtships, love affairs, and friendships all can provide substantial joy, gratification, and esteem for those involved in them. However, in each one of these relationships, intimacy may be difficult to establish and even more difficult to maintain. The continuing need for maintenance activities to sustain a high degree of involvement with intimate others can become burdensome or even oppressive at times, especially in dyads where there is no one else to bear the "responsibilities" of intimacy. Intimate relations always contain a large number of potential problems, such as disagreements, arguments, communication breakdowns, separations, jealousies, coolness, and the withdrawal of favors, that could surface at any time to cause at least temporary disruptions of equilibrium and patterns of integration. In enduring intimate groups, the continuous flow of minor tensions and strains are regularly and successfully resolved. But in those cases where intimacy cannot be maintained and relations disintegrate completely or become transformed into nonintimate ones, the process of disintegration may be marked by considerable anguish, depression, or anger. Thus, it is not surprising that the highest incidence of homicide is among people who know one another best, since this can be seen as a reflection of the strain of maintaining an intimate relationship (Levinger and Snoek, 1972:16).

This strain is probably most nagging in those unfortunate circumstances where people do not really want to remain intimate, but feel they must try— perhaps "for the children's sake" or for their own "respectability" in their community. The result may rarely be as drastic as homicide, but as Davis observed: "Each intimate who experiences the painful tension of the contradictory pressures both to sever and to sustain the relationship will often express it in the little cruelties by which he tries to make the other's life as miserable as his own. The relationship between George and Martha in Edward Albee's *Who's Afraid of Virginia Woolf?* is the paradigm" (1973:209). In this context, we can appreciate why some intimate relations are better dissolved than sustained, despite the pressures of external forces keeping them (superficially) together.

Davis (1973:xii) has contended, "Numerous books on intimate relations are being written today because accelerating social change has drastically eroded the bonds that tied individuals together in the past, causing them to seek outside advice on how to re-establish these bonds (doing consciously, as it were, what their ancestors did spontaneously)." In addition to reading books, people have sought help through participating in groups specially designed to deal with breakdowns in intimate relations and related socio-emotional problems. These special-purpose groups can generally be labeled *experiential groups,* and in the next, and final, section of the chapter, we will briefly review the major forms, aims, accomplishments, and dangers of these groups.

EXPERIENTIAL GROUPS AND THE HUMAN
POTENTIAL MOVEMENT: A BRIEF REVIEW

The essential characteristic shared by all the different specific kinds of experiential groups is their members' common desire to gain more understanding and control of group processes through participation in them.[19] There also are cer-

---

[19] This conception of the major features and forms of experiential groups derives from Shaw (1976: Ch. 10). An excellent bibliography of materials concerning experiential groups devoted to sensitivity training is in Hare (1976:418–419). This bibliography follows Hare's overview of the sensitivity training movement (Appendix 4).

tain of these processes that generally characterize experiential groups. Six of the most prevalent ones have been identified by Lakin (1972):

1. facilitating emotional expressiveness;
2. generating feelings of belongingness;
3. fostering a norm of self-disclosure as a condition of group membership;
4. sampling personal behaviors;
5. making acceptable interpersonal comparisons; and
6. sharing responsibility for leadership and direction with the appointed leader (cited in Shaw, 1976:343).

Although one might tend to think of participants in all experiential groups mainly as people with serious or debilitating socio-emotional or psychological problems, actually only one major form of these groups, the *therapy group,* is explicitly oriented to such people. The other two major forms, the *learning* or *training group* and the *expressive group,* are most likely to have participants who generally would be considered quite stable in social, emotional, and psychological terms. People become members of therapy groups expressly to repair damage to the way they feel about themselves or their relationships with others, but people join learning or training groups to improve their interpersonal sensitivity and effectiveness and to facilitate group communication in their marriages, in schools, or in other organizational or community settings,[20] and they join expressive groups to achieve fuller and more open emotional expressiveness.

"T-GROUPS" AND THE SENSITIVITY TRAINING MOVEMENT

It is possible to view currently popular examples of each of the major forms of experiential groups in relation to the emergence of the learning group—better known as the "sensitivity training group" or "*T*-group"—movement, even though this movement is predated by the efforts of prominent psychotherapists such as Freud, Reich, Klein, and Bion to use group processes for therapy (Back, 1973). Perhaps the most interesting fact about the emergence of this movement is that it was accidental rather than planned. The fortuitous discovery of the potential of the *T*-group as a learning vehicle can be traced precisely to a group relations workshop held in Connecticut in 1946 (Golembiewski and Blumberg, 1970:4).

Attending this workshop were educators, public officials, and other community workers. It was staffed by social scientists, including most prominently Kurt Lewin. At one of the regular staff meetings used to review workshop sessions and assess the progress of participants in them, three participants asked

---

[20]See Golembiewski and Blumberg (1970), Part V, for a collection of articles concerning applications of learning group dynamics to setting like the ones mentioned.

permission to observe the staff group at work. When the staff's interpretation of the behavior of one of these observers was questioned by her, she was asked for her perceptions of it. Lewin found this kind of additional data so useful that he incorporated the feedback and self-analysis of participants into all subsequent training sessions of this workshop. Furthermore, and more importantly, Lewin became so excited about this approach as a general method of group training in human relations, he became a major figure in efforts to provide this type of learning experience for a larger audience. These efforts resulted in the establishment of the National Training Laboratory for Group Development, NTL, which sponsored the first formal program in sensitivity training in Bethel, Maine in 1947.[21]

Since 1947, the NTL has grown substantially, and the T-group techniques that are the core of its sensitivity training programs have been expanded and refined. Golembiewski and Blumberg (1970:5-9) identified the following three major distinguishing features of the T-group:

1. It is a laboratory, in the sense that participants inquire about, explore, and experiment with their behavior in a psychologically safe atmosphere that encourages learning.
2. It focuses on "learning how to learn" about the causes, nature, and implications of our behavior by expanding social and personal awareness, inquisitiveness, and desire to participate in decisions affecting us.
3. It focuses on learning from the "here-and-now" or the experiences of the present moment.

The popularity of sensitivity training programs offered by the NTL has spawned numerous attempts to duplicate their T-group experiences or to use them as a model for experiential group processes with different purposes. For example, the encounter group, which has been widely used in therapy, is a well-known type of experiential group that grew out of the sensitivity training movement of the 1960s (Maliver, 1972; Lieberman *et al.,* 1973). Encounter groups generally involve about ten participants and a leader, and they may meet from several times a week for a few hours to every day for several weeks. In the typical encounter-group session, the leader, a therapist, encourages participants to express in a free and open manner their perceptions and feelings about themselves and others in the group and about how they interact. Since such freedom of expression occurs in a close interpersonal environment, it often prompts emotional outbursts, personal revelations, and intense interpersonal encounters. Therapists use this kind of atmosphere to try to nurture increased interpersonal

---

[21] Golembiewski and Blumberg (1970:4) pointed out, in a footnote, that early T-groups focused more on group processes and development than on individual behavior and sensitivity. They also noted that the NTL functioned initially as part of the Adult Educational Division of the National Education Association, and that in 1966, its name was changed to the NTL Institute for Applied Behavioral Science.

awareness, self-understanding and acceptance, and personal and social growth (Siiter, 1974).

THE HUMAN POTENTIAL MOVEMENT

Expressive groups have also been an outgrowth of the sensitivity training movement. Shaw has suggested that compared with learning and therapy groups, expressive groups place more stress on the hedonistic aspect of social interaction by catering to people who want to make their lives happier by becoming less emotionally inhibited and more expressive. He also noted that these groups have become very popular in recent years, with many of them assuming the character of a fad (Shaw, 1976:339). In fact, the rapid spread of involvement in experiential groups of various types over the past decade and one-half has assumed the quality of a social movement that has gone beyond the original aims of the sensitivity-training movement.

This newer movement has been called the *human potential movement*.[22] Generally, it has been aimed at helping people cope more effectively with emotional problems on both personal and social levels. In pursuit of this general purpose, it has employed group processes having a variety of interesting or unusual orientations, ranging from Zen Buddhism to astrology; mysticism; body manipulation and sensory experiences; art, dance, and dramatic games; and sports. By the early 1970s, over 170 "growth centers" such as the well-known Esalen Institute in California had sprung up in the United States; although they offered a diverse range of activities, in general, encounter group experiences of some sort were at the heart of them. No doubt the movie *Bob and Carol and Ted and Alice* contributed to popular awareness of the human potential movement; no doubt this movie also—along with the mass media in general—produced some popular misconceptions about this movement and the various forms of experiential groups associated with it.

EFFECTIVENESS OF EXPERIENTIAL GROUPS: SOME QUESTIONS AND FINDINGS

Many popular misconceptions about experiential groups undoubtedly concern their nature and aims. These misconceptions are not too difficult to eliminate, at least in general terms, and the comments so far in this discussion have been a brief attempt to do that. However, there are also misconceptions and arguments about the effectiveness of experiential groups that are not as easily answered. Shaw (1976:350-351) has suggested that attempts to achieve systematic knowledge about the effectiveness of experiential groups have been hindered by lack

---

[22]These comments about the human potential movement are based mainly on Maliver's (1974) brief account of it. For a fuller account, see Maliver (1972).

of a generally accepted theory about group experiences and their expected outcomes and by difficulties in trying to measure outcomes such as "sensitivity to the feelings of others" on the basis of vague conceptualizations of them. Despite these problems, research using the self-reports of participants, reports by associates, or objective behavioral measures in a wide range of experiential groups have produced at least tentative support for the conclusion that participation in experiential groups causes actual or self-perceived changes in the feelings and behavior of participants.[23]

More than the usual amount of caution must be exercised in generalizing from or reading into these research findings. For not only may their reliability and validity be somewhat dubious, they also may require qualification concerning the persistence and nature of the changes that were found. For example, even when the desired changes in interpersonal effectiveness and sensitivity, emotional expressiveness, or group communication occur during experiential group involvement, they may not persist long or have the intended consequences when participants leave the laboratory environment of experiential groups and return to the social environments originally producing their socio-emotional problems. Furthermore, it has been shown that participation in such groups can cause severe emotional or psychological disturbances (Shaw, 1976:359).

Though the relative frequency of beneficial and harmful outcomes has not been clearly established, there is evidence documenting at least some cases as severe as incapacitating anxiety, depression, suicide, and hospitalization for emotional breakdown, resulting from group experiences (Lakin, 1972). In addition, Back (1973) cited official statistics reported by the NTL listing 25 serious psychiatric problems among 11,000 participants in industrial training programs. In research concerning encounter groups, Lieberman, Yalom, and Miles (1971) found 9.6 percent of the participants demonstrated clearly harmful consequences of group involvement (cited in Shaw, 1976:358). Presumably, the likelihood of harmful consequences will be greatest in intense encounter-group experiences used for therapy. However, evidently there are also potential dangers associated with less intense group experiences used for other purposes. Apparently, these harmful consequences occur least, and learning occurs most, when participants openly express their feelings in a "psychologically safe" environment. Schein and Bennis (1965) suggested four basic conditions facilitating this type of environment:

1. a group which meets for a relatively long time in an isolated place;
2. a low probability that the group will meet again after the sessions have ended;
3. continual assurance by the training staff that the situation is supportive, non-evaluative, and nonthreatening;
4. an attitude on the part of participants that the group is temporary and game-like (cited in Shaw, 1976:358).

---

[23] For a brief review of this research, see Shaw (1976:352–357).

The presence of, or supervision by, a competent trainer, therapist, or group leader should also be explicitly mentioned as a crucial ingredient of psychologically safe experiential group environments.

Consideration of experiential groups should be interesting and important to most of us because of their current popularity and the potentially beneficial, or harmful, consequences they are capable of producing for their participants. From the standpoint of a small-group sociologist, they are especially interesting because they represent a fascinating topic for research on the uses and effects of small group involvement and also because they demonstrate how systematic knowledge about group emotion, interpersonal sentiments, and other aspects of small groups could be used to help us deal with group relationships in a more insightful, productive, and enjoyable manner. In a sense, then, this book, in presenting such knowledge attempts, clearly in a less intense and dramatic fashion, to accomplish some of the same aims as experiential groups.

SUMMARY

This chapter is the first of the five chapters of Part Two concerning basic concepts, assumptions, and findings about the small group as a sociological phenomenon. It began with a focus on communication because as Golembiewski (1962:90) has suggested, communication may be the most obvious necessity of small-group life. In fact, we have viewed regular face-to-face communication or interaction as a defining characteristic of small groups. Small-group studies of communication structures generally have focused on the organization, content, and effectiveness of communication, and we have looked at assumptions and findings about each of these communication dimensions, taking special note of the possible impact of a group's communication structure on other important aspects of small-group interaction. The studies of communication problems that were highlighted in this chapter focused on the role of communication feedback in sustaining commitment to demanding group goals, such as the conquest of Mount Everest, and the implications of communication barriers for the integration and efficiency of discussion groups. The latter study provided a particularly good bridge to the major topic of this chapter, integration.

This chapter drew an important distinction between integration at the group level and at the interpersonal level. Together, these types of integration concern the forces and relations binding together the group as a whole and its members. Group integration, which is the "glue" holding together the group as a whole, includes such aspects as cohesiveness, structural-functional integration, normative integration, and group emotion. We were mainly concerned in the discussion of group integration with cohesiveness and the aspect of structural-functional integration involving subgroup formation. Since the use of the term *cohesiveness* by small-group investigators often has been quite inclusive, thereby clouding the distinctions made here between various aspects of group *and inter-*

personal integration, we have used it only to refer to member attraction to the group as a whole. We have summarized some of its most important sources and consequences in small groups. The discussion of subgroup formation focused on cliques, which blend forces of interpersonal integration or friendship and structural-functional integration (i.e., the development of a group within a group) to have a potential effect on group cohesiveness. The studies of problems of group integration receiving special attention in this chapter focus on the cohesiveness of adolescent drinking groups and the relationship of cohesiveness to interpersonal conflict in dyads.

Interpersonal integration concerns the sentiments holding together people in interpersonal relationships within small groups. We focused on the nature of patterning of sentiment relations, or the sociometric structure, in small groups, and we examined some of the major antecedents of interpersonal attraction, including rewardingness, propinquity, and similarity of beliefs, as well as some of its major sociological consequences, including its impact on uniformity of behavior and beliefs, communication, and task performance. We paid special attention to studies of problems of interpersonal integration concerning intergroup rivalry and conflict, scapegoating, the entry of a newcomer into a group, and intimacy.

The chapter concluded with a brief discussion of the major forms of experiential groups, which have become popular in recent years as a device to help solve interpersonal problems, increase sensitivity in interpersonal relations, and achieve fuller and more open emotional expressiveness. Our discussion of experiential groups dealt with the emergence of the sensitivity training and human potential movements, along with some questions and findings about the effectiveness of the experiential groups that are at the heart of these movements.

Although this chapter has focused mainly on group communication and integration, it has not been strictly confined to these topics. This is to be expected when small groups are viewed as systems of interdependent relations among their various structural-functional components and when a concept of structural-functional integration is presented to refer partly to this interdependence. The topics beyond communication and integration treated in this chapter included status and leadership structures, social conformity and deviance, coalitions, intergroup relations, group goal attainment, and task performance. These other factors will receive closer scrutiny in the ensuing chapters. The next chapter focuses on patterns and problems of social control.

4

Social Control
in Small Groups

INTRODUCTION

Many of us like to believe we walk to the beat of our own drummer, and are "our own people," doing what *we* want when *we* want to do it. Perhaps because we value so highly our individuality, personal freedom, or sense of our own uniqueness, we often seem to resent being labeled "conformists" or admitting we have given in voluntarily to group pressure. At the same time, though, we tend to dislike or fear at least as much the label of "deviant." However, whatever our personal feelings about conformity and deviance, all of us either conform to social norms or deviate from them to some extent, whenever we interact with people in established social settings.

In effect, sociologists have created a conceptual "trap" wherein they classify all behavior in structured situations either as conforming or deviant. Once we recognize this, it becomes easier to appreciate and understand sociological facts and explanations of conformity, deviance, and social control in small groups. One important fact is that even for the "independent" ones among us, most of our behavior more or less conforms to relevant group norms. Indeed, conformity to group norms, which is established and maintained through processes of social control, is the basis for social order in groups. Without extensive conformity, social interaction would be unpredictable and chaotic.

Although conformity is essential for the establishment and maintenance of organized group interaction, we should not make the mistake of presuming conformity and social order are inevitable wherever people interact. In some cases, consensus about social norms may be slow to emerge, if it emerges at all. For example, our experience has been that student clubs, such as sociology majors, optimistically organized by faculty members, often fail to develop their own normative code and social order as a result of lack of motivation, interest, time, or opportunity for self-direction. In such cases, students' conformity to

108

faculty imposed norms of attendance and of involvement is often quite limited because participation is voluntary and prospective group members do not interact enough or with enough seriousness to arrive at their own consensus about what they should do or how they should interact. That is, their club becomes a *stillborn* group, and its normative order never really emerges.

Limited acceptance of group norms and limited conformity to them are not restricted to members of stillborn groups. Even in groups where interaction has become structured and members generally conform, behavior is seldom completely uniform. Patterns of deviance may emerge among some members amidst more extensive tendencies toward conformity. For example, Vince Lombardi expected total conformity to some very strict training rules from members of football teams he coached. Nevertheless, certain players on his teams regularly sought to circumvent these rules, particularly the one about being in bed by a specified hour. In less cohesive and less successful groups, patterns of deviance may be more pronounced or extensive, as in the case of students who are regularly late for class despite general adherence among other class members to the norm about being on-time.

In the ensuing sections of this chapter, we will examine conformity, deviance, and social control in small groups. From what has been said so far, it should be evident that deviance is as much a fact of group life as conformity, even though it tends to be less prevalent. Thus, although the force of social control in creating patterns of conformity in small groups tends to be impressive, it must be remembered that people *do* deviate in varying degrees from group norms. Sometimes this deviance is minor and has little impact on group structure, or it is innovative and has a constructive effect on group functioning. However, other times it may be quite extensive or disruptive and have serious implications for "normal" patterns of group interaction. The aim of this chapter is to convey the complex and often delicate relationships among social control efforts, conformity, and deviance in small groups.

THE NORMATIVE STRUCTURE, SOCIAL CONTROL, AND RELATED CONCEPTS

THE NATURE OF GROUP NORMS

No form of behavior is intrinsically characterized by conformity or deviance, since conformity and deviance are defined with respect to relevant social norms. Thus, to understand the nature of conformity and deviance, we first must understand the nature of the norms governing contexts such as small groups.

All of us at least implicitly understand the meaning of a group norm, since we all belong to groups and norms are a fundamental component of the social order of every established group. We can understand the sociological meaning of norms in more explicit terms if we consider the definitional work of Homans

(1950) and of Crosbie (1975). Homans captured the general sociological meaning of a group norm when he defined it as ". . . an idea in the minds of the members of a group, an idea that can be put in the form of a statement specifying what the members or other (people) should do, ought to do, are expected to do, under given circumstances" (p. 123). Crosbie extended this definition by conceptualizing a norm as "a shared expectation of an acceptable range of behavior in relation to some value" (p. 69).

The meaning of the group-norm concept can be seen in more concrete terms by considering the work of Sherif and Sherif (1964:164–183, 269–273), concerning adolescent groups of boys in the southwestern United States.[1] Sherif and Sherif found that acceptance into an adolescent gang tended to involve more than simply being skilled at gang activities. For example, they discovered that even though a boy was a skilled basketball player, he did not become a full-fledged member of a gang that includes basketball among its activities unless he learned and adhered to the special expectations shared by gang members about how the game ought to be played. Among these special rules or norms were the expectations: (1) that a gang member should never criticize a fellow's performance during competition; (2) that *during competition,* "it is OK for him to foul if he can get away with it," but (3) that *during practice with fellow gang members,* it is *not* OK to foul (unless he happened to be the leader of the gang).

Since members of gangs and other groups typically engage in more than one type of activity, one would anticipate their behavior to be regulated by more than one type of norm. In the case of the gangs studied by Sherif and Sherif, members were also constrained by norms indicating when they could and could not steal or date a new girl; how they should deal with parents and police, i.e., avoid "ratting" about gang activities; and what their role was in street fights with rival gangs. Thus, group norms can cover a wide range of members' behavior. They can *prescribe* what they are expected or allowed to do, or they can *proscribe* what they are *not* to do. Beyond these basic characteristics of norms, there are others, suggested by Homans' and Crosbie's definitions, that should be understood if we are to have an adequate grasp of the important elements of conformity and deviance situations in small groups.

First, it must be emphasized that group norms are *shared* expectations.[2] This means they are not individual standards for behavior, but instead they are expectations group members *collectively* hold and apply to each other. These expectations may apply to only one group member or role, such as the leader; to some, but not all, group members or roles, such as junior or senior members; or to all group members or roles. However, whatever the intended scope of

---

[1] Mills (1967:Ch. 5) also used Sherif and Sherif's work to introduce his discussion of group norms. Mills' general treatment of norms and normative control in this chapter offers a good, brief introduction to some of the key ideas we will be considering in our discussion of social control in groups.

[2] This discussion of salient characteristics of group norms is based mainly on Crosbie's (1975:69–70) conceptual work.

applicability of an expectation, it must be shared by a majority or powerful minority of group members to have an impact on the group's emergent social order and structure.

Although normative expectations must be shared by group members, not all shared group expectations are normative. That is, group members may expect, in a predictive sense, a certain kind of behavior from another or others in the group without giving approval to that behavior. For example, in certain groups such as clubs or college classes, we might expect a couple of members to be late for meetings because they always have been, but this expectation does not mean that this behavior is normative, or that the group will tolerate it indefinitely. What it means is that behavior may be predictable without meeting norms. Behavior that meets group norms is related to group values and therefore is evaluated as acceptable, proper, or good, rather than merely predictable. There is a qualitative difference between the expectation that one *will* or *is likely to* act in a certain way and the expectation that one *ought to* or *should* act in a certain way. The latter moral connotation separates norms from other sorts of expectations, including shared ones. It is important to recognize this distinction when trying to understand the nature and implications of group norms.

Sherif and Sherif (1969:141) have provided a useful summary of the essential characteristics of social norms by listing what the concept refers to and what it does not:

1. Social norms (do) *not* necessarily refer to the average behavior by members of a social unit, or even to what is typical. The concept has little in common with the terms "test norm" or "age norm" as used in psychology textbooks.
2. Social norms are standardized generalizations that epitomize events, behavior, objects or persons in short-cut form. Like a verbal category or rule, a social norm applies to *classes* of objects (e.g., persons, behaviors, or events).
3. A social norm is *evaluative,* designating both what is valued and what is scorned, what is expected (even ideal) and what is degrading, what ought to be and what ought not to be, what is acceptable and what is objectionable.
4. Being generalizations, social norms typically define a range or *latitude* of what is permissible or acceptable, and a range of actions and beliefs that are objectionable. In other words, social norms take note of the universal facts of individual differences, of varying circumstances, and of novelty by designating ranges of positive and negative evaluation, not absolutes.

Combining Sherif and Sherif's list with the characteristics previously described in this section, we arrive at a conception of group norms as shared group expectations that are standardized generalizations applied to classes of objects, having a moral or evaluative basis, and that prescribe a range of acceptable behavior or proscribe a range of unacceptable behavior, under given circumstances. Since norms are ideas, we cannot observe them directly, but we can infer their existence through observation of patterned regularities in group interaction.

Observers and group members also can discover the boundaries of acceptable behavior allowed by group norms by noticing the circumstances and kinds of behavior that prompt sanctions or social control efforts.

ISSUES OF INTERPERSONAL RELATIONS, NORMATIVE ORIENTATIONS, AND FUNCTIONAL PROBLEMS OF GROUPS

As social rules or guidelines for interaction, group norms can help people in groups orient themselves to one another in an orderly and meaningful way. Parsons (Parsons and Shils, 1951:80–88) has suggested that for norms to be effective guidelines for interaction in any group or society, they must help social actors—or, the interacting people—resolve questions relating to at least four universal interpersonal questions:[3]

1. Are relations among members to be based upon the expression of the feelings they have toward one another, or upon the assumption that those feelings should be suppressed and controlled (i.e., is group emotion to have precedence over normative control, or vice versa)?
2. Is involvement with one another to be total and unbounded (as with parent and child), or is it to be restricted and specific (as with driving instructor and pupil)?
3. Is the significance of the other to be due to the unique relation one has with him or her (as brother or sister, cousin, or friend), or to the fact that (the person) represents a type, or a class, of person (a servant, a client, or an employer)?
4. Is the significance of the other to be due to his (or her) qualities (steady and wise), or to the role he (or she) performs (as a scientist, as an athlete, and so on)?

Mills (1967:75) has proposed that norms can be compared across groups by examining how the members of different groups resolve these four interpersonal issues. While there are various possible combinations of normative responses to these issues, some appear more likely than others. Two in particular can be seen as representing the core of the normative systems of ideal-typical primary and task groups. In ideal-typical primary groups, one would expect to find interpersonal relations oriented to norms prescribing expression of feelings, unbounded or diffuse involvement, and emphasis on unique or particularistic ties and personal or ascribed qualities. In ideal-typical task groups, one would expect to find interpersonal relations oriented to norms prescribing suppression

---

[3]These four interpersonal issues have been briefly summarized from a small group perspective by Mills (1967:74–75). As Mills has pointed out, Parsons originally identified a fifth issue, the "self-collectivity dilemma," but eventually dropped it from his discussion of universal interpersonal issues. We are relying here on Mills' summary of Parsons' work.

of emotions or affective neutrality, restricted or specific involvement, and emphasis on technical qualifications and skill in performing the assigned tasks.

Actual primary groups such as families and task groups such as surgical teams, seldom fully or consistently conform to the combination of normative orientations associated with their respective ideal type. Nevertheless, it seems reasonable to assume that concrete primary and task groups departing substantially or frequently from the relevant ideal-typical normative combinations just described *could* face serious problems of social control, along with other basic group-functional problems. For example, relations among members of a family could become quite complicated and confused if parents and children expected affectionate and personal relations of each other on the one hand *and* on the other hand, limited involvement with each other and treatment based on how much each achieves or how successful each is. It is apparent that these confusing normative inconsistencies could disrupt the bonds of intimacy linking members of this family to each other, as well as the patterns of authority relations between parents and between parents and children and the fabric of cohesion keeping the family together as a whole. In addition, the confusion generated could cause family members to have considerable difficulty in maintaining high levels of conformity to any one of these basic normative orientations, with the result being some amount of social disorganization.

Similarly, one could imagine that the work of a task group such as a surgical team might become quite disrupted if during surgery, doctors and nurses failed to live up to the kinds of normative expectations associated with ideal-typical task groups, or if they mixed conformity to primary-group norms, based on intimate relations outside the operating room, with conformity to task-group norms. Thus, from these examples, it should be evident that knowledge about a group's normative responses to the four interpersonal issues suggested by Parsons can, by itself, provide important insights into the sources of social control, and other group-functional, problems in small groups. Furthermore, on a more descriptive level, knowledge of the ideal types of normative combinations we have identified for primary and task groups offers additional insight into the general nature of these sorts of groups and the kinds of interpersonal patterns we might expect to find in them.

LEVELS OF NORMATIVE STRUCTURE

Official Rules and Informal Group Norms

Not all the rules that are supposed to regulate group behavior actually do so, especially when a group exists within a larger organizational framework and has rules imposed on it by officials of the larger organization. *Official* or *formal rules* dictating administrative expectations for acceptable or proper behavior may not be taken seriously by the people who are supposed to follow them because these people belong to groups in the organization with rules of their own that emerged spontaneously, that conflict with the official rules, and that take precedence over official rules for group members. Often, these *unofficial* or *informal group norms* are unknown even to second-line supervisors as well as to higher administrative officials in industrial and other types of organizations where such norms exist (Haas and Drabek, 1973:139).[4] Dubin (1958) and Dalton (1959), among others, have suggested that these informal group norms are inevitable in organizations because no set of administratively derived rules can be complete enough to cover all the situations or problems confronted by organization members. Furthermore, one would expect that people who belong to groups in organizations will develop their own norms with fellow group members when official rules seem excessively demanding or when they threaten group structures or solidarity. Crosbie (1975:70) has proposed that members of groups in organizations will adopt externally imposed (official) rules as group norms only when the rules are consistent with group values, assuming, of course, members are able to resist enforcement of the official rules.

Crosbie illustrates the nature and implications of conflict between the informal norms of a group and the official rules of its organization with the example of possession of marijuana or alcohol by students living in college dormitories. Possession of these drugs usually violates the rules of a dormitory imposed by college administrations. However, on many college campuses, possession and even use of marijuana and alcohol in dormitories are not only tolerated by those living there, but are also approved. In similar cases where there is a lack of consistent enforcement of violations of the official rules by administrative staff members, it often may happen that people in the organization become confused about whether the official rules must still be taken seriously. Thus, on college campuses, students have assumed that because their dormitory supervisors are ignoring the presence of drugs on their floors, the official rules about drug possession and use were no longer being applied. Under such conditions, they often have come to believe, perhaps on the basis of wishful thinking, that their informal norm that drug possession and use are acceptable if kept discreet, is *also* the operational norm accepted by administrative officials.

Haas and Drabek (1973:140-141) have suggested that when organization members misinterpret how administrators feel about official rules, as in the case we just have described, serious repercussions for members and the organization as a whole could result when administrators decide to enforce the official rules. In particular, there could result outrage from members, a severe rift in relations between organization officials and members, and general organizational strain and instability. To illustrate this point, Haas and Drabek noted the angry reaction from many students that was provoked when college officials decided to

---

[4]Haas and Drabek offer a useful general treatment of "groups within organizations" in their fourth chapter. Included in this chapter is a discussion of the official and unofficial components of the normative structure of organizations, and much of what is being presented in the present section was suggested by Haas and Drabek's discussion.

cooperate with local police in raiding dormitories so that (unsuspecting) students violating college drug rules (and local laws) could be arrested.

Thus, it appears that a discrepancy between official rules and informal group norms and between perceptions about these rules by organization officials and members can lead to serious disruptions of relations in organizations. These disruptions would appear to be most severe when members are strongly influenced by informal group norms and administrators are unclear about their desire to enforce the official rules and act inconsistently. In addition, Gouldner's (1965) research suggests that problems could arise when indulgent officials who were lax in enforcing official rules are replaced by stricter ones, thereby confusing and alienating organization members who had come to rely on indulgency.

Organizational Expectations and Informal Group Responses: The Case of the Bank Wiring Room

Even when official rules or policies are intended to provide fair and equitable treatment of organization members, these rules may not have as much influence on people as the informal norms of the groups to which they belong within the organization. This pattern is illustrated by Roethlisberger and Dickson's (1939) classic study of the "Bank Wiring Room" at Western Electric's Hawthorne plant in Chicago.[5] This study focused on a group of fourteen men who had the job of assembling "banks" of telephone equipment. At the time of the study, the Western Electric management recently had established a piece-rate wage incentive plan that increased pay for each completed piece of telephone equipment. This wage incentive plan was based on the assumption that the workers wanted to increase their earnings. It was believed by management to be a plan that would distribute earnings fairly as well as improve efficiency and productivity. After instituting this plan, management expected that (Broom and Selznick, 1977:146):

1. Since each individual's total wage was determined to some degree by group output, each worker would try to increase output.
2. If the workers exerted pressure at all, it would be to increase the output of the slower workers.
3. To increase his hourly wage rate, each worker would strive to increase his individual average output.

---

[5]This is one of a number of "Hawthorne studies" reported by Roethlisberger and Dickson in *Management and the Worker* (1939), which we cited when discussing the Relay Assembly Room research. Among the books where one can find an account by Roethlisberger and Dickson specifically pertaining to the Bank Wiring Room study is Crosbie's (1975) volume of small-group readings. In addition, Broom and Selznick (1977:145-147) offer an especially good, brief summary of the Bank Wiring Room research. We will draw from both the account in Crosbie, and Broom and Selznick's summary, in discussing this research in this and the next section in this chapter.

Despite the opportunity to improve individual earnings, workers continued to produce at about the same rate as they had before the plan. The researchers were interested in learning the source of the plan's failure. They conducted six months of extensive interviews and observations in the Bank Wiring Room. They discovered that the workers in this room held their own conception of "a fair day's work," which was about two complete equipments per man, and they felt production should not go much above, or below, that level.

In the eyes of these men, they were producing at a level that seemed satisfactory to the company and represented a "hard day's work" to their foremen. They saw the incentive plan and the specter of higher production rates as a threat to their group. They felt that higher production, which they actually were capable of achieving by working harder, might ultimately result in increased company production standards for lower pay. In the face of this perceived threat, the workers developed their own norm of production, which they strictly enforced within their group.

The men in the Bank Wiring Room either did not or were not able to respond to the company's wage incentive plan and its promise of greater earnings. Responding would have meant violating their group's informal production norm, which in turn would have resulted in their being sanctioned by other group members. As we will attempt to make clear in the ensuing discussion of social control, the threat of informal sanctions or punishment from fellow group members often can have more influence on a person's behavior in an organization or the larger society than the lure of formal incentive systems or the threat of official punishment. Once again, it should be emphasized that group members are most likely to voluntarily adopt official or externally imposed rules as their own group norms when the former rules are consistent with the basic values shared by group members.

BASIC TYPES AND CHARACTERISTICS OF CONFORMITY, DEVIANCE, AND SOCIAL CONTROL IN SMALL GROUPS

THE NATURE OF SOCIAL CONTROL: AN INTRODUCTORY ILLUSTRATION

Since we are defining social control as the establishment and maintenance of patterns of conformity to group rules or norms, we have already begun to consider this process in referring to the use of sanctions, or punishment, to enforce conformity in the Bank Wiring Room. In fact, the sanctions used there were quite interesting, and therefore deserve a closer look.

If a man worked too fast or produced at too high a rate, he was ridiculed by other group members as a "rate buster." On the other hand, if a man worked too slowly or produced too little, he was chided by group members for being a "chiseler." While these verbal sanctions often were effective in bringing the output of deviants into line with the group production norm, a form of physical sanction called *binging* also was used at times to bring deviants into line.

Binging was a type of game in which one man might walk up to another and strike him as hard as possible on the upper arm. The victim then was allowed to retaliate with one blow. One of the objects of the game was to see who could hit the hardest. However, binging also was used as a penalty for objectionable behavior (such as unnecessary swearing), as a means of expressing mutual antagonism and settling disputes, and as a way of regulating the output of some of the fastest workers. The latter was one of its most significant applications, and it is well illustrated by the following exchange among co-workers, reported by Roethlisberger and Dickson (1939):[6]

> *First wireman* (to second wireman): "Why don't you quit work? Let's see, this is your thirty-fifth row today. What are you going to do with them all?"
>
> *Second wireman*: "What do you care? It's to your advantage if I work, isn't it?"
>
> *Third wireman*: "Yeah, but the way you're working, you'll get stuck with them."
>
> *Second wireman*: "Don't worry about that. I'll take care of it. You're getting paid by the sets I turn out. That's all you should worry about."
>
> *Third wireman*: "If you don't quit work I'll bing you." (The third wireman struck the second wireman and finally chased him around the room.)
>
> *Oberserver* (A few minutes later): "What's the matter, (second wireman), won't he let you work?"
>
> *Second wireman*: "No. I'm all through. I've got enough done." (He then went over and helped another wireman.)

This description of social control in the Bank Wiring Room makes evident that this process involves norms, potential or actual sanctions, and the processes of conformity and deviance. In the next section, we will consider the meaning of conformity a bit more explicitly and fully than we have so far in this chapter, so that the nature of the related concepts of deviance and social control will be clearer when we discuss them afterward.

TYPES OF CONFORMITY IN SMALL GROUPS

Crosbie (1975:431) has defined *conformity* as "behavior in accordance with the standards and beliefs (including norms) of a group." As we noted earlier, as members of groups most of us conform to a large extent, which makes possible the existence of social order in groups and reinforces group structural effects.

---

[6] These quoted materials appear in a selection from *Management and the Worker* (1939) called "A Fair Day's Work," which is in Crosbie (1975:85-94).

The sort of conformity of interest to small-group investigators is *acquiescent conformity,* which is characterized by voluntarily giving in to the group, rather than conformity-type behavior occurring independently of group influence. Crosbie has distinguished three types of acquiescent conformity: informational conformity, normative conformity, and obedience (pp. 431–436).

Informational Conformity

Crosbie has defined informational conformity as "acceptance of the standards and beliefs of others as evidence for reality" (p. 432). This type of conformity arises when people attempt to ascertain the validity of their own standards, judgments, or beliefs in the absence of clear-cut, accepted, "objective" standards of reference. In this context of subjectivity and uncertainty, people often try to derive a sense of what is valid or correct by checking their standards and beliefs against those of fellow group members. Informational conformity occurs when people revise their standards and beliefs in the direction of others'. As Crosbie has pointed out, informational conformity often differs from cases of normative conformity and obedience, in that the change involved in informational conformity is both public *and* private, which means the conformer actually accepts the group standard or belief as his or her own and as right.

Research by Sherif (1936) concerning the *autokinetic effect* provides an excellent illustration of the concept of informational conformity. Sherif used the autokinetic situation as a prototype for stimuli lacking objective structure (Sherif and Sherif, 1969:119). In a completely dark room, a single stationary pinpoint of light appears to move (autokinesis); the problem for people in this ambiguous situation is to establish a stable and valid sense of the ostensible range of movement of this pinpoint of light. Sherif initially asked subjects to make their estimates alone in the darkened room. After they had made enough of these estimates for Sherif to determine a stable average range for each subject, he then put groups of two or three in the autokinetic situation at the same time.

Sherif found that individual estimates within groups were discrepant at first, but that after a while the estimates began to converge on a common distance. For each group the common estimate was unique, reflecting the original individual estimates of the group members. In the last stage of the research, Sherif had the subjects return to the alone condition and he found that they retained the newly acquired group estimate. Thus, in this experiment, subjects modified their estimates in the direction of information provided by others in their group and held on to these modified estimates after leaving the group, though for how long is uncertain.[7]

---

[7]Sherif and Sherif (1969:119) have suggested that although we might expect social influence to produce informational conformity when group members' original individual judgments are not widely discrepant, "the sky is not the limit for attempted social influence" in

Normative Conformity

Although informational conformity is interesting because it shows the influence of groups on their members, it will be relatively less relevant to us than *normative conformity*. This latter type is defined as "acceptance of the standards and beliefs of others as a means of fulfilling real or imagined (normative) expectations of others" (Crosbie, 1975:432). Unlike informational conformity, it involves the actual or perceived existence of social pressures to follow group norms. Sometimes these pressures are quite subtle, and they often operate in the normal context of group interaction. Whatever their form, these pressures represent social control forces. This more direct relation to social control makes normative conformity more relevant to us in this chapter.

Obedience is "acceptance of real or imagined leadership expectations (or authoritative commands)" (Crosbie, 1975:434). It is more similar to normative conformity, but we will concentrate on obedience in our chapter on leadership and power because it is defined as more relevant to authoritative commands of leaders than to group norms in general. We have already considered an excellent illustration of the meaning of normative conformity in the case of the Bank Wiring Room. The men recognized that there were certain shared expectations about how they were supposed to act and work in their group. They knew that if they violated those norms, they could expect to face pressures from other group members to bring them into line. Thus, we find in this situation the normative element and the actual or anticipated group pressure associated with the concept of normative conformity.

The term *normative conformity* makes quite obvious what referent is being used in defining it. Knowing this referent is important because the general concept of conformity has little meaning or utility in sociological analysis unless it is defined in relation to social standards such as group norms. As Sherif and Sherif (1969:190-191) have observed: "There is no such thing as conforming . . . behavior in the abstract." In order to understand the meaning of the term, first we must be able to answer the question: "Conformity to *what*?" That "what," or referent, is, of course, a social norm.

This should be kept in mind because at times social scientists have seemed to neglect this crucial referent question in developing experimental situations to study conformity. Sherif and Sherif illustrate this point with the example of Asch's classic experimental study of the effects of group opinion on judging the length of lines. In describing this study as a "classic experiment on normative conformity," Crosbie (1975:433) would seem to be among those inviting the Sherifs' criticism. Let us look more closely at Asch's research to gain a better

---

autokinetic situations. More specifically, when an individual establishes his or her own standard and range for estimating movement and then is faced with another person presenting extremely discrepant estimates, the other person's estimates will have little if any effect, even though the experience is a bit unsettling for the person trying to arrive at a stable and valid estimate.

119

sense of the nature of the Sherifs' argument *and* of the meaning of normative conformity itself.

Conformity as Yielding to the Majority: The Asch Line-Judgment Research

Asch (e.g., 1957) devised an experimental situation involving a naive subject and seven to nine confederates that was meant to determine the influence of an incorrect majority opinion on judgments made by naive subjects about the lengths of lines.[8] The confederates were instructed by the experimenter to give the same incorrect judgments in what was represented as an experiment in visual perception. The stimulus materials were two sets of white cards. Each card in one set displayed a single black line (the standard); each card in the second set displayed three comparison lines. On each card of comparison lines, one line was the same length as the relevant standard line, and the other two were easily recognizable departures from the standard length. For each pair of comparison and standard cards, the subjects were to indicate which of the three comparison lines most nearly matched the length of the standard line. This experimental situation is more graphically represented in Figure 5.

For each trial of the experiment, the experimenter showed a pair of stimulus cards. One by one the confederates (whose collusion with the experimenter was unknown to the naive subject) and then the naive subject orally expressed their opinion of which line matched the standard. There was a series of eighteen trials, which consisted of twelve "critical" ones, in which the confederates unanimously gave incorrect responses, and six "neutral" ones, in which the confederates unanimously responded correctly. Since the naive subject gave his opinion last, or next-to-last, on each trial, he repeatedly was placed in a difficult position during the critical trials. On the one hand, the subject knew or thought he knew the correct response. However, on the other hand, seven to nine apparently trustworthy peers (fellow college students) disagreed with him while agreeing with each other.

Using this basic experimental design, Asch placed 123 college students in the minority situation we have described. When subjects were faced with an incorrect majority opinion, they significantly increased their errors, always in the direction of the majority. In fact, nearly 37 percent of the subjects' responses were incorrect, as compared to an error rate of less than 1 percent of all judgments for subjects in a control condition (where there were no confederates and judgments were merely put on paper, trial by trial). Thus, in a substantial proportion of cases, subjects in the experimental condition gave in to group influence and responded incorrectly. Most subjects gave in to the incorrect majority one or more times.

---

[8]Hare (1962:26–29) offers a good, brief summary of this research, and we have used part of his summary in developing the description of Asch's study presented here.

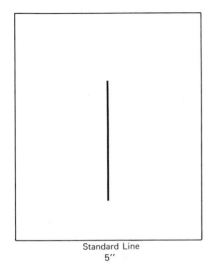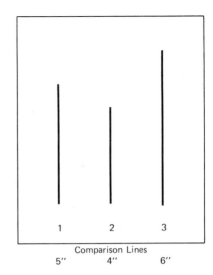

Standard Line	Comparison Lines
5″	5″ 4″ 6″

FIGURE 5. An Illustration of a Pair of Stimulus Cards from the Asch Research (Asch, 1957)

These lines have been drawn to ¼-scale of the lengths shown above, which were actual lengths used in Asch's research. Subjects saw this particular pair of cards on the 4th, 8th, 13th, and 17th trials of the experiment. (There were 18 trials overall). All four trials were "critical"—vs. "neutral"—ones because the majority responded incorrectly. For the 4th and 13th trials, the incorrect majority response was the second comparison line (4″) and for the 8th and 17th, it was the third comparison line (6½″).

Does Group Conformity Actually Occur in the Asch Research Situation? A Closer Look at the Meaning of Conformity

While Asch's results clearly show the impact of social influence, there is some dispute about whether they illustrate the idea of conformity to group norms. Crosbie (1975:434) has proposed that this yielding to majority opinion is normative conformity in the sense that it shows people trying "to be like others in order to gain acceptance and avoid rejection." However, Sherif and Sherif (1969:191) have argued:

> . . . The encounter with such errors (by the majority) is an unusual if not bizzare event in the ordinary run of social life. This (Asch) experimental model does not contain the essentials for studying conformity . . . The referents of conforming behavior . . . are not properly represented by immediate, brief, and sheerly arbitrary social pressures from others. . . .

It might seem we are senselessly nit-picking in focusing on whether Asch's results actually reflect normative conformity. However, in presenting these contradictory interpretations of the meaning of Asch's research, we are able to underscore some important ideas about group conformity. In fact, there are valuable insights on both sides of the argument. The Sherifs' argument that the notion of conformity is meaningless without a clear referent deserves reiteration, and we can see why they have suggested that the (incorrect) majority opinion in the Asch situation represents an "immediate, brief, and . . . arbitrary" referent for conformity when compared to the social norms that govern our behavior in established groups.[9] Nevertheless, this majority opinion does, at least, represent an answer to the question: "Conformity to what?" Furthermore, since most naive subjects gave in to the incorrect majority one or more times, we can assume they felt the influence of the group standard in most cases, which is why Crosbie treated Asch's research as an example of normative conformity.

In general, then, Asch's research indicates that a normative influence process can emerge even in a temporary, trivial, and artificial group situation. This implies that patterns of conformity must be quite strong in established small groups. Further research (e.g., Deutsch and Gerard, 1955; Schulman, 1967) has also suggested that more than one type of conformity may operate under certain conditions of the Asch situation. This means that people may be influenced at the same time by their perception of group norms, their desire to know whether their judgment is correct, and their recognition of what is expected of them by their group leader.

Although this examination of the Asch research has enabled us to emphasize some important ideas about normative conformity in particular and conformity in general in small groups, we must go beyond it to learn more about what happens in groups when people break rules as well as follow them. By shifting focus from Asch's conformity research and Sherif's autokinetic work, to the Bank Wiring Room study, we gain a better grasp of the kind of situation where rule-breaking behavior—or social deviance—is likely to engender social-control efforts, sanctions, and social problems for small groups. Our main focus in the remainder of this chapter will be social deviance, social control, and their dynamic implications for interpersonal relations and the group as a whole.

DEVIANCE IN SMALL GROUPS

The Nature of Social Deviance in Small Groups

In the adolescent gangs studied by the Sherifs, which we mentioned earlier in this chapter, it was considered deviant to criticize a fellow basketball player during competition, to go with a new girl without the approval of the gang, to "rat" to the police or parents about gang activities, or to desert the gang during a street fight (Sherif and Sherif, 1964). In the Bank Wiring Room, it was con-

---

[9]It should be added that the influence of the erring majority was found to be substantially reduced when there were *two* naive subjects facing the majority and when the naive subject was provided with a confederate "partner" who was instructed to respond accurately without exception (Asch, 1957).

sidered deviant to produce significantly more, or less, than two complete equipments per day, to tell a supervisor anything that would be detrimental to an associate, to maintain social distance, or to act in an officious manner (Broom and Selznick, 1977:147). Each of these types of behavior was considered deviant in its respective group setting because it violated an expectation shared by group members about how one *should* act as a member of that particular group. Thus, deviant behavior is not merely different; it is behavior that challenges or violates group norms.

Social deviance in groups and elsewhere can be quite significant and complex in its implications for social order and structural stability in a given social system. In addition, because of the reasons just mentioned as well as the connotation of *deviance* for many people, the sociological meaning of *social deviance* may often be misunderstood. Bredemeier and Stephenson (1962:121–122) have provided helpful clarification about sociological and other meanings and possible implications of this process:

> In discussing deviance, we want to emphasize that we are not discussing what is "good" or "bad" in evaluative terms. We are not even discussing what is functional or (dysfunctional) for the social system or for the individual. We are discussing only the *fact* that sometimes some people under some conditions do not conform to the expectations of other people. . . . Very often it is a good thing that deviation or nonconformity occurs. There are some expectations that we (Bredemeier and Stephenson) would say, from our own ethical point of view, *ought* to be violated. There are some situations to which individuals ought *not* to be "well adjusted"; they ought to deviate for the sake of their own sanity or integrity. Furthermore, the institutional structures of some social systems are (dysfunctional) for the system's own adaptation or integration, and therefore, it would be better off if its members did deviate from institutionalized (normative) expectations. *Successful* pattern maintenance in such conditions might well mean the end of the system. Still further, we would not hesitate to say—again, from the point of view of our own values—that some systems ought not to survive (some families ought to break up, for example); and therefore, if conformity would help the system, we would be all for deviance.
>
> We should also note in discussing deviance we are not necessarily discussing "social problems." Some "social problems" are a consequence of deviant behavior, and some consist of deviant behavior. But (a) not all deviance is a "social problem" and (b) many social problems have nothing to do with deviance.[10]

---

[10] Bredemeier and Stephenson have cited Merton (1961) as an example of an excellent discussion of the general issue of deviance and social problems; they have cited Bredemier and Toby (1960) as an example of an analysis of social problems that either consist of or result from social deviance.

Thus, according to Bredemeier and Stephenson, social deviance may be "good" or "bad" in some ethical sense; it may be functional or dysfunctional for a social system or its members; and it may or may not be a social problem. However, when social deviance occurs in a group and represents a violation of normative expectations held by group members, we can generally expect it to be met by a negative response from group members and by their efforts to control it. Crosbie (1975:510) has suggested that although most small group theorists assume that deviance in groups will produce the reaction just described, there are a few who have proposed that deviance serves a useful purpose in groups by reminding members of the boundaries of acceptable behavior, and that groups recognize this function and therefore try to "induce, sustain, and permit deviant behavior." These latter theorists seem to be suggesting that groups allow deviance in order to control it.

Dentler and Erikson (1959) are prominent among those theorists who have taken this minority viewpoint regarding the functions of deviance in small groups. In addition to proposing that "groups tend to induce, sustain, and permit deviant behavior," they proposed that "deviant behavior functions in enduring groups to help maintain group equilibrium" and "groups will resist any trend toward alienation of a member whose behavior is deviant." After presenting their rationale and some empirical justifications for each of these propositions, Dentler and Erikson illustrated these propositions by reference to a field study by Dentler about isolates and deviant isolates in Quaker work projects and one by Erikson concerning deviant schizophrenics in Army basic-training squads. They concluded the discussion of their admittedly "crude theory" by suggesting a way of testing it more systematically in the laboratory.

DEVIANCE AND SOCIAL CONTROL IN SMALL GROUPS

Apparently, establishment of the general validity of Dentler and Erikson's propositions and "theory" will require the generation of a good deal of additional supportive, and more systematic, evidence. Crosbie (1975:510) has observed: "There is little evidence to suggest that group members actually recognize the benefits of deviance and almost no evidence to suggest that group members actively seek to 'induce, sustain, and permit deviant behavior.' On the contrary, most research evidence suggests that members in most groups react negatively to deviance and actively seek to control it." This effort to control deviance and to maintain patterns of normative conformity is what we mean by *social control,* and we presume the activation of this process to reflect a *desire* to preserve or reinforce existing group norms, patterns, and equilibrium. However, in considering conformity, deviance, and social control, we should keep in mind Bredemeier and Stephenson's suggestion that maintenance of existing patterns may ultimately be more dysfunctional, than functional, for a group.

Even though Dentler and Erikson focused on group tolerance toward deviant members and showed the functions deviants could perform for the group, they still assumed that the group would tolerate deviants or allow them to remain in the group only up to the point where the group perceived deviants to threaten group solidarity. Needless to say, this point is often difficult for group members to define. Dentler and Erikson proposed that a group's sense of the nature of "dangerous" or "extreme" deviance arises from a context of recurrent interaction between conforming members who respect the central group norms and deviant members who test its boundaries. An important idea following from this perspective is that the boundaries of conformity, "acceptable deviance" (if it exists), and "dangerous" or "extreme deviance" may often be redefined as interaction patterns unfold and as the group develops and changes over time.

Thus, in trying to understand the dynamic implications of deviance in groups and the conditions under which social-control efforts will arise, it is necessary to recognize that group members' conceptions of acceptable and unacceptable behavior are not fixed. They vary over time, sometimes in very subtle and unconscious ways. Hence, perceptions of conformity and deviance and efforts to control deviance can only be understood in relation to the nature and importance of the normative expectations shared by group members at any given time.

Types of Social Control in Small Groups

Crosbie (1975:510–512) has summarized a variety of mechanisms used in small groups to control deviance. Four basic types are efforts to: (a) reward conformity, (b) punish and sanction deviance; (c) persuade deviants to conform, and (d) redefine norms so that deviance can fall within the boundaries of acceptable behavior. We can gain a better and more concrete sense of the nature of these general control mechanisms and how they operate in groups by considering some specific types and examples of each.

SOCIAL REWARDS. Social rewards often can produce conformity to central group norms in relatively indirect or subtle ways. That is, group members may conform because they value the consequences of their conformity, rather than because they value conformity *per se*; sometimes they may conform without explicitly thinking about the fact they are conforming. In such cases, group members conform because they are pursuing things that are rewarding to them, such as esteem from other members, or status-deference, or leadership rights, and they realize these rewards are achieved by doing what is valued or expected by other group members (see, e.g., Dornbusch, 1955).

While the appeal of esteem, status-deference, or leadership may be sufficient to induce most group members to conform or perform valued group activities, these inducements may not be enough to produce conformity or value-achievement efforts from everyone in the group. For these others, different or greater rewards may be explicitly offered. Among these rewards could be an opportunity for a larger role in group decision-making, perhaps including a chance to become part of the group's leadership. Sometimes, as in the case of attempted co-optation of deviants or opponents by group leaders, these rewards turn out to be less substantial than they first seemed (Gamson, 1968).

Leaders of groups, which might include groups as varied as trade-union locals, university or corporate boards, college classes, and legislative or executive committees in government, may offer titles or positions of ostensible leadership to deviant or dissenting group members, without any intention of allowing them much impact on group decisions. This attempted co-optation may work as a means of social control if those who are co-opted enjoy their new status, believe it implies some impact on group decisions, *and,* most importantly, begin to feel a greater responsibility—as part of the group leadership structure—to uphold the group norms, policies, and decisions they previously challenged. Of course, co-optation efforts can backfire. Deviants or dissidents supposedly given only the illusion of authority may convert their new status into real power to disrupt or change group norms, goals, policies, or patterns. Their new status may give more legitimacy to their prior deviant behavior, or they may recognize they have been deluded and react angrily to that recognition.

PUNISHMENTS AND SANCTIONS. As we pointed out earlier, rewarding conformity, implicitly or explicitly, is just one of the general mechanisms of social control used in small groups. In fact, when we think of social control, we probably are much more likely to think of control through punishments or sanctions. Crosbie has cited a variety of examples of this type of control, and they include deliberate silence or frowns, derisive laughter, name-calling, isolation, ostracism, physical abuse (such as "binging" or worse), and ultimately, expulsion from the group or even death.[11] Punishments or sanctions as extreme as formal expulsion or the threat of severe physical coercion or death would seem most likely to occur in groups demanding the strictest conformity. For example, one could imagine formal expulsion being used in groups as diverse as sports teams, religious cults, and exclusive social clubs, and formal expulsion and extreme physical threats and abuse being used in groups such as military combat squads, street gangs, and radical political cadres.

Milder sanctions are much more familiar to us than the extreme forms just mentioned. Undoubtedly, all of us have been the target of one or more of them, since we have all, at some time, whether in our family, a class at school, one of our peer groups, or a work group, said or done something objectionable to other group members. Crosbie has cited an example very familiar to college

---

[11]Crosbie (1975:511) has cited the work of Parsons (1951); LaPiere (1954); Blau (1963); Turner (1973); and Roethlisberger and Dickson (1975), as providing illustrations of the use of these kinds of control mechanisms.

students and professors. This sanction takes the form of restless behavior among students, including shifting in seats, shuffling papers, and stacking books and notebooks, meant to inform the instructor that he or she has gone beyond the expected end of the class. Some professors ignore such behavior or fail to see it as a sanction, and soon find they are lecturing to an empty classroom.

PERSUASION, ACTIVATION OF COMMITMENT, AND RESOCIALIZA-TION. Instead of using rewards or punishment, groups may use persuasion as a social-control mechanism. *Persuasion* is an effort by group members to make deviants aware of their deviance, and to influence them to bring their actions into line with the group's normative expectations. One way persuasion may be exercised is through the "activation of commitment" (Parsons, 1963; Gamson, 1968; Schwartz, 1968). This involves reminding the deviant of an obligation to the group, to upholding its norms, or to fulfilling internalized standards learned during group socialization. A concrete illustration of activation of commitment could be a high school or college basketball player who has shouted an obscenity at a referee. His coach pulls him aside and reminds him what it means to represent his school on the basketball court, and that players on his team do not act in such an "ungentlemanly" manner. One would expect such attempts to control deviant behavior to be most effective when deviants value group membership and either want to conform but do not know or have forgotten how they should act, or know they have done the wrong thing and feel guilty enough about it to try to do what is right in the future. In the latter regard, Crosbie has suggested the creation of guilt can be an effective regulator of behavior. Based on our own experiences, it should be easy to appreciate how guilt can act in this way, especially when we have been well-socialized and care about belonging to a group, gaining the approval of its members, or demonstrating our acceptance of its basic values and normative principles.

Another mechanism of social control that may be seen as the basis for successful "activation of commitment," is *socialization, or resocialization.* Socialization involves teaching or otherwise inducing beliefs and forms of behavior conforming to a group's normative expectations. When socialization is effective and members internalize group normative standards, the need for overt forms of social control may be substantially reduced, since members will want to do what the group expects. When people join new and different groups, the socialization process may be seen as one of resocialization, which may result not only in internalization of the new group's standards and values but also in related changes in self-identity.

Resocialization may be voluntarily or even actively pursued to achieve desired changes in one's personality, feelings, or interpersonal skills or adjustment, as in the case of the various experiential groups discussed at the end of the last chapter. However, here we refer to resocialization by group members to control the behavior of new or wayward members to bring their behavior into line with group norms. Sometimes, this control-oriented resocialization can be quite dramatic and coercive, as the purported "brainwashing" of Patty Hearst by her Symbionese Liberation Army captors in the mid-1970's seems to suggest.

REDEFINTION OF NORMS. When a group does not want to, or cannot, expel a deviant member, when it wants that deviant's behavior to be conforming, and when its efforts to control the deviant by the other means suggested here are ineffective, there remains the last resort of redefining the norms. Generally, we would expect this kind of group response in cases where the deviant has high status in the group or is a leader in it (Crosbie, 1975:511). In fact, this kind of redefinition of group norms and members' roles often happens in subtle ways and as part of normal group interaction, and it is a major reason for change in groups (Coser, 1956).

A Social-Systems Approach to Social Control in Small Groups

A DYNAMIC CONCEPTION OF SOCIAL CONTROL IN SMALL GROUPS. The notion that normative structures of groups always are open to redefinition and rearrangement is a valuable insight emphasized in some of the most recent social-systems models (e.g., Buckley, 1967). This idea is related to Homans' (1950) earlier insight that social control is not a separate part of a social system such as a small group—i.e., something purposely "set up" by or imposed upon a system. Rather, as Buckley (1967:165, 166) has suggested, it is "inherent in the (dynamic) interrelations and interactions of elements that make up the system." Buckley elaborated by saying that:

> In cybernetic terms, control is at best only partly pre-programmed in the system structure in anticipation of particular disturbances or deviations; an important part is "error-regulated," in the sense that the (people in a) system (are) continually processing feedback information about (the condition of the system and the nature and amount of deviance in it). The notion of built-in mechanisms of control, on the other hand, implies a pre-programming of constraints, designed to maintain a given structure despite the possibility that later challenges may demand changes of that structure for adaptive flexibility. . . .

> To deny the existence of special mechanisms of control is not to say that we should not focus on special areas—such as the role of group pressure in promoting conformity, or of socialization in producing ordered behavior— as long as it is made clear that conformity and ordered behavior do not exhaust the significance of group pressures and socialization; that is, that the latter are, in fact, also responsible for just the opposite.

Thus, modern social-systems theorists such as Buckley propose a dynamic conception of social control, derived from Homans' earlier work, in which this process evolves from and is an integral part of the network of ongoing social relations, information flows, and exchanges of meanings that are the essence of social behavior in systems such as small groups. The work of both Homans and Buckley suggests that if groups are not successful in regulating themselves by reinforcing patterns of conformity and by controlling deviance, then we can expect to find emerging from the network of ongoing group interaction, tendencies toward structural change of the group. Buckley has said that regardless of increased reliance on explicit controls under these conditions, "we may find such phenomena as collective attempts to redefine or restructure the network of relations and meanings, diffuse manifestations of mental disturbance, deviance of both positive and negative kinds, and intergroup (and intragroup) conflict" (p. 166).

INEFFECTIVE AND EFFECTIVE SELF-REGULATION OF SMALL GROUPS. It should be clear from what has been said so far that the establishment and maintenance of patterns of normative conformity and the emergence and control of social deviance can be quite complex group processes. Each of these processes can arise from a number of different group conditions, can take different forms for different group members, and can have a variety of consequences, functional and dysfunctional, for the group as a whole. There is no guarantee that groups will regulate themselves effectively, for we know that group structures can break down with the loss of substantial group consensus and respect for ostensibly shared normative expectations. For example, there are committees, policy-making groups, juries, clubs, families, and friends whose internal disagreements and instances of deviance are so frequent and serious that despite the attempted imposition of some very strong controls, they are totally unable to conduct business, make decisions, or even interact with each other at all.

We also know there are groups, such as religious, political, or social groups, that maintain such rigid patterns of conformity that they either find their life together very stifling or they eventually find themselves out of tune with, or unable to adapt to, changes in the world around them. For example, imagine a group of parents who originally got together to fight the use of busing to bring about racial desegregation in their school district, and who vowed never to send their children to the public schools as long as buses were used. Further imagine that busing eventually became an accepted practice in this school district despite the protests of this parents' group, but the group continued its fight and continued to expect its members to uphold their vow to keep their children out of the public schools. Under these circumstances of group failure, we might expect continuing membership in the group to be a source of strain for some members who still do not like busing but are concerned about the quality of the alternative education their children are receiving or about the cost of providing that alternative education. Presumably, there are limits to the tolerance of such strain, so that eventually the only ones left to continue the struggle will be the truest of the "true believers,"[12] who thereby subject the whole group to the labels of "deviant" or "extremist" in their community.

In addition to groups that regulate themselves ineffectively or too rigidly, there are others that seem to be able to keep a steady stream of minor deviations by their members within acceptable limits. The effective operation of social control in these latter groups does not necessarily imply that control is typically exercised in an explicit manner or that there is little change in group structure. On the contrary, modern social-systems theorists have suggested that such groups often may react to minor deviations and pressures toward change in the context of normal group interaction, and that in doing so, they may be subtly and often unintentionally or unconsciously modifying group norms and behavior. Thus, redefinition of norms can be an implicit and regular aspect of group interaction, rather than merely the "last resort" type of social-control mechanism described earlier. Groups where there is a steady succession of subtle and implicit efforts to control minor acts of deviance may ultimately find themselves with a set of norms that are different from the ones that guided their behavior in the past. The new norms are likely to be more consistent with the existing desires and needs of group members and with the existing needs of the group as a whole. Such groups may be characterized by an evolving equilibrium and may be said to be in a subtle, gradual, but continual, process of structure elaboration, or *morphogenesis.*

We might expect the features just described to characterize cohesive and happy families that meet the various life-cycle crises or changes of family members by periodically modifying what is expected of each of them. We also might find continuing normative and structure elaboration in community action groups that must alter what they expect of their members each time they move from one type of issue to another or each time their community changes in an important way. When these types of groups remain happy or effective, growth and change will be expected in a predictive sense, and thus, new forms of behavior will tend to become accepted in a normative sense over time.

SUMMARY OF KEY IDEAS OF THE SOCIAL-SYSTEMS APPROACH TO SOCIAL CONTROL. Some of the key ideas from social-systems theory that have been presented here about social control in small groups have been summarized by Homans (1950:295, 301) in the following way:

1. Control is the process by which, if a man departs from his existing degree of (conformity) to a norm, his behavior is brought back toward that degree, or would be brought back if he did depart. The remaining statements hold for both actual and virtual departures.
2. There is nothing new about control, no separate element that we have not already found coming into social organization.
3. The separate controls, that is, the relations between a man's (departure from)

---

[12]Hoffer (1958) added this term to our popular language. It is used here in a general sense to refer to people who are ideological zealots, or zealots in the pursuit of a cause.

a norm and the various consequences of that (deviance), are nothing more than the old relations of mutual dependence (among the basic elements of group behavior including activities, sentiments, and interaction). . . .

4. Control as a whole is effective in so far as an individual's departure from an existing degree of (conformity) to a norm activates not one but many separate controls.

5. That is, any departure activates the system of relations so as to reduce future departures.

6. Punishment does not necessarily produce control. The state of a social system in which control is effective we shall call a state of equilibrium of the system.

The concepts of equilibrium and control we have presented here are not static ones. Rather, they imply that groups having orderly patterns of interaction and effective systems of control are ones where there may be a subtle and gradual, but persistent, pattern of change in group norms and structures. Recognizing the complexity and varied implications (and connotations) of conformity, deviance and social control in groups is essential in trying to understand the findings of small-group investigators. In the remainder of this chapter, we will consider in more detail sociologically interesting research and problems concerning conformity, deviance, and social control in small groups.

GROUP CONFORMITY AND DEVIANCE:
GENERAL ASSUMPTIONS AND FINDINGS

Crosbie (1975:480) has contended "There is no research on deviance *per se* in small groups; only research on conformity." He meant that most of the research concerning deviance in small groups has actually focused on the behavior of nonconformists in conformity experiments. As a result, we generally assume that deviance is produced by conditions opposite to those producing conformity. Thus, for example, if we can assume, as Crosbie does, that the likelihood of conformity increases when there is more group consensus, task interdependence, homogeneity of group members, and cohesiveness, then we would conclude from this perspective that the likelihood of deviance increases when there is *less* group consensus, task interdependence, homogeneity, and cohesiveness.

While in fact it may be *generally* valid to assume that the major conditions inducing deviance in small groups are the opposite of those inducing conformity, this basis for generalizing about deviance in groups may be somewhat dubious in certain cases and may reflect our dearth of direct empirical knowledge about deviance. Crosbie has pointed out that there may be different types of nonconformity, e.g., *independence* based on disagreement with the group and *anticonformity* based on a desire to hurt the group.[13] It may be necessary to ex-

---

[13]Hollander and Willis—e.g., Willis, 1965; Hollander and Willis, 1967—have been among those who have challenged the view that nonconformity could be adequately understood merely by studying conformity. They have emphasized the value of examining this kind of distinction between "independent" nonconformity and "anticonformity," along with some other related ones.

amine these different types separately to gain a fuller and more systematic sense of the reasons, motives, or conditions associated with deviant behavior. This limitation of past research should be kept in mind as we consider more specifically some basic findings about conformity and nonconformity or deviance in groups.

SOURCES OF CONFORMITY AND DEVIANCE IN SMALL GROUPS

We already have suggested that conformity and deviance seem to be affected by the amount of group consensus, task interdependence, homogeneity of group members, and cohesiveness. Crosbie has identified these factors, especially group consensus about normative standards or beliefs and task interdependence, as particularly prominent among those found to be related to conformity and, at least by inference, to deviance as well. To this set, we will add a few more sociological variables, concerning such things as group prestige, goal attainment, size, type of group pressure, and friendship of group members, that have also seemed to have a direct or indirect effect on conformity and deviance in past small group research.

Effects of Group Consensus and Related Factors

Asch's (1957) line-judgment experiments indicate the importance of the amount of group consensus in bringing about group conformity. After all, as we suggested earlier, if potentially deviant subjects in very temporary laboratory groups can be influenced by tacit group pressure to change their opinion to bring it into line with an opposing, and erroneous, majority view, we might reasonably expect group consensus to have an even stronger impact on conformity in *established* groups. Variations of Asch's basic experimental paradigm, where a naive subject faced a unanimous majority of seven or nine confederates who disagreed with him, have clarified the nature and importance of the group-consensus variable (see, e.g., Asch, 1952; 1955).

It should be recalled that in the basic Asch line-judgment situation, nearly 37 percent of the naive subjects' responses agreed with the incorrect responses of the majority.[14] In one variation of this basic situation, the naive subject was given a "partner" who gave the true estimate of the line length. This experimentally arranged partnership decreased the number of times the subject conformed to the majority view. However, if the partner changed to the majority position in the middle of the experiment, the majority's influence regained its former strength. On the other hand, if the partner began with the majority and joined the naive subject halfway through the experiment, the subject was encouraged to give his own—versus the majority's—estimate. In general, when the naive subject was buoyed by the presence of a confederate who disagreed with the major-

[14] Hare (1962:38-39) is once again helpful in providing a concise summary of Asch's research.

ity, the average rate of conformity dropped from 37 percent to less than 10 percent. An interesting aspect of this pattern is that in certain versions of the experiment, the disagreeing confederate sometimes also gave an incorrect answer—though obviously a different one than the majority response. Apparently, any kind of departure from the consensus may encourage deviance in others not committed to group norms, even if the deviants themselves disagree.

In another series of experiments, Asch examined the effect of the size of the opposition on conformity. He varied this size factor from one to fifteen persons. He found that when a naive subject was confronted by a single individual who disagreed with his answers, the subject continued to answer independently and correctly on nearly all trials. When the opposition increased to two, pressure to agree substantially increased, and the naive subject accepted the wrong answer of the majority 13.6 percent of the time. When group size increased to four, and the naive subject faced a unified opposition of three, the subject's error rate jumped even more substantially to 31.8 percent. However, further increases in the size of the majority—up to fifteen people—only increased the tendency to conform to the majority position by a relatively small percentage. Asch concluded that naive subjects tended to remain relatively independent in groups of two and three, where they faced opposition from only one and two people. But when they faced opposition from three people in a group of four, they felt the full force of the majority.

Hare (1976:32–33) has cited a considerable amount of additional experimental evidence produced by other researchers confirming the hypothesis that support from even a single other person increases the number of times a subject will hold out against a majority. It appears the support will be especially effective in encouraging such resistance if it comes from the group leader or some other high-prestige person. It also appears that it is the *relative* size of the majority or *proportion* of group members in it, rather than its absolute size or the number of members in it, which is important in producing conformity, since in a group of two the "majority" influence may be exerted by only one person.

It should be evident that the influence of the majority or group consensus will be significantly enhanced by the presence of explicit and direct forms of social control. Our prior discussion in this chapter of mechanisms of social control should have clearly indicated the types of control used in more natural and enduring groups than the ones found in the Asch situation, to reinforce the influence of group consensus. There also seem to be structural conditions of more established groups that are conducive to widespread consensus about group norms and increase the influence of this consensus on tendencies to conform without necessarily calling forth explicit, direct, or strenuous social control efforts from the context of ongoing group interaction. For example, there is research (cited by Hare, 1976:30) suggesting that the conditions promoting the appeal of group membership or group cohesiveness, such as high levels of group prestige, goal attainment, similarity of members, and friendship among them, will also increase group conformity.

Effects of Cohesiveness

Crosbie (1975:441) has cautioned that we should not interpret the finding that cohesiveness and conformity have similar antecedents as implying that cohesiveness itself affects conformity. Crosbie noted that evidence and arguments from Downing (1958), Mills (1962), Rotter (1967), and Crosbie, Stitt, and Petroni (1973) had cast doubt on other research by investigators such as Festinger, Schachter, and Back (1950), Back (1951), Festinger et al. (1952), and Gerard (1954) that apparently had shown a positive relationship between group cohesiveness and conformity. However, it should be pointed out that these critics tended to raise doubts on the basis of studies or arguments concerning temporary laboratory "groups," including ones in autokinetic or Asch line-judgment situations. Furthermore, they tended to ignore the important distinction between cohesiveness and interpersonal attraction that was discussed in the last chapter. In this context, it does not seem appropriate yet to discard or seriously question our assumption that more cohesive groups tend to have greater conformity. Of course, as Crosbie has implied, it may be, that there is more "forced"—as opposed to acquiescent or voluntary— conformity in more cohesive groups, because group consensus is more important, deviance is less tolerated, and social control is more vigorous and effective when members have stronger attachments to their group.

Effects of Friendship

Even if past research may not actually cast as much doubt on the cohesiveness-conformity relationship as Crosbie has implied, there still may be reason to wonder about the relationship between interpersonal attraction in groups and conformity. In fact, Hare (1962:37) has proposed that friendship within the group increases conformity only if that norm or standard has been set by the group itself. Presumably, friends feel a greater commitment to their *own* shared standards than to ones imposed on them by an experimenter or authority figure outside their friendship circle. Research (Festinger, Pepitone, and Newcomb, 1952) suggests that conformity to such externally imposed standards will be greater when group members are *not* well known to each other rather than when they know and like each other quite a bit. Group members are less likely to develop their own, possibly competing, norms when they are less acquainted with one another, and additionally, group members may feel more reluctant to challenge externally imposed rules and face the prospect of being held personally accountable for their actions when they are unfamiliar with others in the group than when they know each other well and feel comfortable with each other.

Western Electric researchers discovered a positive relationship between friendship and conformity in their study of the Relay Assembly Test Room (Mayo, 1933; Turner, 1933: Whitehead, 1938; Roethlisberger and Dickson, 1939). This setting was where these researchers found the Hawthorne effect, which we discussed in the second chapter, concerning the biasing effects of an experimenter's presence. In addition to this discovery, they found that friendships had an impact on the output rates of the women working in the room. Six women were placed in this room for the research, and two pairs of them had known each other before the research began. Over the two years of the experiment, other friendships developed. As the experiment progressed, similar patterns of fluctuation began to appear in the output rates of women who were friends and sat next to each other. As Hare (1976:31) has noted, these patterns occurred despite the fact the women were making telephone assemblies so fast their conformity to shared output norms seemingly could not have been the result of conscious manipulation by friends. However, when seating arrangements were changed so that friends no longer sat next to each other, high correlations between those seated next to each other disappeared for a while, then reappeared gradually as new friendships developed between those next to each other in the *new* seating arrangement.

Evidently, each pair of women at least unconsciously had created a distinct output norm that had a strong influence on the actual output of the women in it. In this case, then, the norms of the subgroups—or work pairs—had a more compelling impact on behavior in the Relay Assembly Room than output norms of the whole group or other subgroups, and adherence to these subgroup norms tended to be associated with the development of friendships within them.

The Western Electric research suggests that people working in close proximity will tend to conform highly to norms that have evolved in the subgroup formed by their developing friendship. There is also research (Deutsch and Gerard, 1955; Berkowitz, 1957; Thomas, 1957; Camilleri and Berger, 1967; Crosbie, Petroni, and Stitt, 1972) indicating that interdependent—versus independent—task performance in groups (or subgroups) will promote conformity among those working in such a manner.

Effects of Task Interdependence

Deutsch and Gerard's research is noteworthy because they tried to convert the Asch line-judgment situation into more of a group setting for some of their subjects by creating a more interdependent relationship between these subjects and the others involved in their experimental session. They created the interdependence condition by telling subjects they were involved in a competition among twenty groups for a prize of Broadway theater tickets for winning group members. The prize was supposed to be awarded to members of each of the five groups making the fewest errors on a series of Asch line-judgment tasks. Thus, in this condition, naive subjects were made to feel that their individual responses would have a crucial impact on their group's chances for the prize. Not surprisingly, subjects in this more interdependent or group-like task relationship with others—the confederates—in their session were less inclined to resist the group consensus and were more inclined to conform than subjects in the more conventional Asch-type situation.

Deutsch and Gerard's results clearly show that normative social influences are greater in groups with more interdependent task structures, even when the tasks themselves are as trivial or artificial as judging the lengths of lines in a laboratory. Among the other studies that have produced similar results, Crosbie, Petroni, and Stitt's research seems particularly noteworthy. They replicated Deutsch and Gerard's experiment with natural groups that were trying to quit smoking. Since many people have tried to stop smoking without success, it seems worthwhile to report briefly what these investigators did and found for practical as well as theoretical reasons.[15] Needless to say, though, it is recognized that a successful attempt to stop smoking is likely to involve considerably more than what is described in the summary of Crosbie and his colleagues' research.

These investigators informed participants in smoking cessation groups that they hoped to use the more successful quitters as paid research assistants in later research. They told participants in half of the groups (the interdependence condition) that these quitters would come only from the most successful groups and that each person was responsible for the other group members' chances of getting a job. They did not present this responsibility statement to the other half of the groups (the noninterdependence condition). The investigators found that smokers in the interdependent groups were much more successful in reducing and stopping their smoking consumption than were smokers in the noninterdependent groups. Obviously, then, if one wants to quit smoking, he or she should find several other people with a similar commitment and try to establish a reward structure for the group that is tied to *collective* success by group members. Of course, it is difficult to imagine how conformity to the abstinence norm would be checked in such a group, how social control would be effectively exercised, or how effective the group's influence would be once membership was terminated. Despite such practical limitations, this research still provides an interesting example, using natural groups, of further substantiation of the assumed relationship between group task interdependence and conformity.[16]

---

[15]Crosbie (1975:440) has briefly summarized the results of this research, and we are relying on his summary here.

[16]As an interesting aside here, we also might briefly consider research by Janis (1976) showing the difficulties smoking cessation groups can have in achieving their ostensible purpose. In his study of groups of heavy smokers at a clinic designed to help them stop smoking, Janis discovered a seemingly irrational tendency for members of these groups to exert pressure on each other to *increase* their smoking as the time for the final meeting approached. Janis interpreted this pattern, which reflected what he called *groupthink,* as a collusive effort to display mutual dependence and resistance to the termination of the sessions, at the expense of rational or efficient goal attainment efforts. That is, members had developed warm feelings on an interpersonal level and had become strongly attached to the group. They had also formed a high degree of consensus regarding the belief that heavy smoking was an almost incurable addiction that might only be altered by a lengthy period of cutting down. According to Janis, members of one group censured another member who had challenged this belief by asserting that he had stopped smoking since joining the group, and felt others could, too. Due to group pressure, he gave in to the group consensus, resumed

STATUS, LEADERSHIP, AND CONFORMITY: WHO ARE THE CONFORMERS AND DEVIANTS IN SMALL GROUPS?

In trying to consider sources of conformity in small groups sociologically, from a social-systems perspective, we have quite naturally placed most of our emphasis so far on the social structural or group conditions associated with different rates of conformity in the group as a whole. This perspective has led us to concentrate mostly on the direct or indirect effects of factors such as the amount of group consensus, homogeneity, cohesiveness, group prestige, goal attainment, size, the presence of social-control mechanisms, and task interdependence on group rates of conformity (or deviance). While these factors certainly deserve major attention here, a discussion of them still may not give insight into a question likely to interest students of conformity and deviance. This question is, "Who are the most (or least) conforming members of groups?" Perhaps surprisingly, we can address this kind of question in a way that shows the relationship between different aspects of group structure and the group's normative order. In particular, we can examine different levels of conformity among individual group members in a sociological manner by looking at how the status and leadership structures of groups relate to conformity.

Although we will deal more extensively with status and leadership in later chapters, these factors merit discussion here because they have an interesting and important relation to the sociological characteristics of individual conformity patterns in groups. For this discussion, *status structure* refers to the patterning of prestige or esteem relations in groups, and *leadership structure* refers to the distribution of decision-making rights and obligations in groups.[17]

Hare (1976:34–35) has offered a summary of the main group leadership and conformity findings. While we might reasonably infer that leaders and other high-status group members tend to conform at least as much as other group members, we should qualify this inference somewhat to provide a fuller and more systematic sense of the way status and leadership are related to conformity.

Conformity and Emerging and Established Patterns of Status and Leadership

A helpful tool in thinking about the relationship between conformity and status-leadership is Figure 6. Crosbie (1975:481) has suggested two major patterns through this figure. First, a linear and positive relationship exists between status-leadership and conformity in groups where the status and leadership structures

---

smoking, and no longer caused a problem for other members. Apparently, in such groups, members were more concerned with how they got along with each other than with whether they could accomplish the purpose for which the group was established.

[17]These definitions have been suggested by Crosbie (1975), and convey the essential sociological meaning we want to convey through these terms.

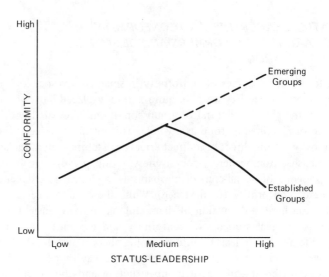

FIGURE 6. Relationships between Conformity and Status-Leadership in Emerging and Established Groups (Crosbie, 1975:481)

are emerging. Second, a curvilinear one exists in groups where these structures are more established. In more established groups, conformity is seen as *highest* for group members in the *middle* of the status and leadership hierarchies and *lower* for members with *low and high* positions in these hierarchies. Figure 6 clearly shows that the difference between the status-leadership and conformity relationships in groups with emerging and established status-leadership structures is a result of a diminished level of conformity among members with higher status and leadership positions. To illustrate this shift in conformity, Crosbie cited an experiment done by Merei (1958).

Leadership, High Status, and Conformity

Merei studied leadership and conformity among nursery school children. In the beginning of his research, he separated the children who were relatively docile and ineffectual in the open playroom from those who were much more assertive and influential (the *natural* leaders). Then, he divided the nonleaders into smaller groups and allowed each of these newly formed groups to play alone with its new set of toys until it formed its own norms and group structures. After group structures had stabilized in these groups, the experimenter introduced a *natural* leader into each one and observed the resulting interaction. The observer found that the new group members first tried to control group activities, but usually with little success. After this initial failure, they tended to conform to group norms, and several of the *natural* leaders gave up their prior aspirations to leadership and became regular group members. However, other natural leaders con-

138

formed for only a limited time, until they were able to climb the leadership hierarchy in their group. After securing a position of leadership, these children reverted back to their initial tendencies to control their groups. This time, though, they were successful, which reflected the leadership position they had earned. In fact, they were able to bring about changes in group behavior. Merei (1958:529) summarized this pattern of change in conformity for the natural leaders in the following way:

> He tries to do away with the group's tradition and lead it on to new ones. He is rejected. He accepts the traditions and quickly learns them. Within the frame of these traditions he soon assumes leadership, and, though reluctantly, the group follows him because he does a good job. He introduces insignificant variations, loosening the tradition. He then introduces new elements into the ritual already weakened by variation.

Small-group investigators have not always recognized the tendency for high-status leaders to conform less to certain norms than other group members in the middle of the status and leadership hierarchies of a group. In fact, Homans (1974:331) acknowledged that he had been mistaken in *The Human Group* in proposing that a group member of high status tended to conform to a high degree to all the norms of his group. At that time, he was thinking of a man in the Bank Wiring Room at the Western Electric plant who was held in high esteem by his co-workers and conformed more closely than any other group member to the *highly valued* output norms of his industrial group.

Leadership, High Status, Personal Freedom, and Idiosyncrasy Credit

In rethinking his original proposition, Homans decided high-status members, especially leaders, conformed closely to *highly valued* group norms, which they may have been most instrumental in creating and establishing in their group, and that high-status members were allowed more freedom to depart from *less important* norms. Homans further assumed that on certain occasions, when groups faced problems, leaders were *expected* to do something *different* from the usual. This special kind of nonconformity or independent behavior is called *innovation* and is what enables some group members to earn and maintain higher status and more authority than most other group members.

If leaders and other high-status group members earn their positions by helping the group resolve problems and, in general, by doing what the group values most highly more often than other group members, it should not be too difficult to understand why they are granted more freedom to act as they wish in matters of lesser importance. By performing the valued activities and behavior from which they derive high status, these people are building what Hollander (1958) has called *idiosyncrasy credit.* This credit is a kind of indebtedness from others that allows a person freedom to act differently from others—whether or not it is in an innovative manner—without losing status in the group. Obviously, though, as leaders use up their credit, less noninnovative deviance will be tolerated by other group members without the threat of sanctions or loss of rank and authority. When leaders or other high-status group members recognize this threat, their rate of conformity tends to increase (Hollander and Julian, 1970). From a social-systems perspective, this reaction of increased conformity by high-status people can be seen to reflect the amount of equilibrium characterizing groups where it occurs.

Medium- and Low-Status Conformity Patterns

Since medium-status group members do less of what is valued in their group, they are not only accorded less esteem and trust, from which status-rank and leadership derive, than high-status members and leaders, but they also earn less idiosyncrasy credit. With less credit, they are less free to deviate. Thus, if medium-status group members wish to attain higher status or even maintain their current rank in the status hierarchy, they must conform at a relatively uniform, moderately high rate.

At the bottom of the status hierarchy of groups are members who deviate more than others of higher status from both central and lesser norms. In some cases, these low-status members would like to conform more, but they lack the ability or opportunity to do so. Despite their low status, these people may still feel part of the group and try to conform as much as possible either because they are satisfied with their group membership or with the rewards they receive by being a group member, or because they perceive the possibility of greater rewards through future mobility. These people pose little or no challenge to group stability or order, since they remain susceptible to the same kinds of constraints or controls affecting members with higher status. Posing a more serious problem for the group are the possibly more numerous low-status members who, as a result of lack of ability or desire or both, deviate fairly often from group norms and eventually become motivationally withdrawn from the group. Crosbie (1975:484) has suggested that the behavior of this latter type of low-status nonconformer rather than that of involved types accounts for the overall high rate of deviance among low-status members.

The circumstances under which low-status nonconformers become isolated from the rest of the group are often quite interesting, and Homans (1974:326-327) has cited a field study by Blau (1955) concerning an interesting case of this sort. Blau studied sixteen agents in a federal law-enforcement agency, paying special attention to one agent who made himself unpopular by violating norms considered very important by other group members. This agent reported to the supervisor of the department that he had been offered a bribe by the management of one of the firms he investigated, and that he had reacted adversely to

the offer and had adopted a threatening posture in general toward the management of such firms.

By reporting the bribe, this agent had created the appearance of trying to
curry favor with the supervisor, which was an act not highly regarded by his
fellow agents. However, he had also violated some other basic expectations of his
group by his behavior. Reporting the bribe earned the disapprobation of fellow
agents for the additional reasons that it was thought unfair to reveal bribes when
the firms faced such a strong temptation to offer them, and that in reporting a
bribe attempt, an agent lost an unofficial hold over the firm that existed as long
as he did not report it. Along with the ill feeling created by this action, this
agent earned disapproval from co-workers because they felt he talked too much,
completed too much work (recall the Bank Wiring Room), and was not very
cooperative when they sought his help with technical problems.

For the various reasons mentioned, this agent not only received little
esteem from the other agents in his department, but in effect was ostracized
from the group as well, since the other agents interacted with him only when
necessary. However, as Homans has noted, this ostracism had an interesting
impact on future social-control efforts. It *removed* him from the influence of
such efforts. In Homans' (1974:327) own words:

> . . . if he holds out against that pressure there is nothing more the group
> can do to bring him back into line, short of physical violence. The group
> has lost its leverage on his behavior. The next time he has a choice whether
> or not to do something they wish him to do, he is the less apt to do it, the
> less there remains for them to take away from him in the way of esteem
> and interaction. He has nothing to lose by not conforming and perhaps
> even something to gain by it if it vexes them: "He does it only to annoy,
> because he knows it teases."

Blau (1955:155) said of this agent:

> To be sure, his deviant behavior contributed to his continued isolation, but
> this position also encouraged lack of conformity. . . . His overproductivity
> had made him an isolate and, once in this position, he became the only
> member of the agency who ignored a very important *unofficial* (under-
> scoring added) norm. The individual who had adapted himself to an
> isolated position could more readily violate the norm of the group.

Who Are the Conformers and Deviants?
Some Summary Comments

We hope the discussion in this section has provided a clear conception of how a
sociologist might answer the question: "Who are the conformers (and deviants)
in small groups?" In general, evidence from past research indicates: (1) low-status
group members have uniformly low conformity rates, although such people

may differ in their attachments to the group; (2) medium-status members tend to have uniformly high conformity rates; and (3) high-status members, especially leaders, tend to conform a great deal when establishing their position and then begin to deviate from norms of lesser importance afterward.[18]

CONSEQUENCES OF CONFORMITY AND DEVIANCE IN SMALL GROUPS

Conformity, Order, and Change

We have tried to suggest that conformity rates in small groups are tied, among other things, to particular types and levels of status in the group. Clearly, then, we are not inclined to accept an overly simplistic structural functional view of group conformity that implies that conformity is inevitable in ongoing groups, that it occurs because members recognize its importance for maintaining order or basic patterns of interaction, or that it occurs because it is a *functional imperative* of group survival.[19]

Surely, some degree of conformity by group members *is* necessary for maintaining order and a viable group. However, we know conformity rates vary over time for groups and their individual members. We also know that groups manage to survive and adapt to changing internal or external circumstances by changing certain aspects of their normative structure. This process of change, which involves re-establishing a group's equilibrium, sometimes may be a relatively chaotic one characterized by deviant actions by group members that first threaten and ultimately help transform the old normative order and equilibrium. As illustrations of this process of structure elaboration, you might recall the examples cited earlier of stable, happy families and successful and enduring community action groups.

In both types of groups, there is likely to be a continuing process of normative redefinition as group members grow and change or as the group changes in its relationship to its environment. The changes in behavior and expectations may not be easily or willingly accepted at first, but the expectation that changes will periodically occur is a key ingredient in the persistence of these groups as happy or successful ones. Of course, conformity to highly valued group norms will accompany the process of normative redefinition, but this conformity sometimes may be to norms that are quite different from ones previously accepted by the group. Thus, while a steady flow of minor deviance, normative redefinition, and change may cause temporary strain or disruption even for the types of

---

[18] A variety of experimental and field studies, in addition to the ones cited here, have been cited by Homans (1974:Ch. 14), Crosbie (1975:481–484), and Hare (1976:34–35) in support of these kinds of assumptions about status-leadership and conformity.

[19] A number of sociologists, including Buckley (1967:23–36), have criticized theorists like Parsons for making assumptions of this type about social systems.

groups just described, the ultimate impact of these processes on the members and their group can be quite beneficial. We should also be reminded that groups maintaining conformity to outmoded or otherwise inappropriate norms can do more to damage, than help, their members and the group as a whole. Conformity and deviance can have potentially functional *or* dysfunctional consequences.

Reactions to Deviance

Since deviance could prompt an ultimately beneficial reassessment of group norms, one might be tempted to conclude group members would occasionally welcome, or perhaps even encourage, instances of functional deviance of this sort. However, there is little evidence to suggest group members tend to recognize the benefits of deviance—other than the special innovative kind—or react positively to deviance, even when it can or does have functional consequences. Instead, research indicates that group members react positively to conformity and try to sanction or control most forms of deviance from most group members.

Although deviant actions by high-status members seem to be tolerated when they concern minor matters or are construed as "innovative," even high-status members are not exempt from sanctions. Their deviance seems to be least tolerated when it violates central group norms or when they have used up their *idiosyncrasy credit*. In fact, research by Wahrman (1970) has indicated that group members may have higher expectations of conformity for members with high status, become more annoyed with deviant actions by them, and deprive them of more friendship and esteem than they would lower-status members for comparable deviant actions.

Wahrman has cautioned that the assumption that high status produces high general expectations of conformity may be too broad. Wahrman's discussion suggests there are a variety of bases for according people high status in a group. These include status characteristics such as race, social class, occupation, and sex that people bring with them from outside the group as well as value-achievement within the group. Thus, one should probably assume the strength of members' conformity expectations for high-status members will vary according to the basis of their high status. If this is true, then it would seem reasonable to conclude from our discussion in this chapter that group members will be most upset with perceived violations of *central* group norms by high-status members who have gained their high status by their performance in the group, but who have used up all or most of their idiosyncrasy credit. This would seem to apply especially to group leaders who have earned their position rather than been appointed to it.

We should not infer from Wahrman's findings that violations of group norms, even central ones, by high-status members will automatically prompt efforts by other group members to sanction them or bring them back into line. In fact, not only do high-status members have more latitude in their behavior than others in the group, by virtue of the importance of their contributions to the group and the idiosyncrasy credit earned in making these contributions, they also have more power to define what is acceptable behavior. Thus, although high-status members may face the greatest disappointment or even loss of respect for their *perceived* violations of *important* group norms, they, especially leaders, are also most likely to escape deviant labels. Furthermore, in times of crisis, leaders often are expected *not* to do what is generally expected of everyone else in the group, but rather to innovate or "deviate" in ways enabling the group to meet the crisis and adapt better to future ones. Of course, such *deviance* is itself a kind of normative expectation tied to leadership, and leaders can anticipate loss of esteem and rank if they cannot fulfill this norm.

We can see, then, that the relationship of high-status deviance to social control and stability or change of the normative order and equilibrium of groups is a relatively complex one requiring some important qualifications to be precisely understood. Indeed, further refinement of our understanding of the relationship of status to social control will be made in the discussion of research in the next section. It should also be recognized that there are certain group structural conditions that are especially conducive to the perception and attempted control of high-status—*and* medium- and low-status—deviance. Research has suggested that in groups where there are conditions like high group consensus and cohesiveness, members are most likely to have stronger general conformity expectations *for everyone* in the group, take a narrower view of permissible behavior, and be less tolerant of deviance. These are the types of findings produced by Schachter (1951) in his classic experimental study of deviation, rejection, and communication, which we cited in the last chapter in the section concerning cohesiveness assumptions and findings. Because this study is a classic and provides much insight about the importance of factors like cohesiveness in affecting how group members respond to deviance as a perceived social problem, we will give it additional attention in the next section, which focuses on studies concerning deviance as a problem of social control in small groups.

DEVIANCE AS A PROBLEM OF SOCIAL CONTROL: A SELECTIVE FOCUS ON RESEARCH

Roethlisberger and Dickson's (1939) study of *binging* and other reactions to deviance in the Bank Wiring Room and Blau's (1955) study of reactions to deviance in a law enforcement agency are excellent examples of the sort of research we will be examining in this section. We will give special attention here to two other studies that allow us to consider more fully the conditions in groups promoting efforts to control deviance, the nature of these efforts themselves, and their implications for group interaction and equilibrium. In addition to Schachter's study, we will focus on research by Gerson (1967) about social rank and punishment of deviants in a college fraternity.[20] Not only are these two studies elucidating and interesting, they also suggest some useful lessons about the treatment of deviance as a perceived problem of social control in small groups. These are lessons we can add to what we have learned from looking at the Bank Wiring Room research and Blau's study of a law enforcement agency.

Parenthetically, we should mention that the focus here on deviance as a perceived problem of social control is not meant to imply that the effects of deviance are always disruptive or dysfunctional in groups. We have already tried to dispel that notion. However, since group members so often view deviance in this manner and react to it as something to be controlled, this kind of focus seemed appropriate for this section. Furthermore, it seemed a convenient way of injecting the social problem theme we have wanted to carry throughout this book into a consideration of research concerning conformity, deviance, and social control.

DEVIANCE, REJECTION, AND COMMUNICATION

Schachter's specific concern was to consider the rejection of a deviate by the group. He guessed that not all groups reject to the same degree and that rejection followed deviance only on certain kinds of issues. Thus, in an effort to gain a more precise understanding of the conditions affecting rejection, he examined the effect of degrees of group cohesiveness and of relevance of an issue to the group's purposes on the degree of rejection of a deviate. He also looked at the effects of these variables on communication and induction within groups.

Schachter's experiment was conducted as the first meeting of a club. He created four types, each one representing a different degree and combination of cohesiveness and relevance. Each club had members who were paid by the experimenter to deviate from and conform to an experimentally created group standard. There was systematic observation of the discussion in each club, and at the end of each meeting members were nominated for committees, and sociometric questionnaires were filled out. The nominations and questionnaire items were the measures of rejection.

The subjects were male college students who volunteered to participate in a continuing club. The four types of clubs formed included one that would discuss movies, one that would discuss psychiatric case studies, and two others that would discuss radio programs and newspaper editorials, respectively. There was a total of 32 clubs, eight of each type; each had from five to seven members and three paid participants who were seen as fellow club members.

[20]The article by Schachter has been abstracted or discussed in many books and articles, including Hare (1962:57–58), Shepherd (1964:75–76), and Darley and Darley (1973:12–13), and reprinted in several others, including Crosbie (1975:518–545). We will draw from these sources and Crosbie's editorial comments in reviewing this study. For Gerson's article, we also will draw from editorial comments by Crosbie, as well as from the original source.

Cohesiveness was manipulated by asking students to indicate their extent of interest in particular clubs and by subsequently placing them in a club in which they had expressed either a high or low interest. The case-study and movie clubs were characterized by high cohesiveness because they consisted of students who had indicated they were "moderately" or "extremely interested" in joining them. The radio and editorial clubs had low cohesiveness because they consisted of students who had expressed a high interest in joining the case-study or movie clubs, and little or no interest in joining the radio or editorial clubs. A subject did not know which club he had come to until the meeting was under way.

Relevance was interpreted by Schachter to refer to "an ordering of group activities along a dimension of 'importance' to the group." He created two degrees of relevance in his experiment. In one condition, subjects were given an activity corresponding to the purpose of the club. This was a condition of relevance. The condition of irrelevance was one where subjects were given an activity having nothing to do with the purpose of the club. Case-study and editorial clubs discussed a case study and a feature article, respectively, and thus, did something relevant to their respective purposes. Movie and radio clubs discussed issues irrelevant to the purpose of the clubs; each began with an appropriate subject but was diverted to an irrelevant issue.

As a result of the experimental manipulations, each type of club represented a different experimental condition. The four conditions created were:

1. high cohesiveness—relevant issue: Case-Study Club,
2. low cohesiveness—relevant issue: Editorial Club,
3. high cohesiveness—irrelevant issue: Movie Club,
4. low cohesiveness—irrelevant issue: Radio Club.

In each meeting, in each condition, the three paid confederates, who also were male undergraduates, played three roles, deviate, mode, and slider. The *deviate* was instructed to disagree with the group throughout the discussion; the *mode* was instructed to agree with the dominant or modal group opinion throughout the discussion; and the *slider* was instructed to begin by disagreeing with the group and then gradually to shift his opinion to agree with the group. Each group was given a story about a juvenile delinquent and asked whether the delinquent should be treated with love and understanding or with punishment. All the groups leaned more in the direction of love and understanding, and the slider initially and the deviate throughout took the opposite position of strong punishment.

The experimenter established the mode and slider roles as controls that were meant to provide evidence of the effect of deviation in contrast to conformity. Comparison of the slider and deviate was thought to provide a test of whether rejection was a result of having temporarily represented a deviant position or of resolutely maintaining a deviant position against all attempted influence.

As suggested earlier, Schachter had two ways of measuring acceptance or rejection of the confederates in each club. He looked at the importance or un-importance of the committees to which these people were nominated by other club members, and he also looked at sociometric ratings of them. On the socio-metric questionnaire, each subject rated other club members in terms of how much he would want them to remain in the group if the group size had to be reduced or the group had to be disassembled. Thus, while nominations indicated the subjects' confidence in the ability of other club members, sociometric ratings provided more of an indication of the perceived congeniality of others in the group.

On the basis of his ingenious experimental design, which he justifiably felt represented a real-life situation for his subjects despite the experimental manipu-lations and controls, Schachter was able to generate data supporting a number of generalizations about reactions to deviants in small groups. These generalizations were presented by him in the form of the following predictions about deviation, rejection, and communication (Schachter, 1951):

1. Persons in the mode and slider roles will be rejected less (if at all) than will persons in the deviate role.
2. With cohesiveness held constant, rejection will be greater in relevant groups than in irrelevant groups.
3. With relevance held constant, rejection will be greater in high cohesive than in low cohesive groups.
4. In the high cohesiveness relevant condition, the amount of communica-tion addressed to the deviate by nonrejectors should increase continuously throughout the meeting. Strong rejectors should reach a peak of communica-tion during the meeting and then decline continuously, and mild rejectors should reach a peak somewhat later and then decline.
5. In all other experimental conditions, communications to the deviate from strong, mild, or non-rejectors should increase continuously throughout the meeting.
6. In all experimental conditions, there should be relatively few communica-tions addressed to persons in the modal role and no increase in communica-tions during the meeting.
7. In all conditions, communications to the slider should decrease during the meeting as the slider shifts from a deviate to a modal position.

In general, then, regardless of cohesiveness or relevance, in all groups the deviate was more likely to be rejected than people who agreed with the group position. However, in groups where cohesiveness was higher and the relevance of the discussion greater, members were more likely to require agreement from others in the group and to reject a member who disagreed. In these groups, there was a marked tendency for members at first to try actively to convert the devi-ate and then to reject him after failing in their conversion efforts. It should be recalled that rejection in these groups meant being nominated for a dull and unimportant committee and being chosen as the person to be dropped from the group, as well as receiving less, and less positive, communications from other group members.

Hare (1976:52) has proposed that evidence from a number of different cultures (e.g., Schachter *et al.,* 1954; Israel, 1956) has indicated that rejection of the deviant is apparently an almost universal phenomenon.[21] According to the research by Schachter (1951) we have just described, people who are able to conform to group norms but do not are likely to face mounting pressure to conform from other group members. In groups that are highly integrated, cohesive, and committed to what they are doing, deviants who continue to resist this pressure can anticipate not only increasing unpopularity and rejection, but also eventually, attempts to isolate or ostracize them.

Especially in groups where there are high degrees of interdependence and uniformity, deviance is likely to be difficult to express and maintain because even the slightest indication of it will be easily recognized and quickly lead to efforts to control it. Asch's research cited earlier suggests that deviants are more likely to be successful in holding out against group pressure if their position is shared by one or more other group members. But, of course, substantial uniformity or consensus implies that there will be few others sympathetic with their deviant position, and the strong conformity pressures generated by this uniformity and by high cohesiveness, commitment, and importance or relevance of the group task, will make those sympathetic to them reluctant to express their sympathy openly. In a sense, then, the uniformity or consensus in these groups is self-perpetuating because it creates strong conformity pressures and nurtures very little tolerance of deviance.

There has been a study done in England (DeMonchaux and Shimmin, 1955) that suggests that deviants who persist quietly and unaggressively in their position may face less rejection because their determined and dignified example encourages others who have misgivings about group norms or policies to express them. Nevertheless, this study does not alter our *general* assumptions that deviants will face rejection and that the amount of conformity pressure and rejection will be greatest in groups with the highest levels of cohesiveness, relevance, and commitment. Apparently, then, groups can be *too* consensual, cohesive, or committed to their tasks or purposes to be tolerant, see the merit in opposing positions, *or* be receptive to *constructive* or *necessary* changes. It is a lonely role to be the voice of dissent or change in such groups. In the face of increasing group pressure and threats of rejection, one wonders how long such defiance will continue *or be allowed.*

Research indicates that group members will give their support to a deviant who eventually conforms (Doise and Moscovici, 1969-1970; Levine, Saxe, and Harris, 1973), rather than leaves the group (Singer, Radloff, and Wark, 1963).

---

[21] Schachter's experimental results have also been replicated by Emerson (1954), in a study of American high school students.

However, imagine the plight of the deviant or dissenter in highly cohesive and consensual groups demanding substantial loyalty from their members—including groups as diverse as college fraternities or sororities, radical political cadres, military combat units, adolescent street gangs, and inner circles of Presidential advisers. One would anticipate that the escalation of conformity or control pressures will eventually lead to psychological or physical removal of the deviant from the group. If so, the main consequence of deviance in such groups is likely to be reinforcement of the normative order and equilibrium the deviant was challenging or threatening.

Certainly there is little evidence from Schachter or from accounts about groups like those just mentioned that show that highly cohesive and *relevant* groups welcome pressures toward change or respond positively to deviants who might create such pressures. For example, we have seen many cases of Presidential advisers or appointees who have been relieved of their duties and jobs not long after voicing their opposition to Presidential policies. Such demotions or firings have frequently occurred *despite* the acknowledged competence of the government official or the public popularity or rationality of the opposition. Instead, they have often occurred merely because the official's action represented disloyalty or dissent. It would seem that deviants or dissenters will be received most favorably—or least unfavorably—and have their greatest impact in groups where members are not, and are not expected to be, "true believers" in the cause or purposes of the group, where they disagree somewhat about group values, norms, goals, or policies, and where their attraction to the group is muted somewhat by the appeal of other, possibly conflicting, groups to which they belong or want to belong.

PUNISHMENT AND POSITION: THE SANCTIONING OF DEVIANTS IN SMALL GROUPS

It has been suggested that college fraternities might be included among groups having little tolerance for deviance from their members. In fact, though, Gerson's (1967) study of reactions to deviance in a fraternity indicates that the amount of tolerance and severity of response will be affected by the rank of a member's position in the group. This study is especially interesting because it was an experiment done in a natural setting and because its results provide further refinement of our conception of the relationship between status and social control in groups.

Earlier, we cited Wahrman's findings that group members have stronger conformity expectations for members with high status, become more annoyed with the deviant actions of such people, and deprive them of more friendship and esteem than they do lower-status members for comparable deviant actions. We also cited Wahrman's own warning about overgeneralizing from his findings. His research implied the need to clarify the circumstances under which high-status deviants might escape serious sanctions that would be applied to lower-status group members for similar deviant actions. In particular, he suggested that we need to know more about the conditions under which group members supplement their possible disappointment, annoyance, or withdrawal of liking or esteem with more overt and severe sanctions for deviance by high-status members. Gerson's research may help provide some of the desired clarification.

Gerson's data were derived from a natural experiment using the 25 members of a college fraternity pledge class as subjects. These subjects were all college freshmen who had been together as members of the pledge class for a period of four months, since their first week in college. During their pledge training, these students had been exposed to an intensive effort by fraternity members to integrate them into the fraternity. This socialization process attempted to create primary relations among pledge class members, initiate primary relationships between members of the pledge class and full-fledged or "active" members of the fraternity, and induce pledges to internalize the norms of the fraternity. At the time of the experiment, this socialization essentially had been completed, and the pledges were full-fledged fraternity members, except for their rite of passage, "help week," and the subsequent formal initiation. Because the pledges had not formally been inducted into the fraternity, they were not allowed by the rules of the national organization to attend meetings of the active body. Thus, they conducted their own meetings, and this fact was an important one in designing the experiment.

At their final meeting, the pledge class was divided randomly into four groups by their pledge chairman. Each group was fairly homogeneous because the pledge class as a whole was fairly homogeneous, due to fraternity selection and pledge training procedures. Each group was then led to a separate room and was informed by an officer of the fraternity that one of the members of the sophomore class had violated a fraternity norm,[22] admitted his guilt, and would have to be punished. They were to discuss the case and individual members of each group were to recommend a just punishment. The identity of the deviant varied for each group so that each was dealing with a person with different social rank in the fraternity. The four groups were given the following four types of members to consider:

Group I: Highest social position; an officer of the fraternity who was very well liked by the membership. He was rated high as an instrumental and socio-emotional leader.

Group II: High social position; best-liked member of the sophomore class; a socio-emotional leader.

Group III: This group did not receive the name of the deviant. They were told "a member of the sophomore class," and were used as a control group or basis of comparison.

[22] The deviant was supposed to have duplicated and sold copies of the fraternity exam files, which was a relatively serious offense within the fraternity.

Group IV: Low social position; not very well liked by the fraternity members.

A panel of fraternity officers was used to help determine the names to be used in creating the different experimental conditions.

The ordinal arrangement of punishments from least to most severe was from formal apology to can never hold office, one-month suspension from active fraternity membership, one-semester suspension, one-year suspension, no eating or sleeping in the fraternity house, and finally, expulsion from the fraternity. All six members of the first experimental group, which considered the deviant member with highest status, recommended the least severe punishment, a formal apology. For the second group, which considered the member second highest in status, one person recommended that the deviant never hold office, three recommended a one-month suspension, and two recommended a one-semester suspension. Five of the six members of the control group recommended the middle punishment, a one-semester punishment, and the other member recommended a one-year suspension. For the fourth group, which considered the deviant with lowest status, one person recommended suspension without specifying a length of time, four recommended no eating or sleeping in the house, and one recommended the most severe punishment, expulsion from the fraternity.[23]

These results clearly show that the severity of recommended punishment varied *inversely* with the deviants' rank in the group. The most lenient punishment was recommended for the highest-status deviant, and recommendations became more severe as the deviant's status decreased. Reactions to the two high-status deviants were generally less severe than the typical response to the control figure; and reaction to the deviant with low status was more severe.

Since Wahrman's results suggest reactions to deviance become stronger as the deviant's status *increases,* Gerson's results seem to pose a contradiction. However, we may be able to explain this apparent contradiction by focusing on the types of groups studied by Wahrman and Gerson and on the circumstances of deviance and social control in each. In doing so, we may provide additional insight into the conditions affecting the relationship between status-rank and social control.

Crosbie (1975:515) has proposed that an inverse relation holds between rank in a group and social control for *low-level,* or *less important,* cases of deviance. However, he also has suggested there is some evidence indicating that when deviance relates to central group values or seriously interferes with group value-achievement, the relation between status-rank and control becomes a direct one. Thus, from Crosbie's perspective, the seriousness of the offense or the extent it threatens group value-achievement or equilibrium, helps explain the contrasting results produced by Gerson and Wahrman. Crosbie cited Sherif

---

[23]Group IV originally had seven members, but one did not respond.

and Sherif's (1967:60) observations of deviance in delinquent gangs to clarify the conditions of these different kinds of relationships between rank and social control:

> The normative regulation of behavior does not apply equally to every member in every sphere of activity. If a norm pertains to a very minor activity, or concerns in-group relations exclusively, the leader and others of high status may violate it with impunity, whereas lower status members may be called to account for similar actions. On the other hand, norms pertaining to important "secrets" to be kept from other groups or adults, or to the very maintenance of the group, require that higher status members conform very closely.

While Crosbie's explanation may offer a satisfactory resolution of the apparent contradiction between Wahrman's and Gerson's results, it does not fully address the implications of these two sets of findings, and in particular, Gerson's findings. For example, Gerson's evidence may not really be inconsistent with the assumption implied by data from Wahrman and others (e.g., Alvarez, 1968) that serious acts of deviance by high-status group members will cause more disappointment, annoyance, and loss of esteem than similar acts by lower-status members, of whom less is expected and who have less esteem to give up. In fact, Gerson's research did not directly focus on such reactions, but instead dealt with more explicit, overt, and harsh forms of punishment for deviance. His results showed that despite the greater loss of trust, popularity, and respect higher-status group members *may* have suffered for committing a relatively serious offense within the fraternity (i.e., duplicating and selling copies of the fraternity files) they still tended to receive less severe overt sanctions for their deviance. We might interpret the combination of these results with the ones from Wahrman as implying that despite *sentiments* to the contrary, group members will be more reluctant to impose more overt and harsh sanctions on deviants with higher status in the group, even in cases where the deviance is relatively serious.

Gerson's study seems to give a better indication than Wahrman's of how group members *actually carry out* their feelings or sentiments toward deviants. This distinction is due to the fact that natural groups were used in Gerson's research, while more artificial and temporary laboratory groups were used in Wahrman's. The pledge groups consisted of members who had known and interacted closely with each other for four months, and they were given an experimental task having substantial relevance to them and their life together in the fraternity. In contrast, Wahrman's "groups" were created in the laboratory, and they consisted of members who were isolated from each other in separate booths, communicated about a relatively abstract task through notes collected, delivered, and manipulated by the experimenter, and hence, did not have to live with, or even meet, the people about whom they expressed disappointment, annoyance, or lack of friendliness or esteem. In view of this contrast, it seems reasonable to conclude that the conditions of social control were more realistic for Gerson's than for Wahrman's subjects, and in reality, higher-status group members seem more difficult to sanction.

Higher-status group members may be more difficult to sanction because they have made superior contributions to the group, have made others in the group indebted to them as a result of those contributions, and have more power in the group than other members. In short, higher-status members are more valuable to the group and have more to say about what goes on in it than other members. As Gerson has noted, "members of a group cannot . . . punish a valuable member as strongly as they could a less valuable one for fear of losing his services to the group."

From a social-systems perspective, we can argue that regardless of the seriousness of the offense, punishment is more likely to be meted out in the manner indicated by Gerson's than Wahrman's results when the contributions of high-status members are perceived to be more valuable and their loss is perceived to have a more damaging effect on group value achievement and equilibrium. Obviously, though, unless high-status members restore themselves to the good graces of other group members by increased conformity and group value-achievement, they can expect to lose their high status and the protection from harsh sanctions it provides. Indeed, by deviating from important group norms, they have already begun their decline in status.

Despite their reluctance to punish harshly high-status members, especially leaders, group members also realize, as Gerson has pointed out, "that any other leadership ambitions of the norm violator have been aborted by his deviance and (they consider) this in levying the punishment. They realize that his social position has decreased because of his deviation from the norms." One of Wahrman's subjects stated this idea rather succinctly in recommending his punishment when he said: "His honor and his bid for an office have been finished and this should complete his punishment." This was purported to be the kind of thinking that prompted then-President Gerald Ford to pardon his predecessor, Richard Nixon, but not the other figures in the Watergate case.

In general, then, it appears that while consistently high levels of conformity to central group norms establish and maintain high rank in a group, continued deviance lowers a person's rank and value and thereby increases the probability of more overt and severe sanctions. Furthermore, on the basis of the research discussed in this section, we can imagine the conditions under which high-status deviants will face the greatest risk of turning adverse sentiments of other group members into punitive actions. These conditions would seem to include: (1) violation of the most central group norms; (2) serious obstruction of group value-achievement; (3) a bankrupt account of idiosyncrasy credit caused by a recent history of deviant actions, declining status, and diminishing importance to the group; and (4) a group that is highly cohesive, interdependent, committed, and in substantial agreement about its norms.

SUMMARY

The main intent of this chapter has been to strip away the moral or value connotations we often impute to conformity, deviance, and social control, and to treat these processes sociologically in terms of their nature, sources, and consequences in small groups. It should be evident by now that small groups, at least under certain conditions, can exercise a substantial amount of influence or control over the beliefs and actions of their members. In fact, in the first chapter we suggested the considerable influence primary groups exercise over their members by socializing them. Socialization is perhaps the most effective means of social control because it operates subtly to induce group members to want to do what the group as a whole expects them to do.

The first step in our treatment of conformity, deviance, and social control in this chapter was to clarify the meaning of each of these ideas in relation to the normative structure of the group. We characterized group norms as shared group expectations that are standardized generalizations applied to classes of objects, having a moral or evaluative basis, and that prescribe a range of acceptable behavior or proscribe a range of unacceptable behavior, under given circumstances. As social rules or guidelines, group norms can help group members orient themselves to one another in an orderly and meaningful way. According to Parsons, norms serve as effective guidelines for group interaction when they help group members resolve basic interpersonal issues regarding how they should express their feelings, how much they should become involved with others in the group, how much emphasis should be given to unique personal ties, and how much relative importance should be attributed to qualities of the person or the nature of his or her performance. Groups may be compared in terms of their respective normative responses to these basic issues, and we may gain some understanding of problems occurring within groups by focusing on these different normative orientations.

For groups in larger organizations, we often find discrepancies between their informal norms and the official rules of the organization. In cases where organizational officials discover deviance from the organization's rules and try to exercise some form of social control over offending group members, the outcome could be turmoil both within the group and for the organization. The study of the Bank Wiring Room provides an excellent illustration of how informal and formal norms can conflict, how much influence is exerted by the informal norms of the group over its members, and what happens to group members when they disregard or violate these informal norms.

We distinguished three types of "acquiescent conformity:" informational conformity, normative conformity, and obedience. Because it implies more social pressure and a more direct relationship to social control, we examined normative conformity instead of informational conformity in this chapter. Obedience is similar to normative conformity in its social pressure and control implications, but since it pertains more to leadership than the normative structure in general, we will examine it in the next chapter. We considered the meaning of normative conformity and group conformity in general by focusing special attention on Asch's classic line-judgment research and the extent it can be seen as representing normative conformity.

In cohesive, harmonious, committed groups with high consensus—including happy primary groups and successful task groups—members are likely to be well-socialized and to have internalized the group's basic normative expectations. Thus, there tend to be few problems of deviance and little need for explicit or overt social control in groups having these characteristics. The weight of members' sentiments establishes and maintains expected and orderly behavior in such groups, even when expectations and patterns of behavior change over time. Without thinking much about it, members of these groups will often act according to group expectations because they are rewarded with affection, respect, or authority for doing so.

Although implicit mechanisms of control may operate fairly effectively in enduring groups with some degree of equilibrium, we cannot assume deviance will not occur nor that explicit forms of social control will not be used in them. Conformity makes social order and an equilibrium possible in groups. However, because socialization, internalization, cohesiveness, task interdependence, task commitment, consensus, homogeneity, the understanding of group norms, the ability to meet them, and other factors suggested as facilitating conformity are not perfectly realized in groups that are in existence for a while, we find deviance in them. Although it may have either dysfunctional or functional consequences for the group, the occurrence of deviance generally produces efforts to control the deviance. The major forms of social control discussed in this chapter were social rewards, punishments and sanctions, persuasion through activation of commitment and resocialization, and redefinition of norms.

The form, seriousness, and amount of deviance and the nature and severity of social control efforts will depend on the extent that factors such as those just mentioned as sources of conformity are present in the group. In addition, deviance and conformity rates of individual group members seem to depend on their rank in the group and whether the status and leadership structures are emerging or established. The likelihood and form of group reactions to deviant behavior also seem to be affected by the rank of the deviant, as well as by the form, seriousness, and frequency of the behavior. Whether and how a group reacts to deviance and tries to control it will influence the structural character of the group and its equilibrium.

In giving special attention at the end of this chapter to two studies of deviance and social control, we attempted to explore in greater depth some important issues raised earlier about the pressures on deviants to conform and the sanctions they face for being or remaining deviants. One of these studies was Schachter's classic experiment on deviation, rejection, and communication, and the other, by Gerson, was about social rank and punishment of deviants in a college fraternity.

Both studies examined at the end of this chapter viewed deviance as a problem of social control, which reveals a general perception by group members of its assumed effects on group value-achievement and equilibrium. This view of deviance by group members in general is not unlike the way authority figures or leaders in groups perceive disobedience. These similar perceptions are to be expected, since disobedience can be seen as a special form of deviance, just as obedience can be viewed as a special type of normative conformity. The special characteristics of disobedience and obedience derive from their relationship to leadership. In the next chapter, we will examine these processes, the process of power, and structures of leadership in small groups.

5

Leadership and Power in Small Groups

INTRODUCTION

We will introduce this chapter with an example. At first glance, this example may seem to have little to do with the content of this chapter. In fact, though, it gives concrete meaning to the key concept of leadership and to some related concepts, while also allowing us to re-emphasize the important notion of functional interdependence that we have used to characterize small groups as social systems. So, read the following brief story carefully, and look beyond its more obvious meaning to try to discover its sociological implications for leadership and small-group functioning.

Imagine you are watching a major league baseball game that is very important for the teams involved in it. This game will decide which team goes to the World Series. It is the bottom of the ninth inning and the home team is behind by one run. There are runners on first and third bases with one out, and the batter has two strikes on him. Because the home team does not have a reliable relief pitcher available for a tenth inning, its manager feels he must try to win in the bottom of the ninth. Thus, in a daring—or foolish, depending on your perspective—move, the manager has ordered a "suicide squeeze" bunt to bring home the man from third to tie the score and get the man on first to second and into position to score the winning run. The man at bat is a weak hitter, but an excellent bunter, and the man who would follow him to bat is the team's best hitter.

Unfortunately, the man at bat disregards the bunt sign and strikes out with his mightiest swing for the fences. This defiant act ends the game and the season for his team, since the man coming from third base is easily tagged out by the catcher. Needless to say, the batter's action arouses the ire of his teammates, especially the ones on base and the one slated to bat next, and his defiance also sufficiently angers his manager to prompt him to levy a $1000 fine for "insubordination." Apparently, the management of his club is quite perturbed, too, because despite the would-be hero's versatility and excellent skills in the field, he finds himself in a uniform of a different team the following year, a team very far from the rank of the pennant contender for whom he had played the year before.

This sad story of team and individual failure offers a good illustration of the nature of leadership, disobedience, and reactions to disobedience in small groups, and it also shows how leadership is related to other basic structural-functional dimensions of groups, such as the normative order, social control, integration, goal attainment, and adaptation. The relationship of leadership to the normative order and to social control (and, by implication, *pattern maintenance*) was explicitly mentioned in the last chapter. In our illustration, social-control elements can be seen in the expectation held by team members that field instructions from the manager, such as the bunt sign, should, and would, be followed, and in the angry response by them to the violation of this expectation. These elements closely parallel aspects of leadership concerning the manager's own expectation that his decision to order a bunt would be followed, his imposition of a fine to accompany his own anger, and the club officials' decision to trade the "insubordinate" player to a worse team. In this case, there are normative expectations that explicitly support the leadership structure and they are reflected in the roles of the manager and higher club officials. These normative expectations also define roles of group members, the players, in relation to that structure. That is, players know they are supposed to obey the decisions of their manager.

Group leaders may translate group norms into authoritative commands or establish new group norms through their authority. In either case, group members who are accepted by others in the group as leaders are given the right to make decisions for the group as a whole and to expect obedience to their orders. It is this element of decision-making that most clearly distinguishes leadership from more general aspects of the normative order of groups. This means the strikeout victim's misfortunes did not stem from his violation of an implicitly understood or unarticulated group norm about what to do when he faced a one-out, two-strike situation with runners on first and third in the bottom of the ninth inning. Nor did his misfortunes stem from his flouting of certain specific official rules of the ball club. Instead, he earned the wrath of his manager and of club officials as well as of his teammates because he violated an explicitly—though furtively—conveyed *order* from his manager that he should have felt obligated to obey.

Thus, in the more general case of social control, group members may feel it appropriate to remind wavering members about proper group behavior and to exert control to bring the deviant's behavior back into line. This social control may operate very subtly in the context of normal interaction between group members, as we suggested in the last chapter. In the more specific case of leadership, one or more particular group members called *leaders* or *authority figures* are granted the right *and responsibility* to make explicit demands on individual group members or on the group as a whole for the purpose of group goal attainment—winning the game, in our illustration. In general, acceptance by the group of a leader's right to make such demands also implies an obligation of compliance and an expectation of punishment from the leader for noncompliance, especially of a willful sort.

Although the role of leadership in group goal attainment and its relationship to the normative order and social control may be the easiest factors to identify in our illustration, it also is possible to see in it some ties between leadership and integration, and leadership and adaptation. Leadership is related to integration in that leaders' efforts often are explicitly aimed at bringing about coordination between members' actions and activities. In our example, leadership overlapped with integration in this sense when the manager called for a play that involved cooperation among three players, the two base runners and the batter. We can see how a breakdown in leadership, reflected in the disobedience, resulted in a breakdown in group integration. Because the batter disregarded his manager's sign, he not only struck out but he also caused the runner coming from third base to be out.

Leadership often may involve group, or interpersonal, integration decisions. It also may involve decisions about group goal attainment that require the group to relate to its environment.. Mobilization of group resources and skills and exchange with its social or physical environment brings a group into the realm of *adaptive* relations. Since another team is part of a baseball team's environment, and mobilizing team resources and skills to try to defeat that other team can be treated as an adaptive effort, the strategy ordered by the manager can be seen as leadership in an adaptive setting of goal attainment. Without becoming unnecessarily immersed in functional terminology, it should be evident from our baseball story that leadership often may blend with a variety of different functional aspects of groups. Thus, the effective exercise of leadership could reflect a substantial amount of structural-functional integration of the group and the existence of a condition of relative balance or equilibrium among the various structural and functional elements of the group.

In this chapter, we will examine the implications of leadership for the nature of the group as a whole, the way it functions, and the way members interact. In addition, we will focus on the processes of interpersonal power, coalition formation, and rebellion. Leaders often become concerned about these processes because each can pose a serious challenge to the stability of a group's leadership structure and the maintenance of its existing equilibrium. Much has been written about leadership, interpersonal power, coalitions, and related phenomena.[1] However, it is not our intention here to review all the literature.

[1] The most comprehensive survey of theory and research concerning leadership and related factors is by Stogdill (1974). Other helpful general reference materials in this area include Homans (1950; 1974), Verba (1961), Hare (1962; 1976), Hopkins (1964), Jacobson (1972), Ofshe (1973), Crosbie (1975), and Shaw (1976). All of these materials will be used to present the main ideas of this chapter.

Our more modest aim is to define key concepts related to leadership and power in small groups; present major assumptions and findings about sociologically interesting and group-relevant sources, characteristics, and consequences of leadership, interpersonal power, and coalitions; and focus special attention on studies concerning problems of leadership and power in small groups.

UNDERSTANDING LEADERSHIP, INTERPERSONAL POWER, AND REBELLION IN SMALL GROUPS

SOME PRELIMINARY CONSIDERATIONS
ABOUT LEADERSHIP AND POWER

Since terms such as *leadership, authority,* and *power* occur frequently in popular usage, we should distinguish how we will use these ideas here. Unfortunately, defining and using these terms tend to be complicated somewhat by the fact that these concepts—especially power—have been defined in a number of different and sometimes inconsistent ways by social scientists and others. In our discussion of basic concepts, we will address some of the sources of the lack of consensus about the meaning of these concepts. We also will try to sort through the conceptual disagreements and ambiguities to provide relatively clear, precise, and straightforward definitions of the key concepts used in this chapter.

The first thing that should be understood is that we will use *leadership* and *authority* interchangeably. This seemed appropriate because our conception of *leadership* tends to resemble very closely conceptions of *authority* typically found in sociology.[2] We indicated in the last chapter that leadership is conceptualized as having a structural basis; the notion of *leadership structure* has been proposed to refer to the distribution of decision-making rights and obligations in groups.[3] Thus, this conception of leadership can also apply to authority in small groups.

The second important point is that the actual exercise of leadership or authority by leaders or authority figures is a form of influence, because it involves an impact on or some degree of control over the behavior of other people. That is, after leadership has been exerted, the targets of this influence act differently than they would have if the leadership had not been exerted. Leadership or authority (we will discontinue using both terms at the same time) is successful or effective to the extent behavior changes in the direction the leader intended or expressed.

By conceptualizing leadership in general terms as a form of influence, we

[2] Sociological conceptions of authority are typically based to some extent on the work of Weber (1946; 1947). We would replace Weber's term *power* with *influence.* However, like Weber's notion of *authority,* our concept of *leadership* refers to *legitimate power* (or influence) that rests on the consent of the governed—the group members—and involves the acceptance of an obligation to obey.

[3] As we noted in the last chapter, Crosbie (1975) is mainly responsible for this conception of leadership structure.

can see its similarity to interpersonal power. Following Crosbie (1975:346), we can define *interpersonal power* as "the ability to cause at will a change in another person's behavior through the promise of reward and/or the threat of punishment." Thus, as forms of influence, both leadership and interpersonal power cause a change in other people's behavior. They also are similar in the sense that both are interactive or social in nature and cannot exist apart from a relationship between at least two interacting parties. At this point, though, the basic similarities between leadership and interpersonal power end.

Unlike leadership, interpersonal power is *not* embedded in a group's social structure. Furthermore, as Crosbie has noted: "whereas both are solicited forms of influence, compliance to a leader is normative, involving a suspension of judgment; compliance to a power source, however, is not normative and involves the very definite judgment of contingent rewards and costs" (p. 346). Leadership is also different from interpersonal power in that it is more likely to be exercised for the benefit of the group and oriented toward collective goals than power is. Interpersonal power is frequently personal or individualistic in nature.

The distinction between leadership and interpersonal power can become blurred in concrete behavior when group members feel little or no obligation to comply with the leader's orders, thus compelling the leader to use promises or threats to gain their compliance. We can see this happen in a case where a street gang and its leader have just lost a fight to a rival gang. The leader's orders to prepare for another fight to try to regain their lost territory and pride are loudly criticized or ignored by gang members. These challenges represent a breakdown of the leader's authority. However, his reminder that he can still pulverize or physically punish anyone in his own gang who continues to defy him is a resort to power to reinforce his shaky leadership.

Leadership and power also can become blurred when leaders make demands of the members of their group that go beyond the legitimate scope of their authority. For example, the street gang leader of the example just given may order members of his gang to rob a local "numbers bank" under the pretense it will enhance the gang's prestige and power in the community, when, in fact, it will do nothing of the kind. The gang members never intended to become involved in such activity, and the gang leader's *real* intention is to enhance his *own* prestige, material standing, and power among his underworld acquaintances. To the extent gang members balk at this directive or perceive it as an abuse of authority, the leader will once again have to rely on his resources of interpersonal power in the group. Of course, if he persists in such demands without gaining the general support of gang members, he may be risking his status as leader.

The examples presented here show how leadership and power can become confused in concrete behavior. Despite the possibility of such confusion, it is important to maintain a clear distinction between these two notions, since, as we have suggested, each has a different role to play in group behavior. In addition, we will discover that challenges to each type of influence tend to be of a different nature and have quite different implications for group structural stability, equilibrium, and goal attainment. Indeed, power exercised *by followers—*especially through the collective action of coalitions—can pose a serious threat to group leadership, stability, and equilibrium. In this chapter, we will want to examine more closely leadership, interpersonal power, and various forms of individual defiance and collective rebellion. In the next section, we will begin exploring in greater depth the meaning and implications of each of these factors by concentrating on the nature and functions of group leadership.

THE NATURE AND FUNCTIONS OF LEADERSHIP IN SMALL GROUPS

To some people, leadership implies the capacity to dictate others' behavior and get one's own way. However, there is a French Proverb that gives a very different picture of leadership: "I must follow for I am their leader."[4] In fact, we have already tried to suggest this latter conception of group leadership in proposing that it is tied to group structure, is based on the consent of other group members, and implies a responsibility to serve the group by making and enforcing decisions for its benefit. Of course, this does not imply that leadership is without its rewards, such as the right to make binding decisions affecting the destinies of group members and the group as a whole. However, to understand fully the nature of group leadership, it is essential to recognize its basis in group consent and its responsibilities to the group as well as the rights or privileges attached to it.

Leadership, Legitimation, and Scope: A Sociological Approach

LEADERSHIP, GROUP STRUCTURE, AND PERSONALITY TRAITS.
By defining leadership as part of group structure and as a product of group interaction and consensus, we have tried to draw attention *away from* a personality trait approach to group leadership. This should be exactly what you would expect from a sociologist. In fact, a stress on structural rather than personality aspects of leadership allows us to reveal more of a sociological nature about the emergence, nature, and effects of leadership in small groups, which is consistent with the general perspective we have tried to maintain throughout this book. In addition, though, this structural approach should discourage the acceptance of dubious assumptions about "natural" leaders or unique personality traits of leaders. Assumptions that a leader in one group will automatically and immediately become a leader in other groups or that all group leaders share the same distinctive personality traits generally have been discredited by research.

[4] This proverb was suggested by Jacobson (1972:129) in his discussion of the nature of leadership.

For example, Hare's (1976:278) review of relevant evidence indicated, "The variety of traits . . . a leader may have is the same as that of any other group member, except that the leader is usually found to have a higher rating on each 'good' trait. While correlations between 'good' personality traits and leadership are generally positive, they are rarely large . . . ." Even Merei's (1958) research about "natural" leaders in new group settings, cited in the last chapter, showed that their initial efforts to assume leadership met with failure, and that only those "natural" leaders who accepted and learned their new group's traditions ultimately were able to ascend to leadership in it.

A sociological approach to leadership does not deny the possibility that certain general types of individual qualities, traits, or skills frequently may be found in group leaders. Indeed, past research has suggested that leaders often are characterized by intelligence, enthusiasm, dominance, self-confidence, social participation, and egalitarianism (Hare, 1976:279). The point here is *not* to deny the existence of these traits in many leaders. Rather, it is to emphasize that focusing on them alone will not help us understand much about the emergence and effects of group leadership. We contend that group leadership cannot be adequately understood apart from the particular group context in which it emerges and functions. Even the personality traits group members may see as "good" in their leaders are likely to vary according to the differing values and needs of different groups.

LEADERSHIP AND LEGITIMATION. An important part of understanding the group basis of leadership is an appreciation of how *legitimation* makes leadership possible. In the last chapter, we proposed that group members earn and maintain positions of leadership, and high status in general, through high levels of group value-achievement and conformity to central group norms. This means that the process of attaining leadership is built on making group contributions that other group members value highly. These superior contributions produce respect and trust that may engender a normative belief among group members that the contributor or contributors ought to have the right (a) to make decisions for the group as a whole and (b) to expect group members to accept and carry them out. The granting of this right to make binding decisions[5] for the group is called *legitimation of leadership* or *authority,* and leaders

---

[5] Gamson (1968:21–22) has suggested that a decision is *binding* in the sense that it can be implemented without the necessity of further review of its content by group members. He has further proposed that this was essentially what Easton (1953:132) meant by the term *authoritative* when he said: "A policy is authoritative when the people to whom it is intended to apply or who are affected by it consider that they must or ought to obey it." However, Gamson's conception of binding decisions placed more emphasis on the capacity to enforce them. According to him, a decision is made binding if "either it is accepted as binding (for whatever reason) *or,* if it is not accepted, legitimate force—or other sanctions, we would add—can be used to implement the decision" (p. 22). Gamson was specifically referring to effective authority, such as the kind *earned* in small groups, not merely to formal or legal authority.

can effectively maintain their special position in small groups only by maintaining the legitimacy of their influence attempts.

The notion of legitimation should help us appreciate the implications of the French Proverb cited earlier, as well as the idea that leadership rests on the consent of the governed. It also should help us understand better the distinction between leadership and interpersonal power. If we substitute *leadership* for *authority* and *small group* for *government* or wherever else it is appropriate, we can gain a better understanding of both leadership *and* power by considering MacIver's (1947:83–87) remarks:[6]

> By social power we mean the capacity to control the behavior of others either directly by fiat or indirectly by the manipulation of available means.
>
> By authority we mean the established *right,* within any social order—like a small group—to determine policies, to pronounce judgments on relevant issues, and to settle controversies; or more broadly, to act as leader or guide to other (people). When we speak of *an* authority we mean a person or body of persons possessed of this right. The accent is primarily on right, not power. Power alone has no legitimacy, no mandate, no office. Even the most ruthless tyrant gets nowhere unless he can clothe himself with authority.
>
> The conclusion immediately follows that the authority (in groups) does not create the order over which it presides and does not sustain that order solely by its own fiat or its accredited power . . . . There is a greater consensus without which the fundamental order of the (group) would fall apart. This consensus plays a different role (in different groups) . . . . But always, whether mainly acquiescent or creatively active, it is the ultimate ground on which the unity and the order of the (group) repose.
>
> We see, then, how inept is the identification of authority with power . . . .

LEGITIMATE SCOPE OF LEADERSHIP.   Thus, it is a leader's legitimate decision-making, rather than exercise of interpersonal power, that can hold a group together and enable it to act collectively. In general, the types of decisions group members allow their leaders to make fall into three broad classes: (1) ones concerning group goal-, or value-achievement, (2) ones concerning interpersonal relations among members within the group, and (3) ones concerning the allocation of group rewards. However, according to Crosbie (1975:215), the right to make these types of decisions will rarely be accompanied by acceptance of a leader's right to make personal decisions for group members involving their behavior or activities outside the group. We can see plainly this limitation of leadership in cases where members of high school, college, or even pro-sports teams accept without question their coaches' dictatorial policies regarding

---

[6] Buckley (1967:179) has suggested using MacIver's conceptual comments to clarify the distinction between leadership or authority and power.

training, deployment of personnel, or game strategy, but greatly resent or rebel against policies concerning matters such as their politics or whom they should date.

Personal decisions of this sort, especially regarding public, political, or racial protest and interracial dating, often have caused severe rifts in authority relations between coaches and players when the coaches have been white and the players black.[7] Of course, white athletes also have become involved in conflicts with white coaches in recent years when they have viewed the coaches as trying to exert too much control over their personal lives *or* their lives as athletes.[8] The controversy over the proper length of hair and the amount of permissible facial hair, which has even found its way into the professional sports realm at times, is a good example of this type of conflict.

We can see that a major problem faced by coaches today is actually a problem universally confronting coaches, and group leaders in general. It is the problem of achieving a sufficiently broad scope of authority to allow them to pursue their leadership responsibilities effectively. For coaches, this means trying to get their players to carry out decisions that will enable their team to win. Obviously, this is a matter intimately tied to legitimacy, or the way group members feel about the nature and scope of decision-making rights of their leaders and their own obligation to obey. In practice, this typically becomes a matter of achieving some consensus about what kinds of decisions leaders should *and should not* make, and of making sure the group and its leaders recognize and accept that conception of leadership as a normative expectation. Group leadership, order, and the achievement of group values and goals may *all* suffer to the extent this consensus is not achieved, leaders fail to appreciate the limits of their authority, or group members do not feel an obligation to obey.

The Functions of Leadership: A Structural-Functional Approach

TYPES OF LEADERSHIP FUNCTIONS. An understanding of the areas in which group leaders are usually granted a right to make decisions (e.g., group goal- or value-achievement, interpersonal relations within the group, and reward-allocation) gives us a sense of the types of functions leaders are expected to perform in small groups. If we view the group leadership role as the type played by executives in organizations, then we can infer from classical theories of organizational management that the primary functions of group leaders are planning, organizing, and controlling.[9] There are variations of these functions, including

[7]See Edwards' (1970) *The Revolt of the Black Athlete* for a discussion of such race-related authority conflicts in sport.
[8]Underwood (1969) offers insight into this conflict from the perspective of the "desperate coach," and Scott (1971) views it more from the athlete's point of view.
[9]These broad categories of executive, or leadership, functions, as well as the variations of them mentioned in the next sentence, come from Stogdill's (1974:30) survey of relevant leadership literature.

coordinating, supervising, and motivating, but in general, these variations can be subsumed by these three broad categories of executive functions just mentioned.

Classical management theories are helpful in suggesting the broad outlines of leadership functions in small groups, but we need to consult the work of social scientists who have studied leadership *in small groups* to gain a clearer and more precise sense of what group leaders are expected to do. According to Stogdill (1974:30), behavioral theorists and researchers have identified the following kinds of group leadership functions in their work:

1. defining objectives and maintaining goal direction;
2. providing means for goal-attainment;
3. providing and maintaining group structure;
4. facilitating group action and interaction;
5. maintaining group cohesiveness and member satisfaction;
6. facilitating group task performance.

This list and our baseball story at the beginning of this chapter show us that group leaders are expected to make decisions concerning all major aspects of group structure and functioning. In particular, they reveal that in trying to mobilize group and personal resources for group goal attainment, which concerns adaptation as well as goal attainment, group leaders must make decisions or carry out actions of the sort that also force them to deal with problems of pattern maintenance, including social control, and integration. That is, in trying to provide direction for group goal-attainment efforts, leaders often have to: (1) clarify and help enforce group norms to maintain order in their group (social control and pattern maintenance); (2) try to hold the group together, coordinate members' behavior, and keep them motivated and happy (integration); and (3) try to facilitate group task performance involving relations with the group's environment, act on behalf of the group for such adaptive purposes, and decide how group members should be rewarded for what they have contributed to the group (adaptation).

Describing the functions of leadership in these terms serves two useful purposes. First, it subsumes other lists of leadership functions under a set of categories that relates directly and meaningfully to the general functional orientation presented earlier during our consideration of models of the small group as a social system. And second, it allows us to add some clarification and refinement to the comments made at the beginning of the chapter about the relationship of leadership to other major aspects of group structure and functioning.

Another useful way of conceptualizing the varied functions of leadership we have just described is in terms of the idea of *completer*. According to Hare (1976:280),[10] this idea implies ideally that a group leader is the member of the group who has the necessary conception of the group's purpose, specific

---

[10]Hare derived this conception of the leadership role from the work of Schutz (1961).

problem-solving skills, concern for intermember solidarity, resources of power, and techniques of control to help the group complete its task when others in the group fail. Surely, this is what the term *leadership* often seems to mean when people use it in casual conversation. However, this interpretation also has relevance to our general structural-functional approach to small groups' social systems. For, as Back (1948) has suggested, whether or not an actual leader fulfills all these ideal functions, he or she will be a major influence in establishing the point at which the group will reach equilibrium along each basic dimension of interaction.

FUNCTIONAL DIFFERENTIATION OF LEADERSHIP. We tend to refer to *the* group leader. Of course, we know from personal experience that leadership functions may be concentrated in a single group member, *or* they may be distributed among several members (Hare, 1976:280). We will consider the distribution of leadership functions at greater length later in this chapter in a discussion of the differentiation of leadership structures. For the time being, though, at least it should be recognized that having more than one leader in a group can have both benefits and costs for the group.

On the benefits side, greater specialization of leadership functions could produce increased leadership efficiency and effectiveness. On the costs side, problems such as malintegration or role confusion could result from having more than one leader in a group. These problems could result if the group has not clearly established how the different leadership roles should be coordinated, or if the particular bailiwicks of different leaders seem to overlap or are unclearly articulated by group norms. Since we have emphasized functions, rather than dysfunctions, in describing leadership, we may tend to minimize these potential problems and costs of particular kinds of leadership structures. However, it is important to realize that the disruptive effects on group functioning and equilibrium of malintegrated, confused, and ineffectual leadership could be as pervasive and strong as the beneficial consequences of good leadership.

Malintegration and role confusion may seem less likely in groups where each leader's particular bailiwick is formally prescribed by the norms of a larger organization. For example, in military groups, status differences are formalized and clear cut, and on this basis both leaders and group members are *supposed to* know exactly what to expect of leadership. However, we have already considered how distinctions between different types of leadership functions, like group functions in general, can become blurred in reality, even when they seem so clearly differentiated in the abstract. Furthermore, we should recognize also that an informal leadership structure may emerge to parallel, replace, or conflict with the official one; this dual leadership structure may cause a great deal of confusion about who is in charge of what, and when.

When leaders or group members are confused about the leadership mandate, or when the authority of leaders is directly challenged or intentionally ignored, leaders may call upon resources of power, along with or instead of legitimate group sanctions, to support their failing or wavering leadership. Nonleaders also may exercise power to gain more control over each other or to get their own way in confrontations with leaders. Power in groups is most threatening to leaders and the leadership structure, and it is most disruptive for group order and equilibrium, when it is exercised collectively in coalitions.

THE NATURE AND DYNAMICS
OF INTERPERSONAL POWER IN SMALL GROUPS

Characteristics and Types of Interpersonal Power

We already have indicated we will be using Crosbie's (1975:346) definition of interpersonal power as "the ability to cause at will a change in another person's behavior through the promise of reward and/or the threat of punishment." Although this concept has been defined in numerous other ways,[11] we have chosen Crosbie's definition because it is clear and simple, while still capturing the sociologically relevant properties of power as an *interactive* influence relationship involving the manipulation and exchange of *rewards* as well as costs. Thus, in our conception of interpersonal power, we are *not* referring to situations where one person can influence the behavior of another regardless of what the other person does. Thibaut and Kelley (1959) have called this type of influence "fate control." Instead, we are applying our power concept to situations where people who are the targets of power attempts *could* act otherwise, even if the alternatives are relatively costly to them.

As Homans (1974:85) has observed in his own exchange-theoretical treatment of power, an understanding of interpersonal power from this perspective implies the need to know the payoffs from a given power relation for *both* the power agent *and* the target. In Homans' view, "power is always a matter of negotiation, implicit or explicit" (p. 87). Crosbie (1975:346-347) has suggested the nature of these power negotiations in the following terms:

> Suppose that a power source wanted his target to choose *A* and the target was reluctant to do so. The source must increase the target's profit for *A*, and we (can conceptualize) . . . four distinct ways of altering rewards and costs to increase the relative profit for *A*. The source may promise to increase the rewards . . . or decrease the costs for (*A*, or) he may threaten to decrease the rewards . . . or increase the costs for (alternative behaviors). The first two are often said to constitute *reward power* and the latter two *coercive power*. For example, suppose a girl wants her boyfriend to take her out to dinner and he wants her to cook dinner in her apartment. In order to get her boyfriend to take her out (behavior *A*), she may promise him something special when they get home (increase

---

[11] Included among references reviewing the different meanings that have been given to *power* by social scientists are Dahl (1957), Riker (1962), Wrong (1968), Jacobson (1972), Stogdill (1974), and Crosbie (1975).

rewards), offer to pay for the dinner (decrease costs), threaten to cook beans and spinach at home (decrease rewards), or threaten to make him do the dishes at home (increase costs). Thus, there are numerous ways by which a person may alter the rewards and costs of others in order to gain power over them . . . .

Resources of Interpersonal Power

Homans (1974:74) has proposed a "principle of least interest" to describe the exercise of power and the change it produces in the less powerful person's behavior. According to this principle, superior power derives from a greater capacity to reward in exchange situations. That is, one person has power over another when that person is more able to reward the other in an exchange than the other is able to reward him. Homans went on to suggest that there may be a number of different reasons why a person possesses this capacity to reward others, and these reasons may vary according to the particular circumstances of different exchange relations. He called these reasons the *bases of power.* We might also call them *resources* of power, and in small groups they are things people possess or control that are valued, needed, or feared by other group members.

It is possible to imagine a wide variety of things that could be used as power resources. For example, Crosbie (1975:347) has mentioned the giving or withholding of approval, assistance, friendship, affection, information, advice, social support, money, opportunities for other rewards, and verbal and physical abuse.[12] He reminds us that any characteristic or possession could be a power resource in interpersonal relations as long as: (1) it is controlled *or* perceived to be controlled by the power agent, and (2) it is either rewarding or costly to the power target. Thus, in order for our power attempts to have any impact at all on others' behavior, we must control *or* appear to control one or more resources of power such as those we have mentioned.

Crosbie (1975:348) has noted that collective support and dependence are two power resources that have attracted a great deal of independent attention among small-group researchers. The use of collective support to wield power is illustrated by the organization of voting blocs in legislative and other types of decision-making groups. The study of this kind of behavior in groups relates to coalition formation, and we soon will give special attention to the meaning and implications of this phenomenon.

Since dependence implies a reliance on others or vulnerability to them, it may seem strange to consider it as a possible resource for *exerting* power. However, according to Berkowitz and Daniels (1963), the explanation for power exercised by "helpless" or dependent people, such as young children, the sick, or

---

[12] One of the most frequently cited discussions of the *bases of social power* is by French and Raven (1959). Jacobson (1972:Ch. 2) offers another, more recent, treatment of a variety of power resources, which draws from French and Raven's work. Both discussions are considerably more extensive and detailed treatments of this topic than the discussion here.

the disabled, may be found in a societal "norm of social responsibility."[13] The main implication of this norm is that people are supposed to feel a responsibility to help or accede to the wishes of helpless, weak, or dependent others merely because they are helpless, weak, or dependent. Thus, dependence becomes a resource of power when dependent people either implicitly or explicitly invoke this norm by emphasizing their helplessness, weakness, or dependency, and when the people whom they are trying to influence comply with it.

Flagrant violations of the norm of social responsibility can have relatively serious psychological (guilt) and social (sanctions from other group members) repercussions for the violators. For example, we can imagine such consequences if a man ignores the objections of his seriously ill and bedridden wife and leaves for a week-long golfing vacation. Nevertheless, research has not yet clarified the amount of power the dependency resource typically provides.[14] We might guess its use would be reduced by a weak acceptance of the norm of social responsibility by the power target, a lack of concern by this person about the possible repercussions of disregarding the norm, the absence of other group members when the norm is invoked, and a reliance on this norm several times in the past. However limited dependence may be as a power resource, it is important to realize it may often be the *only* potentially effective resource low-status group members have at their disposal.

Unlike low-status group members, high-status members—especially leaders—often have several substantial potential power resources available to them. People attain high status and leadership in small groups because they possess qualities or perform services that are highly valued by group members, and these qualities and services become the basis for both power and authority. Of course, it may also be the case that group members will yield or defer to others with high status or authority merely because of their respected position in the group. Furthermore, we should not forget that the processes of attaining high status and leadership in a group will lead to an accumulation of idiosyncrasy credits, which may be applied as a resource in interpersonal power relations.

Leadership as Source and Consequence of Interpersonal Power

Earlier in this chapter, we pointed out how the analytically distinct notions of leadership and power could blend together in concrete cases where leaders seek to maintain their authority in the face of diminished legitimacy. Now we have seen how leadership and power can be closely associated in two further senses. In one sense, the attainment of leadership can generate increased power and provide a greater reserve of power resources. In a second sense, power can

---

[13]Crosbie (1975:348–349) has provided a brief overview of the central thrust of research about dependency power in small groups, and our comments here are based largely on his overview.

[14]Crosbie has cited research by Shure, Meeker, and Hansford (1965) indicating that dependence does not always translate into effective power in pacifist bargaining strategies.

enable group members to acquire authority initially. Since we have been less explicit about the latter sense in which power and leadership or authority may be related, we will let Homans (1974:92) provide additional clarification:

> . . . a (person) may not be able to acquire authority without first acquiring power. A (person) cannot even begin to win authority over another unless the other takes his advice at least once, for if the other never takes his advice, the other can never find that the result rewards him. The difficulty is always to get him to obey the first time, and for that purpose power over him may be necessary. If he can be induced or compelled to obey once, he may obey spontaneously thereafter.
>
> This is in effect what happens in the case of successful military leaders. When an officer is new to a unit and bears no reputation other than his insignia of rank, he may get his men initially to obey his orders through the implication, inherent in his rank, that they ought to obey him and that he can get them punished if they do not obey. But once they have obeyed his orders and have found that obedience leads to victory over the enemy without their suffering unnecessary casualties—once, that is, obedience has led to their gaining reward at least in comparison with possible alternatives—then the officer will have begun to acquire authority over them as well as power. If he is successful enough in this respect, they will come in time to follow him, as we say, blindly. In this case he will never have to use his power. If, on the other hand, obedience to his orders does not result in success, his official power may not be enough to save him. His soldiers will begin to challenge even that. Formal institutions are always being supported or undermined by these more elementary processes . . . .

Since power can help establish authority, and authority can enhance power, we must be careful to keep in mind the distinctive nature of each and the different implications each may have for group structural stability and equilibrium. These distinctions may be most evident when power is used by group members to oppose their leaders. This use of power is likely to have more disruptive implications for the group than disobedience alone, since it is explicitly aimed at changing one or more aspects of group leadership. When this rebellion is organized, it tends to have its most disruptive consequences *and* be most effective. Small-group investigators have studied collective power attempts under the topic of *coalition behavior,* and we will look more closely at the nature of what they studied in the next section.

COALITIONS AND REBELLION IN SMALL GROUPS

The Nature of Coalitions

When leaders, such as the newly assigned military officer in Homans' example, cannot gain or maintain acceptance of their group leadership, they are likely to find themselves faced with halting obedience or outright disobedience. They also may be confronted with active resistance or opposition to their decisions or even to their right to make them. When group members combine forces to form a sub-group that uses the collective resources of its members in an organized effort to influence group decision-making, they constitute a *coalition*. Thus, as we suggested earlier, coalitions are built on the principle "there is strength in numbers," and thereby derive their power from the resource of collective support.

It is unrealistic to assume group leaders will be able to meet the expectations of all group members all the time. Thus, disobedience and unorganized or organized rebellion are recurring possibilities in the life of any leader or group. To understand better the conditions under which group members will combine their resources to oppose—or try to reinforce—group leadership, we will take a closer look at the nature of coalitions, coalition formation situations, and their possible group structural implications.[15]

Gamson (1961) has suggested that coalitions are alliances of convenience formed on a temporary basis for the pursuit of power over group decisions. This conception of coalitions means that the alliances may involve members who disagree among themselves about group values, goals, or activities. However, they will be united by a common desire to change or reinforce one or more aspects of group decision-making. To achieve their aims, they will need to arrive at what Gamson has called "tacit neutrality" on matters going beyond the immediate prerogatives or aims of the coalition.

Coalition Formation Situations and Types of Coalitions

Gamson (1961) has also proposed that "full-fledged coalition situations" contain the following kinds of elements:

1. There is a *decision* to be made and there are more than two *social units* attempting to maximize their share of the *payoffs*. In Gamson's framework, *decisions* are selections among alternatives; *social units* are individuals or sets of individuals which for the duration of the decision follow the same coalition strategy; and *payoffs* are rewards to be derived from decisions, including influence on future decisions.
2. No single alternative will be acceptable to all participants in the situation, or maximize the payoff to all of them.

[15] It should be pointed out that most of the concepts, findings, and insights about coalitions in small groups that we will consider in this chapter are related to or derived from "coalition game" situations that have been experimentally created in the laboratory. (These coalition games have been described by Ofshe and Ofshe, 1970.) Despite the laboratory origins or ties of these ideas and findings, we can assume they will have relevance to collective power efforts in groups outside the laboratory, since a number of the basic aspects of coalition game experiments can be generalized beyond the laboratory. In this chapter, we will concentrate mainly on ideas and findings about coalitions having *general* relevance to leadership in small groups.

3. No participant has dictatorial powers—akin to what Thibaut and Kelley have called "fate control," i.e., no one has initial resources sufficient to control the decision single-handedly.
4. No participant has veto power, i.e., no member *must* be included in every winning coalition.

According to Gamson's first two conditions, coalition situations are ones involving meaningful decisions or issues for more than two group members, in which there is an element of competition or conflict. The third condition states that a dictator cannot be present; the fourth states that no single member can be capable of blocking or holding to a stand-off any possible opposing coalition. The presence of a dictator means that one group member's power or resources of power will always be *greater than* the total power or resources of any possible opposing coalition. The possession of veto power means that one group member will have power or resources *equal to* the power and resources of the strongest opposing coalitions. Together, these four conditions indicate the types of situations where coalitions are possible and can have some impact on group decision-making.

Although coalitions can form in leaderless groups or in groups in an early stage of development,[16] we are most interested here in coalition formation, behavior, and effects in more established groups *with* leaders. In these latter group contexts, we may find either *conservative* or *revolutionary* coalitions (Caplow, 1968; Crosbie, 1975:398). Conservative coalitions typically are ones including high-status members such as the leader and his lieutenants who combine their power resources *in defense of* their vested interest in the status quo. Revolutionary coalitions engage in efforts to *change* the status quo, typically through challenging the decisions of leaders, or even more radically, through challenging their very right to exercise authority. Gamson's conception of the basic elements of coalition situations suggests that coalition formation is unlikely when group leadership is strong; i.e., when the leader has *dictatorial power, veto power,* or strong and diffuse support from group members in general. On the other hand, coalition formation—by rebellious group members and perhaps by leaders and other high-status members, too—is more probable when leadership is weaker and less effective.

We have proposed that coalitions usually are temporary alliances in the sense that they tend to remain in existence only until the issue causing their formation has been resolved or members can no longer sustain their power attempt. It has often been said that "politics makes strange bedfellows." Since this is often true for coalitions, we can readily understand why coalition members would want to dissolve their alliance as soon as it has achieved their desired aims or proven itself ineffectual.

---

[16] Experimental coalition research typically seems to concern coalition formation in groups or pseudo-groups of these types.

Structural Implications of Coalitions in Small Groups

In saying that coalitions tend to be temporary and exercise power rather than authority in the group as a whole, we are implying they exist outside group structure. However, we are not implying they cannot affect group structure, for we have already pointed out that conservative coalitions are aimed at supporting it and revolutionary coalitions attempt to change it. Crosbie (1975:399-400) has elaborated on the potentially important structural implications of coalition behavior in groups:

> ... In contrast to the momentary distortions in group structures caused by the exercise of individual power, the effects of coalition power relations have the capacity for permanence. This is because of the greater number of members involved in coalition relations. When the members of a winning coalition constitute a majority or near majority of members, which they often do, the change that the coalition advocates has the capacity to become normative in the group and incorporated into the group's social order. As a normative element, the change will be enforced by the group members and from that time until the norms are again changed, the members are likely to act in accordance with the new policy. This is not to say that all changes favored by coalitions in a group will alter the group structures, for obviously some changes, such as deciding what the group will do on Saturday night, will be temporary and inconsequential. It is to say, though, that coalition power relations, unlike individual power relations, have a greater potential for changing the stabilized group structures.

The formation and behavior of revolutionary coalitions in small groups capture a number of the basic conceptual ingredients of leadership and power relations considered so far in this chapter. We have learned that they are collective efforts to change one or more aspects of the group decision-making structure, and that they tend to form and be most effectual when leadership is weak or has been weakened and leaders have limited power resources to support their tottery legitimacy.

LEADERSHIP IN SMALL GROUPS

GENERAL ASSUMPTIONS AND FINDINGS

In the next section, we will begin examining in greater depth assumptions about leadership and considering the type of evidence that has been generated to support these assumptions.

*Some Preliminary Considerations
about the Emergence of Group Leaders*

LEADERLESS GROUPS. In considering the emergence of leadership structures in small groups, it should be recognized that some groups may be without a leader, at least for a while, and that leadership can derive either from outside or within the group. To say that a group has no leadership structure means that the group has not conferred the normative right to make decisions for it on any member or set of members. This absence of leadership is most likely to be found in primary or nontask groups having members very similar in ability, external status characteristics, and beliefs, who feel no strong commitment to explicit goal-attainment of any sort. Crosbie (1975:216) has suggested that leaderless groups tend to make decisions through action of the group as a whole, on a relatively democratic basis, or by temporary coalitions of members. He also has pointed out that although individuals in leaderless groups may exert influence over their decisions, this influence is not authority but results from factors such as rank in the group, persuasion, and related power resources.

APPOINTIVE AND INFORMAL GROUP LEADERSHIP. Externally derived group leadership is illustrated by the case of the newly reassigned military officer mentioned earlier by Homans. In such cases, leadership is delegated or imposed by external authority figures and is not initially chosen by group members themselves. This type of appointive, or delegated, official leadership usually is found in groups in formal organizational settings, and the likelihood that official or formal leaders will gain legitimacy in their group depends on how much the group accepts the authority of those who have made the appointment and on the other kinds of factors by which group members earn leadership in groups on their own (Crosbie, 1975:216). In addition to this case, appointive leadership is illustrated by classroom teachers, college department heads, coaches of school or professional sports teams, and formal supervisors of industrial work groups.

Although it is essential to realize that many group leaders initially attain their leadership position through appointment or delegation, we are more interested in what happens within groups to elevate a certain member or set of members to a position of group leadership. As Homans has indicated, formal leaders are likely to have their influence substantially curtailed unless they can earn the respect and legitimacy by which informal leaders gain their authority. Thus, although we will focus mainly on the emergence of informal group leadership, by doing so, we will also consider assumptions and findings having relevance to how formal leaders earn legitimacy in small groups.

LEADERSHIP, PERSONALITY TRAITS, AND THE GROUP CONTEXT. We have already suggested that research has uncovered a number of individual or personality traits, such as intelligence, enthusiasm, dominance, and self-confidence, that have frequently been associated with leaders (Hare, 1976: 279). However, underscoring our previously indicated reluctance to define leadership or account for its emergence in terms of such personality traits, Homans (1974:270) has said:

> For a long time psychologists tried to discover some single trait of personality, or single set of traits, the possession of which was apt to make a (person) a leader. Their results have been meager and ambiguous: no

single trait or set seems to make a (person) a leader with any regularity. The highest correlation links leadership with intelligence as measured by an intelligence test, and we (can) find reasons why this might have been expected, but even this correlation is not very high. Recently the psychologists have contented themselves with saying that leadership does not depend on the personality of the leader but on the nature of the relationship between (the leader) and his followers (see especially Browne and Cohn, 1958). . . .

The importance of the group context and of interaction or exchange between group members is something to which we have already given some attention in considering the processes of status- and leadership-attainment. Homans has noted in this regard: "Field studies of groups suggest a general rule: the same process that wins a person high status in a group is also apt to win him leadership, if the group has any use for it" (p. 270). This means that the rare and valuable services or contributions members provide for their group or at least most of its members, will earn them both high status, and leadership. The difference between high status, *per se,* and leadership, is that a group member gets social approval and respect from the former but also gets the right to make and enforce binding decisions from the latter. The particular kinds of services, contributions, or qualities that earn a person the right of leadership will differ according to the distinctive needs and values of different groups. This reflects the essence of what is meant by the notion that the emergence of leadership in a particular group depends on the nature of the group context and the relationship of leaders to followers in it.

LEADERS AND LEADERSHIP STRUCTURES. By taking a structural approach to leadership, we have tried to discourage the tendency to associate leadership with individuals rather than with the structure of the group in which it has emerged. We want to draw a clear distinction between the factors making particular group members leaders and leadership itself. Furthermore, as trivial as it may seem, we want to emphasize that leaders will not emerge in a group unless factors conducive to the emergence of a leadership structure are present in that group. This idea is important because it suggests an additional distinction between the factors associated with the general emergence of a leadership structure in a group or of a particular type of leadership structure and those associated with the attainment of positions in a group's leadership structure by particular group members. Thus, to provide a general indication of what sociologists know about the emergence of group leadership, we will give attention to factors (beyond rare and valuable services) affecting leadership-attainment by group members; factors affecting the emergence of leadership *structures* in groups; and factors accounting for the emergence of different types of leadership structures in groups. Our approach, then, will be to move from leaders to leadership structures and from leadership structures in general to differentiation of them.

We have said that group members attain leadership (and high status, in general) by performing rare and valuable services for their group, and that the specific nature of these services varies according to the particular needs and values of the group. Along with these contributions to group value-achievement, which can be understood generally in terms of the leadership functions we discussed earlier in more detail, there are other sociologically interesting factors associated with leadership-attainment. We discussed one of these factors, conformity to central group norms, in the last chapter. Researchers also have identified some other factors affecting leadership-attainment, and prominent among them has been rate of participation in group interaction.[17]

TALKATIVENESS, PERCEIVED CONTRIBUTION, AND LEADERSHIP-ATTAINMENT. Laboratory studies of emergent leadership and field studies of established leadership have both consistently shown that leaders participate more often in group activities than any other group members.[18] For example, Bass (1949; 1954) formed discussion groups that had no leader at the outset and found that the group member who talked the most tended to emerge as a leader. Bass' research seems to suggest that members become leaders by having the highest rate of group participation, rather than high participation rate merely being a *product* of becoming a group leader. In fact, it appears that most of the participation-leadership research supports this assumption (Crosbie, 1975:222).

An experiment by Riecken (1958) concerning the effect of talkativeness on the ability to influence group problem-solving indicates the importance of distinguishing between content and rate of participation in generalizing about how participation affects the emergence of leaders. Riecken formed discussion groups that were asked to try to solve three "human relations problems." On the basis of discussion of the first two problems, Riecken derived measures of the relative rankings of members of each group according to their amount of talking or rate of participation. Riecken used these rankings to determine which group member would receive a hint about the best solution to the third problem. In half of the groups, the hint was (secretly) given to the member who had done the *most* talking; in the remaining groups, this hint was (also secretly) given to the member who had talked *least*.

Riecken found that the most talkative group members were more likely to have their solution accepted by other members than the least talkative members, even though the two's proposed solution was exactly the same. Thus, it appears that a member's influence, and attainment of leadership, may be determined less by the actual superiority of his or her suggestions or contributions than by his or

---

[17] Stogdill (1974) has summarized the main findings of research of this sort, especially in his nineteenth and twentieth chapters.
[18] Stogdill (1974:220) and Crosbie (1975:222) cite a number of these studies.

her status as the most frequent talker in the group. This finding may seem to conflict with our earlier assumptions about members' contributions and their attainment of high status and leadership. However, this apparent contradiction tends to dissolve when it is recognized that Riecken's subjects tended to identify quality of contribution to the solution of the problem with amount of talking.

The relationship between talkativeness and perceived contribution could mean that the probability a contribution will be perceived by other group members as good or that a good contribution will be attributed to a given group member will depend on how much the contributor talks. In either case, Riecken's data imply that group members will tend to perceive the contributions of the most talkative members as being more valuable than those of the least talkative ones—even when their contributions are *actually* equivalent in quality. As a result of such perceptions, it will be more difficult for those usually having relatively little say to get their suggestions accepted, their contributions recognized, and their contributions translated into higher status and leadership.

According to Riecken, good solutions to group problems by highly talkative members tend to face the most resistance when these members promote the solutions weakly or with little conviction. On the other hand, good solutions from quiet members have their best chance of being accepted when these people have support from one of the more talkative group members, who presumably acts in a sort of sponsor's role. Interestingly, in Riecken's experiment, neither measured intelligence nor verbal fluency and the extent a person offered and pushed convincing arguments—from an objective point of view—had a significant impact on acceptance of a solution. Riecken also discovered that success in getting a good solution accepted seemed to be affected little by the amount of opposition it aroused, but to be enhanced by a member's ability to gain support from the group.

The main thrust of Riecken's findings has been supported by other research, including an experiment by Jaffee and Lucas (1969).[19] These investigators controlled both quantity of participation and quality (accuracy) by using a confederate in problem-solving groups. In one condition (high quantity-low quality), the confederate was instructed to talk a lot without giving correct answers. In a second condition (low quantity-high quality), this person was told to talk very little but to give the correct answers. Jaffee and Lucas found that the high quantity-low quality confederate was chosen as a leader more often than the low quantity-high quality confederate.

Overall, then, it appears that a high rate of participation in group interaction may be *necessary* for gaining recognition, respect, and acceptance as a leader, and this recognition, respect, and legitimation may not always be justified on objective qualitative grounds. It should be noted, though, for those who

---

[19]This experiment has been briefly reviewed by Crosbie (1975:223-224), and we will draw from this review here.

intend to test this proposition in their next group encounter, that merely talking a lot may not be *sufficient* to earn high status and leadership.

According to McClintock (1963) and Morris and Hackman (1969), a high rate of group participation will not earn these rewards if a member also exhibits a great deal of obnoxious behavior or behavior detrimental to group goal attainment. As Hare (1976:279) has pointed out, "the person who does most of the talking wins most of the decisions and becomes the leader . . . *unless* he talks so much that he antagonizes the other group members." In cases where a member has little of *actual* value to say or contribute, this person may walk a tightrope between the promise of acceptance and deference and the threat of rejection and debasement. At this stage of research on participation and leadership, we do not know precisely how this tightrope will swing or when useless talk will become tiresome or antagonistic in given groups. Thus, one takes an uncertain risk in trying to talk his or her way into leadership without having much that is worthwhile to say.

Once leadership is established in a group, it may be difficult to challenge or replace it merely by trying to talk more than leaders, even if one has more constructive things to contribute. Burke (1974) has suggested that opportunities to talk or gain the attention of other group members may be normatively regulated. This means that ". . . speaking and turn-taking in discussion groups is socially regulated; that the floor is passed from one individual to another, that getting the floor is not simply a matter of deciding to talk and then doing so faster than anyone else. There are rules governing floor transition" (Burke, 1974:841).

Burke's perspective further implies that the most active or talkative members may *become* leaders because people generally tend to conceive of the leader's role as *requiring* high rates of activity and verbal participation. Thus, when people conform to this role conception when leadership has not yet emerged or is very tenuous, members are likely to be willing to grant them the right to make decisions for the group. Once leadership is established, it will be difficult to "steal" discussion turns from leaders because "(t)he floor is turned over to them at least as often as they desire to participate . . ." (Burke, 1974: 841); and they will want to participate a lot, at least partially in response to members' expectations for them as leaders.

FIRST IMPRESSIONS, EXTERNAL STATUS CHARACTERISTICS, AND LEADERSHIP-ATTAINMENT. Along with certain individual qualities, perceived contributions to group value-achievement, conformity, and rate of participation, first impressions and external status characteristics have been identified by small-group investigators as important or noteworthy factors in trying to understand the attainment of leadership by a particular member or set of members in a group (Crosbie, 1975:221-227). Since people often form first impressions on the basis of cues from external status characteristics, it should be evident that it can often be difficult trying to separate the independent effects of each of these two factors. In research by Strodtbeck, James, and Hawkins (1957), we see how these factors can combine with two others, rate of participation and perceived competence, to influence the process of selecting a group leader.

These researchers conducted mock-jury deliberations in which participants were drawn by lot from the regular jury pools of the Chicago and St. Louis courts. After participants in each mock jury listened to a recorded trial, they were instructed to select their foreman and begin their deliberation. According to Strodtbeck, James, and Hawkins, foreman selection was influenced in the following way:

> In more than half of the deliberations, the foreman was nominated by one member and then quickly accepted by the remainder of the group. In about a third of the deliberations the man who opened the discussion and sought either to nominate another, or to focus the group's attention on their responsibility to select a foreman, was himself selected foreman. However, in all instances the selection of a foreman was quickly and apparently casually accomplished. There was no instance in which mention of any socio-economic criteria was made, but this is not to say that socio-economic criteria were not involved. For example, (it was found) that some foremen were selected from all strata, but the incidence was three and a half times as great among proprietors (the highest stratum represented) as among laborers (the lowest stratum). In addition, . . . tabulation shows that only one-fifth as many women were made foreman as would be expected by chance (p. 715).

Strodtbeck, James, and Hawkins' foreman-selection results and their comments about them indicate that group members forced to select a formal leader relatively early in their group involvement waste little time and have little difficulty making this choice, at least where members differ in external status characteristics. They seem to be guided by first impressions based on who shows an early inclination or ability to lead the group, and by external status characteristics—in this case, cues from general societal evaluations of occupational and sex distinctions. These initial choices and the reasons for them seem to have a continuing impact on group interaction, expectations, and decision-making. Strodtbeck, James, and Hawkins found that males talked more than females, that jurors who were higher in occupational status talked more than those with lower occupational status, and that foremen accounted for approximately one-fourth of the total group participation (in the 12-person juries). They also looked at the effects of sex and occupational status distinctions on influence, perceived contribution to group decision-making, and perceived competence as a juror; these effects were found to be similar to those for foreman selection and rate of participation.

These results seem to imply that status evaluations and expectations from the larger society follow people into small groups to affect how they initially act and expect others to act in the group. Thus, since people with high status outside the group are accustomed to initiating interaction and making decisions, they will be more inclined than group members with lower external status to try to do these things after joining a new group. If the group itself has just been formed or for some other reason has no established leader, we can anticipate that group members will encourage or indeed, expect high participation and decisions from members with higher external status. As a result, members' initial status rank and position in the leadership structure of their new group will tend to parallel their rank in other groups and in society in general. As group members' initial expectations become established and normative in nature, leaders—and other high-status group members—will wield relatively more influence than others, and will be perceived as more competent and as making better contributions to the group, which tend to maintain their leadership or high status.

There are many cases where external status characteristics—especially achieved ones like occupational status—are good predictors of the *actual* quality of contributions members can make to their group. Thus, initial tendencies to allow people with higher external status characteristics to talk more and make decisions should tend to be reinforced by the actual behavior of these people in many cases of this sort. However, where external status characteristics—especially ascribed or irrelevant ones such as sex, race, or age—are *not* good predictors, members initially accorded high status and leadership prerogatives in the group eventually may find their position a bit insecure. As we suggested earlier, talkative group members who have little constructive to contribute, may eventually lose the respect of other group members. This means that external status characteristics will not be a firm basis for maintaining high status or leadership in the group, unless they are accompanied by contributions of roughly equivalent rank. This assumption is supported by Strodtbeck, James, and Hawkins' data, for they found that after face-to-face experience, jurors tended to show less respect for those in their group with high occupational status and more respect for those with lower occupational status, in accordance with the actual quality of contributions made by group members.

A CLOSER LOOK AT EXTERNAL STATUS AND LEADERSHIP-ATTAINMENT: HOW DOES COMPETENCE AFFECT LEADERSHIP-ATTAINMENT FOR FEMALES? Strodtbeck, James, and Hawkins' research raises an important question about how the possession of task-revelant skill or expertise generally affects leadership by group members with lowly-evaluated external status characteristics. This is the type of question addressed by Eskilson and Wiley (1976) in their experimental study of sex composition and leadership in three-person problem-solving groups. Although the experimenters manipulated attainment of leadership in this research, their results nevertheless offer some insight into how perceived skill might interact with low external status to affect leadership-attainment as well as performance.

In Eskilson and Wiley's study, the independent variables were leader sex, perceived mode of attaining the leader role (achievement or appointment), and sex composition of the followers (two males, one male and one female, or two females). In the appointed leader condition, subjects drew lots for the leader role. In the achieved leader condition, people became leaders *apparently* as a result of their performance on a spatial perception test given earlier by the experimenters. In fact, in all cases, the leadership position was randomly assigned by the experiments. The findings revealed three main effects of sex of the leader. They were:

> First, male leaders, as predicted, concentrated significantly more than female leaders on recognizable leadership behavior (e.g., instrumentally oriented suggestions, opinions, information, and orienting or integrating statements).
>
> Second, female leader behavior was distinguished by a relatively greater performance of positive affect (or emotionally-expressive) activity.
>
> Third, female leaders were less likely to choose themselves as future leaders than male leaders.

As Eskilson and Wiley have pointed out: "These results scarcely require explanation: they are completely consistent with traditional sex role stereotypes."

These effects of sex on leadership clearly suggest the more limited interest of females than males in conventional leadership behavior. However, there *were* female leaders in Eskilson and Wiley's experimental groups, and it is interesting to see how the perceived manner of leader role attainment and the group's sex composition affected both male and female leaders' role performances and followers' acceptance of them. In regard to the appointment-achievement dimension of leadership, Eskilson and Wiley's research suggests:

> . . . that the norms of female subordination and succorance still have currency among college students *except* when the female attains the superordinate role through (apparent) personal achievement. In the present experiment, females who achieved the leader role showed intense involvement with the instrumental aspect of the group task. However, they simultaneously performed the expected encouraging and tension-relieving behavior. Like some working wives, they took on two jobs . . . In contrast, female subjects who became leaders by chance appeared to conform entirely to the expectations for female behavior: their leadership performance was minimal, and they showed the least involvement in the task . . .
>
> Male leaders, on the other hand, did not differ in leader behavior due to type of leader role attainment. We have speculated that males who (became) leader by chance felt pressed to justify their occupancy of the leader role by acting leader-like. Males who achieved the leader role may

have regarded it as merely their due, and not felt the need to validate their identity through intense effort. We further suggest that the whole notion of achievement may have been less salient for males in the present experimental context because a female experimenter directed all activity (pp. 192–193).

Eskilson and Wiley have proposed that by conforming to traditional stereotypes of the female sex role, appointed female leaders, as opposed to achieved ones, were performing relatively little leader-like behavior and as a consequence, were severely damaging whatever chance they might have had of gaining trust and legitimacy from other group members. Thus, followers could be expected to give less support to appointed female leaders than to achieved female leaders, and much less to appointed female leaders than to male leaders who attained leadership either way. Turning the female results around, we could say that when females feel competent to lead (i.e., in the achievement condition) they will make more intense efforts to lead the group, and their performance of more leader-like behavior will tend to generate more acceptance of their leadership than the behavior of appointed female leaders.

Eskilson and Wiley's data regarding sex composition effects show some interesting differences in both followers' reactions and leaders' performances. The experimenters summarized these findings in the following way:

> . . . Both sexes concentrated more on the task of leader in a sexually homogeneous as compared to a mixed-sex group. We attributed this to the existence of "hidden agendas" in mixed-sex groups which lessen the importance of and concentration on the experimental task. For example, females leading two males performed minimal amounts of leader behavior, and received few requests for direction from their followers, even though they, like all the leaders, were the sole possessors of valuable information. In this case the hidden agenda seems to have required the validation of the norms of female subordination and of male task competency.

> Another striking contextual effect occurred when a male led a mixed-sex group. The male follower challenged the leader, in what we have labelled the "rooster effect." Perhaps the hidden agenda in this context dictated male competition for female appreciation. This competitive behavior was in sharp contrast to the cooperative demeanor of male followers in all-male groups, where task activity was the primary item on the agenda (p. 193). . . .

> In contrast (to all-male groups), task completion did not appear salient to groups of three females. These groups were least effective at completing the (assigned task) despite the fact that female leaders acted more leader-like with two female followers. Perhaps all-female groups redefined the group goal to include concerns which are considered more feminine by society. However, it is interesting to note that female leaders were most

effective when leading mixed-sex followers. The approval and (requests for direction) shown by the single male follower may have enabled the group to successfully achieve its instrumental goal (p. 192).

In combination with the results produced by Strodtbeck, James, and Hawkins, Eskilson and Wiley's data clearly demonstrate the importance of focusing on the specific external status characteristic of sex in trying to account for the emergence of leadership and the success of leaders in gaining and holding legitimacy. The difficulties faced by prospective or actual female leaders were succinctly stated by Nemeth, Endicott, and Wachtler (1976:293) when they summarized the results of their own investigation of women in jury deliberations:

> After a century of struggle to gain the right to serve on juries, females are still viewed, both in the literature and in lawyers' folklore, as being submissive, emotional, dependent and envious . . . In spite of the similarities between the sexes (found in this research with respect to) verdict, interaction style and persuasiveness, males were perceived to be more independent, rational, strong, confident, influential and as more of a leader than were females.

Sex alone may have a significant impact on group members' willingness to accept particular members as leaders. However, we have learned from Eskilson and Wiley that the effects of this variable and other similar ones that might affect attainment of leadership are best understood if we look at the context in which leadership attempts are made and legitimacy is granted. Contextual variables such as the manner in which leadership is attained, by arbitrary appointment or achievement, and the sex composition of the group could have an important influence on how or whether variables such as external status characteristics, first impressions, participation rate, conformity, perceived contributions, or other individual qualities or actions, influence leadership-attainment and performance. Of course, as we noted earlier, these factors may have little or no effect unless they can, themselves, or in combination with other relevant factors, generate a desire among group members for leadership. Furthermore, a particular member's chance of becoming or remaining a group leader may be significantly affected by the *type* of leadership structure that has developed in his or her group. In the next two main sections, we will look more closely at assumptions and findings about the emergence, and differentiation, of leadership structures.

Emergence of Group Leadership Structures

FACTORS AFFECTING THE EMERGENCE OF GROUP LEADERSHIP STRUCTURES. In the broadest terms, leadership structures—or consensus among group members about the distribution of decision-making rights and obligations—will tend to emerge in groups that are explicitly task-oriented, and in which there are differences in members' external status characteristics and in their ability to contribute to group value-achievement and decision-making. These broad generalizations are based on some of the things we have said (in reverse) about leaderless groups or we have just stated about attainment of the leader role. Stogdill (1974:Ch. 21) has provided additional insights about the emergence of leadership structures through his summary of research concerning the effects of various group factors on this phenomenon. He has suggested that this research tends to show that:

> . . . Intermember compatibility and agreement among members about who should lead facilitate the emergence and stabilization of leadership structure (p. 246).

> . . . Attempts to lead are more likely to be successful when the members differ in social status and when they are highly motivated . . . than under the opposite conditions. . . . (G)roups with goal-relevant tasks (enable) leaders to exercise more influence on other members than groups with low goal orientation. . . . Leadership is less frequently attempted on easy problems (pp. 233–234). . . .

> . . . As the size of the group increases, the potentiality for leadership is reduced to a smaller percentage of members. In other words, the chances that a randomly selected member will emerge as leader tend to decrease as the group size increases. Large groups make greater demands for leader skill and competence than small groups (p. 246).

These summary comments, along with what we said earlier, indicate that the emergence of leadership structures in small groups will be fostered by group conditions or factors such as intermember compatibility; consensus about a leader; variations in social status, task ability, and leadership capacity of group members; strong collective commitment to group goal-attainment; the presence of explicit goal-relevant and relatively complex tasks; and large group size. Crosbie (1975:221) has proposed that another potentially important factor in the development of group leadership structures may be environmental stress or crisis. This means that when normal group patterns or equilibrium are disrupted, when group goal-attainment is blocked, or when something similarly upsetting happens to a group, members will become more desirous or accepting of leadership. Indeed, strong, forceful leadership may be more likely under such circumstances. Hamblin (1958) has conducted research on leadership and crises in small groups, and we will discuss it later in our consideration of selected studies about problems of small-group leadership.

IMPLICATIONS OF THE EMERGENCE OF LEADERSHIP STRUCTURES FOR SMALL GROUPS AND THEIR MEMBERS. In considering factors affecting the emergence of group leadership structures, it is important to recognize exactly what is implied by the emergence of this type of structure.

The first thing implied is that group members are willing to give up some of their own autonomy and decision-making prerogatives to allow one or more other group members to make group decisions (Crosbie, 1975:219). This may be a significant concession for many group members, since research by Brehm (1966: 123) has suggested "that people are motivationally aroused by the elimination or threat of elimination of a behavioral freedom, and tend to show increased desires for the eliminated or threatened behavior as well as attempts to engage in it." We are assuming the group conditions or factors we have mentioned as determinants of the emergence of leadership structures will counteract this reluctance of group members to give up personal autonomy or freedom, so that structures of leadership can develop.

A second important implication of the emergence of group leadership structures is that one or more group members are willing to accept the responsibility of making decisions for the group. This is the other side of leadership, viewed from the leader's—rather than followers'—perspective. We already have considered factors accounting for the emergence of certain group members as leaders, but we have not really stressed the element of choice in this matter, except, perhaps, to indicate that females who are arbitrarily appointed leader show little inclination to engage in leader-like behavior. In fact, the acceptance of achieved leadership, by males *or* females, often may develop rather unceremoniously or spontaneously from the context of regular group interaction. That is, group members will tend to grant leadership rights to those among them who participate, conform (to central norms), and contribute most. For those who contribute most, earning leadership may seem a natural extension of the other things they already have been doing in and for the group. Nevertheless, we must remember that leadership is not merely a matter of gaining a lot of approval or high status for one's actions; it also involves the exercise of influence. Thus, it seems worthwhile to consider the conditions under which group members will try to initiate leadership acts.

LEADERSHIP MOTIVATION: PURSUIT AND ACCEPTANCE OF LEADERSHIP IN SMALL GROUPS. Hemphill (1961) has summarized the main findings of four different experiments regarding these conditions.[20] These experiments showed that efforts to lead were encouraged by:

1. Large rather than small rewards promised for task success;
2. Reasonable expectations of successful task completion;
3. Acceptance by others of the individual's leadership attempts;
4. Tasks requiring a high rate of group decision;
5. Possession of superior task-relevant information;
6. Previously acquired status as a group leader.

[20] This presentation of Hemphill's summary comes from Stogdill (1974:239).

Although leadership, in the sense we have defined it, is only possible when other group members have accepted the leader's right to make and enforce binding decisions, a group member's motivation to lead may be significantly affected by the group's *communication* of their acceptance. This is because leadership often involves trying to get others to do what they might not voluntarily choose to do on their own. We have already noted the reluctance people often feel about giving up their personal autonomy. Hence, we might expect the exercise of leadership to arouse negative reactions at times, even as people follow the leader's orders. Verba (1961:155–156) has pointed out the possible implications of these negative reactions for leadership motivation:

> . . . These negative reactions in turn feed back upon the instrumental task and make its accomplishment more difficult because of the possibility that the leader's directives or the leader himself will be rejected or simply because of the increased tension in the group. . . . (T)he lack of satisfactory affective relations will have an effect upon the willingness of the leader to lead, just as it has an effect upon the willingness of the followers to follow. Acceptance by the followers may be looked at as a reward for the leader. If this is the case, the motivation of the leader to assume an instrumental leadership role will be lowered if he is greeted by negative affective relations to his leadership attempts. The motivation to lead, furthermore, will be lowered even if the attempt at instrumental leadership has been both successful (i.e., the group members have followed the directive) and effective (i.e., it has brought the group closer to the instrumental goal).

STABILITY OF GROUP LEADERSHIP.   Despite the potential difficulties and challenges of leadership, we are likely to find a leadership structure and leaders of some sort in most small groups, especially in task-oriented ones that have been in existence for a while. That is, a certain group member or set of members will want to perform the leadership functions and other group members will accept their leadership behavior to some degree. We have identified the conditions and factors accounting for the desire to lead, the emergence of certain group members as leaders, and the development of a structure of leadership in groups. To our understanding of these things we should add that once a leader has been accepted by a group, his or her leadership position and the leadership structure in which this position is embedded tend to be quite stable. In fact, Crosbie (1975:228) has proposed, "the leadership structure is perhaps the most stable of the group structures." Crosbie explained his contention by noting the normative basis of leadership. Establishment of a leadership structure means that group members will feel that leaders should lead and followers should obey, and these normative expectations will be enforced as long as they are accepted in the group.

Leaders will generally want to maintain their positions because leadership offers attractive prerogatives and rewards, despite the continuing possibility of rejection or other negative reactions. These prerogatives and rewards include the right to control group decision-making and the opportunity to encourage activities and tasks in which leaders are superior and discourage those in which they are disinterested or unskilled (Sherif and Sherif, 1969:177). Leaders will reinforce their hold on their position by their taking advantage of these rights and opportunities, especially when the leaders have attained their position by election rather than appointment or usurpation (Read, 1974).[21]

Although leadership tends to be relatively stable in small groups, this does not imply that leaders can always do whatever they wish or act totally incompetently and expect to retain their position. Leaders *are* replaced, sometimes after intense power struggles, and some *even* step down voluntarily. It is important to recall that the norm giving leaders the right to make and enforce decisions for the group *also* makes them responsible to the group to act in its behalf. When leaders do more to disrupt than reinforce group equilibrium, to hinder than to facilitate group goal-attainment, or in some other way to substantially diminish the contributions to the group that initially earned them leadership, they can expect to lose legitimacy. Furthermore, because they are in frequent face-to-face contact with their followers in small groups, group leaders, as opposed to leaders of larger collectivities, may find it difficult to abuse their authority with impunity. Let us be reminded once again about the French Proverb cited earlier: "I must follow for I am their leader."

LEADERSHIP STRUCTURES IN SMALL GROUPS: SOME SUMMARY COMMENTS. A useful way of looking at the nature, emergence, and persistence of leadership, which summarizes both the individual and group components, has been proposed by Gibb (1954:917):

> Leadership is an interactional phenomenon. . . . The emergence of group structure and the differentiation of function of group members depends upon the interaction of those members, and are general group phenomena. An individual's assumption of the leader role depends not only upon the role needs of the group and upon his individual attributes of personality, but also upon the members' perception of him as filling the group role re-

---

[21]In particular, Read looked at the effects of four different conditions of source of authority on a leader's tenure in office. In his experiment, leaders attained their position through: (1) election by the group; (2) appointment by an external authority, who was an expert in the group's task; (3) appointment by an external authority who was unfamiliar with the group's task; or (4) usurpation—i.e., seizing control from another group member who had been elected to the position, by claiming the election was not a good selection procedure and indicating he would like to be leader himself. In all groups, the leader was the same person—who worked as a "stooge" for the experimenter. Votes at the end of the experiment for future leaders of the experimental groups indicated that 74 percent of the votes in groups with elected leaders were for retaining the original leader, 60 percent of the votes in groups with expert appointment were for retention, 47 percent of the votes in groups with nonexpert appointment were for retention, and only 24 percent of the votes in groups with a usurper as leader were for retention.

quirements. These, in turn, vary as the situation and the task alter. In general, it may be said that leadership is a function of personality and of social situation, and of these two in interaction.

To Gibb's comments we can add Read's (1974:203) summary of the findings of his research on sources of authority and legitimation in small groups:

> . . . the leader's source of authority (from election, appointment by an expert, appointment by an external authority without group task expertise, or usurpation) had immediate and lasting effects upon his task influence and evaluation of him by others, even when, for all intents and purposes, he was the same person performing the same deeds. This finding should come as no surprise to theorists who have long argued that the context of power (or influence, in our terms) is as important as its execution, but it should bring comfort to researchers who have been unable to produce solid evidence for so important a variable. In addition, some of the results presented here argue that leader legitimacy cannot be considered a general disposition but involves a complex interaction of attitudes toward the leader and his source of authority, with the leader's actual behavior contributing substantially to his task influence and continuing legitimacy.

We have suggested on a number of occasions that leadership may be exercised by more than one member of a group, and we have hinted lightly that different leaders may perform different types of leadership roles in given groups. In the next section, we will consider some of the basic ways in which leadership can become differentiated or divided among different specialists.

Differentiation of Group Leadership Structures

TASK AND SOCIO-EMOTIONAL SPECIALISTS OR "GREAT MEN"? The two main types of leadership usually distinguished are task and socio-emotional leaders. These types parallel a common conception among small-group investigators of how roles and activities generally become differentiated in small groups, with some seen as more task-oriented (or instrumental) and others as more socio-emotional (or expressive or affective).[22] Hare (1976:302) has cited numerous studies of initially leaderless groups showing the distribution of leadership functions between a task leader and a socio-emotional leader and some others indicating that the group member who receives the most nominations for leadership is not necessarily the one who is liked best. This same kind of differentiation between task and socio-emotional specialists has been found in studies of organized groups. Research has also suggested that when groups do not have a socio-emotional leader, members may be more inclined to "scapegoat" one of

---

[22] In view of the meanings usually given to these terms, we will use *task-oriented* interchangeably with *instrumental*, and, *socio-emotional, expressive,* and *affective* in an interchangeable manner.

their number in an effort to resolve socio-emotional problems (Gallagher and Burke, 1974).

On the basis of what has been said so far in this book, it should be relatively easy to visualize the distinctive kinds of things task and socio-emotional leaders will be most likely to do. Burke's (1967; 1971) research [following the work of Bales and Slater (e.g., Bales and Slater, 1955; Slater, 1955; Bales, 1958)] enables us to gain a more precise understanding of these distinctions, since he attempted systematically, through empirical methods, to separate *task leadership* factors from *socio-emotional leadership* factors. Major aspects of task leadership he identified included providing "fuel" for discussion by introducing ideas and opinions for the group to discuss, guiding the discussion and keeping it moving, providing clarification, providing the best discussion ideas, standing out as the leader in discussion, making the most influence attempts, and being the most successful in influencing the group's opinion. In general, then, task leaders direct and strongly influence group task behavior, make important contributions to it, and are recognized by other group members for performing their leadership role.

According to Burke, socio-emotional leaders tend to do the most to keep relationships among members cordial and friendly, to be most liked, to make tactful comments to heal hurt feelings arising from group interaction, and to try to harmonize differences of opinion. Thus, in general, this kind of leader or specialist tends to concentrate more than the task leader on reducing the frustration, disappointments, and hostilities or disagreements that develop in group interaction, and, as a result, is better liked.

Since the nature of task and socio-emotional leadership functions seem quite different, there might be a tendency to assume that these functions will always or nearly always become separated into two distinct leadership roles played by different group members. This separation is what we mean by *differentiation of the leadership structure* or what Crosbie (1975:216) and others mean by a "pluralistic leadership structure." In recent years, some investigators have begun to question whether leadership differentiation of this sort is as general in small groups as Bales, Slater, and others had earlier proposed. For example, Lewis (1972) has suggested that the same person may play both roles since the roles are not incompatible. Landecker (1970) has indicated that some overlap may help integrate or coordinate group activities. Riedesel (1974) has argued that faulty or biased measures of popularity and expressive leadership in past research may have produced an overestimation of the proportion of differentiated leadership structures in groups. As a reflection of this recent wave of criticism of earlier leadership differentiation arguments, Crosbie (1975:217) has contended that most task groups will have a leadership structure in which:

> . . . the decision-making rights are normatively given to one member who is then expected to direct the group. This leader, who is sometimes referred to as the "great man" leader (Borgatta, Couch, and Bales, 1954),

will direct the group in its task activities, arbitrate interpersonal disputes among group members, represent the group to outsiders, and so on. . . .

Crosbie has added that leaders may occasionally delegate lesser decision-making rights to one or more lieutenants, but this delegation was not a lessening of the superordinate leader's authority, since he or she (a "great woman") could be expected to retain veto power over the decisions of the hand-picked lieutenants. Obviously, our understanding of the emergence or nonemergence of differentiated, or pluralistic, leadership structures remains a bit murky. Rather than trying to count the number of groups in which the leadership structure does or does not become differentiated, it would seem more fruitful to consider the conditions fostering the emergence of this type of structure. This has been a main focus of Burke's (1967; 1968; 1971) research. Thus, we will give it some more attention.

GENERAL CONDITIONS AFFECTING LEADERSHIP DIFFERENTIATION IN SMALL GROUPS. Burke wanted to extend the theory of task and socio-emotional role differentiation proposed by Bales and Slater, and he began this effort by summarizing the key ideas of Bales and Slater's work in the following way (Burke, 1967):[23]

1. In any group's attempt to reach a goal through interdependent, coordinated activity, acts designed to achieve the goal (task acts) give rise to tension and hostility (social-emotional problems). When one person engages in task acts, another is thereby denied the opportunity; in reaching decisions, some ideas are selected over other ideas; some departure from equality of participation must occur because not everyone can act at the same time. Meaningful coordination requires an inequality of participation in task actions.
2. When there is inequality, the person who is highly active in the task area is the primary source of change and of tension and is consequently the target of some hostility. It is his action which deprives action opportunities to others and forces them to adjust their behavior and ideas to accomplish the task.
3. Because the task leader (the person most active in the task area) is himself the principal source of tension, it is unlikely that he would be effective in resolving this tension, and if the tension is to be reduced, someone other than the task leader must assume a role aimed at the reduction of interpersonal hostilities and frustrations.
4. The result, therefore, is the development of task and social-emotional role differentiation.
5. The tendency toward differentiation of task and social-emotional roles (regarding leadership as well as other spheres of group activity) is quite generalized, depending not upon any gross differences between persons, upon preexisting cultural prescriptions, or upon any particular task demand, but rather upon fundamental social processes common to all social systems.

[23] Burke's summary is based mainly on Bales and Slater (1955), Slater (1955), Bales (1956), and Bales (1958).

EFFECTS OF TASK LEGITIMACY AND RELATED FACTORS ON LEADERSHIP DIFFERENTIATION. Burke noted research indicating that the process of differentiation of leadership and group roles in general described by Bales and Slater may not be as general in groups—especially ones outside the laboratory—as these investigators assumed. For example, the emergence of a differentiated leadership structure may be affected by factors such as group size (Levinger, 1964), the degree of familiarity of group members with each other (Leik, 1963), the degree of task-orientation of group members (Mann, 1961), the degree of legitimacy or acceptability in the group of instrumental behavior, and the degree to which the leader is legitimated (Verba, 1961). Implicit in the view that leadership differentiation depends on certain conditions is a question about the *inherent* incompatibility of task and socio-emotional roles. In one of his studies, Burke (1967) addressed this question by considering the conditions under which an inequality of participation in task actions (with the *task leader,* by definition, involved in more tasks than anyone else) leads to a disliking of the task leader, to less socio-emotional behavior by the task leader, and to a separation of the roles of task and socio-emotional specialists. His working hypothesis for this study was:

> . . . the legitimation of task activity in a group (a) prevents high task per-
> formance on the part of one member (or alternatively high inequality of
> task performance) from violating the expectations of group members and
> leading to a disliking of the high task contributor, and (b) frees the task
> specialist from having to concentrate heavily on task activity in order to
> prove himself, and allows him freedom to engage in social-emotional
> activity if he is inclined.

Burke used four- and five-member laboratory discussion groups to test his working hypothesis. He found:

1. Inequality of task participation was correlated with a disliking of the task leader under conditions of low task legitimacy, but not under conditions of high task legitimacy.[24]
2. High task participation by the task leader and competition over the task leader's role were correlated with a reduction in the amount of socio-emotional activity by the task leader under conditions of low task legitimation but not under conditions of high task legitimation.
3. Inequality of participation in the task area was correlated with the emergence of distinct task and social-emotional roles in conditions of low task legitimation, but not in conditions of high task legitimation.

---

[24]To measure "legitimation of task activity," Burke (1967) used observer ratings of the extent that group members exhibited in interaction an acceptance of a "task ethic": i.e., the extent they were concerned about their task of discussing the case assigned to them, arriving at conclusions, reaching consensus, avoiding distractions, assessing goal attainment at any given time, etc. Groups having a high concern for and acceptance of this "task ethic" were placed in a "High Task Legitimacy" category and those having a low(er) concern and acceptance were placed in a "Low Task Legitimacy" category.

According to these results, legitimation of task activity can play an important part in determining whether unequal task participation results in leadership differentiation into separate task and socio-emotional roles. They suggest that such differentiation tends to emerge from the high task participation of the task leader when task legitimacy is low, but not when it is high. Burke proposed that his findings meant the need for modification of the Bales-Slater theory of role differentiation in small groups, and he suggested that this modification might take the following form (Burke, 1967):

1. In any group's attempt to reach a goal through interdependent, coordinated activity, acts designed to achieve the goal (task acts) give rise to tension and hostility *if they go beyond the legitimate, expected level* (and thus constitute a threat).
2. Subject to the condition given in No. 1 above, when there is an inequality of participation in the task area, the person who is most highly active is the primary source of *undesired, non-legitimate* change and is consequently the target of some hostility.
3. The person who is *illegitimately* high in task participation is likely to be preoccupied with task action and, therefore, to engage in little social-emotional activity.
4. Because the task specialist is himself the principal source of tension it is unlikely that he would be effective in resolving this tension, and, if the tension is to be reduced, someone other than the task leader must assume a role aimed at the reduction of interpersonal hostilities and frustrations.
5. The result, therefore, subject to the conditions given in Nos. 1, 2, and 3 . . ., is the development of task and social-emotional role differentiation.

EFFECTS OF BASIS OF LEADERSHIP, GOAL CONSENSUS, AND REWARD SYSTEMS ON LEADERSHIP DIFFERENTIATION AND PERFORMANCE. In a later study, Burke (1971) examined the effects of basis of leadership, goal consensus, and nature of the reward system on task and socio-emotional leadership role performance and differentiation of the leadership structure. He used laboratory discussion groups in this investigation. He experimentally manipulated the basis of leadership by giving one-half of the discussion groups additional instructions to elect someone "to act in the role of discussion leader, to moderate, guide, and keep track of discussion." This elected leader was to be paid 25 cents extra per meeting for this "extra duty." The other half of the groups received no additional instructions, thereby allowing leadership to emerge by itself. Initially Burke intended only to look at these *elected* and *emergent* leadership conditions. However, a third condition, which he called a *counter-election* condition, emerged in the study and was used in the data analysis. In this condition, one person was elected leader, but a different person, in fact, emerged to become task leader by virtue of having the highest rate of task participation.

The consensus condition regarding goal attainment was created by asking group members to explore as many alternative interpretations as possible for the problem before them and then reach agreement on the best single interpretation. The nonconsensus condition was created by asking members of the remaining groups only to explore as many alternatives as possible. Further inducements to achieve consensus in the former condition were given in terms of monetary incentives or penalties. The nature of the reward system, per se, was manipulated by paying all group members the same amount ($1.50) for each meeting (equal pay) or by paying group members (from $1.00 to $2.00) in a manner contingent upon the relative "contributions to the discussion" (differential pay).

In general, Burke found that the basis of leadership had the strongest effect on role differentiation, and that this effect influenced the socio-emotional performance of the task leader. In particular, Burke found support for each of his three hypotheses about leadership role differentiation.[25] His results showed that: (1) there was more role differentiation in the emergent than elected leadership condition, and more still in the counter-election condition; (2) role differentiation tended to be greater in the nonconsensus than consensus goal-attainment condition; and (3) there was no significant impact of equal versus differential pay on role differentiation.

To help understand the leadership basis finding, we can recall Burke's prior research about the effects of task legitimation on role differentiation. In fact, he meant leadership basis to reflect the amount of legitimacy which the task leader has for engaging in task activity. It can be argued that under conditions of less—versus more—legitimacy, task leaders will have to work harder to validate their leadership, will become more preoccupied with task actions, and hence, will engage in less socio-emotional behavior and be less effective at it. Thus, when there is less legitimacy, there is more need for someone else to lead the group through its socio-emotional problems; there also may be a greater likelihood that socio-emotional problems will occur then, since the task leader will be devoting most of his or her energy to demonstrating his or her task "superiority." In Burke's research, task leaders were likely to have to work hardest to gain acceptance in the counter-election condition. Acceptance was likely to be earned more easily in the emergent condition, and most easily in the elected condition, since the election itself is a significant form of acceptance. Thus, we would predict that the likelihood of differentiation will tend to increase from the elected to the emergent to the counter-election conditions, which is what Burke found.

We might expect leadership differentiation to be greater under conditions

---

[25] Overall, Burke tested fifteen hypotheses concerning the effects of basis of leadership, consensus, and nature of the reward system on the relative number of task and socio-emotional functions performed by task leaders, on the relative number of each of these types of functions performed by socio-emotional leaders, and on role differentiation. We are concentrating here on the three concerning role differentiation because they have greatest relevance to our general discussion of leadership differentiation. In addition, since these three hypotheses can be derived from the other twelve, we will be considering key ideas from the others in considering the three role differentiation hypotheses.

with less—versus more—pressure to reach consensus because task leaders tend to act more in the capacity of idea contributor (a task function) than coordinator (a socio-emotional function) when consensus is less important. When task leaders concentrate more attention on task than socio-emotional activity, they leave a greater void in the socio-emotional area, and presumably, this void will be filled by a separate socio-emotional leader.

The finding of no difference between equal and differential pay conditions can be explained in terms of countervailing tendencies. On the one hand, differential—versus equal—pay could be expected to make more competitive the top contributors in the group, including the task leader, as they all strive for the top reward. This competition would lead to the performance of fewer (relative to the other group members) task functions by the task leader, and to a more equal distribution of task actions in the group as a whole. This greater equality of task activity *could* free the task leader to perform more socio-emotional functions, thereby reducing the need for leadership differentiation.

On the other hand, though, competition for rewards in the differential pay condition could be expected to produce a greater preoccupation with task than socio-emotional activity among top contributors, including the task leader, along with a leveling of differences among them regarding such activities. This means that although the task leader might have more time to perform socio-emotional functions, he or she still might be more interested in devoting most of his time and energy to task functions that could earn higher pay. Thus, differentiation ultimately could be necessary in the unequal pay condition, even though the tendency for task functions to be more widely and equally shared in this condition would allow the task leader to perform more socio-emotional functions, *if* he or she chose to do so. These contrary tendencies could explain why Burke found no differences in role differentiation between the two pay conditions.

Burke (1971) has proposed that his results concerning leadership role performance and differentiation indicate that the relative socio-emotional performance of task leaders and the extent they become preoccupied with task behavior crucially affect the emergence of differentiated leadership structures. Apparently, the more a task leader succeeds in performing the delicate juggling act of socio-emotional with task functions, the less likely differentiation is to occur. In addition, this juggling act apparently becomes more difficult when legitimacy and the pressure to achieve group goal consensus are both low.

SOME ADDED CONSIDERATIONS ABOUT LEADERSHIP DIFFERENTIATION IN SMALL GROUPS. One would guess that there is more to the emergence of differentiation of leadership than Burke has found. Furthermore, in drawing conclusions about *leadership* differentiation from his and other ostensible studies of this topic, we must be careful to keep in mind the distinction between leadership—with its normative basis—and other forms of influence and group participation. In fact, Burke found that amount of legitimacy (at least of task activity by the task "leader") may itself be an important determinant of the emergence of leadership differentiation. Crosbie (1975:218–219) has suggested that a consequence of conceptually or operationally confusing leadership with other kinds of influence or related factors could be to miscalculate the number of leaderless groups or the number of pluralistic leadership structures. Obviously, we have more to learn about the emergence of leadership differentiation and how to study it. Nevertheless, merely by searching for conditions contributing to this process, we will be less inclined to accept the apparently dubious assumption that the emergence of leadership differentiation is universal or inevitable in small groups.

Although this discussion of leadership differentiation has drawn attention to socio-emotional, as well as task, functions of leadership, we assume here that the main or ultimate concern of group leaders is to make decisions that facilitate group goal attainment. Thus, although socio-emotional specialists may arise in differentiated leadership structures to handle a group's major socio-emotional problems, the task leader will still tend to be left with major responsibility for group goal attainment. This means that in groups where differentiated leadership exists, the major authority figure will tend to be the task, rather than socio-emotional, leader. Where there is leadership but no differentiation, we are assuming the "great man" (or "woman") will tend to be evaluated more in terms of task than socio-emotional performance, even though both types of functions must be performed.

This emphasis on the task functions of leadership is not meant to encourage a unidimensional view of leadership, especially since we have pointed out the importance of socio-emotional performance for group functioning. In fact, a consideration of *both* task *and* socio-emotional leadership functions does not provide a complete picture of how leaders perform their roles or how leadership affects group interaction and goal attainment. An important added dimension of leadership that allows us to see more of its nature and implications for the group is its style. In the next section, we will consider some important types of leadership styles in relation to the group atmosphere in which each exists.

Leadership Styles, Group Reactions, and Group Performance

THE LEWIN, LIPPITT, AND WHITE STUDIES OF LEADERSHIP STYLES. The classic studies of leadership styles and climates in small groups were conducted by Lewin, Lippitt, and White (see Lippitt and White, 1952). They established three different leadership settings, *authoritarian, democratic,* and *laissez-faire,* and tried to determine the effects of changes in these three leadership settings on such things as group morale and hostility, dependence of members on the leader, and the quantity and quality of group productivity. In this section and the next one, we will consider the nature of the differences between these leadership styles, and then we will consider their implications for the overall atmosphere of group relations and for group performance.

One cannot discuss Lewin, Lippitt, and White's leadership research without first pointing out the important place it occupies both in the small-group research tradition and in efforts to extend and apply small-group findings. Verba (1961:206-207) suggests the importance and recognition gained by this research in saying:

> . . . The techniques and findings of these experiments had an effect on educational and industrial psychology; on leadership training programs in business, government, and the military; on work in the art and science of persuasion; and on community planning. In all these fields there have been follow-up experimental and semi-experimental studies, as well as attempts to apply the findings of the experiments. Furthermore, these studies have been cited as *scientific* demonstrations of the superiority of democratic methods over autocratic ones . . . . (This body of material on democratic and autocratic leadership) represents the most ambitious attempt to connect significant laboratory findings with leadership phenomena as they exist in on-going social systems . . . .

Although four decades have passed since Lewin and his colleagues conducted their research, it continues to have an impact on how leadership styles are conceptualized and studied by small-group investigators. Their first experiment compared the group climate created by authoritarian and democratic leaders, and their second experiment added a laissez-faire leadership condition.[26] In the second experiment, which reinforced the results of the first, four clubs of eleven-year-old boys were formed in a way that made them equivalent regarding certain personal and sociometric characteristics of their members and the degree of interest in the group task. All clubs met in the same clubroom setting, two at a time in adjacent meeting spaces, and they used the same equipment box. Four adults performed the roles of *authoritarian, democratic,* and *laissez-faire* leaders in rotation so that, with minor exceptions, each of the four adults performed each of the three leadership roles in each of the four groups. The experimenters were able to manipulate group activities so that similar ones were pursued in each of the clubs. Their manipulation involved allowing the democratically led clubs to choose an activity and then imposing that activity on the authoritarian-led clubs. In the laissez-faire condition, there were a number of potential activities of the same type as those chosen by the democratically led clubs.

DISTINCTIONS BETWEEN LEADERSHIP STYLES. It is noteworthy that when clubs were under a democratic leader, they chose their own activity,

[26]Hare (1976:293-298) offers an excellent brief summary of this research; and we will draw from it and other secondary sources (including Olmsted,1959:38-42; Verba,1961: Ch. 9; Golembiewski,1962:209-212; Sherif and Sherif,1969:178; Stogdill,1974:Chs. 32,33; Shaw,1976:275-279) in summarizing it here. Among the many original sources one might consult for a more detailed description of Lewin, Lippitt, and White's work are Lewin, Lippitt, and White (1939), Lippitt (1939; 1940), Lippitt and White (1952), and White and Lippitt (1960).

but when they were under an authoritarian one, they had the group activity imposed on them. This distinction regarding amount of choice for group members provides a revealing clue about the difference between democratic and authoritarian—or *autocratic*—leadership styles. A summary of the major ways in which these two leadership styles differed from each other and from laissez-faire leadership in Lewin, Lippitt, and White's research has been offered by Verba (1961:208-209) in the following form:

Authoritarian	*Democratic*	*Laissez-Faire*
1. All determination of policy by the leader.	1. All policies a matter of group discussion and decision, encouraged and assisted by the leader.	1. Complete freedom of individual or group decision, with a minimum of leader participation.
2. Techniques and activity steps dictated by the authority, one at a time, so that future steps were always uncertain to a large degree.	2. Activity perspective gained during discussion period. General steps to group goal sketched, and when technical advice was needed, the leader suggested two or more alternative procedures from which choice could be made.	2. Various materials supplied by the leader, who made it clear that he would supply information when asked. He took no other part in work discussion.
3. The leader usually dictated the particular work task and work companion of each member.	3. The members were free to work with whomever they chose, and the division of tasks was left up to the group.	3. Complete nonparticipation of the leader.
4. The dominator tended to be "personal" in his praise and criticism of the work of each member; remained aloof from active group participation except when demonstrating.	4. The leader was "objective" or "fact-minded" in his praise and criticism, and tried to be a regular group member in spirit without doing too much of the work.	4. Infrequent spontaneous comment on member activities, unless questioned, and no attempt to appraise or regulate the course of events.

In casual conversation, especially about the relative importance of discipline, in group settings as varied as classrooms, factory production crews, athletic teams, and families, people often tend to use the term *democratic leadership* when they really mean the *laissez-faire* type. In fact, as it was applied in Lewin, Lippitt, and White's research, laissez-faire "leadership" has only the faintest resemblance to the conception of leadership we have been using in this chapter. Since it involves little or no active influence or decision-making by the ostensible leader figure, the laissez-faire condition is closer to a leaderless condition than one with an actual leader.

In many cases, the confusion between democratic and laissez-faire "leadership" seems to arise because people assume there is either authoritarian leadership or total *permissiveness,* with the latter condition often called *democratic.* However, Lewin, Lippitt, and White have suggested a way of conceptualizing *and* operationalizing leadership styles with democratic leadership located *between* authoritarian leadership and total permissiveness. This means that although democratic leaders will be less dictatorial than authoritarian, or autocratic, ones, they still will enter into and exercise influence over group decision-making, unlike laissez-faire or *totally permissive* leaders. That is, democratic leaders still will be leaders, despite their encouragement of group participation in the decision-making process. Because there may be a tendency to confuse the democratic and laissez-faire styles, it is important to keep in mind the distinctions just mentioned. Furthermore, since we identified the democratic style as a form of leadership and the laissez-faire style as more reflective of a leader*less* condition, we mainly will be interested here in specific contrasts between the authoritarian and democratic—versus laissez-faire—styles in our discussion of actual leadership styles.

From his summary description of the three leadership climates used by Lewin, Lippitt, and White in their research, Verba was able to reduce the distinctions between authoritarian and democratic leadership to five major ones. According to Verba (1961:209), they can be found in the:

1. Decision method (decisions by the leader versus decision by the group);
2. Time perspective (step-by-step direction versus broad time perspective);
3. Degree of freedom of movement of group members (highly structured behavior controlled by the leader versus freedom of movement within the activity pattern);
4. Group atmosphere (impersonal and cold versus friendly and warm); and
5. Leader's criteria for criticism of the group members (personal and arbitrary versus objective and fair).

THE LEWIN, LIPPITT, AND WHITE FINDINGS. In view of the marked differences between how authoritarian and democratic leaders exercised authority in Lewin, Lippitt, and White's experiments, it should not be surprising that the experimenters found strikingly different group reactions to these two types of leadership. The *amount* of impact of leadership style on group behavior was clearly suggested by Lippitt and White's statement " . . . in nearly all cases, differences in club behavior could be attributed to differences in the induced social (or leadership) climate rather than to constant characteristics of club personnel" (quoted in Hartley and Hartley, 1952:629). The *nature,* as well as impact, of changes in leadership style can be illustrated by the following example, cited by Golembiewski (1962:210–211), of their influence at the individual level: " . . . Sue spent nine meetings in a group with a directive atmosphere. Her behavior, especially in the later sessions, was rated very high on 'dominating ascendance.' She spent her tenth session in a group with a (more) permissive atmosphere. Her 'dominating ascendance' dropped by two-thirds in that session, and dropped further in subsequent sessions." Golembiewski noted that similar changes could be observed for whole groups when they rotated through different leadership conditions.

Since authoritarian leadership evoked two different types of group reactions, there were *four* distinct patterns of group reaction to the experimental manipulation of the leadership style variable. For some group members under authoritarian leadership, the reaction was essentially *apathetic,* while for others under this form of leadership the group reaction was basically *aggressive.* As we have suggested, these different reactions resulted from differences in leadership style and in the way groups rotated through them. For example, some clubs reacted relatively passively when they first experienced authoritarian leadership. When group leadership shifted to a more *permissive* democratic or laissez-faire style, the previously apathetic groups engaged in "great bursts of horseplay between the members" (Lippitt and White, 1952:349). This activity reflected unexpressed group tension, and it disappeared after more meetings in the more permissive atmosphere. However, when one club returned to the authoritarian condition after experiencing democratic leadership, it expressed much more discontent about relations with the leader than it had initially. Another club that was originally exposed to laissez-faire "leadership" became fairly rowdy at the outset and maintained this type of behavior throughout most of the study.[27]

A clear sense of the main thrust of Lewin, Lippitt, and White's findings about the effects of leadership style on group behavior has been provided by Shaw (1976:276). He summarized the results of one of their studies by saying:

> . . . Hostility was thirty times as great in the autocratic as in the democratic groups, and aggression was eight times as great in the autocratic as in the democratic. There was more scapegoating in the autocratic groups than in either of the other two; one group member was frequently made the target of hostility and aggression until he left the group, and then another boy would be chosen for this honor. Nineteen of the twenty boys liked the democratic leader better than the autocrat, and seven of ten liked the laissez-faire leader better than the autocrat. There was no reliable difference in the number of products produced, but the products of the democratic groups were judged to be qualitatively superior to those of the other groups.

[27]These examples were suggested by Sherif and Sherif (1969:178) and Hare (1976:296).

In addition to looking at reactions of hostility, aggression, scapegoating, liking for the leader, and group productivity, the experimenters considered factors such as demands for the leader's attention, the occurrence of "friendly, confiding relations," the tendency to make "group-oriented suggestions," reactions to hostile criticism when the leader was (purposely) absent, and orientation to work in the absence of the leader. Let us look briefly at some results concerning these latter factors to get a richer flavor of what Lewin, Lippitt, and White discovered in their research.[28]

Perhaps because gaining the leader's attention is one of the few ways of achieving higher status in a leader-dominated group, demands for the leader's attention were greater in both types of authoritarian situations than in the other group atmospheres. In regard to "friendly, confiding relations," those in democratic and laissez-faire settings initiated more "personal" and friendly encounters with their leader or ostensible leader, and those in democratic settings tended to engage in more spontaneous "confidential" exchanges than those in the other group atmospheres.

The results concerning "group-oriented suggestions" to the leader indicated that groups under a democratic leader felt freer and were more willing to make suggestions on group policy issues than in the other leadership climates. These results also indicated that the lower level of suggestions in the laissez-faire situation was not due to a feeling of restricted freedom, but instead derived from a lack of a cooperative working relationship between the ostensible adult leader and the other group members.

Groups reacted differently when exposed to hostile criticism by a strange adult (e.g., a "janitor" or "electrician") while the leader was out. In the apathetic groups, members tended to accept individually and internalize the unjust criticism, although in one or two cases they "blew off steam" in aggressive advances toward another group (that was meeting in the adjacent clubroom). In aggressive groups, frustration generally was expressed through aggressive activity toward another group, although in a number of instances members reacted directly to the source of frustration, the hostile stranger. Groups under democratic leadership were more willing to unite in rejection of the real source of frustration, the hostile stranger, and to resist aggression from another group.

While the leader was out (by design), both types of authoritarian groups did very little, the democratic group remained about as productive as it was, and the laissez-faire group became more productive. There were similar patterns of productive activity when the leader was late. Lippitt and White (1952:348) have suggested that the improved performance of the laissez-faire groups when the "leader" was absent seemed to occur because ". . . when the adult left, one of the boys exerted a more powerful leadership and achieved a more coordinated group activity than when the relatively passive adult was present."

---

[28]This brief summary of group reactions is based on summary comments by Lippitt and White (1952), which have been cited by Hare (1976:294–298).

SOME LIMITATIONS OF THE LEWIN, LIPPITT, AND WHITE STUDIES.
Despite its secure place as a landmark in the tradition of small group research,
Lewin, Lippitt, and White's work on leadership styles and atmospheres does have
certain limitations. First, this research from the 1930s seems quite a bit more
consciously ideological than much of the small-group research of the ensuing
decades (Olmsted, 1959:42); but this is not necessarily a source of scientific
weakness as long as the investigation was conducted in a systematic scientific
fashion. Indeed, its consciously ideological flavor, stressing the virtues of democracy in contrast to the shortcomings of authoritarianism, created a great deal of
interest in this work among practitioners of leadership, while at the same time its
experimental methods were a model for many subsequent small-group researchers
considering leadership *and* other aspects of small-group behavior.

More serious limitations can be mentioned. For example, Golembiewski
(1962:211–212) noted that this research was limited by its focus on formal and
externally imposed leadership. Data were not explicitly collected on the emergence of informal leadership; such data might have provided some valuable insights about how groups informally handle leadership and power problems—if
at all—in the face of unsatisfactory externally imposed formal leaders. Certain of
Lewin, Lippitt, and White's results were suggestive in this regard. For example,
there were instances in the practically leaderless laissez-faire condition when
efforts were made to achieve control over the group. It was also shown that
autocratic leaders often had difficulty gaining control over groups that previously had a laissez-faire "leader," and that groups reacting aggressively against
an autocrat may have formed a group that was unified in its rebellious feelings
toward the formal leader. Such suggestive results indicate the potential value of
focusing more fully and explicitly than Lewin and his colleagues did on the
emergence of informal leadership and its possible interplay with different styles
of externally imposed leadership. Furthermore, these results suggest the importance of examining the effects of leadership styles and changes in them when
leadership has emerged from within the group, as opposed to when it has been
externally imposed.

One of the possible dangers of accepting Lewin, Lippitt, and White's
findings at face value is that we might be tempted to exaggerate the beneficial
consequences of democratic leadership and the detrimental consequences of
autocratic or authoritarian leadership for groups and group members. This gets
us back to the ideological tone of their work. We have already noted Verba's
comment that this study has been cited as a "scientific" demonstration of the
functional superiority of democratic over authoritarian leadership. In fact, in
the decades following the original studies, there has been an accumulation of
additional ones by other investigators conducted in industrial, business, workshop, and school environments that tend to replicate the original findings. Most
of these studies have tried to show that a more permissive, friendly, and helpful
leadership style results in more effective or productive groups, as measured by
indicators such as task performance and exam scores (Sherif and Sherif, 1969:

178). In view of these results, one might wonder why we have suggested caution in generalizing from the original ones. Anderson (1963:160), who reviewed studies of this sort in the Lewinian tradition, has offered some cause to wonder:

> *The evidence available fails to demonstrate that either authoritarian or democratic leadership is consistently associated with higher productivity* (italics in original). In most situations, however, democratic leadership is associated with higher morale. But even this conclusion must be regarded cautiously because the authoritarian leader has been unreasonably harsh and austere in a number of investigations reporting superior morale in democratic groups. . . .

REFINEMENTS OF THE CLASSIC APPROACH: BEYOND LEWIN, LIPPITT, AND WHITE. While the caution suggested by Anderson may be in order, his comments do not necessarily warrant rejection of the *main thrust* of Lewin, Lippitt, and White's findings. Certainly, there is no criticism that can diminish the influence these investigators have had on group leadership research. However, the limitations we have noted, along with Anderson's comments, suggest how leadership research inspired by the work of Lewin and his colleagues could benefit from certain refinements of the classic approach. Rather than searching for different effects of ideal-typical conceptions of authoritarian and democratic (and laissez-faire) leadership styles, it would seem more fruitful to consider how the amount of group participation with the leader in decision-making affects the nature of decisions, their acceptability, the leader's legitimacy, and various other aspects of group behavior.[29] If nothing else, we would avoid some of the ideological baggage that has often become associated with "authoritarian" and "democratic" leadership. Furthermore, by interpreting distinctions between leadership styles in narrower, broader, or slightly different terms than the "authoritarian versus democratic" contrast might imply, we can gain a fuller appreciation of how leadership styles can differ and how these differences can affect group behavior.

In fact, substituting *restrictive, leader-centered, directive,* or *supervisory* for *authoritarian* (or *autocratic*) or substituting *permissive, group-oriented, participatory,* or *follower-oriented* for *democratic,* may not lead to drastically different findings or conclusions than we would have predicted from Lewin and his colleagues' original research. Nevertheless, it does help us at least begin to recognize some of the limitations of more *democratic* approaches as well as some of the potential benefits or functions of more *authoritarian* ones. For example, encouragement by the leader of broad or equal participation on the part of the group members could inhibit the efficiency and effectiveness of group decision-making and goal attainment. There are many tasks or goals—especially

[29] Among others, Verba (1961:Chs. 9, 10) has given explicit attention to this "participation hypothesis."

technical and complex ones—that require for their successful completion more frequent participation by the more skillful members, thereby implying the need for a hierarchy of group participation and influence (Horowitz and Perl-mutter, 1955). We could expect more directive than participatory leadership to be more efficient and effective in such cases. In addition, more permissive leadership (as in learner- versus teacher-centered classrooms) may increase the ambiguity of the task situation unless group members have the necessary skills to set and achieve goals on their own (McKeachie, 1954). As Hare (1976: 299) has suggested: "The best arrangement is to combine (leader) style with the characteristics of the (group members), since dull, anxious, or dependent (members) do better with a more directed form of (leadership)."

Hare also has pointed out that in normally autocratic settings such as industrial organizations and the armed services, where leaders are *expected* to be autocratic, efforts to introduce more democratic procedures usually produce member dissatisfaction and low productivity similar to what is found when autocratic methods are introduced in democratic settings. To support this state-ment, Hare cited research by Berkowitz (1953) about conferences in industry and government that showed a negative relationship between leadership sharing and the variables of group attractiveness and satisfaction with the conference. In this conference context, the chairman was supposed to exert strong central control over the meetings, and efforts by other members to make frequent suggestions of problem-solutions were discouraged. However, if the group had an urgent problem, sharing leadership had no relation to member satisfaction, apparently because this was a time of crisis and regular leadership norms were (temporarily) suspended. Other studies in industrial settings have shown a positive relationship between the level of productivity in a shop and the presence of a well-differentiated and more autocratic style of leadership (Gekoski, 1952; Kahn and Katz, 1953). Hare (1976:300) also has cited research with groups as diverse as air corps bomber crews and doctor-patient therapy relationships ("the smallest autocracy") showing superior progress in group performance when groups were under a more directive—versus permissive—leader.

Thus, it appears that we would be poorly equipped to make predictions about the effects of particular leadership styles or about changes in them with-out additional knowledge about the nature of the leadership and the context in which it is being exercised. For example, we also should probably know about such factors as: (1) the nature of leadership expectations held by group members; (2) the way leadership has been attained; (3) whether there is competition between formal and informal leaders; (4) the needs, tasks, and goals of the group as a whole; (5) the task and socio-emotional skills of group members; (6) the nature of authority in contexts outside or including the group; and (7) the general nature of environmental demands, such as task urgency, that might be imposed on the group and its leadership.

SOME PROBLEMS OF LEADERSHIP IN SMALL GROUPS: A SELECTIVE FOCUS ON RESEARCH

Two problems of leadership will interest us in this section. One concerns the emergence of crises in groups and how they affect the relative influence of leaders and the stability of leadership structures. To examine this problem, we will focus on Hamblin's (1958) study of leadership and crises. The other problem of interest here concerns obedience to authority under questionable circumstances. To consider this latter type of problem, we will look once again at Milgram's (e.g., 1963; 1964; 1965; 1973) controversial research, which we discussed earlier in regard to possible legal and ethical problems that can arise in research using deception.

Leadership and Crisis

Hamblin (1958) defined a crisis as "an urgent situation in which all group members face a common threat," and he gave as an example the case of a family confronted with a reduction or loss of income through unemployment, sickness, or death, which in themselves can be traumatizing apart from their economic consequences. His research on leadership and crisis was aimed at testing two hypotheses. The first, called *the centralization hypothesis,* was based on Weber's (e.g., 1946; 1947) writings on bureaucracy. Hamblin pointed out that a crucial feature of all crises is urgency or time pressure, and that according to Weber, bureaucracies developed as a means of responding precisely, unambiguously, and with a minimum of friction to complicated problems requiring solution in a very limited time. Since bureaucracies represent a centralization of authority, Hamblin hypothesized that influence (and leadership) would be more centralized in crisis than noncrisis periods. This means that he expected leaders to be granted more influence during crises. Hamblin's second hypothesis, called *the replacement hypothesis,* assumed that a group would replace its old leader with a new one if the old leader fails to deal adequately with the crisis.

To test these hypotheses, Hamblin used twelve three-person experimental groups in a crisis situation and twelve more three-person groups in a control situation. The experimental task involved a modified shuffleboard game lasting about thirty minutes. Each group of participants was led into the experimental room, where they were given a general but rather vague conception of the nature and rules of the game. They were instructed to try to learn the rules themselves through a trial and error process and by watching a light board. A red light flashed when a rule was violated and a green light flashed when a score was made.

The experimental subjects were college students who were told they were competing with high-school students who had previously competed in a similar experiment. Apparently, these and related instructions were effective in inducing serious involvement, since most groups acted "as though they were in a tournament." In addition, most groups were visibly satisfied as they mastered the rules and attained (experimentally manipulated) scores that were higher than those of the high-school students against whom they were supposedly competing.

The crisis was introduced for the experimental groups at the beginning of the second half of the experiment. After they had mastered the rules and achieved self-satisfaction and confidence, these groups were confronted with a change in the rules. Formerly permissible procedures were no longer allowed, and procedures that had been against the rules became permissible. Furthermore, as soon as participants learned a new rule and received a green light, the rule changed again. The new effect was that participants could not earn a single point after the rules were changed. This meant they first saw their leads vanish and then saw themselves falling farther and farther behind their rivals.

The introduction of the change in rules and its apparent effect on group performance seemed to create a real crisis for Hamblin's experimental groups. They looked more frustrated, engaged in more aggressive behavior, and were quite hostile by the end of the experiment. However, the crisis was not so severe that it appeared hopeless, for all crisis groups continued throughout the experiment to seek, find, and test new procedures. Thus, even in a relatively artificial laboratory setting, the experimenter apparently was able to create the threatening and urgent aspects of "real-life" crises.

The experimenter measured relative influence by noting the suggestions accepted for each group member throughout the game. Using this observational measure of relative influence, Hamblin produced results showing that the influence of group leaders was greater in the crisis situation than in the noncrisis (control) situation. Thus, he supported his centralization hypothesis.

Hamblin's results also supported his replacement hypothesis, for he found that nine of the twelve original leaders in the crisis groups were replaced, while only three of the twelve control group leaders were replaced. More specifically, participants who initially were second in influence rank became the new leaders in every one of the nine cases where the leader was replaced. This did not occur in the control groups. Participants who were initially second in influence rank either tied for third or became third in influence rank in the second half of the experiment. In the three cases where an original control group leader was replaced, it was the member who initially ranked third in influence who became the new leader.

Hamblin noted that his results suggested the occurrence of a struggle for influence in both the crisis and control groups. During the first half of the experiment, members ranking first and second in influence seemed to be competing for the top position. In the crisis groups, the crisis appeared to cause the loss of the top rank to the second-ranking member, with the third group member remaining relatively isolated from the struggle. In the control groups, though, most top-ranking members were successful in maintaining their position of dominance, apparently by forming a coalition with the participants who initially ranked third. This coalition seemed to freeze out of control the member initially ranking second in influence.

Since it is the nature of leadership for group members to expect and depend on leaders to assume major responsibility for resolving group problems, it is not surprising that when the problems are tougher—as in a crisis—group members will depend more on their leaders and accede more to their authority. Indeed, we have said that members attain leadership by making more valuable contributions to group value-achievement than other members. Furthermore, informal leaders maintain their authority by continuing to make highly valued contributions to the group; and by virtue of their position, they are the ones who are expected—in a normative sense—to innovate when group value-achievement is seriously disrupted or the group experiences great stress during a crisis. When they cannot meet the challenge, the group is likely to look elsewhere for someone else with high rank who might do a better job of meeting its needs. In other words, a leader's legitimacy will be most sorely tested during a crisis; and when he cannot do what is expected of a leader, the basis of group support from which his authority derives will erode and make him vulnerable to replacement by other powerful group members. Thus, just as we would expect, the lack of success of the leaders of Hamblin's crisis groups generally meant their downfall and replacement.

Research by Janis (1963) has suggested that the stress of a crisis at least initially pulls groups closer together (i.e., increases their cohesiveness) and makes them more anxious to get things done to reduce or eliminate the crisis conditions. Under such conditions, we can understand why groups will rely more on the people who have led them in the past. We can see this situation concretely in the case of families that must cope with the father's loss of his job when he has been the sole breadwinner. To the extent the family has relied on the father in the past for direction, guidance, and key decisions (because of his economic contributions), they can be expected to rely heavily on him again in the initial stages of their crisis. However, if he fails to find another job, and the mother goes to work to help them meet their economic crisis, we can expect family leadership gradually to pass from the father to the mother. In fact, according to Crosbie (1975:353), family sociologists have tended to find that as the balance of power resources shifts in favor of the mother, as in our crisis example, she will be able to control more of the family decisions *independently* of the previously established husband-dominance leadership norm. We will have more to say about such authority and power relations in the family in our discussion of power research, but for present purposes, we can conclude from our example that crises may upset even well-established leadership patterns if they are not met effectively or if they remain a problem too long.

Since it is not clear that the group members in Hamblin's experiment granted those with the most relative influence the legitimacy needed to make them real leaders, there may be some question about whether his results permit generalizations about actual leaders and leadership under crisis. While there may be ample justification for questioning Hamblin's equating high influence with leadership in his experiment, the relevance of his results to actual leadership and crises should be seen in our example and in the way we tied the results to our general conceptual framework and earlier comments about leadership in this chapter. Hollander (1976:516–517) has cited some additional findings that offer further support for Hamblin's hypotheses and also extend them.

In an experiment by Hollander, Fallon, and Edwards (1974), discussion groups evaluated proposed solutions to urban problems. Half had appointed leaders and the other half had a leader whom they elected themselves. Midway through the discussion, the groups received either a "success" or "failure" report on their progress toward a solution. The failure feedback—a crisis-like situation of stress—*increased* the elected leader's influence substantially, but not the influence of the appointed leader. By contrast, the appointed leader was more influential after the group received success feedback. Apparently, then, a group will depend more heavily on an elected than appointed leader at the outset of a crisis, perhaps because they have already indicated by the election their trust and confidence in him. To gain such trust, an appointed leader first must impress the group with his contributions and ability to lead. Apparently, the success feedback helped the appointed leader to earn such trust and influence, whereas the elected leader did not gain as much through success because it was what the group expected when they elected him. Hollander and his colleagues' study also showed that the high dependence on the elected leader exhibited by the group in the initial stages of the crisis does not last indefinitely. They found that another report of failure made the elected leader's influence drop sharply, perhaps making him vulnerable to the replacement Hamblin would have predicted.

Other research by Fallon (1973) has produced similar results, with the additional finding that the tendency to "rally around" the elected leader after initial failure feedback was more pronounced with male than female leaders. In view of our earlier discussion of sex and leadership, we might have expected this tendency. Another study of leadership and crisis by Edwards (1973) found that in the type of "crisis" caused by ambiguity or the absence of evaluative information about group goal-attainment progress, leaders will also gain influence. Overall, then, these additional studies cited by Hollander, along with Hamblin's, show the important role of crises in reinforcing an informal leader's authority if they are met effectively *or* unseating the leader if they are not.

Obedience and "Malevolent Authority"

Obviously, whether in crisis or noncrisis situations, leaders are not really leaders unless they are obeyed. Thus, a basic problem for leaders is to gain and maintain sufficient legitimacy so that they can expect group members regularly to fulfill their obligation to obey. In our discussion of leadership to this point, our focus has mainly been on how group members gain such legitimacy or how it is threatened or lost. However, as we have also suggested, it is possible for leaders to gain so much legitimacy or to acquire so many power resources to support their authority, that group members may become *too willing to obey*, even when the leader's orders are quite unreasonable, represent an abuse of authority, or violate higher moral principles. Milgram's study of obedience is focused on this other side of the leader-follower relationship.

In our previous discussion of Milgram's research we outlined the basic experimental procedures he used and some of his main findings, along with the ethical and moral issues it raised. Here, we will review the procedures and concentrate mostly on the conditions found or assumed to be associated with disobedience to *malevolent authority*.[30]

Motivated by a concern about the conditions inducing people in Nazi Germany to follow orders to participate in the extermination of the Jewish population, Milgram designed a series of experiments to help him learn more about such destructive obedience. He used a simulated shock-generating machine with 30 clearly marked voltage levels from 15 to 450 volts. From 15 to 60 volts, the voltage levels were designated on the machine as "Slight Shock;" from 75 to 120, "Moderate Shock;" from 135 to 180, "Strong Shock;" from 195 to 240, "Very Strong Shock;" from 255 to 300, "Intense Shock;" from 315 to 360, "Extreme Intensity Shock;" from 375 to 420, "Danger: Severe Shock;" and from 435 to 450 (!), "XXX." Milgram used this machine to determine how far subjects would go in hurting another, "innocent" person, merely because they were ordered to do so by an authority figure, the experimenter.

Milgram led his subjects to believe they were involved in a study of the effects of punishment on memory. Naive subjects were given the role of "teacher" and were instructed by the experimenter to punish each successive wrong answer of the "learner," an accomplice of the experimenter, with an electrical shock level 15 volts more than the prior one, and ranging up to the 450 volts at the end of the voltage scale. The shocks were not real, but the "teachers" did not know this and approached their task in this ostensible "learning experiment" quite seriously.

In the original experiment, there were 40 male subjects between the ages of 20 and 50, who represented a broad cross-section of occupations, including postal clerks, high-school teachers, salesmen, engineers, and laborers. They received $4.50 for their participation, and they were solicited through a local newspaper advertisement. Although the assignment of "teacher" and "learner" roles in each experimental session was supposed to be random, through drawing slips of paper from a hat, this process was actually "rigged" so that the naive subject in each session would become the "teacher." Immediately after drawing

---

[30] An excellent and fairly detailed summary and discussion of this research can be found in Hare (1976:40–48).

role assignments, the teacher and learner were taken to an adjacent room and the learner was strapped into an "electric chair" apparatus. Naive subjects were told that an electrode attached to the learner's wrist was also connected to the shock generator in the adjoining room where the teacher was to administer the shocks.

The learner—or "victim"—was, in fact, a trained confederate of the experimenter, who gave a standardized sequence of responses to the ostensible learning test and to the shocks following wrong answers. As the experiment proceeded, the naive subject was ordered to give increasingly severe shocks for successive wrong answers, despite the complaints, cries of pain and anguish, and eventual silence from the learner. With increasingly higher shock levels, the resistance of teachers to these orders became stronger, and eventually the subjects refused to continue their involvement. Milgram interpreted subjects' behavior up to this point as "obedience," and he was interested in discovering at what voltage level the subjects would defy authority and break off their participation.

Milgram's findings far exceeded even the most pessimistic predictions.[31] Although many subjects gave signs of extreme tension, no one disobeyed before administering 300 volts, at which point five subjects ended their involvement. It is important to realize that the 300-volt level was reached after twenty separate shocks, and at this level, the victim kicked the wall and no longer gave answers to the teacher's multiple-choice questions. Four more subjects refused to obey at the 315-volt level; two refused at the 330-volt level; and one each disobeyed at the 345, 360, and 375-volt levels. However, of the forty subjects in the experiment, *twenty-six* (!) went to the end of the shock series, while only fourteen defied the experimenter before that point. It is revealing to consider the types of remarks made by these latter subjects at the point of their disobedience, to get a clearer sense of what was involved (Milgram, 1963):[32]

(0124)   I think he's trying to communicate, he's knocking . . . . Well it's not fair to shock the guy . . . these are terrific volts. I don't think this is very humane . . . . Oh, I can't go on with this; no, this isn't right. It's a hell of an experiment. The guy is suffering in there. No, I don't want to go on. This is crazy. (Subject refused to administer more shocks.)

(0123)   He's banging in there. I'm gonna chicken out. I'd like to continue, but I can't do that to a man . . . . I'm sorry I can't do that to a man. I'll hurt his heart. You take your check . . . . No really, I couldn't do it.

[31] Milgram had provided fourteen Yale seniors, all psychology majors, with a detailed description of the experimental situation, and asked them to predict the behavior of 100 hypothetical subjects representing a cross-section of the American population from twenty to fifty years old. There was considerable consensus in their responses, with all fourteen students predicting that only an insignificant minority would go to the end of the shock series. The most "pessimistic" of these students estimated that 3 of the 100 hypothetical subjects would go to the end. Milgram also asked the question informally to colleagues, and the most general feeling was that few if any subjects would go beyond the "Very Strong Shock" (240 volts).

[32] Milgram transcribed these remarks from tape recordings of the experimental sessions.

A number of significant questions—both substantive and ethical—have been raised by Milgram's study and its results. Having suggested some ethical ones earlier, we will focus on the substantive ones here. One of the most fundamental of the substantive questions has been stated rather pithily by Gamson (1968:133): "Why do subjects continue to honor a presumed obligation to an experimenter whom they do not know, to accomplish goals which are at best vague and obscure to them and which at the same time involve virtually gratuitous injury to another human being whom they have no reason to dislike?" In addressing this question, we are almost necessarily led to a second important one, about the conditions encouraging people to defy authority of this sort. We will consider both.

Since we know there are occasions when people disobey, rebel against, and even topple their leaders, it should have come as a surprise to find so many of Milgram's subjects obedient. After all, as Gamson has implied, they were instructed to act in an extreme fashion by an experimenter they had not even met before. Furthermore, the sanctions available to the experimenter could give the appearance of being too mild to gain the desired compliance. Since he did not threaten to withdraw the $4.50, he had to rely essentially on verbal prods ranging from "Please continue" to "You have no other choice, you *must* go on" (Milgram, 1963). Evidently, these verbal prods were a great deal more effective than we initially might be inclined to believe. The reason they were tells us something very important about the exercise of authority in small groups or elsewhere.

It can be argued that the subjects in Milgram's experiments accorded the experimenter considerable legitimacy as an authority figure, because he represented the hallowed institutions of "Science" and Yale University. As a result of this legitimacy, the experimenter generally was able to overcome the subjects' reluctance to obey his dubious or personally objectionable orders by reminding them of their *obligation* to do so. Since we have all been socialized to follow orders in a variety of contexts, this reminder from a legitimate authority, who could be expected to assume responsibility for the consequences of compliance, could, and apparently did, exert a great deal of influence. When the situation is a novel or ambiguous one, as in the experiment, we further might expect a higher than usual tendency to yield to authorities people would normally trust. The essence of the operation of this "activation of commitments" mechanism, which we discussed in the last chapter as a basic social control device, has been stated by Gamson (1968:134):

Perhaps the most powerful and common means of social control is simply the conveying of expectations with clarity and explicitness coupled with clear and direct accountability for the performance of such expectations. As long as legitimacy is accorded in such situations, individuals will regard their noncompliance as a failure and any interaction which makes such a personal failure salient is embarrassing, unpleasant and something to be avoided.

The effectiveness of activation of commitments has been clearly conveyed by Gamson's comments and Milgram's results. We have seen this mechanism operate outside the laboratory in a variety of ways ultimately proving destructive for followers and leaders, as well as for victims. Indeed, in cases such as the Watergate conspiracy, where people did some peculiar things for some dubious reasons, the ultimate outcome proved more destructive for the conspirators than their intended victims. Obviously, then, the leadership problem in such cases is *too much obedience*, rather than too little, and it is a problem suggested by our previous discussion in a social control context of the dysfunctions of conformity. It is a problem in the sense that blindly following orders does more, at least in the long run, to harm group members and group equilibrium than help them. The problem can be exacerbated in small groups by the fact that a cohesive group context and widespread consensus about leadership rights can make it very difficult to resist some of the most destructive or ill-conceived orders. Let us not forget that cohesiveness, consensus, and strong leadership are not necessarily guarantees of the long-term stability of a group or the welfare of its members. Recall again the Watergate conspirators, as well as the phenomenon of "groupthink" described at the beginning of this book.

While leaders can use legitimacy to enforce orders that followers find quite objectionable, we can expect their continuing demands of this sort to place a severe strain on their legitimacy and the loyalty of their followers. In fact, even though twenty-six of the forty subjects in Milgram's experiment went to the end of the shock series as ordered, this obedience was accompanied by considerable tension and emotional strain in many cases. For example, one observer noted (Milgram, 1963):

> I observed a mature and initially poised businessman enter the laboratory smiling and confident. Within 20 minutes he was reduced to a twitching, stuttering wreck, who was rapidly approaching a point of nervous collapse. He constantly pulled on his earlobe, and twisted his hands. At one point, he pushed his fist into his forehead and muttered: "Oh God, let's stop it." And yet he continued to respond to every word of the experimenter, and obeyed to the end.

Further research by Milgram (e.g., 1964; 1965) has suggested the kinds of situational factors that might convert the uneasiness of such obedient people into disobedience. In one condition, with forty new subjects, the experimenter left after presenting the initial instructions, and issued subsequent orders over the telephone. Full obedience dropped from twenty-six of forty to nine of forty in this condition, indicating that the physical presence of the authority figure had an important impact on the compliance of reluctant followers. In fact, in this condition, some subjects reported they had administered the shock when they really had not. If the experimenter appeared in person after the subject refused over the phone, he was sometimes able to get the subject to obey again with the prod "The experiment requires that you continue."

Since face-to-face contact is a basic feature of small groups, we readily can appreciate why group leaders are so difficult to disobey, especially when they are established ones with widespread group acceptance. Milgram and others[33] have produced additional results suggesting that the tendency for group members or followers to disobey will be significantly affected by the possibility of support from other members or followers. These results parallel Asch's findings about conformity and deviance in line-judgment experimental situations. However, the crucial difference here is the normative element of legitimacy. When a leader is more widely supported, group members will be less likely to resist his orders, even when disobedience represents a righteous cause for some. Those contemplating disobedience in groups of this sort are usually able to sense the sanctions from leaders *and* the strong and unified censure from other members likely to result from it.

When there is visible resistance to a leader's orders, his legitimacy may be called into question and his influence may be weakened. Under these conditions, disobedience may be easier and more likely. Milgram found that when two people—both confederates—joined the naive subject and refused to administer the shock, 90 percent of the naive subjects also refused. Other researchers also have found that a person will be less likely to obey if others in the same situation do not, or might censure him if he does (see Hare, 1976:49).

Milgram's research offers a chilling reminder of the human potential to act inhumanely to other human beings, merely because someone in authority tells us we should. We may harbor the illusion we would have the strength of will to resist such authority. However, especially when it is exercised by a legitimate leader in an established group where our membership is important or necessary, it will be extremely difficult to overcome our own felt obligation to obey, as well as our fear of informal or formal sanctions. It is surprising how much more important these factors can become to us than the expression of our individual desires or personal conscience. Yet it offers cogent proof of the influence of social structures or in this case, leadership.

Despite the dire implications of Milgram's findings, we know that people in groups do resist, disobey, compete, and rebel against, their leaders. As we implied earlier, the capacity to do these things, *or withstand them,* effectively depends on how well interpersonal or collective power is exercised. In the last major segment of our treatment of leadership and power we will consider basic assumptions and findings concerning the relationship of leaders to interpersonal and collective power attempts. However, before getting to this discussion, we will take a brief excursion into the realm of "applied sociology", to consider some practical advice for leaders. In fact, this excursion is an extension of the types of things we have been considering throughout our discussion of leadership.

---

[33] Hare (1976:49) has cited examples of this other work.

SOME RULES OF LEADERSHIP: PRACTICAL
APPLICATIONS OF GROUP LEADERSHIP KNOWLEDGE

Although they were written nearly three decades ago, Homans's (1950) "rules of leadership" still retain qualities of relevance and utility for leaders today. This is because the general aspects of establishing and maintaining effective group leadership remain the same today as they were then and because Homans had a firm and broad grasp of knowledge about them that he translated into meaningful practical principles. For these reasons and because Homans has managed to summarize a great deal of what we have said here about group leadership, we will briefly consider his "rules" before discussing leadership and power. In considering these rules, it is important to keep in mind the basis of each in sociological knowledge, as well as possible implications for group structure and functioning.

Homans (1950:425–440) identified eleven rules, and we will summarize here the nature and meaning of each one:

1. *"The leader will maintain his own position.* (This means that) a leader will be able to do nothing to lead his group unless he is established as a person from whom authoritative orders will come." (In small groups, a leader will have to achieve and maintain high social rank before being successful in originating group interaction and gaining legitimate authority.)
2. *"The leader will live up to the norms of his group."* (Group members achieve and maintain high rank by conforming closely and frequently to the most central group norms.[34]) "The leader must set an example."
3. *"The leader will lead."* (If a leader is supposed to originate interaction for other group members and make decisions for them, any failure on his part to do so, to take the initiative, will make him that much less a leader. People do not seem to object to clear, firm orders, specifying exactly who is to do what, at what time, and in what way, just because they are orders. Rather, people appear to welcome orders in any situation in which they consider them appropriate, and they would be confused without them. Especially in an emergency concerning the whole group, members will expect the leader to take charge.)
4. *"The leader will not give orders that will not be obeyed.* This is the converse of the last (rule)." (When leaders give orders that are not obeyed, they have, by that fact, undermined their rank, since rank and influence are mutually related, as well as undermined the expectation by group members that future orders will or should be obeyed. Furthermore, nothing does more to create confusion among followers or to lead them to doubt the leader's competence.)
5. *"In giving orders, the leader will use established channels."* (If group members are to understand that a lieutenant's orders must be obeyed, just as the

---

[34] Homans (1950) originally believed that rank and conformity were related in a positive linear fashion. However, he later acknowledged (e.g., Homans, 1974) that this conception probably needed refinement. That is, he later recognized that leaders were allowed some freedom to deviate from less important norms once they established their position.

leader's own orders are obeyed, the leader must maintain the social rank of his lieutenants. This means that he must not "pull rank" unnecessarily in relations with them or override their orders unless it is absolutely necessary, if the leader generally wants their orders followed. The position of lieutenants is maintained not only by the leader's communicating decisions through them but also by allowing them access to him. By asking their advice, the leader helps establish their position. However, it should be recognized that the leader is not asking lieutenants to make decisions for him; to do that might destroy his position. What the leader is doing is asking for advice on which to base *his own* decision. Using established channels also means that leaders will discourage interaction from followers to themselves that does not pass through their lieutenants, especially when it could lead to authoritative decisions.)

6. *"The leader will not thrust himself on his followers on social occasions."* (People who are equal in social rank tend to interact frequently in "social" settings. When a leader interacts frequently with a typical group member, rather than with his lieutenants, who are closer in social rank, the leader is lowering his social rank. If his orders are to be obeyed, the leader cannot afford to do this. Or, if the leader does not lower his social rank, his action may have an equally bad result. Members may expect the leader to originate interaction in "social" settings, just as the leader does elsewhere, and if he begins doing this, he will destroy the relaxed and casual nature of usual association among equals. The leader may embarrass followers, or himself. Furthermore, the leader might encourage followers to avoid his lieutenants in making demands of him, and the leader needs some insulation from this possibility. None of this is to imply that leaders should completely avoid their followers in "social" contexts. Instead, the implication is that in order to maintain their own and their lieutenants' positions, leaders should interact more frequently with them than other group members.)

7. *"The leader will neither blame nor, in general, praise a member of his group before other members."* (The leader is not the only group member who determines social rank; the opinions of other members are important, too. Thus, group members may not be willing to accept the leader's evaluation. When leaders blame a follower in public, they are not only humiliating the follower; they also may be casting some doubt on their own reputation for justice. If they blame one of their lieutenants, they may be undermining their own authority. Occasional public praise of a group member may be admirable, but frequent praise may cause embarrassment by putting undue pressure on the rest of the group to accept an evaluation they may not be ready to accept.) "So praise by all means. Nothing is more important. But praise in private."

8. *"The leader will take into consideration the total situation."* (This implies that group leaders will maintain a dynamic group equilibrium—or one that responds to necessary changes—by taking into account the needs and goals of the whole group and its relations with its environment. That is, group decision should be based on knowledge about the interrelationship of the group's environment, its technology for dealing with it, relations between

the group and its environment, the internal system of the group, and its normative structure.)

9. *"In maintaining discipline, the leader will be less concerned with inflicting punishment than with creating the conditions in which the group will discipline itself."* (When something has gone wrong in the group the leader would be well-advised to ask for an explanation of the mistake from the apparently responsible person and ask how it might be avoided in the future, rather than to bawl out this person without any questions. This approach will accomplish at least four things: (1) The leader will escape punishing an innocent person. (2) If the person apparently responsible is actually responsible, the leader will avoid humiliating this person and lowering his or her rank. (3) The leader may begin to recognize the underlying cause of the problem. (4) By asking for an explanation, the leader may be taking the most effective step toward avoiding the problem in the future. Obedience, like conformity, depends on the self-correcting relationships of the social system, and in these relationships explicit punishment of wrongdoers by the leader may only play a small part. Instead of punishing mistakes, the leader should concentrate more on the conditions in the group as a whole causing a breakdown of authority and try to correct them. This does not mean a leader should never use punishment or sanctions. It is fully justified when the offense is important, when it is a clear case of disobedience, and when responsibility has been clearly established. In fact, the group will expect sanctions to be applied in such cases, and the failure to do so may undermine the leader's legitimacy and acceptance of the group's normative structure. However, in using punishment, a leader must be careful not to ignore the disease in treating its symptoms. Leaders who have established their legitimacy will not need to "breathe down the necks" of their followers.)

10. *"The leader will listen."* (Leaders must be well-informed about their groups if they are to make appropriate and beneficial decisions; and becoming well-informed will involve trying to know their followers as well as possible. This may seem to conflict with the rule about not thrusting themselves on followers on social occasions, but that rule has more to do with situations where several followers are gathered together. Leaders will not violate that rule if they seek interaction with each follower alone.) "The greatest barrier to free communication between leader and follower is the leader's authority. . . ." (The leader must be careful not to make moral judgments or threaten to take action in talking to a follower, for this stifles the relationship with the weight of authority.) "The leader must not only be available— his door must be open—but also keep quiet when he is available." (By listening and accepting, the leader will become better informed and give followers a chance to see problems more clearly by talking about them. The leader will have to give fewer orders when members realize themselves what action ought to be taken. Also, the leader will gain the respect and gratitude of members by taking the time to listen to each one.)

11. *"The leader will know himself."* "If . . . (a leader) must know his men well, he must know himself still better." (Although this rule did not follow from

1

Homans's group analysis, he still believed it important enough to be given special emphasis, too.)

LEADERSHIP AND POWER IN SMALL GROUPS

From Homans's "rules," we are able to gain a better and clearer sense of what leaders should, and should not, do if they want to maintain their legitimacy and authority and use that authority effectively. Obviously, though, not all group leaders follow these rules or other relevant ones; and as a result, they begin to slide from their high and special position in the group. That slide will be marked by a loss of legitimacy, which means they have been unable to retain the trust, confidence, and respect of group members.

Group members may begin to lose faith in, and question, their leaders after experiencing a series of blatant abuses of authority or after a crisis, failure, or lapse has demonstrated their inadequacies. In cases where leaders have severely tested their legitimacy or placed great strain on it, as in Milgram's experiment, it may take only one act of overt defiance that is mishandled or handled too weakly, to begin a ground swell of disobedience. If a leader can no longer rely on "activation of commitments" to contain this disobedience, he or she may turn to interpersonal or collective power to try to control it. Of course, when leaders begin to rely increasingly on power to enforce their decisions and orders, the stability of their leadership is likely to be in serious jeopardy. In this final segment of our treatment of leadership and power in small groups, we will be interested in how both interpersonal and collective forms of power affect group leadership.

LEADERSHIP AND INTERPERSONAL POWER

General Assumptions and Findings

In restricting our focus to interpersonal power as it relates to leadership, we have left broader considerations of interpersonal power in groups largely to others (e.g., Hopkins, 1964; Jacobson, 1972). However, since we already have suggested how interpersonal power can be used to establish or challenge leadership and how leadership can enhance and be enhanced by interpersonal power, there may seem to be little more to say within this restricted focus. In fact, though, there have been studies concerning reactions to the use of different forms of interpersonal power by leaders, and other studies showing the relationship of interpersonal power to the stability of group leadership structures. In particular, in the latter regard, there have been some interesting family studies giving us some detailed insights into the opposition of interpersonal power resources to leadership structures. Thus, there really are a few more things to say about interpersonal power before we consider collective power.

GROUP REACTIONS TO THE USE OF POWER BY LEADERS. Research has suggested that the type of power used by leaders to enforce their orders will affect how group members perceive them. For example, Mulder *et al.* (1965) manipulated the amount of power of leaders by varying the magnitude of rewards or fines that the leader could administer to group members. They looked at how members rated their leaders on a number of attributes after interacting with them.[35] They found that the more power a leader had, the more self-confidence and self-satisfaction members attributed to him. However, as we might have predicted from Homans's "rules of leadership," ratings of the leader as a "nice fellow" and the degree of preference for him as an associate in a social situation, were negatively correlated with the amount of a leader's power. Thus, more powerful leaders tend to be ones in whom members may have more confidence and to whom they may grant more legitimacy, but they are not people with whom regular group members are likely to become friendly.

Similar findings about reactions to more and less powerful leaders have been produced by Johnson and Ewens (1971). Their study focused on a worker's perceptions of a supervisor who either used his power to produce unfavorable outcomes for the worker (i.e., exercised "coercive power"), believed he was using coercive power (but actually could not affect the worker's outcomes), or did not exert control over the worker's outcomes and did not believe he could. In contrast to the other power conditions, the supervisor exercising coercive power was perceived as unfriendly and self-assured—even if he did not realize the consequences of his power were coercive. In addition, workers expressed greater confidence in their impressions of the powerful than nonpowerful supervisors.

Other research by Schlenker *et al.* (1970) has suggested that the amount of compliance gained by a leader using coercive power will depend on the leader's behavior after communicating the threat. When the threat is followed by *accommodative behavior* (i.e., behavior benefiting both the more and less powerful parties in the relationship), the target of the threat is more compliant than when the powerful person is *exploitative* (i.e., tries to gain benefits for himself at the expense of the other).

In subsequent research concerning the effects of switching between coercive and reward power on target compliance, Schlenker and some other colleagues (Schlenker *et al.,* 1976) found that the initial selection and use of a particular form of power will set the tone for later interaction by affecting the target's perception of the source of power. In particular, an initially noncredible threatener (noncredible coercive power) or an initially credible promisor (credible reward power) will produce a more cooperative and benevolent climate and make the target more responsive in the future to alternative power modes than

---

[35]We are relying on Shaw's (1976:265–266) brief summary of this research. We will also use Shaw as a basis for discussing studies by Johnson and Ewens (1971) and by Schlenker et al. (1970), in the following paragraphs (p. 266).

will their opposites (credible coercive power or noncredible reward power). These latter forms of power will be more likely to produce an initally competitive and malevolent climate in which there will tend to be higher resistance to alternative power modes in the future.

Evidently, then, leaders will be better off relying on reward power (or empty threats) than coercive power (or disingenuous promises) to gain immediate compliance, and especially, to establish a climate where compliance can be expected in the future. Of course, when leaders believe they need threats rather than promises, they are probably indicating their faltering legitimacy and influence. Apparently, the detrimental consequences of the coercion may be offset somewhat when it is followed by accommodation rather than exploitation. Accommodation may not completely patch up the leader's problems, but exploitation can be expected to make them worse.

Crosbie (1975:349-350) has suggested a number of factors that could affect the likelihood that a group member will try to mobilize his or her power resources to resist a leader's orders. Included among them are:

1. the member's distrust of the leader or the strength of the belief that the leader will act against the member's interests;
2. the importance of the member's interests or the magnitude of profit the member expects to gain by defying or challenging the leader;
3. the amount of uncommitted resources the member has at his or her disposal;
4. the magnitude of opportunity costs or the opportunities the member must forego from his or her use of resources;
5. the member's self-confidence or the probability with which he or she expects the leader to give in; and
6. the positive or negative consequences the member expects his or her actions to have on future interaction with the leader and other group members.

Normally, leader-follower relations are supposed to involve a suspension of reward-cost or self-interest considerations. However, when a follower is not well-integrated into a group, no longer trusts his or her leader, and has a conflict of interest with him or her, this normal relationship of leadership may be converted into one of interpersonal power. If so, the considerations raised by Crosbie may then apply and enable us to predict when the disgruntled group member will attempt to resist or challenge the leader.

INTERPERSONAL POWER AND THE STABILITY OF GROUP LEADERSHIP. The key to understanding when individual group members will try to exert power against leaders is less likely to be individual distrust than distrust by the group as a whole. We must keep in mind that leadership and legitimacy are not individual matters, but are embedded in group norms and structures. Thus, even when a leader has lost the trust of a particular member, who would rather act some other way or have the leader act in a different way, the leader may still be able to rely on the resource of his or her legitimacy and the active support of other group members to maintain control over wayward or potentially threatening members.

Even when leaders enjoy substantial legitimacy, they may still face opposing power attempts from members who disagree with them, are poorly integrated into the group, *and* have considerable power resources of their own. In fact, though, since legitimate leaders tend to have a greater reserve of power resources than others in the group, they may have more difficulty with less powerful than more powerful members in many instances. As we noted earlier, group members with no other power resource than their own dependence, may, at times, find it a quite potent means of getting their own way in dealings with leaders.

On the basis of our prior discussion in this chapter, we can assume less legitimate leaders will have more difficulty enforcing their orders and winning power struggles than more legitimate ones, especially if they must consistently rely on threats, rather than persuasion or promises. Furthermore, leaders probably will be more vulnerable to replacement in power struggles with followers who have been almost as powerful, if they cannot deal effectively with group crises or problems (Hamblin, 1958). These generalizations would seem to apply especially to leaders who have emerged from within the group and maintain their position by continuing to make valued contributions to it and its members. Research by Katz *et al* (1957) has suggested that when emergent leaders have difficulty establishing themselves, they may become highly vulnerable to replacement if they must lead the group on tasks imposed by someone else that they would not have chosen themselves.

The replacement of one leader by another could result in relatively little change in leadership or other group structures. Group members may expect the same basic things of the new leader as they did of the old, and the new leader may run the group in essentially the same way the old leader ran it in the past. The only significant change, apart from getting used to a new personality in charge, may be in the relative power of the old and new leaders. However, a change in leaders could mean a significant change in leadership as well, especially if the replacement process reflects or creates a substantial shift in the distribution of power resources in the group. A study by Wolfe (1959) about power and authority in the family gives us some insight into the dynamic elements that can characterize changes in power and leadership in small groups.

Leadership and Interpersonal Power in the Family: A Selective Focus on Research

The purpose of Wolfe's study was to examine several possible sources of interpersonal power in the husband-wife relationship and their effects on the family leadership or authority structure. He divided leadership structures for the families in his interview sample into four basic types:

1. The *wife-dominant type* was found in families in which the wife's range of authority was considerably larger than her husband's.

2. The *syncratic type* was found in families in which there was nearly a balance of relative authority and the shared range was equal to or greater than the combined individual ranges of authority of the husband and wife.
3. The *autonomic type* was found in families having a nearly equal balance of relative authority but the husband's and wife's combined individual ranges were greater than their shared range, i.e., the husband and wife had separate but equal areas of decision-making.
4. The *husband-dominant type* was found in families in which the husband's range of authority was considerably larger than his wife's.

Wolfe used his interview data to examine the relationship between these family authority structures and the accompanying distribution of major family power resources. By looking at his results, we can gain a better sense of how changes in power resources can cause basic shifts in leadership *structures* as well as in leaders.

Wolfe's main findings concerning power and authority were the following ones:

1. Husband-dominant families are generally high on mean annual income and on general social status; wife-dominant families are generally low on these two variables. Since family income and status tended to derive from the husband, this finding supports the hypothesis that husbands who are generally more successful in income and job have more power and derive more authority in the home than husbands who are less successful.
2. Wives in husband-dominant families are less likely ever to have worked or to be currently working outside the home than wives in any other authority type. Working outside the home gives wives more power and enables them to achieve more authority than wives who do not work.
3. The spouse who is the dominant authority figure in the home is generally most likely to handle the family money and bills. This means that control of family financial resources will be either a basic source or a reflection of family authority. This control may be expected to reinforce authority in either case.
4. Wolfe proposed that the strong need for love and affection on the part of the wife is a source of power and authority for the husband (or vice versa, we would add). He found relatively little difference in this need among husband-dominant, syncratic, and autonomic families, but a much lower need in the wife-dominant families. This suggested a reinterpretation of his finding. He proposed that a strong need for affection is a source of power for the other spouse only under special circumstances (e.g., when one has no other significant resources), but a weak need enables the person to develop and exercise more freely his or her own power. That is, a wife or husband not seeking emotional support from a spouse may tend to feel quite free to exercise power from other need-resource bases, while one who needs continual affection (and has few other sources of gratification) may fear the loss of this affection if she or he tries to gain too much authority.

5. The authority of the wife increases over the years of marriage so that husband-dominant wives tend to be younger, and wife-dominant wives are older. A relative increase in the wife's resources and a decrease in her need for those of her husband, over the years, may account for this pattern, since they will tend to increase the relative power of the wife.

From Wolfe's findings we can clearly see how shifts in power resources (e.g., employment of wife *or* husband, control of family financial resources, need for affection in the family) can substantially alter the structure of leadership authority in small groups. Crosbie (1975:353) has noted that, along with a number of other similar kinds of studies in family sociology, Wolfe's research strongly supports the argument that the distribution of power resources in a group plays an important mediating function between the influence specified by the norms of the leadership structure and the actual influence in ongoing interaction. Wolfe's research also suggests that women, or men, may be able to overcome general societal expectations about how authority ought to be distributed in families in their culture if they develop a power base that is substantially inconsistent with the societal leadership norm.

COALITION FORMATION AS A PROBLEM OF SMALL GROUP LEADERSHIP

Especially in larger groups, it may be quite difficult for individual group members to develop power resources on their own that will be able to match the authority and power of leaders. However, by combining their resources with those of others also disagreeing with the leader, individual group members can substantially increase their chances of success in power encounters with leaders. A subgroup of members who combine resources in this way to influence group decisions is called a *coalition*. Although we might be more inclined to view coalitions as opponents of leadership, we should remember that there are also "conservative" ones that form in defense of the prevailing leadership structure. However, in this section, we will focus on coalition formation as a *problem* of small-group leadership, which means we will be more concerned with "revolutionary" than "conservative" coalitions.

Revolutionary coalitions can be a problem of leadership in the sense that they cause substantial disruptions and transformations in the patterning of leadership in small groups. Of course, this does not imply a particular value judgment about the failure or success of such coalition efforts, but it does indicate the amount of power they can exert to bring about group change. We noted in our initial consideration of coalitions that revolutionary ones are unlikely to form when leaders are strong, i.e., when they are dictators or have substantial veto power. In this section, we will consider in more detail the conditions of their formation and their possible implications for group leadership.

Formation and Composition of Revolutionary Coalitions

Caplow's (1968) coalition studies indicate that revolutionary coalitions are more likely to include medium- and low-status members than high-status members. Crosbie (1975:398) has cited three reasons that might explain this type of coalition composition. First, group members with medium and low status have the most to gain by a change in the group structures. Second, weaker members with inadequate power resources of their own are more likely to recognize the need for a coalition. And third, weaker members are more attractive coalition partners because of their more limited resources.

The attractiveness of weaker group members as coalition partners is explained by Simmel's (1950) "tertius gaudens"—or "third who enjoys"—principle we discussed in the first chapter. Since these people are too weak to control decisions by themselves, even in coalitions, they enjoy the position of being sought after for their support by each of the more powerful members trying to form a coalition. Although they are limited, the resources of weak group members may still be enough to swing the balance of power in favor of a particular coalition. When this happens, weak members will have "superadded power" (Crosbie, 1975:398).

Both Caplow (1968) and Gamson (1961) have offered explanations of the paradox that "weakness is strength." According to Caplow, the weak member is appealing because he can be dominated within a coalition. According to Gamson, he is attractive as a coalition partner because he contributes a smaller proportion of the resources to it. Gamson assumes that coalition members will hold a *parity norm,* prescribing that members ought to get from coalition agreements payoffs that are proportional to their resources, or what they contribute to it. If this is true, more powerful group members will be most attracted to others having only enough resources to make a prospective coalition a successful one, because the more powerful members will maximize their payoffs in this type of coalition.[36]

Perceived Support for the Leader and Upward Mobility as Determinants of Revolutionary Coalition Formation and Behavior

Although they may be logical or appealing coalition members, medium- and low-status members may not always be interested in revolutionary coalitions, even when others want them to join. Michener and Lyons (1972) have conducted an experiment in which they examined conditions under which low-status members would be most attracted to such coalitions. In particular, they considered the effects of the prospects of upward mobility by low-status members and perceived strength of support accorded the leader, on the activation of revolution-

---

[36] For an excellent general summary and assessment of major theoretical perspectives on coalition formation, see Gamson (1964).

ary coalitional behavior by low-status group members. They hypothesized that such coalitional activity would be activated when there is a lack of potential upward mobility and a perceived lack of support for the leader by others in the group.

The subjects were female undergraduates[37] who participated in groups of three.[38] Although subjects believed that their group consisted of one high-status member and two with low status, all were actually assigned low status. The mobility factor was manipulated when subjects received their role assignments. Each received written instructions indicating either that she might move up to a high-status (leadership) position during the second half of the experiment (Mobility condition) or that she had no chance of attaining a high-status position (No Mobility coalition). The factor of support for the high-status leader was manipulated through the use of opinion messages sent to subjects, ostensibly from the other low-status group member. Perceived Support for the leader was induced by sending messages indicating extremely positive impressions and evaluations of the leader by the other low-status member. The No Support condition was created by sending messages indicating extremely negative impressions and evaluations. The No Support messages also gave the impression that the other low-status member opposed the leader and would consider a coalition.

These manipulations were used in a context where subjects worked on a judgmental task over several trials. During each trial, the low-status members could engage in coalitional behavior to try to take control of decision-making prerogatives (regarding reward distribution) from the higher-status group member. Possible motivation for coalition activity was created by indicating to low-status subjects early in the experiment that the leader intended to usurp the lion's share of winnings from group goal-attainment for herself. Subjects were given an opportunity to redistribute rewards in some way other than that stipulated by the leader. They believed the situation allowed the low-status members, by acting in a coalition, to force a redistribution. This redistribution could not be achieved by one person acting alone. Michener and Lyons wanted to discover how the mobility and support factors affected the desire of low-status group members to engage in coalitional behavior to seize control of their group under such conditions.

The experimenters found stronger pro-coalition attitudes when there was no support than when there was support for the leader. They also found that

[37]Females were used because Michener and Lyons believed they would provide a stiff test of their hypotheses. Prior research (e.g., Vinacke, 1959; Uesugi and Vinacke, 1963) had suggested that females (as compared with males) did not like to form coalitions against each other, but instead preferred to convert potentially antagonistic situations into cooperative ones.

[38]Each subject began with two others, and this three-person "group" allegedly functioned as a unit through the experiment. In fact, each person was run individually, with written communications ostensibly from the other two subjects in the session being supplied by the experimenter.

subjects engaged in more extreme efforts to form redistributive coalitions in No Support conditions. Subjects made stronger efforts to form coalitions as the trials of the experiment progressed, and this was especially marked in the No Support condition. Thus, once again, we see clear evidence of the importance of legitimacy in determining whether leaders will be resisted or challenged, even when the legitimacy is based on support from just one other (low-status) member in a group of three.

Although the data did not demonstrate an effect of the mobility factor on either attitudes or activity regarding coalition formation, information from a questionnaire following the final experimental trial suggested how variables related to mobility affected subjects' behavior. For example, analysis of this information showed that while nonmobiles believed recalcitrant activity would "have no effect" on mobility possibilities, mobiles felt it "might lessen my chances." Thus, mobiles viewed revolutionary activity as precluding promotion. They seemed to appreciate the inherent contradiction between rising to the top of the status system by conformity to the standards of high-status members and subverting the status system by revolutionary coalitional activity. Michener and Lyons speculated that if the mobiles believed (much more than the nonmobiles) that the leader would strongly disapprove of forced reward reallocation, or if the mobiles valued the status hierarchy more highly than nonmobiles, then mobility would have affected the dependent variables. However, the mere possibility of upward mobility and the belief insurgence would preclude mobility were not enough by themselves to deter radicalism among mobiles, or make them significantly less inclined toward it than nonmobiles. Some of the post-experimental data offered support for these speculations.

Some Additional Factors Affecting Mobilization
of Revolutionary Coalitions

Another experimental study, by Lawler (1975), has indicated some additional factors affecting the frequency and severity of coalitional activity by subordinates against a leader. Lawler used male subjects who participated in triads consisting of a leader (who was a confederate) and two subordinates (the subjects). He was interested in the effects of inequitable reward allocations, the likelihood of leader retaliation, and status differences between potential allies, on mobilization of revolutionary coalitions. In regard to the first of these factors, he found that inequitable, as opposed to equitable, group leaders induced more frequent and more severe revolutionary coalitions. He induced Equity through having the leader allocate collective winnings in accordance with relative status. In the Inequity condition, the leader usurped 70 percent of the collective winnings, rather than the 50 percent justified by his (assigned) status-rank, and gave the other group members the remaining winnings in accordance with the relative status-rank of each.

Lawler pointed out that his treatment of inequity extended Michener and Lyons' research in two important ways. He noted:

. . . First, in contrast to the correlation data on perceptions of inequity, the present research manipulates inequity and clearly demonstrates its causal influence on insurgent coalitions. Second, in the Michener and Lyons study, coalitions automatically *reallocated* the group's outcomes, providing subjects with "perfect information" on the results of a revolutionary coalition. While in the present research, coalitions destroyed a portion of the leader's outcomes and the coalitional success was uncertain because it depended on the response of the leader to the insurgency. This uncertainty enhances the importance of the inequity finding. Even when confronted with such uncertainty, subordinates more readily coalesced against an inequitable leader (p. 174).

In Lawler's study, the importance of inequity was further illuminated by questionnaire data. He found that inequity aroused more anger toward the leader and induced lower endorsement for the leader's hegemony, i.e., reduced his legitimacy. Inequity increased the extent the coalition was perceived as necessary to protect a member's interest; to decrease the extent subordinates were reluctant to coalesce because of their monetary stake in the group; and to increase both subordinates' sense of common interest and their expectations of support for the coalition from each other.

Lawler pointed out that "expected-other-support" for insurgent coalitions was clearly the most important cognitive determinant, among those examined, of coalition frequency and severity. These expectations are important because as Michener and Lyons' study suggested, they affect the way subordinates feel about joining a coalition. When expected support for the coalition is lower—or expected support of the leader is higher—subordinates tend to take a more cautious approach, push less adamantly for a coalition, and make more moderate proposals. Needless to say, the result of both subordinates adopting this approach would be lower coalition frequency and severity.

As we noted, Lawler also looked at the effects of the likelihood of leader retaliation and status differences between subordinates on mobilization of revolutionary coalitions. In regard to manipulation of the retaliation variable, instructions informed subjects either that leaders usually retaliated about 90 percent of the time when subordinates opposed them (high-likelihood-of-retaliation) or that leaders usually retaliated about 10 percent of the time in such cases (low-likelihood-of-retaliation). Leaders retaliated by keeping an even larger share of the collective winnings. Status differences were manipulated by assigning subjects either equal or unequal status weights (ostensibly based on their respective levels of relative task competence). In both status conditions, the leader (confederate) was awarded a status weight of 50 percent, ostensibly based on his superior task ability. It was found that the threat of leader retaliation produced more severe coalitional action on one of the three experimental trials, and that status differences aroused perceptions of different interests of subordinates. However, in general, no significant effects of likelihood of retaliation *or* status differences were found regarding frequency or severity of coalitional activity.

Lawler summarized the main thrust of his results in the following terms:

> It is not only dissatisfaction that is important to coalitional responses to inequity, but the fact that subordinates expect others to share their disenchantment and be receptive to mobilizing insurgent action. Inequity probably increases subordinates' sense of "common position" *vis-à-vis* a leader and engenders a "class consciousness" that is reflected in mutual expectations of support. The significance of expected support as a mediating mechanism suggests that future applications of equity theory to collective movements should examine the criteria persons use to infer that others are likely to be receptive to coalitional proposals and the means through which subordinates communicate their discontent to each other....

Lawler's comments are an appropriate note on which to end this chapter. He has offered us substantial insight into mobilization of revolutionary coalitions, and in doing so, has further emphasized the importance of inequity in the allocation of rewards in this mobilization process. By emphasizing inequity, he has provided a transitional link between our consideration of leadership and power in this chapter and our treatment of status relations and reward allocation in the next one.

SUMMARY

This chapter has covered a wide range of topics concerning leadership and power in small groups. It defined leadership in terms of its relationship to the social structure of the group rather than to one or more specific personality traits. It proposed the notion of *leadership structure* to refer to the distribution of decision-making rights and obligations in groups. When group members grant one or more of their fellow members the right to make binding decisions within a particular scope for the group as a whole, they provide legitimation of their group's leadership or authority. Leaders can only effectively maintain their special position in small groups by maintaining the legitimacy of their decisions and influence attempts.

Leaders perform a variety of functions for their group, including coordinating, supervising, and motivating. These and other types of functions generally can be subsumed under or related to the functional categories of pattern maintenance, goal attainment, adaptation, and integration that were presented in our earlier discussion of functional models of the small group as a social system. The basic functions of leadership may be performed by specialists in a *differen-*

tiated or *pluralistic* leadership structure, or by individual "great men" who assume most or all of the major responsibilities of leadership themselves.

The main difference we have proposed between leadership and power as forms of influence is that compliance to a leader is normative, involving a suspension of personal judgment, while compliance to a power source is not. We have suggested that power relations involve definite considerations of rewards and costs, and we have defined the concept of power as "the ability to cause at will a change in another person's behavior through the promise of reward and/or the threat of punishment" (Crosbie, 1975:346). Leadership and power can become tightly intertwined in actual small-group interaction because a group member may not be able to earn a position of leadership in the group without first effectively exercising power. Once established as a leader, this person may use this special position and its prerogatives to reinforce or enhance his or her power base.

Power may be exercised at the level of individual interpersonal relationships or at a collective level in small groups, and we considered power at both levels in relation to group leadership. One of the most interesting resources people use to exercise interpersonal power is dependence, and it has attracted considerable interest among small-group investigators. We looked at the nature and uses of dependence as a power resource of weak or low-status members of small groups.

At the collective level, support from other group members is used as a power resource by coalitions. Coalitions are subgroups that employ this resource of collective support in an organized effort to influence group decision-making. They may be *conservative,* if they are concerned about defense of the existing leadership structure and leaders, or *revolutionary,* if their aim is to change the status quo or challenge leadership. We were mainly concerned with revolutionary coalitions, and the structural implications, especially for leadership, of their rebellious activity. However, we also considered in more general terms the characteristics of coalitions and coalition formation situations.

The major focus of our discussion of assumptions and findings in this chapter was on leadership and how power relates to leadership. In considering the emergence of leadership structures in small groups, it should be recognized that some groups may be without one, at least for a while, and that leadership can derive either from outside or within the group. We looked at how factors like talkativeness, high levels of perceived contribution to group value-achievement, perceived competence, good first impressions, and positively evaluated external status characteristics facilitate the attainment of leadership by particular group members. *Structures* of leadership were assumed to emerge under group conditions that include: intermember compatibility; consensus about who should be leader; variations in social status, task ability, and leadership capacity among group members; strong collective commitment to group goal attainment; the presence of explicit goal-relevant and relatively complex tasks; and large group size.

An important implication of the emergence of group leadership is that group members have surrendered willingly some of their personal autonomy and decision-making prerogatives to allow one or more other members to make decisions for their group. A second, and related, important implication is that one or more group members have accepted willingly the responsibility of making group decisions, along with the prerogatives of leadership. There are various factors affecting the desire to lead a group, but once an individual who has been motivated by this desire achieves the acceptance or legitimation of the group, this person is likely to enjoy a relatively stable base of support for his or her influence, since the leadership structure tends to be an especially stable aspect of group structure. Of course, leaders are not totally secure in their position. Just as competent performance in group activities can lead to the attainment of leadership, incompetent performance—especially during a crisis—can lead to a leader's replacement. In addition, it happens, occasionally, that leaders voluntarily give up their special status. In either case, though, change of *leaders* does not necessarily imply a change in the *leadership structure,* since the role expectations and performance of new leaders may be similar in most respects to prior patterns of leadership.

When leadership structures become differentiated or pluralistic, the main functional distinction tends to be between task and socio-emotional specialists. We examined a number of important factors, including task legitimacy, basis of leadership, goal consensus, and the nature of reward systems, affecting how much leadership differentiation occurs in groups and how task and socio-emotional leadership functions are performed.

To understand the nature and implications of group leadership, it is important to know the *style* of leadership as well as whether or how it is differentiated. We looked at the classic studies of leadership styles by Lewin, Lippitt, and White, and considered how authoritarian, democratic, and laissez-faire styles differed and how they affected the socio-emotional atmosphere of the group, liking for the leader, and group productivity. We focused mainly on comparisons between authoritarian and democratic leadership. From this comparative perspective, some of the major findings produced by Lewin and his colleagues were that: the atmosphere of authoritarian-led groups was more hostile; democratic leaders were much better liked; the products of democratically led groups were qualitatively superior, though not greater in number; and the absence of the democratic leader had little effect on productive activity in the group, while group members did very little when the authoritarian leader was absent.

Despite the importance of Lewin, Lippitt, and White's contribution to group-leadership research and to small-group research in general, their work has some limitations—as is the case with all research. These limitations stem from such factors as the researchers' focus on appointive but not informally achieved leadership and their use of ideal-typical conceptions of different leadership styles. Although some have even questioned the validity of the major findings in the Lewinian tradition, which clearly imply a more favorable view of the democratic style, it can be argued that Lewin, Lippitt, and White's research has revealed a number of interesting and important aspects of the relationship of leadership styles to group atmosphere and group performance. Furthermore, it has provided direction for more recent studies focusing on the effects of different leadership styles and levels of group participation in decision-making on various aspects of group interaction.

Studies by Hamblin of the effects of crisis on leadership and by Milgram of patterns of obedience to *malevolent authority* were given special attention because they provided interesting and important insights about problems of leadership in small groups. To illustrate the applicability of small-group knowledge about leadership to practical problems of actual group leaders, a number of basic "rules of leadership" developed by Homans were cited and discussed.

In the discussion of interpersonal power assumptions and findings, we focused on member reactions to leadership as a function of the amount and type of power exercised by leaders and on the use of power to oppose leadership structures and leaders. In the latter regard, we considered Wolfe's research concerning power and authority in the family, which shows how shifts in power resources can substantially alter the structure of leadership or authority in small groups. In regard to collective power, we considered factors affecting the mobilization of revolutionary coalitions, as well as some possible implications of such coalitional activity for the stability of leadership structures in small groups.

6

Status Relations and Reward Allocation in Small Groups

INTRODUCTION

In some groups, such as cliques of adolescent boys, certain members consistently earn a great deal of respect and deference from fellow members because they are big, strong, athletic stars, while others are regularly demeaned or ridiculed despite also having a strong interest in sports, because they are relatively weak and unathletic. These evaluations of the relative worth and importance of group members indicate how status relations are patterned in these groups, and status relations are the major concern of this chapter.

On some professional sports teams, there are rookies with multi-million dollar contracts who sit on the bench while veterans paid much less make the contributions that regularly win games. The resulting frictions between these two groups of players and between the underpaid veterans and team management can be construed as the outcomes of distributive injustice or inequity, which are an important aspect of status relations and hence, an important topic in this chapter.

We hope these brief examples of status relations and reactions to reward allocation add some clarity to the main topics of this chapter. Of course, we already have implicitly or explicitly encountered elements of status relations on a number of occasions in discussing communication, integration, social control, and leadership in the previous chapters. In fact, we concluded the last chapter with Lawler's treatment of how perceptions of inequity in the allocation of rewards affect the mobilization of revolutionary coalitions. It should be evident from what we have seen so far that status relations are a pervasive aspect of the small group as a sociological phenomenon.

THE NATURE OF STATUS, STATUS INCONGRUENCE, AND DISTRIBUTIVE INJUSTICE

In this chapter, we will expand our focus to matters such as the expression of status evaluations, the establishment of group status structures, and the nature and effects of diffuse status characteristics, status generalization, status incongruence, and distributive injustice or inequity.

STATUS AND STATUS STRUCTURES IN SMALL GROUPS

Status and Social Organization

Although the concepts of *status, status-rank,* and *status structure* have been used on many occasions in prior chapters, we have not really said much yet about the nature or meaning of these ideas. It is not mere coincidence that we have mentioned status-related factors many times in our prior discussion of small-group literature, since the general notion of *status* has received a great deal of attention in small-group research. In fact, Freese (1974) has observed that the capacity of status conceptions to organize social interaction has long been appreciated by sociologists.[1] He has proposed that the nature and importance of status conceptions can be understood in the following terms:

> . . . We can know who an actor is and how he can be expected to behave if we know *what* he is, what statuses he occupies, whether ascribed or achieved. Occupation, race, sex, age, and education level are examples of status characteristics which provide considerable information about a person and thus orient the behavior of others to him. That stereotypes which collect about statuses may often be false when applied to a single individual is of less consequence than the fact that if people believe them to be true, they will respond in predictable ways. Moreover, a halo effect may develop about such characteristics which provides expectations for conduct in circumstances not normally germane to the status . . . (pp. 174-175).

Status Differentiation, Evaluations, and Ranking

Thus, Freese's comments suggest that statuses are social characteristics enabling others to identify us, locate us in the social structure of groups or the larger society, predict how we will act, and decide how to interact with us. Although this conception may seem to be a fairly clear and straightforward interpretation of the meaning of *social status,* some may be bothered by what it does not say. For many of us at least intuitively seem to associate the nature of status

---

[1] He noted that the origins of this idea in sociology could be traced at least to Simmel (1908) and to Park (1928).

with evaluations and rankings. On a conceptual level, these *implications* of *status differences* can be separated from the nature of the underlying status itself, but in analyses of the dynamics of concrete status relations the implications tend to become blended with the more strictly interpreted core status concept.

Golembiewski (1962:117–118) has proposed that small-group investigators tend to accept a conceptual interpretation of status as "relative position on a group roster of a 'number of individuals ordered . . . with respect to the comparative degree to which they possess or embody some socially approved or generally desired attribute or characteristic'" (Benoit-Smullyan, 1944). From this conception, we readily appreciate the tendencies for people to perceive differences on a particular status characteristic (such as sex, age, race, occupation, group task ability, etc.) in different evaluative terms ("better" or "worse"), and for a group of people with differentially evaluated states of one or more status characteristics (e.g., male and female on sex) to be ranked or located in a hierarchy. According to Berger, Cohen, and Zelditch (1966), the starting point for understanding the nature of status characteristics is the recognition that they are differentiated for purposes of social interaction. The importance of recognizing these differences in states of status characteristics is that they represent differential evaluations of social worth, form the basis of group status structures, and have implications for group interaction. Thus, although statuses are not *intrinsically* evaluated or ranked, we can see why people tend to view them in terms of their evaluated relative worth or rank.

General and Specific Status

Golembiewski (1962:118) has noted that there are certain factors that contribute to confusion and disagreement about the precise meaning, measurement, and use of status and status-related concepts. In particular, two basic types of status, one *specific* and one *general*, are often discussed, but they are sometimes undistinguished or even equated. General or overall status-rank—e.g., as leader—should not be confused with the specific status components—e.g., task performance level, participation rate, popularity, sex, occupation—from which it derives. This confusion could obscure the existence of potentially important status incongruence. In addition, failure to account for all of the major specific components of general status-rank, or for the relative weights assigned to these components, could lead to a miscalculation of the nature of status-attainment or the evolution of the status structure in groups, or it could lead to a miscalculation of the impact of status relations on group interaction or group structural stability. The fact that the identification of these components and their relative weights often can be difficult methodological problems means that some caution may be necessary in generalizing from status research.

Some Further Conceptual Distinctions:
Ascribed and Achieved Status, External and Group-Derived
Status, Prestige and Esteem

Another potentially important distinction is between ascribed and achieved status, or between characteristics such as sex, race, and age, assigned to a person at birth or during the life cycle and characteristics such as educational and occupational attainment gained through personal achievement. A parallel kind of distinction having greater relevance to status analysis of groups is between externally derived status characteristics and ones resulting from group involvement. The importance of this latter type of distinction was shown by Strodtbeck, James, and Hawkins's (1957) jury research, which we considered in the prior discussion of leadership. In this study, they showed that the strong initial impact of external status characteristics (i.e., occupation and sex) tended to recede somewhat over time in favor of the quality of the contributions jurists *actually* made to group decision-making. Later in this chapter, we will examine other studies showing the effects of external and internal (group-derived) status characteristics on group interaction.

One further conceptual distinction regarding the nature of status deserves mention. It is between prestige and esteem. Although these two terms are often used interchangeably, a worthwhile distinction can be drawn between them. *Prestige* can be viewed as social honor or deference granted to a person on the basis of his or her status or position in the social structure of a group. *Esteem* can be conceptualized as social approval or respect granted to a person *independently of status-rank* for performance in a particular status or position in the social structure of a group. The nature of each of these forms of estimation of social worth, and the relationship between them, can be clarified somewhat through the use of a concrete illustration.

Let us use a college fraternity for this example. In this fraternity, the status of president has the highest rank and hence, is the most prestigious, while that of pledge has the lowest rank and is therefore least prestigious. Peter is the current president of the fraternity, and his predecessor is Joe. Joe was an imaginative, energetic, and effective leader who established a good reputation for the fraternity on campus and encouraged both academic and athletic excellence for its members. Peter, on the other hand, is dull, lazy, and ineffectual as president, though he is a nice guy. Although both Joe and Peter have occupied the same high-prestige position, Joe earned a great deal of esteem from fraternity members for his excellent job as president while Peter is earning little or no esteem—indeed, quite the contrary—for the way he has handled the job.

There are also the cases of the two pledges, David and Bob. David is able to maintain high grades, a starting position on two varsity athletic teams, and active involvement in the Sociology Club and other extra-curricular organizations while also diligently carrying out his duties as a pledge. In contrast, Bob spends most of the day either sleeping, watching television, or drinking beer at the local bar. He has frequently skipped classes, earned poor grades, and balked at most of the assignments he has been given as a pledge. Thus, although both David and Bob occupy the same low-prestige status in the fraternity, David is highly esteemed for his role performance as a pledge while Bob is disparaged.

From this illustration, it should be clear that a person's status or position in the structure of his or her group can vary in the amount of prestige accorded it, and that the prestige level will depend on the particular values used by the group to estimate its social worth. Just as prestige may vary, so may esteem. Thus, people in more and less prestigious positions in a group may earn higher or lower amounts of esteem as a result of their actual or perceived role performance in their position.

Aspects of Status and Status Structures

It should be evident by now that understanding the nature and dynamics of status relations in groups often is not a simple matter. A *status* may refer to a position in the group structure, to which people attach certain behavioral expectations, or it may refer to or imply the particular evaluation or ranking the given position is perceived to represent. Thus, it might be said that the status (position) of group leader has a great deal of status (implying the amount of prestige attached to its high rank). In such cases, it is usually clearer to use *position* or refer to its relative rank or evaluation more explicitly. It is also important to recognize that a *general* status such as leader may have several *specific* status components or characteristics. These characteristics may be ascribed (like sex) or achieved (like popularity), or they may be externally derived (like sex, once again, or occupation) or internally derived (like popularity again or participation rate or task performance). Furthermore, by virtue of the perceived quality of a person's role performance in a general status or position, he or she may be highly or lowly esteemed.

The expression of sentiments about the statuses of group members may form a pattern, and the stabilization of this kind of pattern in groups marks the establishment of the *status structure.* Crosbie (1975:177) has defined a status structure as "the patterning of prestige relations in groups, the expression of deference and debasement among group members." This means that a status structure reflects the regular manner in which members defer to and debase each other because of the relative positions they occupy in the group structure.

As Crosbie has pointed out, although people make status evaluations in the early stages of group development, these evaluations tend to be of a general or diffuse nature for group members. Clear-cut patterns of differentiation in these status evaluations tend to become stabilized in a hierarchical status structure as group members become better acquainted with one another and achieve a relatively stable consensus about their evaluations. The achievement of the consensual basis of the status structure implies the prior development of some important shared values among group members. Once stabilized, the status structure can have a substantial impact on various aspects of group interaction, including opportunities to act, origination of interaction and activities, exercise of influence, distribution of rewards, and even how members perceive and judge each other. We will look more closely at how status relations and status structures affect group interaction in our discussion of status-related assumptions and findings.

STATUS INCONGRUENCE AND DISTRIBUTIVE INJUSTICE

The Nature of Status Incongruence

It was noted earlier that a failure to identify the salient *specific* status components serving as the basis of *general* statuses of group members could easily lead status investigators to overlook the existence of status incongruence. This could be a serious oversight because status incongruence may have dynamic implications for group interaction patterns. To understand how this status condition can affect group interaction, we must recall what it means. We first discussed the meaning of this concept several chapters ago in describing Homans's exchange theory, so it seems worthwhile to review it here. In general terms, status incongruence exists when individual group members have different or inconsistent rankings on specific status characteristics the group as a whole considers important. This condition has also been called *status inconsistency,* and its opposite, when rankings on different specific status characteristics are "in line with" each other, has been termed *status congruence, status consistency,* or *status crystallization.*

Let us use a hypothetical group to illustrate the meaning of status incongruence and congruence. In this group, there are men and women and blacks and whites of varying occupations and ages. It might be a jury, for instance. Assume the members of this group tend to believe men have greater social worth or importance than women and that in similar terms, whites are better than blacks, middle-aged people are better than younger or older people, and professional and managerial jobs are better than blue collar and manual ones. Like it or not, this is not too different from the way we often evaluate differences of sex, race, age, and occupation in American society.

One member of this group is a middle-aged black woman who is employed as a college professor. Another member is a young white man who works as a trash collector. A third member is a middle-aged white man who is a bank vice-president. There are others in this group, but these three are enough for the purpose of illustration. We can see that the first person ranks high on age and occupation, but low on sex and race; the second ranks high on sex and race, but low on age and occupation; and the third ranks high on all four status characteristics of sex, race, age, and occupation. Hence, the first two cases are ones of status incongruence, and the third illustrates status congruence. In the latter case, we are assuming these are the only status characteristics that matter to group members, which is probably a dubious assumption once group members have interacted with each other for a while, or that his rankings on other salient characteristics are consistent with these.

As this and the other two cases might suggest, calculating the *degree* of status incongruence or congruence for individual members or the group as a whole (a matter of addition of individual cases) can be complicated quite a bit by the different relative weights individuals and the group assign to the different specific status characteristics that matter to them.[2] To the extent there is difficulty in assessing the degree of status incongruence, there also may be problems predicting its effects. But we still need to know why it is important to assess how much status incongruence exists in a group. That is, we need to give more explicit attention to the kinds of significant effects status incongruence can have on group interaction and equilibrium. At this point, some general types of effects of status incongruence will be considered, and in the treatment of status incongruence research later on, these effects will be considered in more detail.

Status Incongruence, Strain, and Status Equilibration

In the most general terms, status incongruence is assumed to cause psychological discomfort for the individual experiencing it, along with discomfort for others with whom he or she interacts.[3] It is further assumed that people will try to avoid this discomfort, stress, or strain, by bringing their various discrepant ranks into line or by maintaining congruence across them. The process of restoring balance across ranks or maintaining congruence, called *status* (or *rank*) *equilibration,* is believed not only to reduce the individual feelings of discomfort presumably associated with status incongruence, but also to reinforce existing group structures (Crosbie, 1975:305).[4]

What is missing from this conception of the dynamics of status incongruence and status equilibration is an explanation of the discomfort that is supposed to set the equilibration process in motion. According to McCranie and

[2]Fleishman and Marwell (1977) have presented research indicating the complexity of the status incongruence phenomenon. They have proposed that measuring status incongruence should not only include comparing a person's statuses on several objective indices, but also the person's frame of reference—since statuses of a relevant comparison person can have significant effects on reactions to status incongruence. They have also suggested that other psychological factors like the importance to an individual of particular status dimensions, knowledge of others' statuses, and strength of his expectation that ranks on certain dimensions are related, should be examined along with frame of reference in studying status incongruence. This is a much more sophisticated conception of this phenomenon than has been used in most status incongruence research.
[3]McCranie and Kimberly (1973) have cited a number of sources reporting research that has tended to be consistent with this assumption.
[4]Zelditch and Anderson (1966) have noted that interest in status equilibration or rank balance goes back at least to Weber (see, e.g., 1946).

Kimberly (1973), there are at least two general explanations. One is that status incongruence produces discomfort by creating "conflicting expectations" for interacting people (Goffman, 1957; Zaleznik, Christensen, and Roethlisberger, 1958:58–66; Jackson, 1962; Malewski, 1966). The other is that conflicting expectations create the discomfort of status incongruence, but an "injustice" process also explains part of this strain (Homans, 1961:248–255; Geschwender, 1967; Sampson, 1969).

"Conflicting Expectations" Interpretations of Status Incongruence Effects

McCranie and Kimberly have summarized the core of these two arguments in the following way. Each of a person's ranks on a set of specific status characteristics is associated with certain expectations for behavior. When ranks are congruent, as in the case of the middle-aged white male bank vice-president in our hypothetical group, behavioral expectations are noncontradictory. However, when ranks are incongruent, as in the case of the middle-aged black female college professor, behavioral expectations are contradictory. Two different conceptions of conflicting expectations seem to be used by those proposing this explanation. One appears to be that every rank is associated with expectations governing status relations between interacting people, whether or not these people perceive themselves as peers (Zaleznik, Christensen, and Roethlisberger, 1958:359; Homans, 1961:248–255). This view of status relations implies that a general or overall assessment of rank is made of a person, with this general assessment built on an accumulation of ranks on specific status characteristics (Hyman, 1942:58–66; Gordon, 1958:246; Galtung, 1966:154; Zelditch and Anderson, 1966:246; Tumin, 1967:26). If a person's specific ranks are congruent with each other, others will expect to relate to him or her as either a superior, peer, or inferior (assuming *their* ranks are *also* congruent). That is, a person's specific ranks provide others with a clear picture of his or her overall status-rank. In our hypothetical group, we would expect the bank official to be rather unambiguously perceived as having superior or high status. On the other hand, if the specific ranks of a person are incongruent, others will be confused about how to approach or interact with this person, because the incongruence will provide contradictory indicators of overall status-rank. This could be expected to happen in interaction with the middle-aged black female professor in our hypothetical group. Others may not know whether to interact in terms of her lower-ranking characteristics of race and sex or her higher-ranking characteristics of age and occupation. Thus, status incongruence creates ambiguity for others in social interaction (Zaleznik, Christensen, and Roethlisberger, 1958:359; Homans, 1961:248–255).

A second conception of conflicting expectations is that the type of specific status characteristic, as well as the overall status-rank and the relations among specific status-ranks, has a bearing on the expectations governing status relations and group interaction. A number of investigators have treated specific status characteristics from a social psychological or exchange perspective using concepts such as *investments* (e.g., training, seniority), *rewards* (e.g., money, social approval), and *costs* (e.g., taking responsibility, working long hours) to define different types of them (Homans, 1961:248-255; Geschwender, 1967). From this perspective, status incongruence has been viewed mainly as a matter of discrepancies between investments and rewards and/or costs. Homans has suggested that these discrepancies generate conflicting expectations and ambiguity or uncertainty about the general status relationship for people associated with this situation of status incongruence.

Status Incongruence and Distributive Injustice: A Social Exchange View

This social exchange view links status incongruence to distributive injustice, which is the second major condition or process assumed to cause reactions to status incongruence. The close association between these phenomena assumed by Homans was suggested earlier in the book when we looked at how his exchange framework was applied to the case of ledger clerks and cash posters. In this case, ledger clerks had a more demanding job, were generally regarded by others in the billing office as more skilled and responsible, and tended to be older and more experienced in the company than cash posters. Yet ledger clerks received the same weekly pay as cash posters. In addition, they suffered the "indignity" of being taken off their own job to help out with the "inferior" one of cash posting. They felt they were being put "down" when they were given the temporary afternoon cash-posting assignment, which they perceived as a loss of status-rank as well as autonomy.

According to Homans, this was not only a case of status incongruence, but one of injustice as well. In his words (Homans, 1974:246):

> The ledger clerks . . . were superior to the cash posters in investments and in costs, but only equal or even inferior to them in some rewards. It was the fact of rewards being out of line with their rank on the other two dimensions (of seniority and job responsibility) that made their condition one of distributive (in)justice . . . They were not driven to open revolt, but they were vexed and they complained. Their complaints, addressed to both the management and union and still unsuccessful at the time the investigation ended, were directed toward bringing their rewards into line, toward establishing just conditions. That is, they asked for more pay than the posters and they asked that they be no longer temporarily assigned to posting.

Though the ledger clerks certainly felt that they were victims of injustice, they were also concerned about their status. If it really was superior, why

did some of the posters refuse promotion to it? There was a highly symbolic element in their demand for more pay. It was not the size of the
difference between their pay and the posters' that concerned them, but
only that there should be *some* difference, "to show that their job was
more important." They were not just being unfairly rewarded: they were
being treated in such a way as to throw their superior status into doubt.
Perhaps there are no pure cases of distributive injustice; perhaps it always
comes mixed with status anxiety.

The linking of distributive injustice to status incongruence within the
exchange framework was first explicitly proposed by Homans, and his model
of injustice has been further developed by several others (e.g., Kimberly, 1962;
1966; 1967; Adams, 1963; 1965; Geschwender, 1967; Kimberly and Crosbie,
1967; Anderson *et al.*, 1969; Sampson, 1969; Zelditch *et al.*, 1970; Berger *et al.*,
1972; Berger, Conner, and Fisek, 1974; Cook, 1975; Donnenwerth and Törnblom, 1975). Distributive justice theorists generally assume that people will
tend to develop an expectation that rewards or profits (rewards minus costs)
ought to be proportional to investments. When this norm is met, feelings of
justice or equity are predicted. When it is violated, feelings of injustice or inequity are predicted.

Social Exchange and Status Value Models
of Distributive Justice and Injustice:
Similarities and Contrasts

In addition to the exchange model, the other major theoretical interpretation
of the justice and injustice processes is a status value formulation (e.g., Berger
et al., 1972). Cook (1975) has pointed out that both theoretical perspectives are
concerned with the reactions of people to the ways in which rewards are allocated in social systems like small groups, and she has noted a number of the
common elements of them. For example, both assume (Cook, 1975:373):

1. Rewards are allocated on the basis of the possession of particular social
   characteristics (Berger *et al.*, 1972), investments (Homans, 1961; 1974), or
   inputs to exchanges (Adams, 1963; 1965).
2. A justice rule (Homans, 1961; 1974; Adams, 1963; 1965) or referential
   structure (Berger *et al.*, 1972) defines what is just or equitable.
3. A comparison process based upon the justice rule or referential structure determines the rewards individuals can legitimately expect to receive (Homans,
   1961; 1974; Berger *et al.*, 1972).
4. Violations of legitimate expectations result in psychological reactions (e.g.,
   anger, dissatisfaction, guilt) and/or behavioral reactions that attempt to
   restore equity or justice.

Cook has added one further important condition to the distributive justice
process. From Berger, Conner, and Fisek (1974), she proposed that along with a

well-defined distributive justice norm, justice situations also must include well-defined expectation states. That is, people must know which states of relevant status characteristics they possess in order to determine what reward levels to expect. The importance of knowledge of states of status characteristics for determining the outcome of the justice process has also been emphasized by McCranie and Kimberly (1973).

The status value formulation of distributive justice and injustice was developed because its creators believed that the exchange model failed to account for the nature and importance of status value in distributive justice and injustice, usually gave incomplete attention to the comparison process by which people identify similarity or dissimilarity of status characteristics, failed to account for the distinctively normative character of the justice and injustice processes, and failed to provide meaningful and precise definitions of these processes (Berger *et al.*, 1972:144). To help rectify these perceived deficiencies of the exchange model, the status value theorists have given special emphasis to the structural aspects of the justice, injustice, and equilibration processes. That is, they have focused on the process by which, independently of "strictly local comparisons" of one specific individual with another, meaning is given to rewards and expectations are formed about the way they should *legitimately* be distributed. They saw these structural aspects as largely neglected in the exchange model, and they formulated their conception of justice-related processes in terms of the status significance of rewards instead of their exchange value to provide a basis for understanding them.

The Nature of the Status Value Model
of Distributive Justice and Injustice

A key notion in the status value model is the concept of a *referential structure.* Referential structures are stable and generalized frames of reference that give meaning to local comparisons between specific individuals so they can determine first, the status significance of specific social characteristics and rewards possessed by them, second, how rewards like their own should legitimately be distributed, and third, whether or not they have been fairly or justly rewarded. The difference between a strictly local comparison and one based on a referential structure can be seen in the following example.[5] Imagine that Joan Jones is a university professor of surgery who earns $30,000 a year. If she compares herself and her income with only one other specific person, say another person in her department named Bill Williams, she is making a strictly local comparison. If she extends her comparison to include more generalized categories of people similar to herself in some salient respects (e.g., surgeons in private practice, surgeons in university medicine, university professors, or perhaps female doctors

[5] This example was generally suggested by Berger *et al.* (1972:135–136).

or professional people), her comparison is a "referential" one. It is the activation of some kind of referential structure that is presumed by status value theorists to set the stage for justice-related processes. By looking beyond Bill Williams to a more stable and generalized standard or frame of reference, Dr. Jones presumably can gain a more secure sense of whether or not she has a *legitimate right*—justice is a moral issue—to feel underpaid by her university.

It should be evident from this example that in the status value conception, the creation of feelings of injustice and what to do about them will depend on what referential structure, if any, is chosen. Berger and his colleagues did not try to analyze how this choice is made,[6] but they proposed that the entire justice process is renewed every time a person changes his or her referential structure. Thus, we might conclude from this view that the stability of groups where referential comparisons regarding rewards take place depends on the stability of referential structures activated in them. With each change there will be a redefinition, a formation of new expectations, and a reassessment of justice. In concrete reward-allocation situations, justice therefore may be seen as a recurrent process in which balance, tension, and resolution of behavior fluctuate through time.

In addition to formulating their status value model to give more emphasis to the structural features of the justice process, Berger and his colleagues have used it to try to clarify how people will act in justice and injustice situations (e.g., Anderson *et al.*, 1969; Anderson and Shelly, 1970; 1971). They assumed that justice situations would be balanced status situations that would in turn be relatively stable, as long as the referential structure did not change. Injustice situations were, on the contrary, assumed to be unbalanced and unstable, and, like status incongruence situations, to produce tension and pressure for change. Since justice and injustice involve normative considerations, we might expect the tension and strain of injustice to have moral overtones, and reactions to the injustice of undercompensation to be inspired and marked by moral indignation and righteousness. Needless to say, the injection of the moral element into such reactions could make underpayment situations quite volatile. Injustice investigators also have suggested that *over*payment—receiving *more* than one has a legitimate right to expect—may be uncomfortable and create instability in reward-allocation situations.

---

[6] They did not examine how particular referential structures come to be seen as similar to a person's own situation for three main reasons. First, they felt these matters had gained considerable attention in other justice investigations and therefore were more studied, and understood, than the structural aspects of the process of primary concern to them. Second, they viewed the choice process as a complex one in which status value played only a part. And third, they believed choices would be influenced by the structure of the specific social system in which they are made. This, too, would have complicated their analysis beyond what they intended in their status value model. Berger *et al.* (1972) looked at the justice process from the point at which a specific referential structure had already been activated.

Local and Referential Comparisons,
Anomie, and Distributive Injustice

By including the component of a referential structure in their conception of the justice and injustice processes, status value theorists have given a stricter interpretation than exchange theorists of the conditions needed to produce justice or injustice feelings and reactions. Status value theorists have proposed that strictly local comparisons, without referential structures, will tend to create anomie, or confusion about how to define one's reward situation, but will not create a feeling of justice or injustice. Anomie may be accompanied by anxious or uneasy feelings and a desire to change—or clarify—the situation, but according to Berger *et al.* (1972:123) the problem in such settings will *not* be to protest injustice. They have argued that formulating comparisons only as local ones can obscure the justice process and its implications.[7]

As we have noted, in Homans's terms, the ledger clerks were clearly the victims of injustice, despite the fact that that all ledger clerks and cash posters in their company received the same weekly pay and the ledger clerks could not earn more money for a comparable job elsewhere. However, perhaps the ledger clerks compared themselves with others *generally* having their relative seniority and job responsibility in jobs of other kinds, and concluded from this referential comparison that they ought to be paid at least slightly more than the cash posters. The fact that more directly relevant referential comparisons with other ledger clerks in their company and other women with jobs such as their own in other companies gave them no basis for feeling unjustly treated may have made their dissatisfaction and complaints more a matter of status anxiety or incongruence than of injustice. After all, as Homans (1953) himself pointed out, the "status problem" was not an acute one. It produced no change, there was no further revolt beyond the complaints to management and the union, ledger clerks were *generally* not unhappy with their pay, and general morale in the billing office was fairly good. Perhaps if directly relevant referential structures had provided a basis for normatively expecting a higher relative wage, the reactions of ledger clerks would have been stronger, more persistent, and more disruptive. Lawler's study of revolutionary coalitions, which we discussed earlier, already has indicated the potentially significant impact of injustice feelings on the stability of leadership, leadership structures, and group equilibrium.

---

[7]Berger *et al.* (1972:124) have identified six ways in which formulating comparisons only as local can cloud understanding of the justice process. First, anomie and unjust states may be confused. Second, some just states may be incorrectly identified as unjust ones. Third, some unjust states may be incorrectly identified as just ones. Fourth, collective injustice cannot be distinguished from individual injustice. Fifth, situations in which it is oneself who is unjustly rewarded are not distinguished from those in which the other person is unjustly rewarded. And sixth, it is not even possible to always correctly distinguish overreward from underreward.

The Role of Perceived Skill Rank
in Creating Justice and Injustice

Status value theory implies there is good reason to question Homans's (1961: 248-255) argument that the conflicting expectations and injustice processes are produced simultaneously by status incongruence or rank inconsistency. This theory suggests, instead, that anomic status situations and the conflicting expectations of status incongruence in general should be clearly distinguished from distributive injustice. According to McCranie and Kimberly (1973), a person's knowledge of another's skill rank or relative level of task competence will be the crucial variable affecting whether a conflicting expectations or injustice process occurs in reward-allocation situations. Earlier, we noted Cook's (1975) emphasis on this knowledge factor as an important element of injustice situations. Combining her insights with those of McCranie and Kimberly and the status value theorists, we conclude that people must have a clear sense of which states of salient status characteristics such as skill they possess in order to choose an appropriate referential structure that will tell them what reward they deserve. In the absence of such knowledge, people may feel confused or have conflicting expectations. However, with this knowledge—and the activation of a referential structure—their problem will not be anomie or conflicing expectations when there is rank inconsistency concerning rewards; rather it will be injustice.

The reason for McCranie and Kimberly's emphasis on skill rank as the focal criterion for assessing the fairness of rewards, along with overall status-rank, can been seen in Kimberly's (1962; 1966; 1967; 1970:84-89) model of the relationship of skill and reward to other basic types of status characteristics or ranks. Kimberly defined four general types of ranks: position, performance, skill, and reward. Position is defined as a set of norms that specify one's tasks in the division of labor or general social structure of a social system (e.g., pledge master and pledge in a fraternity). All positions in the system are considered to be ranked relative to one another. Performance is defined as how well the individual conforms to the norms specifying his or her position. Skill is conceptualized as the amount of position-relevant competence the individual possesses. Rewards refer to both the psychic (e.g., prestige, esteem) and material (e.g., money) gratifications received by an individual in a given position. Position, performance, skill, and reward are seen as connected by a specific set of cognitive relevance bonds. Skill is viewed as the cause of performance, and thus as the legitimate (just) basis of holding a certain position and receiving certain rewards.[8] Status value theorists would say that the relationship among these elements in a given situation would derive its status significance and become interpreted in terms

[8]McCranie and Kimberly recognized that for various reasons (e.g., lack of motivation), an individual may not perform up to his or her skill level. However, in their model, it is assumed that an individual will perform as well as he or she is capable (i.e., that performance and skill levels will be consistent).

of a particular distributive justice norm through activation of a pertinent referential structure of some sort.

In addition to these four types of status-ranks, McCranie and Kimberly proposed another that they called *symbolic rank*. The term refers to attributes of an individual that people believe, correctly or incorrectly, to be indicators of skill level (e.g., sex, race, age, educational institution attended, occupation). In the juries of Strodtbeck, James, and Hawkins's (1957) research, which we discussed earlier, the external status characteristics of occupation and sex seemed to be salient *symbolic ranks*. Kimberly's model treats symbolic ranks as *diffuse* indicators of a person's skill rank that become cognitively salient only under certain conditions (Berger, Cohen, and Zelditch, 1966). We might guess they will be especially salient in the early stages of group development or just after new members have been introduced into a group, because assessment of rank on skill factors relevant to group goal-attainment often will be difficult then.

The Effects of Perceived Skill Rank and Injustice or Conflicting Expectations on Group Interaction and Goal-Attainment

Knowledge or lack of knowledge about skill on group tasks could have a significant impact on group interaction and goal-attainment in task-oriented groups through either the injustice or conflicting expectations process. When people know how much task skill they have and how well they have used it, they are able to form normative expectations about what status-rank and reward level they deserve. If their status-rank or reward is less (or more) than expected, they will feel unjustly treated. The resulting anger or outrage, or guilt in the case of overreward, could seriously disrupt individual task performance and relations with other members in the group task process, depending on the victim's position and how adversely the victim's performance is affected by the perceived injustice.

When group members are unsure about their own or others' relative task competence, they may become uncertain about where they and others belong in the group's division of labor and status hierarchy, and about how rewards ought to be allocated in the group. When there is ambiguity about these kinds of things coupled with incongruence across diffuse status-ranks, conflicting expectations may result. If so, people may become confused about the relative performance levels to expect of group members, including themselves. This could hamper group, as well as individual, task performance. If the group task process is a highly integrated or interdependent one, requiring close member cooperation or coordination, it, too, could suffer from the ambiguity, awkwardness, or antagonism in interpersonal relations that could result from conflicting status expectations.

STATUS STRUCTURES, STATUS RELATIONS, AND REWARD ALLOCATION IN SMALL GROUPS

GENERAL ASSUMPTIONS AND FINDINGS

Having discussed the meaning of the key concepts for this chapter, we will now use these concepts to examine major assumptions and findings about status structures, status relations, and reward allocation in small groups. We will begin this discussion by focusing on status evaluations and the emergence of status structures in small groups.

Status Evaluations and The Emergence of Status Structures in Small Groups: A General Research Review

Since leadership is a general type of group status—albeit with special rights and responsibilities—we can derive some insights about the emergence of status evaluations in small groups from our prior discussion of the emergence of group leaders. Crosbie (1975:178, 225) has proposed that first impressions, external status characteristics, and performance affect both processes. We have considered how all three factors have influenced group status and leadership in juries, in our discussion of Strodtbeck, James, and Hawkins's (1957) research. In fact, the emergence of status and leadership or influence structures has been a major focus in the study of task-oriented small groups.

Berger, Cohen, and Zelditch have identified two traditional lines of research concerning the emergence of status and influence hierarchies in task groups. One has demonstrated the development of such structures in groups whose members were initially undifferentiated in status, while the second has shown the relationship between prior status differences among group members (i.e., external or diffuse status differences) and the emergence of influence and prestige orders in the group. Some examples of major findings in these two research traditions have been cited by Berger and his colleagues (Berger, Cohen, and Zelditch, 1966:30–31), and we will briefly describe what these findings have shown.[9]

THE EMERGENCE OF STATUS STRUCTURES IN GROUPS INITIALLY LACKING EXTERNAL STATUS DIFFERENCES: A GENERAL OVERVIEW OF FINDINGS. Bales and his colleagues (e.g., Bales *et al.*, 1951; Bales, 1953; Heinicke and Bales, 1953; Bales and Slater, 1955) have produced evidence indicating that task groups with members who are status equals regarding external characteristics of age, sex, color, education, and occupation tend to develop stable structures of influence and prestige.[10] These structures

---

[9]Our review of these findings is based mainly on Berger, Cohen, and Zelditch's review.
[10]Berger, Cohen, and Zelditch use the term *power-prestige order* in reviewing this research and in discussing the emergence of status structures in general. It seems more consistent with the conceptual framework we have developed to substitute "influence" for "power,"

246

are important in shaping the distribution of opportunities to perform, in the distribution of performances, in the distribution of evaluations of member contributions, in the overall evaluations of group members, and in the relative influence of different members on the group's ultimate decision. These behaviors are highly correlated and form stable patterns of differentiation. Taken together, these patterns have been designated by Berger, Cohen, and Zelditch as the "observable power-prestige order" of a group.[11] Heinicke and Bales (1953) and Bales and Slater (1955) have suggested that the differentiation processes for status and influence fluctuate over time and seem to produce tension and conflict. Apparently, there is a *status struggle* preceding the establishment of the status and influence or leadership hierarchies. Once these structures are stabilized, they tend to have a continuing impact on performance opportunities, performances, group evaluations, and relative influence on decision-making, as the group shifts from task to task. That is, evaluations and interaction on new tasks tend to be shaped by the structures of influence and prestige existing during the pursuit of prior ones.

SOME DISTORTING EFFECTS OF PREVIOUSLY ESTABLISHED STATUS PATTERNS: A SPECIFIC RESEARCH FOCUS. Sherif, White, and Harvey (1955) have shown that reliance on previously established status patterns can have a distorting effect on current assessments of members' performances; this distortion may at least temporarily reinforce the status patterns that existed before.[12] They conducted a field experiment involving two groups of boys at a summer camp. Each group had been together long enough to develop a relatively stable status structure. The investigators hypothesized: "Variations in judgments made by an experimentally formed group of a member's performance on a task which is of common significance to the group and which provides few external anchorages (i.e., is unstructured) are significantly related to the status of that member." In particular, they expected to find that under conditions of ambiguous performance, members with higher status would be more likely to have their performance overestimated, and that members with lower status even might have their performance underestimated. This hypothesis was implied by the results of Harvey's (1953) earlier experimental study of status relations in informal groups.

To test this hypothesis, Sherif, White, and Harvey introduced a "game" into camp activities. This game involved having each member in a group throw a series of handballs at a target while the other members each judged his accuracy. To make performance ambiguous, the researchers covered the target (consisting

---

since the former is a broader term subsuming both power and leadership. It seems appropriate to allow the inclusion of leadership, since—as we have already indicated—status and leadership emergence can be closely related.

[11] We would refer to them as the "observable influence-prestige order" or perhaps as the structures of leadership (when legitimation exists) and status.

[12] This summary is based on the original article and Crosbie's (1975:185) summary of it.

of a set of concentric circles) with a denim cloth, so it was difficult to judge how close each throw came to the center. The experimenters were able to determine actual performance because they wired the target. As hypothesized, the performance of high-status members was overestimated, and the performance of low-status members was underestimated, with the extent of over- or underestimation being positively related to status rankings. It is noteworthy that neither status-rank nor estimated performance was significantly correlated with actual performance, since this fact underscores the distortion produced by past status-rank in this case where performance was ambiguous.

Sherif, White, and Harvey proposed that among more established groups having more structural stability and solidarity than their experimental groups, the relationship between status-rank and performance judgments would be closer than what they found. They also indicated there was evidence that actual skill tended to be given *relatively greater* weight in judgments of the group with a less stable status structure. Thus, the amount of distortion produced by a status structure will depend on how stable it is.

Sherif, White, and Harvey's research suggests that group members tend to rely on established status-rank or specific rank characteristics to make performance judgments when performance is ambiguous. When they are not as confident about the overall rank of those whom they are judging, their performance evaluations are likely to become more closely related to actual skill rank. The groups of campers these researchers studied were relatively homogeneous or undifferentiated in regard to social characteristics that might have served as *symbolic ranks;* and hence, the boys could not rely much on diffuse or external status characteristics for indirect performance assessments. However, in many groups, members are *not* the same in age, sex, social-class background, or other potentially salient status characteristics of this sort, and in these groups, we can expect such characteristics to have a significant influence on performance assessments and other important types of status-related evaluations.

THE EMERGENCE OF STATUS STRUCTURES IN GROUPS HAVING EXTERNAL STATUS DIFFERENCES: A GENERAL OVERVIEW OF FINDINGS. According to Berger, Cohen, and Zelditch, past research tended to show that when task group members are differentiated regarding salient diffuse or external status characteristics, these characteristics determine the nature of status and influence or leadership structures that develop in task-oriented groups. For example, the jury research by Strodtbeck, James, and Hawkins (1957) indicates that sex and occupational prestige differences can affect choices of jury foremen, participation, influence, and perceived competence. Torrance (1954) studied the consequences of differences in formal Air Force rank for decision-making in "permanent" and "temporary" three-man bomber crews.[13] The "permanent" crews had been together as a unit for several months before the experiment, and

---

[13]This research has been summarized by Hare (1976:138–141), and we are using his summary here.

the "temporary" ones had been formed on an *ad hoc* basis for the experiment and contained members who had no prior experience together. Torrance looked at the relative influence exercised over group decisions by the pilot, navigator, and gunner in both types of groups. He found that formal rank was positively related to influence, although this relationship was more evident in the permanent crews than in the ones brought together temporarily for the experiment. Hurwitz, Zander, and Hymovitch (1953) observed effects of professional prestige on interaction in conference groups that were similar to the Air Force rank effects found by Torrance. Katz and his colleagues (Katz, Goldston, and Benjamin, 1958; Katz and Benjamin, 1960; Katz and Cohen, 1962) have shown that in biracial work groups, whites initiate more interaction than blacks, talk more to other whites than blacks, and even blacks talk more to whites than other blacks (Berger, Cohen, and Zelditch, 1972).[14] Caudill (1958) has produced evidence revealing the effects of position in the hospital hierarchy on participation in administrative conferences in a psychiatric hospital, and Zander and Cohen (1955) have shown how position in a university hierarchy affects simulated committee discussions of students. In a study of consequences of age heterogeneity in adult decision-making groups, Ziller and Exline (1958) found that the effect of age on participation was related to the sex of group members, who were teachers ranging in age from twenty-one to sixty-three. In male groups, the older members talked most, and presumably gained the most status and influence, while in female groups, the younger teachers talked most (Hare, 1976: 201).

According to Bergen, Cohen, and Zelditch (1966:30), research concerning groups with heterogeneity on external status characteristics generally showed that differences in these characteristics produce the same result that prior experience of members interacting with one another produced in the Bales group, where members were intially equal in status. That is, both external status differences and prior experience shape the development of stable patterns of influence and prestige in groups. However, an important additional fact has been revealed about the impact of external status characteristics: this factor operates not only when it is directly related to the group task, but often even when it has no obvious or direct relevance to the task. In noting this fact, Berger, Cohen, and Zelditch (1966:31) also observed that:

> . . . While it is not unexpected that prestigeful mental health specialists would have an impact on groups discussing mental health problems (Hurwitz, Zander, and Hymovitch, 1953), it is somewhat surprising that Air Force rank should determine interaction in a projective discussion task

---

[14] There is little doubt that race continues to have a strong effect on influence and prestige orders in most groups today. However, its relative salience as a specific status characteristic should be less where racial prejudice is less among group members of both races. Or, where it remains salient the evaluation of it may be relatively higher today, at least for blacks who have been affected by movements or events raising black consciousness and pride.

(Torrance, 1954). Indeed, Torrance shows the same pattern of results for four different tasks of quite varying degrees of relationship to the role of Air Force officer.

They went on to say that their point of departure for their own work was the repeated finding that:

> When task groups are differentiated with respect to some status characteristic external to the task situation, this differentiation determines the observable (influence) and prestige order within the group, *whether or not the external characteristics are related to the group task* (emphasis added).

Diffuse Status Characteristics, Status Generalization, and the Evolution of Influence and Prestige Orders in Small Groups: From Berger-Cohen-Zelditch and Beyond

THE NATURE AND ACTIVATION OF DIFFUSE STATUS CHARACTERISTICS. From this point of departure, Berger, Cohen, and Zelditch went on to clarify their conception of a diffuse external status characteristic, and to identify the properties of situations in which they expected these characteristics to be activated. They defined an external status characteristic as a social characteristic with differentially evaluated states that are associated with other specific traits such as mathematical ability or diligence and that are also associated with more vague, unspecific, and general traits such as "ability," "skill," or "morality." The last feature, connecting external status characteristics to diffuse traits, led them to refer to these characteristics as *diffuse*. When external status characteristics serve as diffuse indicators of group task skill, they constitute what Kimberly has called *symbolic ranks*.

According to Berger, Cohen, and Zelditch, we can expect diffuse status characteristics to be activated when: (1) two or more group members are required to interact or work together to complete a task; (2) there is a differential evaluation of the task outcomes such that a particular outcome is perceived as "success"; (3) there is a desire to achieve the "success" outcome; (4) a specific social characteristic is believed to be instrumental to task success, and that characteristic is positively evaluated; but (5) there is ambiguity about which states of this instrumental status characteristic should be assigned to whom; and (6) differences on one or more external status characteristics provide the only socially salient basis for differentiating among group members. In this kind of situation, Berger, Cohen, and Zelditch assumed that there will be pressure on people to assign states of the instrumental characteristic to facilitate the achievement of a successful task outcome. In addition, people will infer such states from states of diffuse status characteristics because they constitute the only basis for inferring anything about relative standing in the group. They asserted that the social beliefs, or stereotypes, attached to diffuse status characteristics perform the same function in interaction that would be performed if people had had prior experience with each other.

Once people have been assigned states of the instrumental status characteristic on the basis of their states on ostensibly or actually relevant diffuse status characteristics, they also will have specific performance expectations associated with their instrumental status. For example, a varsity football player (external status) may be expected to be a star player on his fraternity volleyball team (performance expectation) because it is assumed he is *generally* an excellent athlete (instrumental status characteristic). Whether or not they are fully justified, such performance expectations may become a basis on which performance opportunities and evaluations, influence, and perhaps even performance itself become distributed in groups. Thus, the levels of task skills and other instrumental characteristics that are inferred from diffuse characteristics or symbolic ranks can become the basis of a group's influence and prestige orders.

STATUS GENERALIZATION FROM DIFFUSE STATUS CHARAC-TERISTICS AND MORE SPECIFIC ONES.   The fact people may generalize from football to volleyball ability reflects the basic generalizing potential Berger, Cohen, and Zelditch have assumed for diffuse status characteristics. The essence of their theory about the operation of these characteristics in task-oriented groups is that, in the absence of other information, members will infer each others' task abilities by generalizing their external status conceptions, even when the group task is not obviously relevant to the external status differences. Furthermore, influence and status structures can be assumed to result from task performance expectations that had generalized from the diffuse status differences (Freese and Cohen, 1973). Predictions relevant to this theory have been tested in experiments by Moore (1968) and Berger, Cohen, and Zelditch (1972); and confirming evidence has been reported.

The theoretical work of Berger, Cohen, and Zelditch about status characteristics and status generalization inspired a number of studies that have led to elaboration and refinement of the original theory. For example, Freese (1969) tried to create a generalization effect by discriminating people on a characteristic that was not diffuse.[15] He believed that if differentiation in influence and prestige resulted from conceptions of specific task ability, then perhaps such conceptions would generalize not only from a diffuse status difference but also from any other known differences in specific task performance, if they seemed relevant. He predicted that if two or more task-specific performance attributes were directly related to each other, then people would develop conceptions of each others' abilities at a different group task by generalizing from task-specific performance attributes whose distribution in the group was already known. The

---

[15] This summary is based on Freese and Cohen (1973).

observable influence and status structures in the group were predicted to result directly from this generalization of specific performance expectations, and this was what Freese found.

ELIMINATING STATUS GENERALIZATION. In a subsequent study, Freese, along with Cohen (Freese and Cohen, 1973), used his insights gained from the study just described to try to discover how status generalization might be neutralized. Freese and Cohen were interested in the neutralization or elimination of status generalization because they recognized that significant consequences were suffered by many victims of such stereotyping. Their research strategy was to superimpose experimentally the generalization effect Freese had demonstrated upon the generalization effect of diffuse status so that they were operating at cross-purposes. Freese and Cohen wanted to show that under certain conditions, diffuse status generalization (e.g., stereotyping according to sex, race, age, etc.) could be eliminated by substituting an alternative based on performance attributes contradicting diffuse status expectations. The purpose of their theory and investigation was to identify conditions when performance differences, of a specific-kind, whose relevance to a task is *not* known, would determine beliefs about group task ability that might otherwise be generalized from diffuse status characteristics.

The specific research approach used by Freese and Cohen involved manipulating differences on the diffuse status characteristic of age within experimentally created task-oriented dyads. Their subjects were junior college females between the ages of eighteen and twenty-one who were paired in the experimental condition with either an eleven-year-old girl or a thirty-eight-year-old woman. The pairing was done with the aid of a closed circuit television monitor. The partner, either the girl or the woman, was introduced on the monitor so that she was visible to the subject. During this introduction, the partner, or at least the ostensible partner, stated her age and other information indicative of her age. All those who were led to believe they were interacting with an eleven-year-old girl actually confronted the same videotaped standardized presentation on their monitor, and the same sort of thing happened to those who thought they were interacting with a thirty-eight-year-old woman. Since the experimenters wanted to break down the effects of a status differential, they deliberately tried to establish as big a differential as possible with their manipulations.

After establishing this initial status differentiation, the experimenters then discriminated the dyad members in terms of a *general performance characteristic* that was inconsistent with the initial status differentiation. By *general performance characteristic* they meant "any combination of specific task abilities that are consistently evaluated and symmetrically related," and they induced states on it by using tests of fictitious abilities known as "Meaning Insight" and "Contrast Sensitivity." Subjects performed a group task that ostensibly required "Spatial Judgment" ability, and they were encouraged to take their "partner's" advice if they judged it would be helpful. Feedback each subject received from or about her "partner" was, in fact, controlled by the experimenter.

Through their manipulations, Freese and Cohen created two basic experimental conditions relevant to their theory: High Diffuse Status-Low General Performance Characteristic (HS-LP) and Low Diffuse Status-High General Performance Characteristic (LS-HP). They also used four additional control conditions: High Diffuse Status (HS), Low Diffuse Status (LS), High General Performance Characteristic (HP), and Low General Performance Characteristic (LP). On the basis of their theory, they made predictions about differences between conditions regarding the tendency to reject influence attempts by the other group member. They predicted that HS-LP would not differ from LP and that LS-HP would not differ from HP because they expected the generalization effect of the specific "Meaning Insight" and "Contrast Sensitivity" ability factors, i.e., the general performance characteristic, to override the generalization effect of the diffuse status characteristic of age. They also made predictions about HS and LS from theoretical work by Berger, Cohen, and Zelditch (1966) and Moore (1968), and about HP and LP from Freese (1969). They predicted that HS would be greater than LS and that HP would be greater than LP with respect to rejecting influence attempts.

All of these predictions were confirmed by Freese and Cohen's data. When subjects were discriminated only by age, they assumed positions of relative influence and prestige consistent with their relative age. However, when subjects were also discriminated by a general performance characteristic, the generalization effect of this factor eliminated the effect of diffuse status differences. That is, when states of S and P were inconsistent, HS subjects had a significantly *lower* rate of rejecting influence attempts—they were *more* likely to be influenced— than LS subjects. Influence patterns tended to be the same in the HS-LP as LP condition and in the LS-HP as HP condition.

Freese and Cohen reported an independent study of racial interaction by (a different) Cohen and Roper (1972) that produced results similar to their own. In their experiment, Cohen and Roper used groups of two black and two white junior-high-school boys matched on social class and attitudes toward school. The researchers were interested in discovering whether members of these interracial groups would alter their status and influence relations if they had knowledge and experience of superior black competence on a training task preceding regular group task interaction. They expected on the basis of Cohen's (1972) research that without the training task to induce superior black competence perceptions, whites would be dominant. Cohen had named this phenomenon of white dominance in interracial work groups *interracial interaction disability.*

In the experiment, black subjects taught white subjects how to build a transistor radio. This training task preceded the *criterion task* of "Kill the Bull," a cooperative game designed to meet the conditions assumed by Berger, Cohen, and Zelditch to activate diffuse status characteristics. The general performance characteristic consisted of competence in building the radio set and in teaching someone else to build one. The task characteristic on which measures of influence and prestige were taken consisted of ability at "Kill the Bull." Cohen and

Roper found that manipulation of the general performance characteristic had a strong effect on interaction during the game. That is, participation rates of blacks increased significantly in groups where the general performance characteristic was introduced, even when the training tasks were not described as relevant to the game. However, in the control condition, where this experimental treatment was absent, whites dominated interaction during the game.

Cohen and Roper (1972:643) summarized the main thrust of their results in the following way:

> Unless the expectations for black competence held by both whites and blacks are treated (with a contradictory general performance characteristic), whites will dominate the interaction in the criterion game. When expectations of the whites are treated by having the whites serve as "students" of the black "teacher," behavior on the game approximates an equal status pattern. The strongest treatment involves spelling out the relevance of the training tasks (general performance characteristic) to the criterion game.

Cohen and Roper's research, focusing on racial differences, may suggest the practical importance of Freese and Cohen's theoretical work concerning elimination of the generalization effects of diffuse status characteristics even better than Freese and Cohen's own research. We can gain a sense of these practical implications from Freese and Cohen (1973:193) themselves: [16]

> We are encouraged by (the) results (produced by us and Cohen and Roper) in view of the extent to which status generalization permeates social behavior. Anyone who has ever possessed a low state of a (diffuse) status characteristic—such as blacks, women, youth, and others—have been a victim of the generalization effect of such a characteristic. To infer that a black is lazy because he is black, or that a woman is illogical because she is female, or that a youth is irresponsible because he is young is to perpetuate at least a disservice and at best an indignity. Yet, apparently under certain conditions such generalizing is normal. The problem from a theoretical view is to specify conditions which can be interposed to dissolve it. (Our) theory . . . specifies some conditions and isolates key elements that can be developed into a potential treatment. . . .

Freese (1974) has suggested that the main implication of his research with Cohen, and Cohen and Roper's research, is that despite the potential symbolic significance of diffuse status differences, a simultaneous and inconsistent ranking of group members by performance, even when the task relevance of such a ranking is ambiguous, has an inhibiting effect on generalization from states of diffuse

---

[16]Practical—as well as theoretical—implications have also been considered by Cohen and Roper, who were concerned about how their results and results of similar kinds of studies applied to school desegregation.

status. When there is a general performance characteristic ranking of this sort, participation rates, status evaluations, and influence seem *not* to be a function of diffuse status generalization. Freese proposed that this effect of a general performance characteristic probably occurred because a condition of Berger, Cohen, and Zelditch's (1966) was not met. Specifically, this condition is that a diffuse status characteristic provide the only social basis for ranking people in the group. In trying to provide further refinement of the theory of diffuse status generalization, he addressed the question: "When will observable (influence) and prestige in task groups *not* (emphasis added) be determined by a prior (diffuse) status order even though there exists no other rank order in the group?" Thus, Freese wanted to identify additional parameters for the status generalization theory, and in particular to determine when status unequals will tend toward equality in influence and prestige relations. This, of course, was opposite the main thrust of the original diffuse status generalization theory.

CONDITIONS FOR STATUS EQUALITY IN INFORMAL TASK GROUPS. Using the same type of experimental situation he had earlier employed with Cohen (Freese and Cohen, 1973), Freese (1974) created conditions causing an inversion of the status generalization effect. This inversion occurred when group members were exposed to an increasing number of status unequals as comparison persons. These new people were not group members but possessed additional discriminating characteristics that contradicted diffuse status evaluations and were similar but not explicitly relevant, to group tasks. The comparison persons appeared on the closed circuit television monitor after the subject was introduced to her partner. A new experimenter also appeared on the subject's screen immediately afterward to report and explain scores on three bogus tests of performance, which measured fictitious abilities, for all participants in the laboratory who had previously been tested. In this way, this new experimenter was able to manipulate the subject's comparison persons and her state of the general performance characteristic at the same time. If the subject was in a high status condition—i.e., was paired with a younger girl—with three comparison persons, she was given low test scores and three other individuals (supposedly elsewhere in the laboratory) who were of the same relative age (and low status) as her partner, were given high scores. If the subject was in a low status condition—i.e., was paired with the older woman—with three comparison persons, she was given all high test scores and three other persons who were of the same high status as her partner were given low scores. Each of the comparison persons was supposed to have taken one and only one of the three fictitious ability tests the subject had taken, and each supposedly had taken a different one. No scores were reported for the subject's ostensible partner, and subsequently the subject learned her partner had taken no tests.

In a second condition of the experiment concerning comparison persons, one comparison person and one of the subject's tests were deleted. In a third condition, two of the comparison persons and two of the subject's tests were deleted. For all three of the experimental conditions we have described, comparison people appeared on the screen only long enough to state their name and age and receive their scores, and they did not reappear. Thus, the subject was free to decide for herself whether or not these people had relevance to her subsequent *interaction* with her *partner*. In the baseline control condition, there were no comparison persons and no tests of performance were used. This control condition was taken from Freese and Cohen's (1973) prior experiment.

Freese found that HS subjects were less likely to be influenced than LS ones when no comparison person was present. When one was added, Freese found no difference between HS and LS subjects in influence rates. With two comparison people, influence rates began to invert, with HS subjects becoming more likely to be influenced than LS ones. With three comparison people, this inversion effect on influence rates became more pronounced.

Thus, it was shown that differentiation in influence as a function of diffuse status differentiation decreased as the number of comparison people (providing contradictory stimuli) increased. Freese's results also imply that diffuse status differentiation has a *negative* or *inverse* impact on the development of influence and status structures when two or more comparison people of this sort are present. In Freese's (1974:188) words, his results meant:

> With no comparison actors, status unequals appear to behave as unequals. With one, status unequals appear to behave as equals. With two or three, status unequals again behave as unequals, but not because of their (diffuse) status inequality. In the latter cases, observed differences in power and prestige correspond, not to the (diffuse) status differentiation between (a person) and (another), but to the performance differentiation between a person and the comparison actors. The same differences might be observed if a person is treated on general performance characteristics without comparison actors.

REFINING STATUS GENERALIZATION THEORY: SOME SUMMARY COMMENTS. In refining status generalization theory, Freese has shown that the halo effects of diffuse status characteristics can be reduced systematically by the apparently more powerful halo effects of differences in general performance characteristics present among group members or members and comparison people outside the group. In another study, Freese (1976) found that his conception of the effects of general performance characteristics also needed refinement. He discovered that the consistency of group members' specific performance ranks is apparently a necessary condition for the subsequent development of influence and prestige hierarchies. If experimental subjects were consistently ranked, prior to task interaction, on specific performance characteristics not defined as instrumental to their task, differentiation in task influence resulted. If they were inconsistently ranked on these characteristics, no differentiation in task influence occurred. In the latter case, subjects were equally likely to reject influence attempts.

EVOLUTION OF STATUS STRUCTURES FROM INITIAL STATUS EQUALITY: FURTHER RESEARCH DIRECTIONS. Having concentrated in this part of the chapter mainly on theory and research clarifying the conditions under which differences on diffuse status characteristics affect the evolution of influence and status structures in groups, or on the conditions neutralizing the diffuse status generalization effect, we will conclude by considering how status structures evolve when group members begin as status equals. That is, we will shift from the research tradition inspired by Berger, Cohen, and Zelditch's work on diffuse status generalization to the earlier one inspired by Bales and his colleagues. Although we have already considered the main thrust of this latter line of research, Fisek and Ofshe (1970) have pointed out that there is at least one significant gap in it that had not been addressed until their work. They suggested there had been no reports providing a detailed description and analysis of changes in members' behavior as they moved from being status equals at the beginning of group interaction to a condition in which they were differentially ranked in a status structure. Their research was intended to provide some clarification of this status evolution process.

In their investigation, Fisek and Ofshe created three-person discussion groups composed of male college freshmen who had no prior contact and did not differ in any obvious manner regarding age, social class, or race. The task on which these groups worked was the development of a problem that was supposed to be used as the subject for a group decision-making study. The data in this study were derived from observation of group discussion from its start to its resolution or approximate resolution forty minutes later.

The data revealed two different paths of status evolution in the discussion groups that were studied. Although all began with apparent status equality of their members, about half of the groups displayed marked differentiation in member participation as early as the first minute of group interaction, while the remaining groups displayed near equality in initial participation and seemed to evolve dominance structures during the course of members' interactions. For the former groups, Fisek and Ofshe assumed that variables reflecting socialization differences had an immediate impact on the distribution of participation and related status evaluations through different self-conceptions of members and in different behavior styles that in turn served as cues in interaction. In these groups, the predisposing tendency toward inequality showed up almost immediately in the emergence of a dominant member who controlled an approximately fixed proportion of available opportunities to speak throughout the discussion. Apparently, he achieved his high rank without a status struggle. These groups also displayed the typical association found between a member's participation rank and his rank on each of three evaluation variables, guidance, ideas, and task ability.

In the remaining groups, members had no immediate predisposition toward inequality. Structured differential participation patterns evolved over the course of group discussion. However, the process of establishing these patterns had more fluctuations, and the ultimate participation structure seemed less developed and clearly differentiated, than in the former groups. In regard to status evaluations, members of the groups that did not immediately differentiate themselves on participation apparently were unable to develop differentiated conceptions of their relative competencies that were correlated with their participation ranks. That is, unlike the other groups, these latter groups did not develop a status structure that corresponded to the structure of differential participation. This was a surprising finding for the researchers, and they speculated that it may have occurred because the members of these groups did not have enough time to interact and form their evaluations, even though they had been able to establish a structure of participation.

Combined with the evidence concerning the groups that quickly became differentiated, this unexpected finding provided fuel for Fisek and Ofshe's interpretation of the general process of status evolution in task groups. In presenting this argument, they asserted that (Fisek and Ofshe, 1970:343-344):

> There is a crucial point about the sequence of events that task groups move through during the process of developing status structures which can be clarified by (our) data. . . . The question is the following: In the course of the interaction among group members do individuals first develop differentiated beliefs about each other's abilities and then adjust their behaviors such that those individuals who are believed to be more competent receive deference and thereby are moved into positions of leadership, or is the sequence of events one in which differentiated structural positions are evolved first with the recognition (or perception) of differential competence developing after individuals begin performing leadership roles? Obviously, both of these sequences result in the typically observed final correlation between participation level and beliefs about competence.

> The data presented . . . make it possible to differentiate between the two possible sequences and strongly support the second conceptualization of the process. In the case of the groups that display initial differentiation in participation it is obvious that the group members participate differentially in the group's activity as early as the first minute of the discussion session. It is also clear that perceptions of differential competence among group members are in evidence by the close of the session and that participation rank is positively related to perceived competence. We have therefore observed a situation in which there was both initial behavioral differentiation and systematically related cognitive differentiation by the close of the session. In the case of the groups that display initial behavioral equality, it is clear that by the close of the session the group members have become differentiated with respect to participation but do not display cognitive structures in which participation rank is associated with conceptions of each other's competence. In this case, we have observed a situation in which behavioral differentiation has recently occurred and there is no correlated cognitive differentiation.

Since Fisek and Ofshe's initially undifferentiated groups failed to develop patterns of evaluation of competence that were correlated with their structured differences in participation and dominance, the researchers could not conclude unequivocally that the patterning of differential participation and dominance in groups causes the evolution of patterning in status evaluations. If these groups had been allowed to interact for a longer period of time, they might have shown this process of status evolution, which seemed to occur in the initially differentiated groups. What seems clearest from Fisek and Ofshe's research is that in both the initially undifferentiated and the initially differentiated groups, group members did *not* develop differentiated cognitions or evaluations of each other's abilities *before* they established patterns of differential participation and dominance. Thus, although Fisek and Ofshe have not provided a definitive demonstration of how influence and status structures evolve in small groups, their results offer some valuable insights about such structural evolution, and help refine some of the ideas presented earlier in this chapter about the emergence of status structures.

Status Incongruence and Distributive Injustice in Small Groups

EFFECTS OF STATUS INCONGRUENCE. We have suggested that when group members have dissimilar rankings on two or more status characteristics, they may experience the effects of status incongruence. The most immediate effect is likely to be psychological discomfort or strain. According to McCranie and Kimberly (1973), researchers have tended to explain this effect in terms of conflicting expectations or feelings of injustice or both. Following McCranie and Kimberly, we will try to maintain a conceptual separation between cases of conflicting expectations and status incongruence in a broad sense, and cases of distributive injustice where people have perceived a normative violation in the way reward, skill, and other salient ranks have been associated. McCranie and Kimberly have proposed that in cases of conflicting expectations deriving from rank inconsistency, people *do not know* the skill rank of others. This is unlike distributive injustice where people recognize a clear discrepancy between reward, skill, and other "investment" ranks. We will use the term *status incongruence* to refer to the conflicting expectations case where people lack crucial knowledge about status factors like skill rank.

McCranie and Kimberly's distinction between status incongruence and distributive injustice seems especially appropriate for task-oriented groups, because the amount and type of knowledge members have about skill rank is likely to be a crucial determinant of how they will interact with each other in task roles. Without a clear conception of relative skill levels, they may not be able to arrive at assessments of the fairness of their own or others' positions and rewards or determine the general rank of others as superior, equal, or inferior to their own.

That is, with ambiguity or uncertainty about skill rank in task-oriented groups, distributive injustice is not likely to arise, but status incongruence may arise, if members develop conflicting performance expectations from rank inconsistency. Thus, status incongruence involves status ambiguity or a lack of social certitude. We want to consider in this section how this status ambiguity or uncertainty may affect group interaction.

Macrosociological Findings

Crosbie (1975:306) has noted that most of our knowledge about the effects of status incongruence has come from macrosociological research focusing on consistencies and inconsistencies between societal status characteristics, that would be external, diffuse, or symbolic ranks in small groups. He also gave a number of examples of what this research has shown. For example, Hughes (1945) studied minority (females and blacks) professionals (doctors, lawyers, and engineers) in organizations in the 1940s and found that their employers often tried to minimize the potential problems arising from the status incongruence they could create by segregating them from co-workers, clients, and the public. They frequently were assigned library and laboratory research jobs where interaction with others was minimized.

Lenski (1954; 1956) looked at status incongruence regarding discrepancies in income, occupation, education, and ethnicity and found a positive relationship between status incongruence and liberal voting behavior. He explained his findings by proposing that people experiencing status incongruence might prefer liberal politicians because these politicians may seem to be more likely to support changes of the things in society making incongruent people, like themselves, incongruent.

In looking at discrepancies among rankings on occupation, education, and ethnicity, Jackson (1962) found that highly incongruent people reported a higher incidence of psychosomatic illnesses than congruent and moderately incongruent people. In the same vein, Kasl and Cobb (1967) found that parental status incongruence affected the mental health of their children. Crosbie has pointed out that these two studies could be seen as implying that psychological withdrawal may be another response to status incongruence, along with segregation and support for social change. An extreme form of withdrawal is suicide, and Gibbs and Martin (1958) have reported a positive association between status incongruence and suicide.

Small Group Findings

In contrast to the macrosociological studies of status incongruence, small-group studies have produced less striking findings of its effects. Crosbie (1975: 306) has explained: "This is, in part, the result of the fact that status inconsistency in groups is less pervasive than societal inconsistency. A member of a group spends only part of his time in interaction with other group members but a member of society spends all of his interaction time with other members of society. Also, the lack of striking effects is the result of the fact that small-group researchers have not paid as much attention to status inconsistency as they should have." Nevertheless, if status inconsistency or incongruence can have dramatic effects on individual behavior in the larger society, we would expect it to be able to produce at least some disruption of interaction patterns in small groups. In fact, according to Crosbie, the small-group studies that have been conducted regarding status incongruence have suggested such disruptive consequences, as well as efforts to control them.

We have already considered the tension, dissatisfaction, and complaints Homans (1953) assumed to result from status incongruence in the utility company accounting office he studied. There may be some question about whether this case represents distributive injustice or staus incongruence in the more general sense. However, whatever the form of their rank inconsistency, the ledger clerks felt "aggrieved." Unfortunately, though, we do not learn from Homans's research how the quality of the ledger clerks' work or their relations with the cash posters were affected by the failure of management and their union to respond to their complaints and rectify their rank inconsistency. We need to turn to other research to discover how variables such as quality of work and the nature of interpersonal relations might be affected by status incongruence.

In one example of research of this sort, Adams (1953) studied the effects of status congruence and incongruence on fifty-two, eleven-man Air Force medium bombardment crews.[17] His research staff identified a number of status dimensions of the crew members that were believed to be important to these men. The status criteria were classified by Golembiewski (1962:125) under three functional roles: *individual prominence* (including crew position importance, education, military rank, length of service), *group task facilitation* (including combat time, reputed ability, and amount of flying time), and *sociability* (or popularity). In interpreting his results, Adams applied the status congruence and incongruence concepts more at the group than individual level.[18] He found that crews with moderate status congruence were superior in technical performance to crews with high or low status congruence. He also found that crews acted in a more harmonious and trusting manner and demonstrated more friendship and intimacy as status congruence increased.

The productivity finding is interesting because it indicates that there may not be a linear relationship between status congruence of groups and the quality of their technical performance. In considering this result, Golembiewski suggested that the type of task may influence the nature and direction of this relationship. He observed: "Some degree of status congruence probably contributes to increased productivity on many tasks through such means as improved

[17]This study has been summarized and discussed by Golembiewski (1962:124–126); and we are relying on his comments here.

[18]Sampson (1963) has pointed out that the status congruence factor may be viewed as a characteristic of the social structure and as a characteristic of a particular unit of that structure, e.g., an individual person. This means one can meaningfully refer to the extent a group has evolved a congruent status structure, or to the extent a given individual's status-ranks are congruent.

communication and cooperation. But high status congruence (or low incongru-ence) may be 'externally' dysfunctional on many tasks when the small group is in a formal organization" (p. 126). Two major dysfunctions of this type were suggested by Adams. First, formal crew leaders may become more considerate and thus less willing "to organize and structure activity," i.e., more interested in socio-emotional functions and less interested in task-oriented ones, when they have high popularity. Indeed, their popularity may be a *result* of such an orienta-tion. Second, high status congruence for a group implies a "close integration of the crew." Thus, it may provide security against external authority of the larger organization as well as reduce fear of this outside authority, which might other-wise induce high technical performance (Golembiewski, 1962:126). Although group harmony and superior technical performance are not necessarily contra-dictory, especially where groups select their own goals and tasks, we might ex-pect informal interpersonal relations in a cohesive and harmonious group to revise production norms handed down by external authorities. This is what the Western Electric research suggested, and we will return to this theme in the next chapter.

Thus, status congruence or incongruence may have a complicated relation-ship to group task performance with the interpersonal harmony induced by high congruence and the disharmony (or reduced harmony) produced by high incon-gruence. Further evidence of the effects of status congruence and incongruence of groups on interpersonal relations in them has been reported by Exline and Ziller (1959). These researchers manipulated the status congruence of members of small discussion groups with respect to the status characteristics of voting power and task ability. They found that congruent groups were more congenial and developed more discussion consensus than incongruent groups. Apparently, incongruence created concern about power relations and it may have encouraged upwardly mobile members to contend for positions of high status-rank and influence. According to Golembiewski (1962:126), this concern about power relations was revealed through emotionally based interpersonal conflict.

STATUS INCONGRUENCE AND "ASSOCIATIVENESS": A TEST OF A THEORY. In a more recent study of the effects of status congruence and in-congruence, Fleishman and Marwell (1977) tested Galtung's (1967) highly re-garded theory of "rank and social integration." Galtung did not isolate the status incongruent person from his social setting. Instead, he explicitly considered the status ranks of those with whom the incongruent person normally interacted. He derived this perspective at least partially from the fact that the dependent variable of main concern to him, "associativeness," was conceptualized to be intrinsically interpersonal in nature. This variable refers both to the frequency and amount of interaction, and to the affective nature of the relationship. Fleishman and Marwell tested three axioms from Galtung's theory: the first, Galtung's most significant one, was that status incongruence would decrease associativeness; the second was that a lower number of status-ranks held in common by people would make their relation less associative; and third was that a lower number of "topdog links" (or shared *high* status-ranks) would make a relation less associative.

Fleishman and Marwell's study is important because, as they pointed out, there had been a conspicuous lack of research on Galtung's theory despite the high regard in which it was held. This lack of research may have been a result of some studies that seemed to cast doubt on the explanatory power of the status incongruence variable. Fleishman and Marwell noted that the problem in using status incongruence as an explanatory factor in past research was that the researchers could not disprove the alternative explanation that the dependent variable was an additive function of a person's ranks on the status dimensions being considered, regardless of discrepancies between these status-ranks. Early studies of status incongruence (e.g., Lenski, 1954; 1956; Goffman, 1957; Jackson, 1962) seemed especially vulnerable to criticisms of this sort, because several subsequent studies have shown that the variance explained by simple additive models is increased only slightly when relations between ranks are included (e.g., Treiman, 1966; 1970; Broom and Jones, 1970; Laumann and Segal, 1971; Jackson and Curtis, 1972; Olsen and Tully, 1972). In other words, these latter studies have suggested that evidence of the unique effects of status incongruence is very limited.

A possible reason suggested by Fleishman and Marwell for the difficulty in generating independent effects of status incongruence may be the lack of attention to the status-ranks possessed by people who are especially salient to those with rank inconsistency. Galtung's theory is significant in the emphasis it places on this social milieu factor. The typical conflicting expectations explanation of the discomfort caused by status incongruence is that people in incongruent situations cannot agree on which of the incongruent person's ranks should serve as the basis for structuring their interaction. In this perspective, the incongruent person wants to be treated in terms of his highest rank, while others try to emphasize his lowest rank, presumably because each wants to maximize his *own* relative standing in the situation. Since others cannot develop a clear conception of the status of the incongruent person or predict how he will act, a common definition of the situation does not develop, smooth coordination of interaction is hindered, and the incongruent person experiences embarrassments and disappointments (Lenski, 1956:458–459; Goffman, 1957:276; Jackson, 1962:470; Sampson, 1963:162; Fleishman and Marwell, 1977:2).

According to Fleishman and Marwell, the conflict that is assumed to characterize status incongruence situations should be reduced if status incongruent persons associate with another or others occupying the same incongruent ranks. In this case, both presumably would interact on the basis of their shared high status. Thus, two bartenders having Ph.D.'s in sociology should get along well. However, we would expect conflict and tension to arise if either of these bartenders should deal with the uneducated owner of the bar, since most likely both the bartender and owner would want to structure their interaction around a different status dimension. As Fleishman and Marwell (1977:2) suggest: "The pattern of rank positions held by others may thus diminish or aggravate the conflict experienced by status-inconsistent individuals."

The injection of social context and interpersonal comparison factors into Galtung's theory and Fleishman and Marwell's test of it, makes Fleishman and Marwell's research an especially interesting and important contribution to the status incongruence literature. Their research consisted of a survey experiment, in which subjects responded to a questionnaire describing a hypothetical situation and asking them to predict the reactions of the two people described in the story.[19] Subjects were presented with stories concerning the rank positions of two individuals, named Smith and Jones, on two status dimensions, which was the situation on which Galtung focused. Each of Smith's two ranks and Jones's two ranks was treated as a separate independent variable with two states, high or low. Four stories were used in which these two characters were either Air Force pilots, aspiring actors, businessmen, or graduate students. Smith and Jones occupied ranks on two dimensions, ability and job status, which suggests the potential relevance of Fleishman and Marwell's findings to distributive injustice.[20] However, since Fleishman and Marwell believed that subjects would strongly expect these ability and job status ranks to be closely related, and since these ranks incorporated several others (including knowledge, skill, income, and power) mentioned by Galtung as relevant to status incongruence theory, their research could be viewed as a critical test of his model. That is, unsuccessful predictions under these conditions would seriously challenge its validity.

What Fleishman and Marwell found tended to offer general support for Galtung's theory and hence, justification for continued interest in the effects of

---

[19] Fleishman and Marwell believed their use of the role-playing approach would produce *greater* external validity than the typical laboratory approach using behavioral responses to artificially created status. Their stories were ones involving statuses of great significance in the lives of the characters in these stories. In this respect, the stories were thought to be closer to meaningful "real-life" status inconsistencies than would have been possible in a laboratory experiment.

[20] Fleishman and Marwell's subjects were asked to play roles in a reward-allocation situation in which they were to indicate their reactions to being awarded a high- or low-status job or, as a graduate student, a lucrative fellowship or no financial aid at all. Each story indicated that awarding jobs on the basis of ability was the best or usual procedure. However, in cases of incongruence involving high ability and award of a lower-status job, conflicting information was given to rationalize this situation. With this rationalization and the fact they received little indication of the *specific* task skills needed to do the new job, subjects may have experienced some of the ambiguity presumably associated with conflicting expectations in cases of status incongruence, *along with* some feelings of unfair treatment. In the latter regard, they probably had enough information to choose a referential structure of some sort to serve as a basis for justice assessments. Thus, we see here the possible *blending* of elements of status incongruence and distributive injustice in a way perhaps not anticipated—and certainly not dealt with—by McCranie and Kimberly. The crucial ingredient telling us which process, or how much of either, operated, would be the choice of a referential structure, according to status value theorists. Due to the nature of Fleishman and Marwell's research, we cannot really determine the extent to which referential comparisons were activated, thereby ultimately leaving unclear how much their results apply to status incongruence or distributive injustice theory.

status incongruence, and perhaps distributive injustice as well. They used two measures of associativeness. One was an index of the amount and frequency of interaction, and the other concerned the affective aspect of associativeness or how tense and uneasy, or pleasant, the relationship was perceived to be. To the researchers, the most important aspect of their results was their finding of strong support for Galtung's key first axiom which proposed that status incongruence would affect associativeness. This support was especially striking because each associativeness index consisted of just two or three items that were only moderately correlated.

Their support for the second axiom, concerning sharing of ranks and associativeness, was more equivocal. The interaction effect between Smith's job-status dimensions and those of Jones was the most reliable effect in the data, appearing on every item within each index of associativeness. In contrast, the effect of shared ability ranks was not statistically significant. Fleishman and Marwell interpreted the weaker effects of shared ability compared to job status or reward ranks as implying that ability may have been a less salient status dimension than reward. However, they noted Galtung's assumption that both dimensions would be equally salient, and they indicated the need to investigate further the effects of variations in relative salience.

Galtung's third axiom, predicting that sharing of high ranks would cause more associativeness than sharing of low ranks, was not confirmed by Fleishman and Marwell's data. However, the researchers cautioned against premature modification of this aspect of Galtung's theory. They suggested the need for future investigation of the effects of shared ranks in cases having a greater disparity than they had created between high and low ranks on each status dimension.

Although they did not generate support for Galtung's third axiom, or full support for this second one, they viewed the fact that they produced strong support for the first axiom as their most important result because it directly contrasted with negative or indeterminate results of other recent status incongruence studies. Their finding of clear-cut effects on associativeness suggested that a difficulty in prior research may have been a failure to account for effects of the social frame of reference or process where people compare their own rank consistency or inconsistency with the configuration of ranks possessed by others. It might be added that the specific content of their finding concerning the effects of status congruence and incongruence on associativeness is in line with a main thrust of the findings of Adams (1953) and Exline and Ziller (1959) that we described earlier. Collectively, they imply that groups with greater status incongruence will have more unsettled and unharmonious interaction patterns.

STATUS INCONGRUENCE AND STATUS EQUILIBRATION IN SMALL GROUPS: "STREET CORNER SOCIETY" AND OTHER STUDIES. If status incongruence really has disruptive or dysfunctional implications for group interaction, we also might assume it will produce a desire to control or eliminate it. Sampson (1963) has suggested that in both Adams's and Exline and Ziller's research, there is evidence that status incongruence is undesirable and that people subjected to status incongruence want to establish congruent status structures. This latter tendency is called status equilibration, as we noted earlier. It appears among Adams's Air Force crewmen in the dissatisfaction and frustration of those in incongruent situations, who viewed themselves as inappropriately placed in their group. Exline and Ziller suggested that if conditions of their research setting had allowed it, the incongruent discussion groups in their study might have changed toward a congruent status structure. Whyte (1943; 1955) has presented an interesting case study that more clearly reveals how group members may control status incongruence.

Whyte's classic study of "street corner society" provides insight into status equilibration or the maintenance of status congruence in informal groups in its treatment of bowling and social ranking in the "Norton Street Gang" (1955: 14-25). The Nortons were thirteen young men in their twenties, and they had a well-established status structure with one member Alec occupying the bottom rung of the status ladder with another member Tommy. During the period Whyte observed the Nortons, bowling was a favorite group activity, and Alec was one of the members who bowled quite a bit. In fact, despite his low performance and status regarding other activities, Alec saw himself as a good bowler and he frequently excelled during the week when he bowled with Frank, Long John, Joe Dodge, and Whyte himself (who was a participant observer). However, Whyte's position was really outside the group, Frank and Joe had relatively low statuses in the group, and only Long John had fairly high status. But even Long John did not have much influence in the group, since his high position derived from his friendship with the three top members, Mike, Danny, and the leader of the Nortons, Doc.

On Saturday nights when the group was all assembled, Alec's score differed from what it was during the week. He had several chances to prove himself, but each time he had "an off night" and he failed. Whyte used one particular match to illustrate how Alec's rank in bowling with the whole group was kept in line with his overall rank in the group. Doc had the idea of climaxing the season one year with an individual competition among group members. He persuaded the owner of the alleys to contribute ten dollars in prize money to be shared among the top three scorers. The competition was limited to the ten members who bowled most regularly during the season. Alec wanted to use this occasion to demonstrate his superiority as a bowler over the other Nortons, and after the first four frames he was ahead by several pins. At this point he turned to Doc and said, "I'm out to get you boys tonight" (p. 20). But then he began to falter, and as one mistake followed another, he stopped trying. Between turns he went out for drinks, so that he became "flushed and unsteady on his feet." He threw the ball carelessly, trying to give the appearance he was not really interested in the competition. As Whyte (1955:20) noted: "His collapse was sudden and complete; in the space of a few boxes he dropped from first to last place." Of course, his dismal finish was in perfect agreement with his overall standing in the gang.

We gain an appreciation of the dynamics of status equilibration among the Nortons while they bowled, from the following comments by Whyte (1955: 21-22):

> Several days (after the match) Doc and Long John discussed (it) with me.
> *Long John:* I only wanted to be sure that Alec or Joe Dodge didn't win. That wouldn't have been right.
> *Doc:* That's right. We didn't want to make it tough for you, because we all liked you, and the other fellows did too. If somebody had tried to make it tough for you, we would have protected you. . . . If Joe Dodge or Alec had been out in front, it would have been different. We would have talked them out of it. We would have made plenty of noise. We would have been really vicious . . . I asked Doc what would have happened if Alec or Joe had won.

> They wouldn't have known how to take it. That's why we were out to beat them. If they had won, there would have been a lot of noise. Plenty of arguments. We would have called it lucky—things like that. We would have tried to get them in another match and then ruin them. *We would have to put them in their places* (emphasis added).

Thus, as a result of heckling by group members and Alex's own reluctance to create status incongruence, he was kept "in his place." In this example, we see the capacity of an established and congruent status structure in a group to maintain itself in the face of potential disruption. Alec's own role in this case is especially interesting, because he possessed the ability to do much better—which was even briefly exhibited in the big match—but he was unable to translate that ability into a performance that might raise one of his ranks. His downfall was not just a result of heckling and other control mechanisms employed by the rest of the group. It seemed to be at least as much a result of his own reduced effort. According to Crosbie (1975:307), additional evidence (e.g., Katz, Epps, and Axelson, 1964; Hoffman, 1972) suggests that the anticipation of status incongruence may cause a reluctance to perform well, or a self-inhibition of performance, among most low-status group members.

Although there is not consensus among past researchers about how, or how much, status incongruence affects social behavior, it seems evident from the studies we have reviewed concerning this phenomenon in small groups that status incongruence can have a number of disruptive or dysfunctional effects.[21] For example, incongruent groups or ones low in status congruence can be expected to have more dissatisfied members, less friendliness, mutual trust, and "associativeness," and be less cohesive than congruent ones. Furthermore, it appears that groups that are highly incongruent will be less productive than ones that are

---

[21] Additional research (Roethlisberger and Dickson, 1939:379-584; Homans, 1950:48-155; Clark, 1958) reporting similar kinds of results as the ones described in this section, has been reviewed by Homans (1974:202-211).

congruent or only moderately incongruent. Since status incongruence can confuse people and make them feel uncomfortable, which in turn may produce the effects just mentioned, we can assume that the occurrence, or anticipation, of incongruence by group members will activate equilibrating processes like those described in Whyte's case study of bowling in the Norton Street Gang.[22]

Once congruent group structures have become established and stable, status equilibration tendencies can be expected to reinforce and maintain the existing structures. In groups in equilibrium, these tendencies arise as members perceive the development of incongruent conditions. Crosbie (1975:305) has also suggested that if control is impossible in the existing structural context of a group or the incongruence has become extensive, the desire for status congruence may lead to a change in group structure that will make new forms of congruence possible. For example, it might involve re-evaluation of certain status dimensions or abolishing certain ones (e.g., diffuse characteristics like sex, race, or age) as aspects of overall group status.

EFFECTS OF DISTRIBUTIVE INJUSTICE. Having considered the effects of status incongruence on group interaction, it should be easier to imagine how the special case of rank inconsistency called *distributive injustice* affects the patterning of group behavior. Although some effects parallel those of status incongruence in general, there are some distinctive effects of injustice resulting from the salience of reward inconsistencies when people have normative expectations about how rewards should be allocated. In particular, people who perceive themselves as unjustly rewarded may react with a sense of moral outrage or guilt to their injustice, and in the former case especially, they may direct their anger at a particular group member or set of members whom they perceive to be the cause of their condition. These targets of reactions to injustice often will be part of the group's leadership structure, if it has one, since allocation of rewards is typically a responsibility or right of leadership. Thus, reactions to injustice could have a disruptive impact on the structural stability and equilibrium of a group. As Lawler (1975) has suggested, when victims of

---

[22]Berger and Fisek (1970) have studied how members of task-oriented groups form performance expectations in the face of rank inconsistency, and how these expectations are related to the group's influence and prestige orders. That is, they were concerned with the basic status incongruence and equilibration issue of how people form predictable relations with each other in the face of ambiguous stimuli. They postulated two alternative mechanisms, a "balancing" mechanism and a "combining" mechanism, by which expectations could be formed in this situation. In the case of the former mechanism, it was assumed that where rank consistency existed, expectations would be formed to correspond to the actual ranks. However, where rank inconsistency existed, it was assumed that the balancing mechanism would cause a cognitive alteration in the conception of rank relations—e.g., ignoring ranks out of line with others—and that expectations would be based on the cognitively altered and balanced conception. The combining mechanism was assumed to shape expectations on the basis of a combination or average of the performance information contained in the states of status characteristics of people in congruent or incongruent situations. Berger and Fisek's experimental results provided support for the combining mechanism formulation.

injustice combine forces to form a revolutionary coalition, the consequences could be especially disruptive.

Since the consequences of overreward intuitively might seem to be relatively harmless or undramatic for group behavior, there may be a tendency to overlook this form of injustice when considering reactions to rewards. However, it too represents a normative violation—getting "too much" versus "too little" —and therefore qualifies as injustice. In group contexts where overrewarded members must interact with others who are justly rewarded or underrewarded, overrewarded members could feel quite uncomfortable, presumably as a result of guilt or embarrassment. Thus, along with an examination of results concerning the apparently more dramatic implications of underreward, we will also consider what research has shown about the effects of overreward on group interaction.

Injustice and Structurally Unbalanced Situations

In our earlier discussion of the concepts of distributive justice and injustice, we noted the assumptions by status value theorists (e.g., Anderson *et al.,* 1969) that justice situations tend to be balanced and stable and injustice situations tend to be unbalanced and produce strain and pressures toward social change. Anderson, Berger, Zelditch, and Cohen concentrated their attention on reactions to unbalanced situations involving injustice and examined five classes of these situations. For each, they focused on two people, p and his or her referent, o. For these two people, they limited their perspective to dichotomous rankings (positive or high and negative or low) on the reward factor and one other status characteristic, ability. They assumed that a referential structure would be activated when ability and reward ranks were inconsistent.

The five classes of unbalanced situations were: (1) cases in which p is overrewarded, while o is justly rewarded; (2) cases in which p is underrewarded, while o is justly rewarded; (3) cases in which both p and o are unjustly rewarded in the same way; (4) cases of maximum system imbalance where both p and o are unjustly rewarded but in opposite ways; and (5) cases where p is justly and o unjustly rewarded. Using this perspective, they reviewed past research, and analyzed p's reactions in terms of behavior toward three kinds of significant others: namely, referents, sources, and audiences. They defined a *referent* as another person—the o to whom we have already referred—with whom p interacts or expects to interact. They defined a *source* as a person perceived by p as capable of evaluating him in regard to his level of ability and as controlling reward allocation in the situation. And they defined an *audience* group as referring to people who are unable to evaluate which state of ability p possesses, but can recognize that p possesses a highly valued reward state.

Reactions to Overreward: The Adams Research Tradition

The evidence reviewed by Anderson and his colleagues (Anderson *et al.,* 1969; Anderson and Shelly, 1970; 1971) regarding cases where p is overrewarded and o is justly rewarded has largely been produced from an experimental situation like the one originally developed by Adams (see, e.g., Adams and

Rosenbaum, 1962; Adams, 1963; 1965; Adams and Jacobsen, 1964). In it the experimenter—as source—instructs the subject *(p)* that he is clearly not very competent on the ability required for successful task performance. The way this was accomplished is indicated by the following verbatim quote from the description of justice (Low-dissonance) and overreward (High- and reduced-dissonance) manipulations used in one of Adams's experiments (Adams and Jacobsen, 1964):

From the time that the subjects reported for work the sequence of experimental events was as follows:

1. The subjects first filled out the standard application for employment used by the University, which requests demographic, educational, and previous employment data. This lent realism to the employment situation and provided a partial basis for later manipulation of perceived qualifications.

2. The subject took the "Ohio Test of Proofreading Aptitude," which consisted of 20 spelling words and a passage of text containing 10 typographical errors. The subject's alleged performance on this test also served as a basis for manipulating perceived qualifications.

3. The experimenter studied the application form and test results in the subject's presence and proceeded with the induction appropriate to the condition to which the subject had been assigned. The differential inductions were as follows:

High- and reduced-dissonance conditions (HD and RD):

Well, you don't have nearly enough experience of the type we're looking for. We were hoping to find someone who had previously had actual job experience correcting publishers' proofs of a manuscript. It's really important that this be done by someone who is experienced in this sort of work. It takes special training to have the skill necessary to catch all the sorts of errors that can creep into the proofs. They will have to be returned to the publishers soon, and we can't afford to have any mistakes slip by. (Pause.) Your score on this proofreading test isn't really satisfactory either. Would you wait here just a moment (Brief exit).

(High dissonance conditions—HD): Well, I guess I'll have to hire you anyway, but please pay close attention to the instructions I will give you. If there's anything you don't understand, don't hesitate to ask for clarification. This job on the surface sometimes appears deceptively easy. Since I'm going to hire you, I'll just have to pay you at the rate I quoted you, which is 30 cents per page.

(Reduced dissonance condition—RD): Well, I guess I can hire you anyway, but I can't pay you at the regular rate of 30 cents per page. I can only pay you 20 cents per page, because your qualifications aren't sufficient. Please pay close attention to the instructions I will give you. If there's anything you don't understand, don't hesitate to ask for clarification. The job on the surface sometimes appears deceptively easy.

Low-dissonance conditions (LD):

This is fine; you're just what we were looking for. You meet all the qualifications that were required, and your score on this proofreader's test looks very good. So far as pay is concerned, you probably are aware that we pay 30 cents per page. This rate is standard for work of this kind done by qualified people.

Using this version of the experimental situation or a variant involving payment by the hour (Adams and Rosenbaum, 1962; Adams, 1963) instead of on a piece-rate basis, Adams and his coworkers looked at how work output was affected by the overreward (HD and RD) and justice (LD) conditions. The data were presented in two ways, in terms of the quantity of work done, and in terms of its quality. Adams's theory predicted that overpaid subjects, working on an hourly basis, would try to reduce their injustice and the discomfort presumably associated with it, by producing more work than justly paid subjects. In this way, they could compensate for their overpayment with an input of extra effort. In the piece-rate situation, Adams expected overpaid subjects to cut down on quantity so that the *quality* of their work would be better. His reasoning was that the rate of reward was fixed and subjects could only manipulate their investments of the quantity and quality of their work to compensate for their being overpaid. However, if they increased quantity as in the hourly pay situation, they would increase their reward, which might make them feel more guilty. Thus, by trying instead for better quality work *on each piece,* they could compensate for their high rate of pay, which in turn would reduce the absolute amount of money they received for their work.

The findings produced by Adams (1965) and his associates (Adams and Rosenbaum, 1962; Adams, 1963; Adams and Jacobsen, 1964) and by others (e.g., Arrowood, 1961) supported Adams's assumptions about reactions to overpayment when people are paid by the hour and on a piece-rate basis. In regard to the latter results, Adams (1965:286) has proposed that the reduction of income by concentrating more on quality than quantity in piece-rate situations implies that the need to reduce injustice can be a more potent motivation than the desire to maximize monetary gains.

Apparently, then, Adams and his coworkers have provided a clear demonstration of the effects of overreward on work output. Their results seem to suggest that overpaid people who know the source is aware of their overpayment will try to do a lot of work (in an hourly pay situation) or high-quality work (in a piece-rate situation) to try to convince the source their ability level is really higher than initially estimated (Anderson *et al.,* 1969). If the source evaluates their ability more highly, originally overpaid subjects will feel less overpaid, depending on how closely the source's ability evaluation corresponds to their pay level. This reassessment could also benefit overpaid people in their relations with others who are justly paid *or underrewarded.* They too, like the source, can create discomfort (guilt or embarrassment) for overpaid subjects, especially if they are fellow group members, unless an effort is made to reduce the injustice in some way. Indeed, others in a group who are more competent but are paid the same *or less,* may feel resentment and express hostility not only toward the source, but also toward those who are overpaid. If efforts to reduce their own and others' perceptions of their receiving more than they deserve are unsuccessful, overpaid people in groups or other reward-allocation situations can be expected to try to avoid as much as possible both the source and referents who are paid differently. Or, if their tension or strain is excessive, they may even leave the group or situation entirely.

People who are overpaid may temporarily or permanently leave the group where their injustice originated because they are unlikely to feel comfortable, to interact easily with others who are paid fairly or are underrewarded, or to gain much esteem within their group. According to Anderson *et al.* (1969), the people who might grant overpaid people high esteem for their high level of reward will be *outside* the group or immediate reward-allocation situation. Thus, overpaid group members may not only leave their group to escape the tension they feel there because of their overpayment; they also may leave or look outside the group to find more appreciative audience groups. They can expect contempt or disdain within the group, especially if they intend to keep their reward. They are likely to feel a lot more comfortable in the company of people unfamiliar with their qualifications, but who are impressed with their high reward. For example, a full professor of sociology at a university may fail to impress his departmental colleagues with his professional qualifications for his high rank. However, when this professor interacts with people outside the department on university committees or in local civic groups, he may be greatly respected because he is a full professor.

Although Adams and his coworkers have provided concrete evidence that supports *some* of the assumptions presented here about reactions to overreward, most of these assumptions have been based on an abstract conception by Anderson *et al.* (1969) of the reactions overpaid people have at their disposal to try to deal with their overpayment. That is, even though these assumptions about reactions involving sources, referents, and audience groups may follow logically from injustice theory and Adams's data, there is little direct or indirect systematic support for many of them. Thus, what has been said about reactions to overreward should be viewed cautiously.

Beyond Adams: Criticisms, Suggested Refinements, and
Further Studies of Overreward

Further cause for caution is provided by additional studies that have failed to replicate Adams's findings and have even called into question whether Adams was actually looking at reactions to *injustice.* According to Cook (1975:372), the main objection to Adams's injustice interpretation of his data has been that his experimental manipulation threatened the self-esteem of ostensibly overpaid subjects. Therefore, his results (at least in the hourly pay situation) were due not to injustice but to a defense of self-esteem according to Andrews and Valenzi (1970) or to attempts to maintain prior perceptions of self-qualifications according to Friedman and Goodman (1967).

In an article following his theoretical formulation of reactions to inequity, Anderson (Anderson and Shelly, 1970) also raised a criticism of Adams's experimental procedures. He and Shelly argued that rather than producing perceived injustice, the procedures created pressure on subjects to produce for the source (experimenter) because he challenged their qualifications and made them feel he was giving them a break. To provide a better test of the effects of overreward, Anderson and Shelly redesigned the "Adams experiment" for their own research. They designed their experiment with two main objectives. First, they wanted to use an overpayment manipulation free from social pressures from the experimenter on subjects. Second, they wanted to test a prediction that some subjects might try to resolve the presumed imbalance in their overpayment situation by changing their perceptions of their job qualifications. In the former regard, they tried to create a state of inequity by suggesting a referential structure and without "any admonitions to the subject to pay close attention or any expressions of annoyance on the part of (the experimenter)." To test their prediction about changing ability perceptions, Anderson and Shelly used two kinds of "inequitables" (or overrewarded subjects): "mobiles" and "immobiles." Mobiles were told the proofreading test "usually" predicts accurately how good a proofreader a person is. The immobiles were told the test "always" predicts how good a proofreader a person is. The researchers found no statistically significant differences in the quantity or quality of work done between equitables, mobile inequitables, and immobile inequitables.

Anderson and Shelly interpreted their negative results as implying that in eliminating the disapproving attitude of the experimenter, they may have eliminated a necessary condition for the creation of feelings of overreward. They suggested that experimenters using Adams's paradigm may have unwittingly created situations in which this necessary condition, disapproval from a significant other, was met, *even though Adams's theory had nothing to say about this condition.* However, a subsequent study (Anderson and Shelly, 1971) failed to provide support for this assumption.

Despite their negative findings, Anderson and Shelly were not ready to give up on injustice theory. They recognized that evidence from studies of "real-life" work groups existed indicating that overreward could sometimes create considerable strain. To reduce the murky state of knowledge about overreward and clarify the conditions likely to create this state of injustice, Anderson and Shelly suggested that researchers should try to create experimental analogs to the "real-life" overreward situations. In particular, they noted two problems requiring special attention in such research. First, they indicated the need to create a credible referential structure seen to be relevant to the task performed by subjects. Anderson and Shelly admitted that they may not have done this. Second, they pointed out that the reward-allocation situations studied probably should be ones that endure over time—as opposed to temporary laboratory settings—or represent a threat to a person's self-esteem. In general, then, it seems that if we are to gain more confidence in the assumptions and findings of injustice investigators, they must develop a more refined conception of the conditions creating perceptions of inequity. In addition, they must provide clearer evidence that cases of presumed injustice actually represent *normative violations* for those experiencing or observing them.

We have given a lot of attention to cases of underreward because they have received quite a bit of attention from injustice researchers and perhaps more importantly, because this research illustrates the limitations of current knowledge about reactions to injustice in general, both in small groups and in the larger society. We will be much briefer in considering possible reactions to other cases of injustice or situational imbalance. In summarizing these reactions, which have been suggested by Anderson and his colleagues' (Anderson *et al.,* 1969) status value formulation, it should be remembered that many of the assumptions about them are as much in need of systematic empirical confirmation as the assumptions about reactions to overreward.

Reactions to Underreward

As opposed to overreward, underreward is assumed to produce anger, dissatisfaction, or moral outrage. We can get a sense of how underreward affects people from Homans's case study of the ledger clerks. On the basis of this case, we would predict that victims of underreward will try to approach the source to impress upon him their legitimate claims (e.g., high ability) for higher pay. In cases where injustice is more clearly evident than in Homans's billing office, failure to respond to victims of underreward can be expected to produce more strain and perhaps have more disruptive effects on group leadership. The amount of disruption is likely to depend on how many underrewarded group members there are and whether they organize a coalition to protest their injustice. As for the relations between underpaid people and equitably paid referents, we might expect the victims of injustice to have neutral feelings toward those who are equitably paid, since equity is what is *supposed to* occur. However, those who are fairly paid may feel sympathy toward those less fortunate than themselves. Anderson and his associates have proposed that in regard to audience groups, underrewarded people are likely to avoid them, since they will be indifferent or give them little esteem for their low level of reward.

Reactions to Shared Inequities of the Same Kind

According to Anderson *et al.,* sharing similar inequities is likely to draw people together. We already have noted our assumption that underpaid group members may want to combine their (limited) individual resources to form a revolutionary coalition. We also might expect overpaid subjects to seek association with one another, but for different reasons—to help each other hide their overreward from the source or to provide mutual support in the face of contempt or disdain from the source or others. Fleishman and Marwell's (1977) research, which we discussed earlier, indicates that the sharing of reward ranks, *per se,* has a strong effect on associativeness. The added element of shared injustice should make this relationship even stronger. We would expect over-rewarded or underrewarded people to relate in the same way collectively to audience groups as they do individually.

Reactions to Maximum Imbalance

Cases of *maximum* (system) *imbalance* are ones involving people who are unjustly rewarded, but in opposite directions. In this case, victims of under-reward may try to convince the source a mistake has been made, while over-paid people probably will try to avoid both the source and those who have been underpaid. If victims of underreward cannot convince the source to alter their reward level in this situation, their failure will tend to reinforce their perception of the source as arbitrary and incompetent or both. Under such conditions, these people are likely to become alienated, hostile toward those who are overpaid, and to seek to withdraw, unless they can and want to form a revolutionary coalition with others like themselves.

Reactions to Just Rewards in Situations
with Unjustly Rewarded Referents

One further case of injustice should be mentioned, even though its basic elements have generally been covered. It is the case that combines people who are fairly rewarded with referents who are not. Despite their own fair treat-ment in such cases, equitably rewarded people still may feel uncomfortable in the face of overrewarded or underrewarded referents, because the existence of others' injustice suggests the source may be unreliable or incompetent and may treat justly rewarded people like themselves unfairly in the future. People who are fairly rewarded will probably feel sympathy for the underrewarded and dis-dain or hostility toward the overrewarded; and they may become angry with audiences who fail to appreciate the ability of the underrewarded or who honor the overrewarded.

Structural Effects of Reactions to Injustice in Small Groups

Since sources are typically leaders, reactions to injustice in groups may have implications for the stability of group leadership structures, and in turn for the structural stability and equilibrium of the group in general. The legitimacy of the leader is likely to be seriously weakened by his perceived unfairness as a source, especially when *fairly* rewarded group members begin to doubt the fair-ness or competence of the leader because they can see examples of injustice around them. On the other hand, research by Michelini and Messe (1974) sug-gests that when leaders are perceived as fair in their allocation of rewards, their legitimacy and influence may be enhanced even when orders include a threat. In particular, they found that negative affective reactions to a threat resulted only when the threatener demanded an unfair share of rewards for himself. We might infer, then, the way people react to the influence attempts of leaders as sources when a justice norm is present and salient will depend more on their degree of fairness than the degree of coerciveness of their influence.

With Michelini and Messé's findings, we see additional evidence of another possible structural effect of distributive injustice in small groups. It appears that the task ahead for injustice researchers is to clear up the equivocal findings and provide systematic confirmation of the numerous possible implications suggested by injustice theorists for group structures. The recent work of status value theorists and researchers seems to offer the most fruitful direction for investigators interested in structural implications of injustice in small groups; and that is why this work has received primary emphasis in our discussion of the nature and effects of injustice.

PROBLEMS OF STATUS RELATIONS IN SMALL GROUPS: A SELECTIVE FOCUS ON RESEARCH

In the concluding sections of this chapter, we will focus special attention on three studies concerning interesting and potentially significant problems of status in groups. One study is by MacNeil, Davis, and Pace (1975) and concerns a serendipitous finding about group status displacement under stress. The second is by Short and Strodtbeck (1963) and is about the response of gang leaders to status threats to their leadership or influence. The third is a study by Pearlin (1975) about status and stress in marriage.

Group Status Displacement Under Stress

MacNeil, Davis, and Pace noted that there had been phenomenological evidence indicating that people in high stress situations may behave in ways contrary to established status and role expectations, even in well-stabilized natural groups (e.g., Leighton, 1945). However, because of the ethical limitations of experimentally manipulating stress or creating extreme forms of it merely for research purposes, there have been relatively few experimental reports of the effects of real and severe stress on members of natural groups. Thus, the results of MacNeil, Davis, and Pace's fortuitous experimental opportunity to study disruptive stress and status relations in a natural group are especially interesting and valuable.

The original aim of MacNeil, Davis, and Pace's research was to develop methods of sociogramming informal (natural) groups of teenaged boys through the use of a disguised technique. The members of these groups were high-school students at a boarding school. The unfortunate fortuitous event that changed the course of the researchers' study was the severe stress created in one group as a result of the accidental death of one of its members a few hours before its scheduled participation in the experiment.

The death occurred because this member had accepted the challenge of the group leader to chug-a-lug a fifth of vodka; it was made especially traumatic by the fact that possession of alcohol by these boys was a violation of both boarding school rules *and* state laws. In addition, after the tragedy, the party, held after dark in the school ground woods, broke up and the boys returned unobtrusively to their dormitories, leaving the body. About an hour later during bed check, school authorities realized the dead boy was missing, aroused the group members, asked where they had been, and located the body of the missing boy. The police entered the scene and took statements from each boy.

When Davis arrived, the police had finished taking initial statements. After spending time alone with the boys and listening to their story, he asked them if they still were interested in participating in the experiment, which was scheduled to begin in one hour. After deliberating among themselves, they decided they would "really rather do that than just sit around here waiting for the police—and anyway we don't want to miss the steak feed" (p. 294). The "steak feed" was payment for participation in the experiment since the boys were not allowed to have cash. The researchers considered the consequences of proceeding, and decided to follow the group's wishes.[23] Thus, a new condition—extreme stress—was added to their study.

MacNeil, Davis, and Pace's study involved three sociometric devices for measuring group membership and member status within the group, with member status based on a criterion of effective initiative in two cases and perceived self-performance and performance of other in-group members in the third. The three measures, in chronological sequence of administration, were: (1) a *disguised sociogram* for the selection and initial structuring of groups, administered about one month before; (2) a *highly unobtrusive* measure called the *"baseball sociogame"* (a baseball throw and judgment task); and (3) an *undisguised situational sociogram* administered immediately after the group's participation in the sociogame. In addition to the high-stress group, there were two other natural groups of boys from the boarding school who were involved in the research.

The baseball sociogame used by MacNeil, Davis, and Pace was a modified version of the game used in Sherif, White, and Harvey's (1955) research, which we discussed earlier, to obtain unobtrusive measures of performance evaluations. On the basis of this prior research, we normally would expect performance evaluations derived from the sociogame and from situational sociogram questionnaire items following it to be highly correlated with status rankings obtained from the initial sociogram questionnaire. However, we might reasonably expect the introduction of stress to disrupt a group's status relations and upset at least

---

[23] The authors expressed their feeling that denying participation would have been interpreted as punitive by the boys. They were concerned with not letting them down since their relationship with the boys was that of nonauthoritarian, older friends. It should also be noted that the editor of *Sociometry*—in which the article appeared—received legal assurance that the publication of this article in no way placed the subjects at risk. He also commended the authors "for their extensive efforts to protect the rights of their subjects."

the immediate evaluations members have of each other. MacNeil, Davis, and Pace predicted that in the stressed group, perception of member performance would digress from the established and previously measured status rankings of the group members, and this would reflect member involvement in the immediately preceding stress-causing situation. Since changes in status evaluations caused by the immediately stressful situation could be unconscious, the investigators guessed that these changes might be more likely to show up on more unobtrusive measures like the sociogame instrument than on more direct or overt measures. Furthermore, they expected that a more direct approach, such as asking direct questions about how members performed overall in the immediate task or how they stand relative to each other in contribution to group activities, would result in responses based on long-term experience—i.e., rankings tied to the established status structure.

The researchers found, as they expected, that in the two groups not experiencing stress, the rankings of members based on the sociogame perfectly matched their rankings obtained from the disguised and situational sociograms. Also as expected, the results for the stressed group departed from this pattern. While their rankings derived from the relatively direct or overt situational sociogram matched the ones obtained from the earlier disguised sociogram, the more disguised baseball throw sociogame gave different results. Analysis of judgmental error in the sociogame revealed drastic displacement of members' rankings within the stressed group. Individual roles in the activities leading to their trouble were related directly to the displacements.

Using pseudonyms, the researchers described the radical shifts in rank caused by the tragedy.[24] Martin, the group leader and initiator of the party and challenge resulting in the death of one of the group's members, was "put down" from first to fifth place among the six members. He was one of the two members of the group who received negative net error scores for their performance in the sociogame. Thus, the role of initiator that usually earned Martin the highest rank in the group, this time led to his debasement on the disguised sociogame instrument because the activities he initiated produced extreme stress and tragedy for the group.

Leaper, the only other group member to receive negative net error scores, was displaced from fourth to sixth (and last). He earned his disesteem by having been the one who smuggled the liquor onto the school grounds for the party and by strongly backing Martin during the evening's activities.

Alky and Kent were displaced because of other shifts in rank. Alky went from third to fourth, and Kent from fifth to third. Rabb, who was the lieutenant, was ranked number one by an overwhelmingly high positive score in the base-

[24] The researchers learned the roles played by group members in the tragedy through an open conversation with the boys after it happened. These roles were later confirmed by an official investigation. The acquisition of this information from the boys clearly reflected the trust accorded the researchers by group members.

ball throw sociogame. Although he attended the party, he had tried to prevent it, and during the party, he tried to end the activities at an early hour.

Lucky, who had occupied the lowest rank in the group before the tragedy, was displaced upward to the second rank by member responses in the sociogame. Later investigation of the illegal party and death revealed that he had no role in these activities. He was not even there. In fact, before the party began, Lucky had left school without permission, defying school regulations, Martin, and the group. Though he was in trouble with school officials, obviously his absence did not hurt him in the group. On the contrary, we see here a case where deviance or disobedience (not attending the party) gained a low-status member at least tacit and temporary group approval and much higher status because the tragedy had drastically altered what the group viewed as valued and proper behavior.

A significant question raised by MacNeil, Davis, and Pace's findings concerns the long-term impact on a group's status structure, as well as its leadership, integration, and social control patterns, of a crisis or tragedy of the magnitude experienced by one of their research groups. We previously considered experimental research by Hamblin (1958) indicating that leaders who cannot handle environmentally created crises will be replaced. However, here we have a case where the leader and others in the group *were responsible for* the crisis. In such cases, can we expect the group ever to return to the way it was?

MacNeil, Davis, and Pace were interested in this question of the extent that the covertly detected shifts in perception of fellow group members would affect the future structure of the stressed group. Unfortunately, though, circumstances did not allow them to pursue this interest. Following their participation in the illegal party and related tragedy (and the experiment), the group was broken up. All except Lucky were expelled from the school and went in different geographic directions.

THE RESPONSE OF GANG LEADERS TO STATUS THREATS

The second study about status problems to which we will give special attention here is by Short and Strodtbeck. It examines the status equilibration process from the perspective of high-status members threatened with a drop in rank and influence. It involves observations and interviews with delinquent gangs. The researchers presented eight cases of gangs where gang leaders faced threats to their status. They were interested in the tendency for threatened leaders to instigate outgroup aggression as a means of reaffirming their high status and leadership. Short and Strodtbeck believed that this happened because of the limited resources possessed by gang leaders for internal control of their group, *especially* when their status is attacked. Let us consider the cases they examined.

In one gang, the King Rattlers, Duke is the leader. He is a good fighter and has attained his leadership position in this conflict-oriented gang by being good with his fists and by playing it very cool. The social worker involved with this gang reaffirmed Duke's status by working through him and was quickly successful in suppressing intergang fighting. Duke's leadership style is derived mainly from his coolness and his ability to negotiate in intergang councils and to control his boys.

Despite his coolness, Duke was implicated in a shooting incident involving other members of his gang and was sent to jail. The boys eventually "beat the rap," but they were held in detention for two and one-half months. While Duke and the other jailed members were away, new officers were "elected" by the social worker and group, with the understanding that when Duke returned he would again be leader. However, despite the group celebration of this event, when he actually returned, no formal recognition was made of his leadership. To reassert his leadership, Duke became much more aggressive. The boys approved of his aggressiveness, and were willing to engage in the fights with other gangs he tried to instigate. After a brief period of conforming to the most broadly held group norms of aggressive behavior, Duke resumed his "cool" image that had distinguished him from other gang members. Short and Strodtbeck interpreted the adoption of tough, highly aggressive behavior by Duke as his way of clarifying the uncertainty about his leadership that had arisen because of his detention in jail.

In the second case, the status threat arose from a social worker's failure to understand the previously existing leadership structure. In this case, involving a leadership clique known as the "Big Five," a worker who had been successful in reaching, and reducing the delinquency of gang members, suddenly discovered that a group of his boys was following another boy in predatory and assaultive delinquency. It was learned that this new leader had been in jail during the several months the worker had been with the gang, and the worker had been relatively unaware of the boy's existence and totally unaware of his prior leadership status. After the boy's release from jail, this former leader organized some "lower-echelon" gang members and led them in various acts of aggressive delinquency. This behavior was well under way before the worker understood it, but when he did focus his attention on this aggressive subgroup, he was able to control it by "capturing" their leader.

A contrasting case is the third one. It concerns the return from Army duty of a leader of the Midget Lords, a segment of a large conflict-oriented gang complex known as the "Nation of Lords." It resulted in what Short and Strodtbeck called "The Great Train Robbery." In this case, Johnnie was the leader who had been away in the service. Upon his return, he was introduced to the gang's social worker. The worker was unable to gain control over or "capture" Johnnie immediately, and, in fact, had difficulty getting along with him and the clique that was most closely involved with him after his return. One night, while returning from a party, Johnnie and his clique made a spur-of-the-moment decision to hold up the car of the train in which they were riding. They beat one man and took cash from passengers. The researchers suggested that if this "dramatic demonstration of toughness and daring" had been successful, it would have re-established Johnnie's leadership role in his clique and solidified the subgroup.

In the fourth case, the major figure is Lawrence, who was an influential member of a gang having no single and most influential leader. To maintain his high status, Lawrence had to play a central role in many of the varied group activities. On one occasion, a party, Lawrence found it difficult to play this central role because he had no money to spend, which was a source of embarrassment to him. While several of the other gang members had jobs at the time, Lawrence did not. Mainly as a result of his embarrassment, Lawrence expressed his disapproval of the party and urged the gang members to join him in breaking it up. When they refused to go along, he did not push the issue any further. Instead, he borrowed money from the social worker, probably because his status in the group made asking for money from another member untenable.

During the course of the party, another member of the Chiefs, Lawrence's gang, went after a member of the Cobras with a hammer. Lawrence helped the social worker restore order. Short and Strodtbeck have suggested that the social worker's loan and his request for help enabled Lawrence to re-establish his high status in the group after his earlier effort to "save face" by breaking up the party had failed and had created some ambiguity about his status.

The fifth and sixth cases are parallel. Both involve a social worker's problem in dealing with a highly aggressive boy who had an established role of instigating delinquent episodes. In one of these cases, the boy, Commando, was known for his daring and for being in the middle of whatever was happening. He instigated trouble in a way that brought attention to him, and he set a style of violence by sometimes carrying a shotgun. The worker first tried to control Commando by exposing him to public ridicule, by calling into question his toughness and bravery in front of the rest of the group. But the effect of this approach was the opposite of what was intended. Commando continued to demonstrate to the group he was not "chicken" and that he *was* somebody, until the worker stopped his ridicule. The approach that had the desired effect was a more nurturant relation in which the worker impressed Commando privately with his responsibility, as a leader, for limiting conflict. However, the social worker still had the feeling that in a conflict situation in which he was not present Commando would find it difficult not to "sell wolf tickets" (i.e., make a challenge) to rival gang members and instigate conflict. To him, aggression seemed to be the way to achieve a stable high rank in the gang.

A comparable case involved Bill, a tough and influential member of the Pizza Grill Boys. However, after winning a fight Bill seemed unable to do what was necessary to convert his advantage into a general high status. Short and Strodtbeck suggested that both this case and the prior one involved inflexibility in role shift after aggression, which indicated that flexibility was needed for a boy to cope effectively with leadership responsibilities in these gangs.

The seventh case concerns Gary, one of the three most highly ranked members of the King Rattlers. This case is interesting because it indicates that the outcome of competitive sports activities, even when supervised, may release a need for status equilibration that produces overt aggression. Gary was captain of one of the two pool teams from his gang. The other team won their division play, and Gary's team finished second. In the championship playoffs, Gary's team was eliminated in the first round, while the other team finished fourth and earned individual trophies for their performance. The trophies seemed to reemphasize Gary's failure in his own formal leadership position. This perceived failure happened at a significant time. Gary had emerged as one of the two top members among the Rattlers, since Duke had gotten a job and a wife and was, at this point, spending less time with the gang. Gary's apparent effort to reaffirm his high status after it was threatened by his team's poor performance in the tournament took the form of a "strong-arm" incident. His gang placed a high value on this activity, and after the tournament competition was over, Gary and two members of his team strong-armed a man. The teammates held him and Gary hit him, and took $18.

The final case is different from the others because it involves a group of whites who thought fighting was "square." They were more interested in using drugs, primarily in pill form. In a situation where another white gang strongly encouraged them to become involved in opposing "wade-ins" at a local beach to protest racial segregation, this gang initially "expressed considerable racial hostility" and "talked about getting into the coming battle." When the battle occurred, though, they chose to separate themselves from the milling hostile crowd gathering on the beach, despite insinuations from the other gang that anyone who did not fight was "chicken." Thus, this gang responded to the invitation to engage in aggressive behavior under these highly provocative circumstances with withdrawal, rather than aggression. Of course, this reaction was consistent with their norms.

Short and Strodtbeck suggested that from a practical standpoint of understanding gang functioning, this last case may be much less valuable than the others, since retreatists (such as drug users) tend to drift away from large gangs into isolated retreatist cliques. Presumably, these cliques pose much less of a "social problem" to the surrounding community than the large conflict-oriented gangs. From a theoretical standpoint, the contrast between the final type of gang and the other seven cases seems substantially more significant. This contrast suggests that there is a dependence between group norms and modes of status reaffirmation. Threatened leaders or high-status members in the first seven cases acted aggressively because aggression was highly valued and normatively expected in their groups. In the final case, even strong provocation did not generate aggressiveness. Indeed, the response of this gang was to get "high" on pills. Thus, a threatened leader would be more likely to try to show how competent he was at enjoying a drug "trip" than to show his prowess as a fighter.

Short and Strodtbeck concluded their article with some interesting comments about the role of social workers in controlling gang conflict. Cloward and

Ohlin (1960:176) had proposed earlier, "The reduction in (gang) conflict may reflect the skill of the social workers, but another explanation may be that *the advent of the street-gang worker symbolized the end of social rejection and the beginning of social accommodation* (their italics). To the extent that violence represents an effort to win deference, one would logically expect it to diminish once that end has been achieved." Short and Strodtbeck responded by suggesting that instead of interpreting the presence of the social worker "solely as symbolic of the interest of the larger society," his presence could be seen as having a stabilizing influence on the leadership structure. In performing this function, they believed the worker reduced the frequency of status-maintaining aggressive acts by leaders. They also believed that a gang recognized its obligation to the worker as a *quid pro quo* for his services *and* for the additional status earned within the gang world by gangs having a worker. Both of these ideas relate to status-maintaining mechanisms in more immediate social systems—i.e., the gang itself and the gangs of the area—rather than to the "end of rejection" in a more amorphous context of middle-class society.

Status and Stress in Marriage

The final study about status problems we will consider in this chapter is by Pearlin. It focuses on the relationship between differences in the status origins of husbands and wives and the stresses they experience in their marital group. His concept of stress has particular sociological relevance to group interaction because he regards it as: (1) involving emotional disturbance; (2) being a response to the specific circumstances of specific role areas rather than a generalized personality characteristic demonstrated across all the roles a person performs; and (3) being created not only by crises but also by continuous circumstances of "normal" or daily interaction. The data for this study were derived from an interview schedule administered to a cluster sample of 2,300 respondents in an urbanized area of Chicago.

Pearlin suggested that "love notwithstanding, . . . some couples do make invidious status comparisons between themselves and their spouses and . . . vital elements of marital exchange are influenced by whether one must, as he (or she) regards his (or her) mate's origins, cast his (or her) gaze upwards or downwards" (p. 348.) He found that it was not inequality *per se* that was related to intense stress (such as feeling very bothered, tense, bored, frustrated, unhappy, worried, and neglected in daily life with one's spouse). He discovered that what was more significant was the *particular pattern* of inequality. That is, when a spouse comes from a status background lower than his/her partner's and thus marries up, this person is not disposed to stress. When a spouse comes from a status background higher than his/her spouse and thus marries down, he/she is especially vulnerable to stress. The relationship of these patterns of inequality to marital stress was a central focus of Pearlin's analysis, and much of his article was aimed at elaborating and explaining how stress was influenced by the relations between these external status dimensions. As he noted: "When one feels himself (or herself) a loser in a marriage marked by inequality, there are likely to be problems in inter-action and exchange. . . . (W)hether or not one experiences loss depends on the importance . . . (attached) to status. But when a sense of loss does occur, there is also a very good chance that stress will occur, too. Thus, status inequality and stress become linked, (as I have shown), through status values and intervening disruptions in marital relations" (p. 348).

Pearlin tried to substantiate these statements by examining four aspects of interaction and exchange in relationship to status inequality. These aspects were: (1) the reciprocity of marital exchange (with *exchange* used in the exchange theoretical sense suggested in an earlier part of this book); (2) the exchange of expressiveness or intimate communication; (3) the exchange of affection; and (4) the sharing of values. First, Pearlin considered how each of these factors was affected by marital status inequality, and then he looked at how each could become an intervening condition mediating individual feelings of stress.

The major thrust of Pearlin's results is perhaps best expressed in his own words:

> Taking a broad view of marital transactions, then, it is clear that status conditions and status values have a very real presence. The equitableness spouses perceive in the general give and take of their marriages, the nature of the communications they engage in, the affection they experience from one another and the values they share are all influenced by their status characteristics and the way these characteristics are combined to give form and structure to the marriage itself. Status inequalities are remarkably persistent influences on marital transactions, resisting any changes brought about by mobility that occurs after the marriage, and resisting also what would seem to be the powerful levelling effects of continued and intense interaction that takes place for a large number of couples in the sample over a period of many years.

> It might appear that the penetrating and durable influence exerted by status inequalities on the sorts of transactions we have been looking at is a reflection of the different and, perhaps, clashing norms and standards that people of different social backgrounds bring to marriage. This cannot explain the relationships we have seen, however, since those who have married up have marital experiences very different from those who have married down, although each group has a disparate status relative to their respective mates. The marital disruptions that have been examined are not, therefore, a simple result of differences in custom and attitude. The ex-planation lies, instead, with status values and the meaning such values give to inequalities. Thus, it is not marrying a person of lower status back-ground that matters; it is having married down while striving to move up that is most apt to bring disruption to marital exchange. The sense of loss is keenest among these people, for it involves the sacrifice of something they prize—status. Such loss and deprivation then colors the appraisal of

reciprocities and further separates and divides couples in ways that hinder marital exchanges. But, whereas the hypogamous strivers (or those marrying down in Pearlin's terms) may experience detachment from their spouses and disruption in marital relations, people with the same status goals who have married up are outstandingly likely to experience marriage as involving equitable and gratifying exchange. Thus, social status becomes part of the fabric of husband-wife interaction, one of the conditions that shapes the appraisals and defines the value of elements (exchanged) in the marriage (pp. 351, 353).

Pearlin did not want to imply by his analysis that status inequality and status striving were of pre-eminent significance for stress in marriage. Indeed, he pointed out that their prevalence must be seen as relatively limited. These two status conditions occur together only in a minority of marriages and their impact on marital stress is mediated by other factors. He aimed instead to show how status factors could contribute to such stress. An important insight to be gained from his work for the treatment of marital problems is that status inequality by itself may be of little or no consequence for stress. The impact of inequality is likely to depend on the meaning and value marital partners attach to it. Thus, it is *status consciousness* rather than *status differences per se,* that deserves the attention of marriage counselors. When people who marry partners of lower status *also value status advancement,* there may be a tendency for them to experience daily marital relations characterized by disaffection and a sense of loss. These conditions may tend to create emotional stress and marital instability through disruptions of reciprocity, expressiveness, affection, and sharing of values in the small group of husband and wife.

SUMMARY

This chapter focused on patterns and problems of status relations and reward allocation in small groups. The capacity of status conceptions to organize social interaction has long been appreciated by sociologists. Status characteristics enable others to identify us, locate us in the social structure of groups or the larger society, predict our actions, and decide how to interact with us. We began this chapter by considering a number of important status-related concepts, including status differentiation, status evaluations, and ranking. When the expression of sentiments about the statuses of group members forms a stable pattern, a status structure has been established.

A major focus of the discussion of assumptions and findings about status relations was on diffuse or external status characteristics and their relation to status generalization and the evolution of influence and prestige orders in small groups. This type of research has largely been produced or inspired by Berger, Cohen, Zelditch, and their colleagues. Among the most important contributions to this recent research tradition has been Freese and Cohen's attempt to identify the conditions under which status generalization is likely to be neutralized or eliminated. Their research is important because status generalizations can often translate into vicious and unjustified forms of stereotyping. Apparently, states of "general performance characteristics" that are inconsistent with states of diffuse status characteristics can have the neutralizing effect Freese and Cohen were interested in finding.

In the discussions of status incongruence and distributive injustice, which both represent forms of rank inconsistency, we made an effort to maintain a conceptual distinction between these two conditions. Although both involve psychological discomfort and can disrupt group interaction patterns, the discomfort associated with status incongruence generally is presumed to involve conflicting status expectations, status ambiguity, and a lack of social certitude. In contrast, distributive injustice is presumed to involve a violation of *normative* expectations about the allocation of rewards. We considered results concerning the effects of status incongruence on variables such as group performance and *associativeness*. We gave special attention to the process of status consistency maintenance, or status equilibration, revealed by Whyte's classic study of status ranking and bowling among the young men of the "street corner society."

The treatment of reactions to distributive injustice was guided mainly by the conceptual and empirical work of investigators operating from a status value perspective. The possible effects of overreward were distinguished from those of underreward. In the case of overreward, special attention was given to research done or inspired by Adams, concerning the effects of overpayment on worker productivity in hourly and piece-rate pay conditions. Reactions to injustice were generally considered in relation to sources of rewards, referents, and audience groups.

In the concluding sections of this chapter, three studies about problems of status relations in small groups were given special emphasis. One concerned a serendipitous finding about group status displacement under stress. The second was about the response of gang leaders to threats to their status. The third concerned status and stress in marriage.

7

Group Task Performance

INTRODUCTION

While some groups such as families are not especially concerned about producing anything tangible, there are others whose *raison d'être* is productivity or tangible goal attainment. For example, business conference groups, city councils, university committees, juries, and political caucuses are formed to make recommendations or decisions affecting not only themselves but also, and perhaps more importantly, the members of larger organizations, or communities, or the society in general. Sports teams are, or are supposed to be, concerned with defeating their opponents. Airplane flight crews aim at the tangible goal of getting their passengers to their desired destination on time while also keeping them happy. Engineering construction crews are supposed to try to build buildings, bridges, dams, roads, or whatever else they have contracted to do, as quickly, competently, and inexpensively as possible. Men and women in factory production teams are faced continually with efficiency ratings and production quotas regarding their work on products or pieces of products reflecting the gamut of consumer or public tastes and needs. The list of groups of this general sort could go on and on. For our purposes in this final chapter, it is most important to recognize that they are all task groups and that we are interested in this chapter in learning about some of their most important patterns and problems while they are at work in pursuit of group goals.[1]

[1] Zander (1977) has focused on "groups at work" in a book that draws from the group and organizational psychology literature and his own rich experiences in meetings and offices and as a high-level university administrator. It attempts to blend practical observation, research findings, theory, and suggestions for further research in a way that clarifies a number of recurrent problems of organizations and groups at work in them. They are interesting problems, like recruiting and removing members, secrecy, group motivation and performance, reactions to leaders, creating and coping with new regulations, group harmony and disharmony, and group efficiency; and Zander has proposed that they have often been

Throughout this book, we have considered a variety of aspects of group task structure and process. We began with some comments about how decision-making groups sometimes get diverted from rational decision-making procedures as a result of "groupthink;" we mentioned the relationship of task groups to primary groups; we described the normative orientation of group task roles; we discussed leadership differentiation in terms of its separation into task and socio-emotional roles; and we cited a number of assumptions and findings concerning task variables like group problem-solving, task complexity, and productivity. In concentrating on group task performance in this chapter, we bring into sharp relief this most fundamental aspect of a great many small groups. In particular, we will consider some basic aspects of group task performance; look at a collection of general assumptions and findings about factors associated with group task performance; give special attention to research with sports teams about how cohesiveness and related factors affect or are affected by group task success; and conclude with a discussion of group task performance in organizations based on a reconsideration of the Hawthorne studies.

BASIC ASPECTS OF GROUP TASK PERFORMANCE

GROUP TASKS, PURPOSES, AND GOALS

In this section, we will give more explicit and fuller attention to the meaning of the group task and task orientation concepts than we did in previous chapters. Shaw (1976) has offered some clarification of the nature of group tasks by discussing them in relation to group purposes and goals. He has said:

> A group forms and continues its existence for some purpose; when this purpose no longer exists, the group disintegrates unless a new purpose can be established. There may, of course, be more than one group purpose. The purpose is usually labeled "group goal," but sometimes it is referred to as "group task." Group goal and group task are not necessarily coextensive, although they are interrelated and may in some instances be identical. That is, the task faced by the group may constitute its goal, and when that task is completed, the group will have no further basis for existence. An example of this is a committee appointed for the purpose of making recommendations concerning the disposition of money available for student support. The task of the group is to prepare a statement of recommendations, and completion of such a statement is its goal. But in many instances, the task may be only to achieve a subgoal that must be attained in order to reach the ultimate goal of the group. For instance, a group may

---

neglected by social and behavioral scientists. Hopefully, along with Zander, the chapters of Part Two of this book, especially including the present one, will shed light on some of these problems as they relate to task-oriented small groups, since the treatment of task groups here overlaps to some extent with Zander's treatment of work groups and organizations. Zander's book is a useful general reference tool both for those having a practical need to deal with the sorts of issues he examines and for those interested in pursuing research in this area.

have as its goal the improvement of the educational system in a particular community. In attempting to realize this goal, the group may have to complete a number of tasks, such as raising money for library books, recruiting highly qualified teachers, etc. Whether the task faced by the group at any particular moment is direct achievement of its ultimate goal, as in the example of the committee making recommendations, or whether it is merely to achieve a subgoal, as in the example of the educational improvement group, the characteristics of the task may be expected to exert a strong influence upon group process (pp. 293–294).

Although we have distinguished primary groups from task groups, we should not think that primary groups do not have purposes, goals, or task activities. The goals and purposes of primary groups, such as families, may be diffuse (e.g., socializing their members and making them happy), but these groups do have goals, just like more task-oriented ones. As Shaw has suggested, groups exist to pursue *some kind* of purpose, and we have partially defined small groups in terms of a distinctive shared purpose among members. Similarly, concrete primary groups, just like more task-oriented ones, frequently engage in task activities, although the proportion of time spent on such activities in primary groups is, by definition, less. Thus, we know many families spend a lot of time doing things such as expressing love or hate for each other, trying to smooth over hurt feelings or creating and exacerbating them, playing or fighting with each other, building self-identities and esteem or tearing them down, and pursuing moral or spiritual activities such as religion. However, we also know they engage in many task activities, ranging from the more mundane ones of washing dishes, cutting the lawn, and painting the house to ones of broader significance such as deciding where to live, where the children should go to school, how they should be raised, and how to finance their college education.

Hare (1976:234) has proposed that in the broadest terms, "the definition of the task is the definition of the situation, and differences in behavior which appear between 'situations' are the most general indication of differences in tasks." This task conception is clarified somewhat by his added comment that "(s)ince the task is, in the most pertinent sense, what the group members subjectively define it to be as they respond to the *situation* in which they find themselves, all the internal features of the social system are likely sooner or later become relevant to task specification" (p. 233). More clarification of this notion of group task is indicated by the six variables Hare proposed to describe it. Each one was thought to be implicit in the directions for any task:

1. the kind of task;
2. the criteria for task completion;
3. the rules (or roles) which must be followed;
4. the method of imposing the rules;
5. the amount of stress on the members; and
6. the consequences of failure or success (p. 232).

Hare's conception of group tasks in terms of these six variables indicates their relation to the range of major structural-functional features of groups. However, to gain a clear sense of the distinctive nature of tasks themselves, we need to go beyond these six descriptive features, and certainly beyond defining tasks in broad situational terms. We need to know the relationship between tasks and goals, for instance. In this regard, Hare's suggestion that a *group task* is usually viewed as "the stated objective of the group's activity" (p. 232) is not especially helpful, since we typically define a *group goal* in this way. Shaw's (1976: 303) suggestion that a task is "that which must be done in order for the group to achieve its goal or subgoal" is more helpful, because we can see a means-end relationship between tasks and goals. However, since we might want to speak of *task goals* and *socio-emotional goals,* further refinement seems necessary.

If we conceptualize *group tasks* in general terms as the means to achieve group goals or objectives, then we should also have a narrower meaning for *task-oriented* behavior and activities, so that notions such as *task goals* and *socio-emotional goals* will make sense. The meaning we are applying to *task-oriented* in this book can be understood in terms of the distinctions discussed earlier between task and primary groups, and task and primary role orientations. Steiner (1974:2) has proposed that "(t)he acknowledged function of (task-performing) groups is to provide products or services that are valued by some segment of society...."

This conception of task orientation suggests it involves activities and roles that are more oriented toward explicit and tangible goals than ones having a socio-emotional orientation. We saw this kind of distinction in our discussion of leadership role differentiation.[2] In our discussion of social control, we noted some basic normative orientations that are more characteristic of task than primary or socio-emotional roles. In general, we proposed that task roles are expected to be performed with less emotion and more objectivity, involve a more restricted relationship with others, and place more emphasis on technical qualifications and skill in performing assigned jobs than primary or socio-emotional roles. To avoid confusion, it is important to keep in mind the distinctions we have drawn here between task and socio-emotional roles, activities, and goals, and the difference between "task orientation" in this narrower sense and "group tasks" in general.

TYPES OF GROUP TASKS

In general terms, there are a number of different types of tasks that groups and group members may pursue. Steiner (1974) has described some basic forms of these group tasks in the following way:[3]

---

[2] Burke's (e.g., 1967) research, which we discussed earlier, offers substantial clarification of the nature of task and socio-emotional role differentiation in small groups.

[3] Excerpts from Steiner (1974) Task-Performing Groups, Morristown, New Jersey: General Learning Press.

1. *Additive tasks:* Some tasks entail parallel but coordinated actions by two or more persons. When several people shovel snow from a pathway, each performs the same acts while endeavoring to stay clear of his closest coworkers. When young men participate in a tug-of-war, each person braces his feet, grasps the rope, and flexes his muscles. Shoveling snow and pulling on a rope are one-person tasks, but more can be accomplished by several persons working simultaneously than by a single individual working alone. Peeling potatoes and stuffing envelopes for a political campaign are similar jobs; one person's contribution is added to that of another, and the group's total accomplishment equals the sum of the individuals' accomplishments. A recipe for group success is comparatively simple: each member should do as much as he can while maintaining needed coordination with his colleagues. Although the recipe is simple, adhering to it may not be . . . (pp. 11–12).

2. *Disjunctive tasks:* Whenever a choice must be made between distinctly different options, neither compromise nor addition is feasible. Tasks of this kind are called *disjunctive* because they have an "either-or" quality. The group must select someone's solution and reject all others. The rope-pulling task could be made disjunctive by permitting only one member of the group to pull at a time. . . .

   When tasks are disjunctive the potential accomplishment of a group is established by the competence of its most qualified member. But actual accomplishments may fail to match the group's potential because the ideal recipe for collective action (i.e., letting the most competent member do all the required work to the best of his ability, and having the group accept his output as their own) is unknown or is not followed (because the group does not know who is most competent or is not willing to let him act entirely in its behalf) (p.13).

3. *Compensatory tasks:* Some tasks that cannot profitably be subdivided are amenable to a compromise solution. If what is needed is an accurate estimate of the weight of a parcel, the number of cars in a parking lot, or the temperature of a room, the independent judgments of several persons may be averaged. It is probable, of course, that some members of a group are better judges than others, but if no information concerning the competence of members is available, the resultant average may be the best decision that can be rendered. . . .

   A nondivisible task that permits compromise is *compensatory* when the relevant abilities of individuals cannot be ascertained and when individuals' prejudices may be presumed to generate errors that cancel one another. Under these circumstances, the best recipe for (collective) action requires everyone to reach his own private solution and specifies that disagreements be resolved by computing the statistical average of the individual judgments. A group will fail to follow this recipe if some members abstain from "voting" or if some defend their own estimates so vehemently that they are accorded greater weight than others. It may be surmised that compensatory tasks occur rather infrequently in real life and that they may not be recognized as such when they do occur (pp. 13–14).

4. *Conjunctive tasks:* It is sometimes the case that people who work simultaneously on a nondivisible task can do no better than the least competent

person permits them to do. Thus, the speed at which mountain climbers can ascend a cliff is established by the slowest-moving member of the team, and the distance that can be traversed by a column of marching soldiers can be no greater than that which the weakest can manage. A task of this kind is said to be *conjunctive* because the members of a group must move in unison. Of course, individuals may elect to work independently on such a task, but if they choose to function as a group each must adjust his behavior to the capabilities of the least proficient.

The recipe for collective action requires the least competent member to do his best and specifies that all others adjust their behavior to his. This recipe may not be followed because almost everyone's progress is impeded by the ineptitude of a single person. Consequently, motivation may sink so low that the group gives up, or the group may attempt to better its fate by expelling its poorest members . . . (p. 14).

5. *Divisible tasks:* Most of the tasks performed by groups are far more complex than pulling on a rope . . . or estimating the temperature of a room. Group tasks typically involve the simultaneous or sequential performance of several different kinds of activities. Winning a football game requires blocking, tackling, throwing and catching passes, deciding which play to try next, and many other specialized actions. Reaching a good decision concerning the Bay of Pigs invasion would have required that facts concerning each of several distinct issues be determined and presented, that the implications of the facts be derived, and that those implications be carefully weighed. It is characteristic of complex tasks that they can be divided into smaller parts and that each part can be performed by a different individual or subset of individuals. This, of course, is a major reason why groups sometimes excel on such tasks; no single member is required to perform all phases of the job, and one person's strengths can complement another's weaknesses. . . .

A complete recipe for a divisible task will specify the parts into which the whole should be broken, who should do which part, and the temporal order in which the parts should be performed. The recipe will be more elaborate than one for a nondivisible task because there are many different kinds of activities (subtasks) to be performed . . . (p. 15).

In proposing his "recipes" for collective action regarding each of the various types of tasks he identified, Steiner was suggesting how groups and group members should act to successfully achieve their goals. Successful group task completion and goal attainment are supposed to be the main concern of members of task-performing groups, even though they often get drawn into "having a good time," "goofing off," and other sorts of digressive socio-emotional activities as a result of the informal structure they develop to deal with the pressures of the task-oriented or formal one. Understandably, then, a major concern of investigators of task-oriented behavior in small groups has been to identify the factors affecting successful group task completion and goal attainment. Steiner's work indicates the importance of accounting for the type of group task, and in particular, constraints placed by the task on the group. These constraints might include: "whether the task can be divided into parts, each of which is performed by a separate person; whether the various parts can be performed simultaneously or must be completed in some specific temporal order; and how the contributions of different individuals can be combined" (Steiner, 1974:11).

GROUP TASK PERFORMANCE

GENERAL ASSUMPTIONS AND FINDINGS

There is a great deal about group task performance that we have already covered explicitly or implicitly in our prior considerations of communication, integration, social control, leadership, and status aspects of small groups. Indeed, since so much of the small-group literature is about task-oriented groups of one sort or another, it would have been difficult to avoid exposure to group task behavior in considering these other group aspects. Thus, this part of the chapter on general assumptions and findings about group task performance provides an opportunity to pull together and review many of the scattered ideas about this topic that were presented earlier. It also demonstrates once again the structural-functional interdependence we have proposed as a basic feature of small groups as social systems. Beginning with the structural property of group size and covering in succession, factors of communication, integration, social control, leadership, and status relations, we will look at how group task performance is affected by or affects the various basic structural-functional dimensions of small groups we have been examining in this book. In doing this, we will be summarizing the main thrust of what small-group investigators have learned so far about group task performance.[4]

Group Size and Group Task Performance

According to Shaw (1976:187), the effects of group size upon group task performance are a function of the type of task that the group must complete. Studies of these effects (e.g., Ziller, 1957; Frank and Anderson, 1971; Steiner, 1972) have suggested that group performance increases with increasing group size when the task is either additive (based on the sum of individual efforts) or disjunctive (of an "either-or" type and based on the effort of the most competent member), and that group performance decreases with increasing group size when the task is conjunctive (based on the effort of the least competent group member). Shaw interpreted these effects of group size and type of task to be the result of task norms governing how individual resources can be used by the group, as well as the probability that people competent on the task will be members of the group.

---

[4]This summary derives mainly from the extensive reviews of group task performance research and literature by Hare (1976) and Shaw (1976).

Communication and Group Task Performance

According to Hare (1976:343), research has suggested that feedback from receivers to senders of messages increases the accuracy of messages transmitted through a communication network, so that groups maximizing free flow of communication tend to be more accurate in their judgments—even though they may take longer to arrive at a decision. An exception to this pattern was found in a study by Knutson (1960). In this research, task performances concerning preparation of a public health pamphlet were compared for quiet and noisy or very vocal groups. It was found that the quiet groups had difficulty getting organized, but performed better at the task once they did. The noisy groups spent too much time talking and worked too fast. Additional research about communication and task performance reviewed by Shaw (1976:152) indicated to him that decentralized communication networks tended to be most efficient when group tasks were more complex, while centralized networks tended to be more efficient when group tasks were relatively simple. According to Mills (1967:85), research about effects of group success has generally shown that members in more successful as opposed to less successful groups, tend to communicate with each other more freely and clearly, and to coordinate their activities more closely.

Integration and Group Task Performance

COHESIVENESS AND GROUP TASK PERFORMANCE. A major integration variable frequently studied in regard to group task performance is cohesiveness. Groups that are more cohesive tend to work harder regardless of outside supervision, and they tend to be more productive if they are motivated to perform well (Hare, 1976:340). We would assume from our prior discussion of cohesiveness that groups will be more motivated to perform well when their goals and tasks are of their own choosing, rather than coercively or arbitrarily imposed on them. Research has also suggested that group task success will enhance group cohesiveness, implying that the relationship between cohesiveness and group task performance is mutually reinforcing.

INTERPERSONAL ATTRACTION AND GROUP TASK PERFORMANCE. The relationship between friendship or interpersonal attraction and group productivity seems a bit more complicated than the cohesiveness relationship. On the one hand, pairs of close friends were found to be more efficient in problem-solving than pairs of strangers (Husband, 1940), and ratings of proficiency for six-man reconnaissance units from the same army regiment were highly correlated with the proportion of intraunit friendship choices (Goodacre, 1951). According to Hare (1976:209), this positive effect of interpersonal attraction may be the result of higher *morale* or *attractiveness* of groups containing the most friends, and of the increased ease of communication in groups that are more friendly.

Research has also shown, on the other hand, that if too much time is spent by friends in socio-emotional activity, group productivity will be less. As we have seen from the Western Electric Hawthorne research, group output may be reduced, too, when members informally conspire to lower it. An experimental study by Schachter and his colleagues (Schachter *et al.*, 1951) suggest that efforts of the group to impose a work slowdown will be more effective if group members are more friendly.

Further evidence from Berkowitz (1956), concerning member liking and group effectiveness of bomber crews, indicates that groups in which members are not highly attracted to one another may still be capable of effective task performance. It appears from his research that group cohesiveness and task commitment can affect the relationship between interpersonal attraction and group effectiveness. In particular, he found that crews who were not very friendly were still effective if their members shared a high regard for their job in the air corps (Hare, 1976:340). Although friendliness may not be a requirement for group effectiveness, it appears that effective groups may become more friendly. Berkowitz also found that bomber crews receiving high ratings from superiors tended to associate with each other more frequently during off-duty hours than crews receiving lower ratings.

COOPERATION, COMPETITION, AND GROUP TASK PERFORMANCE. Another important integration-related variable having an impact on group task performance is the extent to which group members are cooperative or competitive in their task orientation. The classic research in this area was conducted by Deutsch (1949). For his experiment, he divided an introductory psychology class into ten five-person groups that were to meet for a three-hour problem-solving session each week for five consecutive weeks. Involvement in the experiment replaced regular class participation during this period. In the first week, the ten groups were observed and rated as they discussed a human relations problem. Ratings of discussion productivity were then used to pair off equivalent groups. For the five pairs, one half was randomly assigned to the cooperative condition, while the other half was assigned to the competitive condition.

The cooperative and competitive groups were distinguished by their reward incentive system. In the former groups, members were given instructions indicating that the group as a whole would be rated in comparison with the efforts of four other similarly constituted groups. They also were told that the grade or reward each member received would be the same and determined by the relative position of the group in contrast to the four other similar groups. Competitive groups were instructed that each member would be rated in comparison with the efforts of the other four members in his group, and that the grade or reward each would receive would be different and determined by relative contributions of each member to the group's solution of its problem.

In his summary of Deutsch's main findings, Hare (1976:245)[5] proposed that in comparison with the competitively organized groups, the cooperative ones had the following productivity-related characteristics:

1. *Stronger individual motivation* to complete the group task and stronger feelings of obligation toward the other members.
2. Greater *division of labor* both in content and frequency of interaction among members and greater coordination of effort.
3. More *effective intermember communication.* More ideas were verbalized, and members were more attentive to one another and more accepting of and affected by each other's ideas . . .
4. More *friendliness* was expressed in the discussion, and members rated themselves higher on strength of desire to win the respect of one another. Members were also more satisfied with the group and its products.
5. More *group productivity.* Puzzles were solved faster, and the recommendations produced for the human relations problems were longer and qualitatively better. However, there were no significant differences in the average individual productivity as a result of the two types of group experience, nor were there any clear differences in the amounts of individual learning which occurred during the discussions.

Social Control and Group Task Performance

It appears that the major connection between group productivity and social control concerns the production norms actually accepted by group members, as implied by our earlier comments about cohesiveness and group task performance. Apparently, when external authorities try to impose output standards not in accord with informal group norms established by workers or task group members themselves, actual group output will be in line with the informal, rather than external or formal standards.

The capacity of groups to enforce their own informal standards is likely to be greater in more cohesive groups. Evidence from Hughes (1946) indicates that when group members are bound together by a common and salient ethnic identity, such as being Black or Puerto Rican or Irish, they may develop a strong capacity to enforce norms not in line with ones leading to maximum efficiency of the larger organization (Hare, 1976:50-51). In the plant he studied, management tried to introduce workers from one ethnic group into three-man work teams whose members worked closely *and* nearly all shared membership in a second ethnic group. The workers already in these work teams were "old-timers" and generally they forced the newcomers to quit through obvious forms of social pressure. However, one three-man team with its members all newcomers from the

---

[5] Hare (1976:239-245) has also offered an excellent review and discussion of this study.

same ethnic group was able to remain on the job, even though they were not fully accepted by the other workers. Hughes found that in another part of this plant, women from the same ethnic group as the male newcomers management had tried to introduce, were partially accepted by other women workers in a context where each worker could work *independently.* In this context, social pressure from "old-timers" was not likely to be as strong because the newer women could effectively work outside the informal group context. In fact, Hughes found that the women belonging to the same ethnic group as the male newcomers were not members of informal cliques of other workers in their part of the plant, *and* did not conform to the informal production norms set by these cliques (Hare, 1976:51).

Although informal production norms may often be at odds with official norms or goals of larger organizations, this is not necessarily the case. In fact, when informal and formal or official norms coincide, the informal social control system will strengthen tendencies to conform to norms leading to maximum efficiency of the larger organization. Furthermore, even when group members do not accept official or external cultural justifications for organizationally-imposed goals and tasks, their performance may still be consistent with what is expected by the organization. We see this latter tendency in studies of military combat units showing that the motivation to fight derived more from primary group norms and attachments in these units than from more diffuse strategic or political goals or feelings of patriotism. Much of this research is from World War II. In their study of the German Army in the final months of the war, Shils and Janowitz (1948:281) observed: "It appeared that a soldier's ability to resist is a function of the capacity of his immediate group (squad or section) to avoid social disintegration."

In a related but more recent study involving Israeli soldiers at outposts in a battlefield situation, Shirom (1976) found that combat performance was not related to normative commitment to societal values or goals legitimizing combat behavior, the most important being the objectives of war. Instead, the effectiveness of these units was associated with favorable evaluations of their commanders and the social integration of the unit. According to Shirom, his results indicated "in a combat unit, characteristics of the interpersonal relationships might be the most powerful predictors of individual soldiers' combat performance . . ." (p. 419).

In our discussion of leadership, it was suggested that group effectiveness or success in achieving its own goals tends to reinforce a leader's control over the group. This implies that social control efforts will also be made easier and more effective by successful group task performance. In fact, according to Hare (1976:257), some evidence has shown that members of groups which had continuing success tended to accept the group's solution to a problem, rather than their own solution. Similarly, group success can be expected to increase conformity through its positive effect on cohesiveness.

Leadership and Group Task Performance

In regard to leadership, research has suggested that group effectiveness is often closely tied to leadership effectiveness. This seems especially easy to appreciate for groups where leaders have earned their status by virtue of their performance, and the group task is a divisible one requiring effective coordination by the leader or is a nondivisible one on which the leader's own competence will be the main or sole criterion of group success. In his "contingency model of leadership effectiveness," Fiedler (1964; 1967; 1971) has *defined* the effectiveness of leaders of task-oriented groups in terms of the performance of their groups, and he has proposed that leadership effectiveness depends on the situational context in which a particular type of leader is operating. In linking leadership effectiveness and group task performance, Fiedler (1971:8) has suggested that "(t)he group is the leader's instrument, just as the orchestra is the conductor's instrument. And the conductor is considered good to the extent that his orchestra plays well or poorly."

Fiedler's connection of leadership effectiveness to the situation in which leadership is exercised involves a conception of two types of leadership styles and a notion of the "favorableness" of the situation for the leader. He considered *task-motivated* and *relationship-motivated* leadership styles. The former is one where the task group leader's main satisfaction derives from successful task performance, while the latter is one where the task group leader's main satisfaction comes from successful interpersonal relations with group members. We can see that these styles parallel our earlier conception of the major form of leadership differentiation.

Fiedler formulated a classification of group situations based on his belief that the leader's style of interaction with followers was affected by how much power and influence the leader could exert over them. Three major factors entered into his classification: (1) the leader's position power (based on varying degrees of legitimate influence, reward power, or coercive power); (2) the structure of the task (its capacity to be programmed, including decision verifiability, goal clarity, goal-path multiplicity, and solution specificity); and (3) the personal relationships between leader and members (affective relations, trust, acceptance). Fiedler considered the most favorable situations for leaders to be ones where the leader-member relations were good, the task was highly structured, and the leader's position power and influence were strong; he considered the most unfavorable situations as ones where the leader-member relations were poor, the task was unstructured, and the leader's position power and influence were weak.

Fiedler developed his contingency model by re-analyzing previously collected data from studies involving groups as diverse as high-school basketball teams, land surveying parties of civil engineers, Air Force bomber crews, military tank crews, experimental problem-solving groups, boards of directors, and management personnel. On the basis of these studies, he determined which leadership style (task-motivated or interpersonal) was required in which kind of situation

(defined in terms of favorableness). His conclusion was that task-motivated leaders tended to perform better than relationship-motivated leaders in very favorable and in relatively unfavorable situations (where strong leadership is required), and that relationship-motivated leaders tended to perform better than the task-motivated ones in situations of intermediate favorableness.

Earlier, we pointed out that leadership style could affect group task performance when leadership style is conceptualized as authoritarian or democratic. In particular, research by Lewin, Lippitt, and White has suggested that although groups with democratic leaders may not produce more than ones with authoritarian leaders, the products of democratically led groups are likely to be *qualitatively* superior to the products of autocratically led groups. However, these results might be modified somewhat if "democratic" and "authoritarian" were interpreted in less extreme terms than in Lewin and his colleagues' research.

Status Relations and Group Task Performance

The earlier discussion of the effects of status relations indicated an interesting connection between status incongruence and group task performance. Adams's (1953) study of bomber crews has suggested that this relationship may not be a linear one. Evidence from this study revealed that groups with moderate status incongruence were superior in technical performance to groups with low incongruence or with relative congruence and to ones with high incongruence. Lawler's (1975) research on revolutionary coalitions implies that in the underreward case of rank inconsistency, there may be a greater likelihood that the relationship to group task performance will be linear than for status incongruence in general. It can be assumed that as the amount of perceived underreward increases in a group, dissatisfaction and the desire to protest will increase, and this increased discontent could seriously distract from or undermine group task efforts. Although the results are somewhat equivocal, it seems that reactions to overreward will affect group task performance in a different way than underreward. Depending on how they are rewarded, overrewarded members *might* try to increase either the quantity (in hourly pay situations) or quality (in piece-rate situations) of their work output to compensate for their overpayment. However, in addition to the fact the precise patterns of reaction to overreward have not yet been clearly established by researchers, it should be recognized that when overrewarded members must cooperate with underrewarded members or either type must interact with fairly paid members, the consequences for group task performance are likely to be disruptive and detrimental.

According to Hare (1976:138), research has suggested that since groups that are well organized tend to be most productive, any shifts in status or any discrepancies in the criteria for establishing status in the group will result in more activity in the socio-emotional area. This increase in socio-emotional activity will be motivated by a desire to re-establish the organization and status structure or resolve possible conflicts or confusion created by the shifts or discrepancies, and it can be expected to reduce productivity.

Klein and Christiansen (1969) have proposed that groups with goal consensus are likely to have higher performance levels when they have more consensus about leadership status (called *focused leadership*). They assumed that high status consensus, especially concerning leadership, will contribute to better group performance because the social structure of the group will be more clearly defined, interaction will be easier, and status conflict will be less. They also believed such groups to be more attractive to their members. In regard to leadership consensus, Klein and Christiansen hypothesized that groups with more focused leadership—or greater consensus about their leader—would be more successful, since they saw focused leadership as an indication of the extent that group members could concentrate on goal attainment. Their results concerning basketball teams, reinforced by similar findings produced earlier by Heinicke and Bales (1953), supported this hypothesis. However, some care should be exercised at this point in generalizing from their results, because a later study of basketball teams (Melnick and Chemers, 1974) produced a positive correlation between the average group consensus score for leadership and the level of group success, but it was not statistically significant.

The basketball studies by Klein and Christiansen and by Melnick and Chemers are part of a recent series of studies concerning sports team success. This recent research is interesting because it involves a number of different types of sports teams, but it is important because it has possible implications for understanding group success in general. In addition, it is worth our attention because it shows the confusion that can result when researchers fail to develop and use consistently a precise conception of "cohesiveness." The next section will be devoted to a consideration of the literature concerning "cohesiveness" and sports team success.

"COHESIVENESS" AND GROUP TASK SUCCESS: A SPECIAL FOCUS ON SPORTS TEAM RESEARCH

Our understanding of the relationship among cohesiveness, related factors, and team success has been complicated somewhat by apparent inconsistencies in the results of past studies in this area.[6] However, recent investigators of cohesiveness and team success have recognized these ostensible inconsistencies, and as a consequence, some—e.g., Landers and Luschen (1974) and Nixon (1974; 1976a: Ch. 4; 1976b; 1977a; 1977b)—have tried to explain them and thereby clarify the relationship of team success to cohesiveness and some other similar, but distinct, sociologically interesting factors. The confusion in interpreting this literature results from the fact that some researchers have apparently reported a

---

[6]This section is based mainly on conceptual and empirical treatments of this topic by the author (Nixon, 1974; 1976a:Ch. 4; 1976b; 1977a; 1977b).

negative relationship between cohesiveness and team success, while others seem to be reporting a positive relationship. For example, the research of Fiedler (1954; 1960), who studied basketball teams; McGrath (1962), who studied rifle teams; Lenk (1969) who studied Olympic rowing teams; Veit (1970), who studied soccer teams; and Landers and Luschen (1974), who studied bowling teams, suggests there is an inverse relationship between cohesiveness and team success. However, the research of Myers (1962) concerning rifle teams; Stogdill (1963) concerning football teams; Vos and Brinkman (1967) concerning volleyball teams; Klein and Christiansen (1969) and Nixon (1976b; 1977a; 1977b) concerning basketball teams; McIntyre (1970) concerning flag football teams; and Landers and Crum (1971) concerning baseball teams, suggests that cohesiveness and team success tend to be positively related. Furthermore, Martens and Peterson (1971) investigated basketball teams and seemed to uncover mixed findings about this relationship. To complicate matters even more, Melnick and Chemers (1974) failed to reveal *any statistically significant* relationships between basketball team success and their measures of "cohesiveness."

The ambiguous picture presented on first glance at this collection of data is made somewhat clearer when one takes into account the different conceptualizations of "cohesiveness" in these studies, along with the different types of teams and sports examined in them. Although these considerations do not resolve all the apparent contradictions, they seem to offer a systematic basis for explaining at least most of them and for providing a clearer interpretation of the relationship of team success to cohesiveness and to a number of other similar kinds of factors (Nixon, 1977a).

In an earlier publication, I proposed that: "Probably the most important insight gained from a close examination of the apparent contradictions in the cohesiveness-team success literature—aside from an understanding of how these factors relate to each other—is that there are factors which have often been confused with cohesiveness that seem to be associated with team success in unexpected ways" (Nixon, 1976b:430). The relationship of cohesiveness—considered as attraction *to the team as a whole*—to team success is not unexpected. In fact, a close inspection of the literature employing direct measures of cohesiveness in the strict sense we have interpreted it here generally reveals a positive relationship between this factor and team success. That is, it has been found that teams placing greater importance on team membership tend to be more successful, and that more successful teams tend to be more attractive to their members.

The results concerning interpersonal attraction and team spirit or morale are a bit more surprising. In regard to interpersonal attraction, it appears that the team's task performance structure must be taken into account in interpreting its relationship to team success. On the basis of prior conceptual work by Allport (1924) and Fiedler (1967), Landers and Luschen (1974) suggested a broad distinction between sports teams with *interacting-type* task structures and those with *coacting-type* structures. This distinction parallels the one we suggested earlier between divisible and additive task structures (Steiner, 1974), and it concerns the way in which group members' individual performances are combined during group task performance or in the pursuit of group success, which, of course, is team victory in this context.

In the case of interacting-type groups, members engaged in the group task combine their different, specialized skills—for instance, as a center, guard, wide receiver, quarterback, etc. in football—in an interdependent pattern of interaction or teamwork during goal attainment efforts. For coacting-type groups, members more or less independently—without direct interaction—perform similar or identical tasks, and their group performance is an additive function of the independent individual performances of group members, as in the case of skiers competing as members of a team. In addition to football teams, rugby, basketball, hockey, baseball, volleyball, soccer, and lacrosse teams offer examples of interacting-type groups. Along with ski teams, golf, bowling, wrestling, boxing, gymnastics, crew, rifle, track and field (individual events), tennis (singles competition), and swimming (individual events) teams illustrate the concept of a coacting-type group.

When interpersonal attraction evidence is considered in light of this task factor, it generally shows that for interacting-type teams, harmonious relations, though not necessarily highly intimate primary ones, among team members tend to promote, and be promoted by, team success. Apparently, when members of these teams find their close teamwork rewarded by victories, they tend to feel friendlier toward each other; this harmony makes effective teamwork more likely in the future. On the other hand, if teams requiring interaction among teammates are not successful, these team members come to dislike, resent, or feel antagonistic toward those teammates who are part of their group's poor performance. As Homans (1974) has suggested, high rates of interaction (or teamwork) under rewarding circumstances, such as team victory, will create more positive interpersonal sentiments than similar rates of interaction under more negative circumstances, such as defeat. Of course, losing also makes efforts of team members to cooperate effectively more difficult in the future.

Results concerning coacting-type teams suggest a negative, rather than positive, association between interpersonal attraction or harmony and team success. That is, for coacting-type teams, members can work as rivals on their relatively independent tasks, as in the case of two fiercely competitive downhill racers vying for the top position on their national ski team. Thereby they can *enhance* the overall performance level of their team. The crucial aspect of the task performance structure of such teams for the relationship between interpersonal harmony and team success is that they do not rely on high rates of cooperative interaction among their members to achieve success. In fact, in this sense, they barely qualify as real groups during competition. Lenk's study of German Olympic rowing teams has shown that intensification of internal conflict can lead to improvement in group performance (for coacting-type teams) *if* they can stay together despite that conflict. The key to understanding how these groups hold together is team success. As mentioned already, more successful teams—whatever their task structure or level of internal conflict—tend to be more cohesive than less successful ones. Thus, highly successful coacting-type teams that achieve their victories at the expense of harmonious relations among team members will tend to cohere as long as they remain successful.

We might intuitively expect the relationship between team spirit and team success to be a positive one. After all, as Zander (1974:65) has suggested, ". . . in spite of the individual athletes who make headlines when they strike off for themselves, team spirit is the rule rather than the exception in sports. In fact, both amateurs and professionals generally feel that a team can't become a winner without it." Other remarks by him have also implied that teams placing a high value on group success may increase their effort, desire, and productivity as a result of that strong team success orientation (Zander, 1974). However, while evidence has been produced indicating that team task commitment is related to team success in the expected positive direction, there also has been evidence suggesting that team spirit—interpreted as group emotionality—may be *inversely* related to team success, at least for certain kinds of teams (e.g., Nixon, 1976b). This latter finding merits additional comment.

Nixon (1976b) found that basketball teams placing *less* importance on being "psyched-up" before games were more likely to be winners than those placing more importance on such enthusiasm. This possibly counter-intuitive finding may be explained by the argument that successful teams are ones highly committed to winning, but that tend to pursue victory in a cool, rational, business-like fashion. Teams seem especially likely to approach competition in this less emotional way if they have a winning tradition enhancing their confidence. Thus, it may be that past success molds confidence which, in turn, makes possible a less emotional and more poised approach that enhances a team's future chances of victory.

While this argument has a relatively logical basis, and some empirical backing, it may need some qualification according to the level of aggression involved in the sport. That is, it has been speculated on the basis of casual observation for the most part, that the relationship between group emotionality and team performance may be an inverse one for teams involved in less aggressive *noncontact* sports, but a positive one for teams involved in more aggressive *contact* sports (Nixon, 1977a). The main justification for these assumptions is that contact sports involve unusual behavior—interpersonal *violence*—demanding unusual motivation, which might include achieving a high level of emotional tension before competition.

Since the accomplishment of a superior level of team performance in sport generally requires substantial commitment to task proficiency and effective individual performances by team members, we would expect more successful teams to be ones placing relatively more emphasis on instrumental than expressive or socio-emotional concerns. This would seem to imply that interacting-types teams will be more successful when they have more favorable leadership climates, coacting-type teams will be more successful when they have less favorable climates, and hence, both types of teams will benefit more from a *task-oriented* than *relationship-oriented* leader. Evidence from Fiedler (1954; 1960), Klein and Christiansen (1969), and Veit (1970) provide general support for the argument that members of more successful teams tend to prefer more instrumentally oriented teammates and leaders, while members of less successful teams tend to prefer teammates and leaders who are more relationship-oriented.

In assessing the current state of literature about cohesiveness, related factors, and team success, one is led to the tentative conclusion that the evidence actually shows or implies the following tendencies (Nixon, 1977a:42):

1. Higher levels of cohesiveness (when measured directly) tend to be related to better performance for interacting- and coacting-type teams engaged in contact and noncontact sports.
2. More harmonious interpersonal relations among teammates tend to be related to better team performance for interacting-type teams engaged in contact and noncontact sports.
3. Less harmonious interpersonal relations among teammates tend to be related to better team performance for coacting-type teams engaged in contact and noncontact sports.
4. Lower levels of group emotionality tend to be related to better team performance for interacting- and coacting-type teams engaged in noncontact sports.
5. Higher levels of group emotionality tend to be related to better team performance for interacting- and coacting-type teams engaged in contact sports.
6. More instrumental—vs. expressive—orientations during goal-attainment activities tend to be related to better team performance for interacting- and coacting-type teams engaged in contact and noncontact sports.
7. Higher levels of past team performance tend to be related to better team performance in the future.

We hope these assumptions will not be seen as having potential relevance only within the realm of sport, despite our introductory comments for this section. Our intent in presenting them here has been to suggest that sports teams may be useful vehicles for learning about small group interaction in a more general sense. The factors we have considered in relation to sports team success are likely to have relevance to group success in competitive task environments outside sport as well as in it. In particular, sports team research suggests that an analysis of the antecedents and consequences of task group success may include factors such as cohesiveness, interpersonal harmony, group emotionality, the relative emphasis on instrumental (task) or expressive (socio-emotional) concerns during goal attainment, and the type of task performance structure. Furthermore, the analogies sometimes drawn by football coaches, generals, and others between football and war—though prone to exaggeration—probably contain an element of truth, and suggest that even the distinction between amounts of aggression in group task activities might occasionally be helpful in clarifying how group effectiveness is achieved and what consequences it has.

With the exception of the last variable, it may seem that sports team investigators have uncovered little new in their studies of group success. After all, we have already encountered the major factors identified by them as associated with winning and losing, along with others, in our prior consideration of general assumptions and findings about small group task performance. Nevertheless, the sports team research has general sociological value for a number of reasons, not the least of which is that it adds more data to the process of understanding group task performance. We have tried to point out how a close inspection of the sports studies reveals the importance of distinguishing between cohesiveness and related factors, especially interpersonal harmony, and of accounting for the type of task structure in trying to determine how factors such as interpersonal harmony affect and are affected by, group success. In addition, this research has indicated that group success and variables such as group emotionality and interpersonal harmony (in coacting-type groups) may be related in unexpected ways. Obviously, these and similar kinds of findings need to be systematically replicated a number of times in independent investigations. Future research also should try to determine how the various antecedents and consequences of group task success are related to each other in the task performance process, as well as to the level of success itself, and future researchers must also begin to identify the relative direct or indirect causal impact of each of the various antecedents on group task performance and effectiveness.

Perhaps the most interesting insight from the research on sports team success concerns the way past group success seems to affect future success. I have tried in the past to summarize the essential nature of this relationship suggested by available data, in the following terms (Nixon, 1976b:434, 435):

. . . (Past) studies . . . suggest that a tradition of past success reinforces the conditions which make future success more likely . . .

In a sense, though, to say that past success produces the conditions which breed future success is begging the question (of how a group creates the conditions predisposing it toward maximum task performance). Certainly, . . . mastery of technical skills, as well as pride in those skills, contribute a great deal to a (group's) chance of success. However, it must also be recognized that there are social, structural, and cultural conditions of groups which enable their members to make maximum collective use of their technical skills, and also conditions which can block team members' realization of their collective potential. At this time, though, it is difficult to be much more specific than to say that the sociocultural conditions promoting top performance for competitive groups like sports teams are most likely to be encouraged when group members feel that their group membership and the development of competitive excellence *for their group* are enjoyable or otherwise rewarding experiences.

It seems that the critical filter through which such experiences ultimately tend to be viewed and evaluated is whether the (group) is a success or a failure in competition. Indeed, it seems that success may often be the sole link tying members to each other and to their (group) in the case of coacting (-type groups) . . . .

GROUP TASK PERFORMANCE IN AN ORGANIZATIONAL SETTING: THE HAWTHORNE STUDIES REVISITED (ONE LAST TIME)

The Hawthorne Research and Carey's Criticisms

This discussion of group task relations would be incomplete without returning to the Hawthorne studies a final time, especially since some social scientists have subjected them to some rather harsh criticisms. We will consider the nature of some of these criticisms and a response to them, and we will suggest the overall significance of the Hawthorne research for small group and organizational investigators and members. In addition, we briefly will look at some findings in the Hawthorne tradition, focusing on the effects of primary or informal group relations on organizational goal attainment.

Few would dispute the importance of economic incentives in inducing work performance. However, Roethlisberger and Dickson's (1939) research at the Western Electric Hawthorne plant, which we have discussed or cited so many times before in this book, raises a question about the amount of independent influence exerted by such incentives on workers when they are involved in small groups in their workplace. Even the "father" of the "Scientific Management" school of organizational analysis, Taylor (1903; 1911), who placed a great emphasis on economic rationality, nevertheless recognized the possible constraining effects of group membership on the pursuit of economic self-interest in industry. In an effort to overcome "gold-bricking" among workers, Taylor persuaded men in a steel mill to shovel coal from coal cars individually rather than in groups. Once they were released from the influence of the group, they were able to earn 60 percent more wages ($1.85 per day, rather than the customary $1.15) and were no more tired than working at the old pace.[7]

Despite the widespread influence of the Hawthorne studies in social science and, to a lesser extent, in organizations, they have not been without critics. Certainly the most scathing has been Carey (1967), who argued, among other things, that the Hawthorne researchers grossly and without an adequate empirical basis, overstated their case. Their case, he proposed, was essentially that social satisfactions derived from primary relations in the workplace, were more important determinants of work behavior in general and output in particular than were any of the physical conditions (e.g., rest pauses, hours of work, lighting, temperature, humidity, etc.) and economic factors (e.g., financial incentives) to which they originally directed their attention. To gain a better sense of the

---

[7] This example was cited in Hare (1976:50).

actual contribution of the Hawthorne studies to our understanding of work groups in organizations, we will briefly consider Carey's major criticisms and then subject *them* to a critical perspective by considering Shepard's (1971) response to Carey.

Carey outlined the five major stages of the Hawthorne research as the Relay Assembly Test Room Study (new incentive system and new supervision), the Second Relay Assembly Group Study (new incentive system only), the Mica Splitting Test Room Study (new supervision only), the Interviewing Program, and the Bank Wiring Observation Room Study.[8] The unanticipated discovery of the significance of social or group factors in the workplace occurred during the first stage of this research. This discovery was stated by one of the researchers as "the great *éclaircissement* . . . an illumination quite different from what . . . had (been) expected from the illumination studies" (Roethlisberger, 1941:15).

This "éclaircissement" inspired the latter stages of the research and became the main focal point of the entire series of studies at the Western Electric plant. Like the first stage, the second and third stages were partially controlled studies "designed to check on" the conclusion from the first stage "that the observed production increase was a result of a change in the *social situation* . . . (and) not primarily because of wage incentives, reduced fatigue or similar factors" (Viteles, 1954:185). The interviewing program, which was the fourth stage, was intended to explore worker attitudes. The final stage focused on informal group organization in the Bank Wiring Room, where *binging* and similar sorts of informal social control devices were observed. Carey limited his critical comments to the first three stages, since the first stage was viewed by him as the key study and the second and third were seen as efforts to reconfirm and supplement the findings of the first stage.

It might be recalled from our initial consideration of the Relay Assembly Test Room and the discovery of the "Hawthorne effect," that the output of the women in this room increased substantially over the period they were observed, and that this increase (of about 30 percent over two years) apparently had little to do with manipulated alterations in physical conditions of the work environment. According to the researchers, it mainly was due to a change in "mental attitude" of the employees resulting from different methods of supervision (Pennock, 1930:297-309; Roethlisberger and Dickson, 1939:189-190). This change in mental attitude was largely described in terms of a more relaxed "relationship of confidence and friendliness . . . such . . . that practically no supervision is required" (Pennock, 1930:309).

Thus, in Carey's view, the Hawthorne researchers ultimately explained the observed change in "mental outlook" and the related increase in output in terms

---

[8]These five Western Electric Company studies were conducted between 1927 and 1932, and their results have been reported in a number of places (e.g., Pennock, 1930; Mayo, 1933; Turner, 1933; and of course, Roethlisberger and Dickson, 1939). The results of the original illumination experiments were first reported by Snow (1927).

of changes in supervision and consequent changes in group interaction. He suggested that this explanation was advanced after competing ones concerning changes in the work task and physical setting, reduced fatigue caused by rest pauses and shorter hours, and the new incentive system, were eliminated by the investigators. According to Carey, the first two of these competing explanations were eliminated in the first stage of the Hawthorne studies, and the third was eliminated after the completion of the next two stages. In the second stage, there was a focus on the effects of the payment system. In this phase of the research, women in the Second Relay Assembly Group were given the same preferred incentive plan used in Stage I. Under this preferred plan, individual earnings were based on the average output of the five women in the test room, rather than the average output in the whole department of about 100 women. As in the first stage, the introduction of the new pay plan produced an almost immediate increase in output, this time of 12.6 percent. The experiment caused so much discontent among the other women in the department, who also wanted the preferred system, that it was ended after only nine weeks, with a consequent 16 percent drop in output for the five women in the test room.

Carey maintained that the experimenters rejected the seemingly more obvious financial incentive explanation of these fluctuations in output, and instead chose an explanation based on intergroup rivalry resulting from the establishment of the second experimental group. He asserted that this interpretation was based on little solid evidence. In addition, he saw it as reflecting a failure to appreciate that the change in the payment system alone (in Stage II) produced as much increase in output in about two months as was produced in about nine months by the combination of the change in the pay system and a change to more congenial supervision (in Stage I).

Stage III used the Mica Splitting Test Room to test the combined effect on output of change to a separate room, change in hours, and the introduction of rest pauses and friendly supervision. In this context, an increase in output (of between 16 to 20 percent for about a year)[9] was recorded for the five women in the test room. Despite the apparent implications of this test for the significance of the supervision factor, Carey argued that it had little scientific utility. In particular, he contended that a comparison between the first and third stages of the investigation could not demonstrate the relative importance of the supervision and financial incentive factors because in Stage III: (1) the incentive system differed from the disliked one at the beginning of Stage I and the preferred one introduced after it; (2) the type of work (mica splitting versus assembling relays) differed; and (3) the experimental changes differed. Carey went on to assert that even if one accepted the comparability of the results of Stages I and III, the investigators' treatment of their evidence did not provide

[9] Here, as elsewhere, Carey noted a discrepancy in the reported increase between Roethlisberger and Dickson (1939:148), who reported a 15.6 percent rise over fourteen months, and Pennock (1930:307), who reported a 20 percent increase over twelve months.

a convincing case for the superiority of supervisory and other social factors over economic incentives in explaining output.

According to Carey, a very important aspect of the Stage III results was that when changes in supervision, hours, etc. were introduced *without a change in the incentive system,* no overall increase in total weekly output resulted—only a less than compensating increase in output per hour when shorter hours were worked. In his view, these results, along with the ones from Stages I and II he stressed, cast serious doubt on Roethlisberger and Dickson's (1939:575-576) conclusion that: "none of the results (in Stages I, II, and III) gave the slightest substantiation to the theory that the worker is primarily motivated by economic interest. The evidence indicated that the efficacy of a wage incentive system is so dependent on its relation to other factors that it is impossible to separate it out as a thing in itself having an independent effect."

Even after looking more closely at the evidence from Stage I, which he viewed as "the only study in the series which exhibits even a surface association between the introduction of (friendly supervision and resulting social factors) and increased output," Carey found little to substantiate the major conclusion of the Hawthorne researchers. Although this assessment and the kinds of critical comments mentioned before represent a strong attack of the Hawthorne research by themselves, Carey proposed that his critical examination "by no means exhausts the gross error and incompetence in the understanding and use of the scientific method which permeate the Hawthorne studies from beginning to end." He added to this admittedly radical criticism some observations about methodological deficiencies. In particular, he noted the lack of adequate experimental controls, the dubious reliability of generalizations based on experimental groups of only five subjects, and the biasing effect of preconceptions from earlier studies on the interpretation of results from later stages of the research. Carey's overall assessment was that the results of the Hawthorne research did little to support the various components of the "human relations approach," but were surprisingly consistent with the "old world view about the value of monetary incentives, driving leadership, and discipline." Indeed, he was so unimpressed with the scientific merit of this research, that he found it "incapable of yielding serious support for any sort of generalization whatever."

Response to Carey's Critique

It is difficult to imagine a more harsh set of critical comments than those expressed by Carey about the Hawthorne studies. In response to Carey's radical critique, Shepard (1971) has argued that Carey may have discarded "the baby with the bath" in leaping from his potentially useful specific criticisms to his general assessment of the Hawthorne research as "worthless scientifically." Shepard tried to show where Carey had overstated his case, and in doing so, he wanted to present a more balanced view of the actual scientific value of this research.

Shepard contended that in fact, the various Hawthorne investigators, including Roethlisberger and Dickson, have provided a more balanced view of the causes of different output levels than Carey suggested. For example, rather than arguing for the causal significance of only one social factor or of "purely social rewards" alone, Roethlisberger and Dickson (1939:185) actually said:

> Throughout the course of the experiments matters, vitally important to management, such as hours of work, wage incentives, and methods of supervision, had been examined. The mere fact that carefully conducted experiments failed to provide conclusive findings on these subjects was in itself very illuminating. Hitherto management had tended to make many assumptions as to what would happen if a change were made in, for example, hours of work or a wage incentive. They now began to question these assumptions and saw that many of them were *oversimplified* (emphasis supplied). They began to see that such factors as hours of work and wage incentives were not things in themselves having an independent effect upon employee efficiency; rather, these factors were no more than parts of a total situation, and their effect could not be predicted *apart from the total situation* (emphasis supplied).

According to Shepard, Carey misinterpreted the Hawthorne researchers when he attributed to them the assumption "that wage incentives were relatively unimportant and incapable of independent effects" (Carey, 1967:409). While they did state that the effects of wage incentives could not be understood apart from the social context in which they were administered, these investigators did not view them as "relatively unimportant." Thus, in Shepard's view, Carey failed to see the multiple causation approach *actually* advanced by the Hawthorne researchers. In this same vein, Shepard suggested that Carey was, at best, misleading in leaving the impression that the researchers used a single factor, style of supervision, to explain level of employee satisfaction. In trying to interpret their results through a social filter applied to the "total situation," it seemed unlikely that they would be content to propose "friendly supervision" alone, as the answer to problems of worker satisfaction and morale.

Shepard also criticized Carey for being somewhat myopic in implying that knowledge of the social context, which could not be neatly quantified, did not qualify as admissible evidence. By ignoring the nonquantitative arguments or denying their validity, Carey may have failed to see how social or group factors *interacted with* economic incentives and other aspects of the formal organizational structure to shape employee output and morale. While this myopia may have had an important effect on how Carey interpreted the contribution and findings of the Hawthorne studies, his decision to exclude from consideration the fourth and fifth studies may have been even more important—and shortsighted.

In particular, we have already seen how the informal norm of production developed and enforced by the men in the Bank Wiring Room curtailed their output—despite the financial gains that could have been made by those who exceeded it. The reason for this norm and its enforcement *may* have been an effort by workers to maximize long-term income and protect their jobs. Nevertheless, it was obviously not this economic incentive *by itself* that caused their restriction of output. Thanks to the Hawthorne researchers, we are encouraged to focus on the mediating role of the informal social system created by the men in the Bank Wiring Room in explaining their behavior. This emphasis on the social or group setting is the major and most enduring contribution of the Hawthorne research, and this contribution is not diminished by the various substantive and methodological weaknesses or limitations identified by critics. Carey might have been able to see this contribution more clearly if he had concentrated more attention on the Bank Wiring Room Study. However, even without focusing on this study, it should have been more evident to him that the main implication of the Hawthorne research was *not* that financial incentives—or perhaps even the physical setting—were *unimportant* in explaining worker productivity and morale. Rather, it was to discourage explanations based on any single factor—whether it was financial incentives *or* supervisory style—that did not take into account the social or group context in which it exists or operates.

The danger in accepting too literally Carey's broad conclusions about the scientific merit of the Hawthorne research along with his numerous legitimate criticisms of a more specific sort, is that one could be left with the impression that the "old world view" of behavior in organizations is valid, while the "human relations approach" is not. If so, there might be a tendency to overlook the effects of informal group structures and processes, in favor of the formal structure of the organization, in trying to explain this behavior. This could be a serious oversight, for we have seen too much evidence throughout this book about the effects of informal group membership, structures, and processes, to ignore their possible impact on behavior in settings where group formation can occur.

Informal Groups in Formal Organizations: Further Research and Comments

The existence of informal groups in formal organizations raises basic questions about how formal organizational structures, pressures, and demands affect the formation of these groups and the behavior of the organization members belonging to them. It also raises questions about whether the structures and processes of these informal groups will have predominantly dysfunctional effects on organizational goal attainment. Small-group researchers are likely to be more interested in the former types of questions, while organizational researchers are more likely to be interested in the latter. However, both types of questions suggest interesting and potentially fruitful research directions for investigators of small groups *or* organizations.

For small-group investigators, the area of informal groups in organizational environments or other kinds of environments, is relatively unexplored territory, when compared to the amount of work done on the internal system of groups. Of course, the emphasis on interaction within relatively autonomous groups can be explained by the extensive reliance on laboratory experiments with artificially created groups to learn about small-group behavior. This is not to demean the contributions of laboratory researchers. However, by getting out of the laboratory into the field and by looking at groups in organizations and in the larger society, we are bound to learn more about small groups, as well as their social environments.

Most of the research concerning informal task groups or primary groups in organizations has involved industrial, business, military, or educational organizations,[10] which means that other kinds of organizations such as political parties, trade unions, hospitals, and prisons, have been largely neglected by group investigators. Research such as Roy's (1959-1960) classic participant observation study of "banana time" for factory machine operators, has shown how informal group interaction develops in response to jobs that are extremely routinized and boring. There is no clear indication how this group interaction affected productivity, but Roy described how a regular pattern of interruptions in the work routine (e.g., "banana times," "peach times," etc.) made monotonous jobs more tolerable, and enabled workers to avoid "going nuts."

In another study of informal intergroup relations in a piecework machine shop, Roy (1954) focused on a shop "syndicate" that was indicative of the existence of intergroup cooperation in the lower levels of a factory social structure. Roy suggested in his report of this research that an informal network of intergroup relations may arise to "get the work out" in officially deviant ways when official rules and directions encourage inefficiency rather than efficiency or reflect formal administrative incompetence of some sort. Thus, in certain cases, the circumventing of the formal structure by members of informal groups may actually have functional as opposed to dysfunctional, consequences for organizational goal attainment. As Roy has pointed out, this possibility implies that we should be careful not to automatically attribute rationality or logical behavior to management, while labeling informal work group behavior as essentially irrational, illogical, or dysfunctional. It appears that at least in some cases the labels should be reversed, if they apply at all.

The combination of Roy's insights with findings of organizational functions (e.g., in military combat units) and dysfunctions (e.g., in the Bank Wiring Room) of informal group relations in other studies implies that the effects of informal structures can vary in different organizational contexts and may have a complex relationship to formal structures and organizational goal attainment. Nevertheless, it should be evident from what we have said in this section and elsewhere in this book about groups in organizations, that an understanding of

[10] See Dunphy (1927:11-31), for a brief overview of research concerning primary groups in organizations of various sorts and in urban communities.

the nature of these informal structures (and processes) and their effects is important for both organization members and researchers. In fact, Whyte's (1949) study of human relations in the restaurant industry indicates that ignorance of informal patterns of organization by members of the organization can seriously disrupt the work flow and the efficiency and effectiveness of the organization.

Of course, an understanding of the informal side of organizations is also important to small group researchers. However, unlike organization researchers who might tend to overlook the effects of informal groups, small group investigators must be careful not to overlook the possible impact of the organizational environment on the group. As Whyte (1951) has suggested, small-group researchers must recognize the limitations of studying groups "in isolation," without regard for the "perspectives of large institutional structures." In addition, according to Roy (1954), researchers who study informal group relations in larger organizational or institutional settings should be prepared to find the formation of networks of interacting groups, which adds another dimension to small-group research that has not received much attention up to this point.

In this section and in prior parts of this book, we have cited examples of research concerning a variety of natural groups in a variety of social environments. For instance, we have paid considerable attention to the Hawthorne research and to Homans's study of clerical workers in an accounting office. We also discussed Blau's study of workers in a federal law-enforcement agency; Sherif's investigation of intergroup rivalry between boys at a summer camp; MacNeil, Davis, and Pace's research on status displacement in informal groups of boys at a boarding school; and Shirom's study of the performance of military combat units. In addition, we have briefly considered Roy's research on informal relations in factories. Of course, there are other studies of this sort, concerning adaptive relations, that we have cited or discussed or perhaps, that we have missed entirely. However, if the ones just mentioned are any indication, increased attention to linkages between groups and their environments is likely to produce some fascinating and important contributions to the small-group literature.

SUMMARY AND CONCLUSION

In this chapter, an effort was made to consolidate the various assumptions and findings about group task performance appearing in previous chapters and add to them so that a more coherent and detailed picture of basic patterns and problems of small groups at work could be provided. To understand the nature of these patterns and problems, it is important to recognize the distinctions that can be drawn between task and socio-emotional roles, activities, and goals. It is also important to distinguish between "task orientation" and the broader concept of "group tasks," which could refer to the means to achieve either "task goals" or "socio-emotional goals." We tried to clarify these basic conceptual distinctions concerning group task performance, while also considering a number of different types of group tasks. Steiner's work indicates it is important to account for the type of group task, and in particular, constraints placed by the task on the group, in trying to analyze what makes task groups successful.

Beginning with the structural property of group size and covering in succession, factors of communication, integration, social control, leadership, and status relations, we examined general assumptions and findings indicating how group task performance is affected by or affects the various basic structural-functional dimensions of small groups considered in prior chapters. In doing so, we summarized the main thrust of what small-group investigators have learned so far about group task performance.

We gave special attention to a tradition of sports team research that has focused on cohesiveness, some related factors, and group task success. We have highlighted this research for a number of reasons. For instance, a careful consideration of it helps reveal the importance of distinguishing between cohesiveness and other similar, but distinct, factors, in trying to analyze the causes and effects of group task success. In addition, this research suggests that in trying to understand the relationship of the interpersonal harmony factor to group task success, it may be necessary to account for the nature of the group's task performance structure. It appears from this research that group success and variables such as group emotionality and interpersonal harmony (in coacting-type groups) may be related in unexpected ways. Perhaps the greatest value of this sports team research, beyond emphasizing the significance of certain conceptual distinctions, is that it suggests some potentially fruitful points of departure for future studies about group task performance processes and the factors shaping and shaped by them.

If one treats group task behavior in relation to the function of adaptation, attention is drawn to how this kind of behavior or its resulting products and services directly or indirectly involve a group in a relationship with its environment. In the last part of this chapter, we focused on such adaptive relations by looking at group task performance in an organizational setting. In particular, we re-examined the Hawthorne studies in terms of Carey's harshly critical perspective, considered some responses to Carey, and then tried to assess the general contribution of the Hawthorne research to our understanding of the task behavior of informal groups in formal organizational environments.

Although a number of Carey's specific criticisms of the Hawthorne studies seem justified, there is a danger in accepting too literally his broad conclusion about the negligible scientific merit of this research. That is, we could conclude from Carey's assessment that the "old world view about the value of monetary incentives, driving leadership, and discipline" in organizations is valid, while the "human relations approach" is not. This could be very shortsighted, since we have seen much evidence in this book revealing the effects of informal group membership, structures, and processes on group task performance and on relations of group members and the group as a whole to formal organizational officials and constraints. We cited two additional studies by Roy at the end of this chapter showing how organizational goal attainment can be affected by informal group and intergroup behavior.

It is noteworthy, and entirely appropriate, that the review of research about group task performance tied this dimension of small groups to elements of each of the other basic structural-functional dimensions examined in previous chapters. These kinds of ties are just what we would expect if task-oriented groups conform to a model of small groups as social systems and if interdependence is an apt way of describing the relations among basic structural-functional components of groups. In fact, the interdependence of elements of communication, integration, social control, leadership, status relations, reward allocation, and group task performance has been a recurrent theme throughout this book, along with other social system concepts such as dynamic equilibrium and structure elaboration.

We have implicitly or explicitly used social system and functional ideas on many occasions to interpret the meaning of findings from small group research. In addition, the use of these ideas has reminded us that small groups can be treated as discrete social units with distinctive structures, processes, functional needs, and problems separate from the sentiments, actions, and problems of their individual members. This is a major insight to be derived from applying the sociological perspective to small groups and it is one we meant to emphasize throughout this book by focusing on the small group as a sociological phenomenon. We hope that by approaching small groups from this type of perspective, we have made it at least a little easier to understand some of the most salient or recurrent patterns and problems we confront as small group members. If it has made small-group experiences more interesting or enjoyable or easier to handle and control, it has accomplished more than any social scientist could reasonably expect from a book.

References

ADAMS, J. STACY 1963 "Toward an understanding of inequity." Journal of Abnormal and Social Psychology 67: 422–436.

ADAMS, J. STACY 1965 "Inequity in social exchange." Pp. 267–299 in L. Berkowitz (ed.), Advances in Experimental Social Psychology, Vol. 2. New York: Academic Press.

ADAMS, J. STACY and PATRICIA R. JACOBSEN 1964 "Effects of wage inequities on work quality." Journal of Abnormal and Social Psychology 69: 19–25. (Copyright 1964 by the American Psychological Association. Reprinted by permission.)

ADAMS, J. STACY and W. B. ROSENBAUM 1962 "The relationship of worker productivity to cognitive dissonance about wage inequities." Journal of Applied Psychology 46: 161–164.

ADAMS, STUART 1953 "Status congruency as a variable in small group performance." Social Forces 32: 16–22.

AKERS, RONALD L. 1970 "Framework for the comparative study of group cohesion: The Professions." Pacific Sociological Review 13: 73–85.

ALBERT, R. S. 1953 "Comments on the scientific function of the concept of cohesion:" American Journal of Sociology 59: 231–234.

ALEXANDER, C. NORMAN, JR. 1964 "Consensus and mutual attraction in natural cliques: A study of adolescent drinkers." American Journal of Sociology 64: 395–403.

ALEXANDER, C. NORMAN, JR. and ERNEST Q. CAMPBELL 1968 "Balance forces and environmental effects: Factors influencing the cohesiveness of adolescent drinking groups." Social Forces 46: 367–374.

ALLPORT, FLOYD H. 1924 Social Psychology. Boston: Houghton-Mifflin.

ALVAREZ, R. 1968 "Informal reactions to deviance in a simulated work organization: A laboratory study." American Sociological Review 33: 895–912.

ANDERSON, BO et al. 1969 "Reactions to inequity." Acta Sociologica 12: 1–12.

ANDERSON, BO and ROBERT K. SHELLY 1970 "Reactions to inequity, II: A replication of the Adams experiment and a theoretical reformulation." Acta Sociologica 13: 1-10.

ANDERSON, BO and ROBERT K. SHELLY 1971 "Reactions to inequity III: Inequity and social influence." Acta Sociologica 14: 236-244.

ANDERSON, RICHARD C. 1963 "Learning in discussions: A resumé of the authoritarian-democratic studies." Pp. 153-162 in W. W. Charters, Jr. and N. L. Gage (eds.), Readings in the Social Psychology of Education. Boston: Allyn and Bacon.

ANDREWS, I. R. and E. R. VALENZI 1970 "Overpay inequity or self-image as a worker: A critical examination of an experimental induction procedure." Organizational Behavior and Human Performance 5: 266-276.

ARONSON, ELLIOT 1972 The Social Animal. San Francisco: W. H. Freeman.

ARROWOOD, MARTIN 1961 Some Effects on Productivity of Justified Levels of Reward under Public and Private Conditions. Unpublished Ph.D. Thesis, University of Minnesota.

ASCH, SOLOMON E. 1952 Social Psychology. Englewood Cliffs, New Jersey: Prentice-Hall.

ASCH, SOLOMON E. 1955 "Opinions and social pressure." Scientific American 193(5): 31-35.

ASCH, SOLOMON E. 1957 "An experimental investigation of group influence." From Symposium on Preventive and Social Psychiatry, Walter Reed Army Institute of Research. Washington, D.C.: U.S. Government Printing Office.

BACK, KURT W. 1948 "Interpersonal relations in a discussion group." Journal of Social Issues 4: 61-65.

BACK, KURT W. 1951 "Influence through social communication." Journal of Abnormal and Social Psychology 46: 9-23.

BACK, KURT W. 1973 Beyond Words: The Story of Sensitivity Training and the Encounter Movement. Baltimore: Penguin.

BACK, KURT W., STEPHEN BUNKER, and CATHERINE DUNNAGAN 1972 "Barriers to communication and measurement of semantic space." Sociometry 35: 347-356.

BALES, ROBERT F. 1950 Interaction Process Analysis: A Method for the Study of Small Groups. Cambridge, Massachusetts: Addison-Wesley.

BALES, ROBERT F. 1953 "The equilibrium problem in small groups." Pp. 111-161 in T. Parsons, R. F. Bales, and E. A. Shils, Working Papers in the Theory of Action. Glencoe, Illinois: Free Press.

BALES, ROBERT F. 1956 "Task status and likeability as a function of talking and listening in decision-making groups." Pp. 148-161 in L. D. White (ed.), The State of the Social Sciences. Chicago: The University of Chicago Press.

BALES, ROBERT F. 1958 "Task roles and social roles in problem solving groups." Pp. 437-447 in E. E. Maccoby, T. M. Newcomb, and E. L. Hartley (eds.), Readings in Social Psychology, 3rd ed. New York: Holt, Rinehart, and Winston.

BALES, ROBERT F. 1959 "Small-group theory and research." Pp. 292-305 in R. K. Merton, L. Broom, and L. S. Cottrell, Jr. (eds.), Sociology Today: Problems and Prospects. New York: Basic Books.

BALES, ROBERT F. et al. 1951 "Channels of communication in small groups." American Sociological Review 16: 461–468.

BALES, ROBERT F. and EDGAR BORGATTA 1955 "Size of group as a factor in the interaction profile." Pp. 396–413 in A. P. Hare et al. (eds.), Small Groups: Studies in Social Interaction. New York: Knopf.

BALES, ROBERT F. and PHILIP E. SLATER 1955 "Role differentiation in small decision-making groups." Pp. 295–306 in T. Parsons et al. (eds.), The Family, Socialization and Interaction Process. New York: Free Press.

BALES, ROBERT F. and FRED L. STRODTBECK 1951 "Phases in group problem solving." Journal of Abnormal and Social Psychology 46: 485–495.

BANDURA, ALBERT 1969 Principles of Behavior Modification. New York: Holt, Rinehart, and Winston.

BASS, BERNARD M. 1949 "An analysis of the leaderless group discussion." Journal of Applied Psychology 33: 527–533.

BASS, BERNARD M. 1954 "The leaderless group discussion." Psychological Bulletin 51: 465–492.

BAVELAS, ALEX 1950 "Communication patterns in task-oriented groups." Journal of the Acoustical Society of America 22: 725–730.

BENOIT-SMULLYAN, EMILE 1944 "Status, status types and status interrelations." American Sociological Review 9: 151–161.

BERGER, JOSEPH et al. 1962 Types of Formalization in Small Group Research. Boston: Houghton-Mifflin.

BERGER, JOSEPH et al. 1972 "Structural aspects of distributive justice: A status value formulation." Ch. 6 in J. Berger, M. Zelditch, Jr., and B. Anderson (eds.), Sociological Theories in Progress, Vol. 2. Boston: Houghton-Mifflin.

BERGER, JOSEPH, BERNARD P. COHEN, and MORRIS ZELDITCH, JR. 1966 "Status characteristics and expectation states." Chapter 2 in J. Berger, M. Zelditch, Jr., and B. Anderson (eds.), Sociological Theories in Progress, Vol. 1. Boston: Houghton-Mifflin.

BERGER, JOSEPH, BERNARD P. COHEN, AND MORRIS ZELDITCH, JR. 1972 "Status characteristics and social interaction." American Sociological Review 37: 241–255.

BERGER, JOSEPH, THOMAS L. CONNER, and M. H. FISEK (eds.) 1974 Expectation States Theory: A Theoretical Research Program. Cambridge, Massachusetts: Winthrop.

BERGER, JOSEPH and M. HAMIT FISEK 1970 "Consistent and inconsistent status characteristics and the determination of power and prestige orders." Sociometry 33: 287–304.

BERGER, JOSEPH, MORRIS ZELDITCH, JR., and BO ANDERSON (eds.) 1966 Sociological Theories in Progress, Vol. 1. Boston: Houghton-Mifflin.

BERGER, JOSEPH, MORRIS ZELDITCH, JR., and BO ANDERSON (eds.) 1972 Sociological Theories in Progress, Vol. 2. Boston: Houghton-Mifflin.

BERKOWITZ, LEONARD 1953 "Sharing leadership in small, decision-making groups." Journal of Abnormal and Social Psychology 48: 231–238.

BERKOWITZ, LEONARD 1956 "Group norms among bomber crews: Patterns of perceived crew attitudes, 'actual' crew attitudes, and crew liking related to aircrew effectiveness in Far Eastern combat." Sociometry 19: 141–153.

BERKOWITZ, LEONARD 1957 "Effects of perceived dependency relationships upon conformity to group expectations." Journal of Abnormal and Social Psychology 55: 350–354.

BERKOWITZ, LEONARD and LOUISE R. DANIELS 1963 "Responsibility and dependency." Journal of Abnormal and Social Psychology 66: 429–436.

BERSCHEID, ELLEN and ELAINE WALSTER. 1969   Interpersonal Attraction. Reading, Massachusetts: Addison-Wesley.

BLALOCK, HUBERT M., JR. 1970 An Introduction to Social Research. Englewood Cliffs, New Jersey: Prentice-Hall.

BLAU, PETER M. 1955 The Dynamics of Bureaucracy. Chicago: The University of Chicago Press.

BLAU, PETER M. 1963 The Dynamics of Bureaucracy, 2nd ed. Chicago: The University of Chicago Press.

BLAU, PETER M. and W. RICHARD SCOTT 1962 Formal Organizations: A Comparative Approach. San Francisco: Chandler.

BORGATTA, EDGAR F., ARTHUR S. COUCH, and ROBERT F. BALES 1954 "Some findings relevant to the great man theory of leadership." American Sociological Review 19: 755–759.

BOSSARD, JAMES H. S. 1945 "The law of family interaction." American Journal of Sociology 50: 292–294.

BREDEMEIER, HARRY C. and RICHARD M. STEPHENSON 1962 The Analysis of Social Systems. New York: Holt, Rinehart, and Winston.

BREDEMEIER, HARRY C. and JACKSON TOBY 1960 Social Problems in America. New York: Wiley.

BRODBECK, MAY 1959 "Models, meanings, and theories." Pp. 373–403 in L. Gross (ed.), Symposium on Sociological Theory. New York: Harper and Row.

BROOM, LEONARD and F. LANCASTER JONES 1970 "Status consistency and political preference: The Australian case." American Sociological Review 35: 989–1001.

BROOM, LEONARD and PHILIP SELZNICK 1977 Sociology: A Text with Adapted Readings, 6th ed. New York: Harper and Row.

BROWNE, C. G. and THOMAS S. COHN (eds.) 1958 The Study of Leadership. Danville, Illinois: Interstate Printers and Publishers.

BUCKLEY, WALTER 1967 Sociology and Modern Systems Theory. Englewood Cliffs, New Jersey: Prentice-Hall.

BURKE, PETER J. 1967 "The development of task and social-emotional role differentiation." Sociometry 30: 379–392.

BURKE, PETER J. 1968 "Role differentiation and the legitimation of task activity." Sociometry 31: 404–411.

BURKE, PETER J. 1971 "Task and social-emotional leadership role performance." Sociometry 34: 22–40.

BURKE, PETER J. 1974 "Participation and leadership in small groups." American Sociological Review 39: 832–843.

BYRNE, DONN 1969 "Attitudes and attraction." Pp. 35–89 in L. Berkowitz (ed.), Advances in Experimental Social Psychology, Vol. 4. New York: Academic Press.

CAMILLERI, SANTO F. and JOSEPH BERGER 1967 "Decision-making and social influence: A model and an experimental test." Sociometry 30: 365–378.

CANNON, WALTER B. 1939 The Wisdom of the Body, 2nd ed. New York: Norton.

CAPLOW, THEODORE 1964 Principles of Organization. New York: Harcourt, Brace, and World.

CAPLOW, THEODORE 1968 Two Against One: Coalitions in Triads. Englewood Cliffs, New Jersey: Prentice-Hall.

CAREY, ALEX 1967 "The Hawthorne studies: A radical criticism." American Sociological Review 32: 403–416.

CARLSON, EARL R. 1960 "Clique structure and member satisfaction in groups." Sociometry 23: 327–337.

CATTELL, RAYMOND B. 1948 "Concepts and methods in the measurement of group syntality." Psychological Review 55: 48–63.

CAUDILL, WILLIAM 1958 The Psychiatric Hospital as a Small Society. Cambridge, Massachusetts: Harvard University Press.

CLARK, J. V. 1958 A Preliminary Investigation of Some Unconscious Assumptions Affecting Labor Efficiency in Eight Supermarkets. Unpublished D.B.A. Thesis, Harvard Graduate School of Business Administration.

CLOWARD, RICHARD A. and LLOYD E. OHLIN 1960 Delinquency and Opportunity: A Theory of Delinquent Gangs. Glencoe, Illinois: Free Press.

COCH, L. and J. R. P. FRENCH, JR. 1948 "Overcoming resistance to change." Human Relations 1: 512–532.

COHEN, A. M. and WARREN G. BENNIS 1962 "Predicting organization in changed communication networks." Journal of Psychology 54: 391–416.

COHEN, ELIZABETH G. 1972 "Interracial interaction disability." Human Relations 25: 9–24.

COHEN, ELIZABETH G. and SUSAN S. ROPER 1972 "Modification of interracial interaction disability: An application of status characteristic theory." American Sociological Review 37: 643–657.

COLLINS, BARRY E. and HAROLD GUETZKOW 1964 A Social Psychology of Group Processes for Decision Making. New York: Wiley.

COOK, KAREN S. 1975 "Expectations, evaluations, and equity." American Sociological Review 40: 372–388.

COOLEY, CHARLES H. 1909 Social Organization: A Study of the Larger Mind. New York: Scribners.

COSER, LEWIS A. 1956 The Functions of Social Conflict. New York: Free Press.

CROSBIE, PAUL V. 1972 "Social exchange and power compliance: A test of Homans's propositions." Sociometry 35: 203–222.

CROSBIE, PAUL V. (ed.) 1975 Interaction in Small Groups. New York: Macmillan. (Reprinted with permission of Macmillan Publishing Co., Inc. Copyright 1975 by Paul V. Crosbie.)

CROSBIE, PAUL V., F. A. PETRONI, and B. G. STITT 1972 "The dynamics of corrective groups." Journal of Health and Social Behavior 13: 294–302.

CROSBIE, PAUL V., B. G. STITT, and F. A. PETRONI 1973 "Relevance in the small groups laboratory." Mimeographed, University of Arizona.

DAHL, ROBERT A. 1957 "The concept of power." Behavioral Science 2: 201–218.

DALTON, MELVILLE 1959 Men Who Manage. New York: Wiley.

DARLEY, JOHN M. and SUSAN A. DARLEY 1973 Conformity and Deviation. Morristown, New Jersey: General Learning Press.

DAVIS, JAMES A. 1966 "Structural balance, mechanical solidarity, and interpersonal relations." Pp. 74–101 in J. Berger, M. Zelditch, Jr., and B. Anderson (eds.), Sociological Theories in Progress, Vol. 1. Boston: Houghton-Mifflin.

DAVIS, KINGSLEY 1948 Human Society. New York: Macmillan.

DAVIS, MURRAY S. 1973 Intimate Relations. New York: Macmillan. Reprinted with permission of Macmillan Publishing Co. Inc. Copyright 1973, by Murray S. Davis.

DeMONCHAUX, CECILY and SYLVIA SHIMMIN 1955 "Some problems in experimental group psychology: Considerations arising from cross-cultural experiments on threat and rejection." Human Relations 8: 53–60.

DENTLER, ROBERT A. and KAI T. ERIKSON 1959 "The functions of deviance in groups." Social Problems 7: 98–107.

DENZIN, NORMAN K. (ed.) 1970 Sociological Methods. Chicago: Aldine.

DEUTSCH, MORTON 1949 "An experimental study of the effects of cooperation and competition upon group process." Human Relations 2: 199–231.

DEUTSCH, MORTON 1959 "Some factors affecting membership motivation and achievement motivation in a group." Human Relations 12: 81–95.

DEUTSCH, MORTON and MARY E. COLLINS 1958 "The effect of public policy in housing projects upon interracial attitudes." Pp. 612–623 in E. Maccoby, T. M. Newcomb, and E. L. Hartley (eds.), Readings in Social Psychology, 3rd ed. New York: Holt, Rinehart, and Winston.

DEUTSCH, MORTON and HAROLD B. GERARD 1955 "A study of normative and informational social influences upon individual judgment." Journal of Abnormal and Social Psychology 51: 629–636.

DOISE, WILLEM and SERGE MOSCOVICI 1969–70 "Acceptance and rejection of the deviant within groups of differing cohesiveness." Bulletin de Psychologie 23: 522–525.

DONNENWERTH, GREGORY V. and KJELL Y. TÖRNBLOM 1975 "Reactions to three types of distributive injustice." Human Relations 28: 407–430.

DORNBUSCH, SANFORD M. 1955 "The military academy as an assimilating institution." Social Forces 33: 316–321.

DOWNING, J. 1958 "Cohesiveness, perception, and values." Human Relations 11: 157–166.

DUBIN, ROBERT 1958 The World of Work. Englewood Cliffs, New Jersey: Prentice-Hall.

DUNPHY, DEXTER 1963 "The social structure of urban adolescent peer groups." Sociometry 26: 230–246.

DUNPHY, DEXTER   1972   The Primary Group: A Handbook for Analysis and Field Research. New York: Appleton-Century-Crofts.

DURKHEIM, EMILE   1927   Les Règles de la Méthode Sociologique (The Rules of the Sociological Method). Paris: Librairie Félix Alcan.

EASTON, DAVID   1953   The Political System. New York: Knopf.

EDWARDS, HARRY   1970   The Revolt of the Black Athlete. New York: Free Press.

EISMAN, BERNICE   1959   "Some operational measures of cohesiveness and their interrelations." Human Relations 12: 183–189.

EMERSON, RICHARD M.   1954   "Deviation and rejection: An experimental replication." American Sociological Review 19: 688–693.

EMERSON, RICHARD M.   1966   "Mount Everest: A case study of communication feedback and sustained group goal-striving." Sociometry 29: 213–227.

ENOCH, J. REX and S. DALE McLEMORE   1967   "On the meaning of group cohesion." Southwestern Social Science Quarterly 48: 174–182.

ESKILSON, ARLENE and MARY GLENN WILEY   1976   "Sex composition and leadership in small groups." Sociometry 39: 183–194.

EXLINE, RALPH V.   1957   "Group climate as a factor in the relevance and accuracy of social perception." Journal of Abnormal and Social Psychology 55: 383–388.

EXLINE, RALPH V. and ROBERT C. ZILLER   1959   "Status congruency and interpersonal conflict in decision-making groups." Human Relations 12: 147–162.

FELDMAN, RONALD A.   1968   "Interrelationships among three bases of group integration." Sociometry 31: 30–46.

FELDMAN, RONALD A.   1969   "Group integration and intense interpersonal disliking." Human Relations 22: 405–413.

FESTINGER, LEON   1950   "Informal social communication." Psychological Review 57: 271–282.

FESTINGER, LEON   1953a   "Laboratory experiments." Pp. 136–172 in L. Festinger and D. Katz (eds.), Research Methods in the Behavioral Sciences. New York: Holt, Rinehart, and Winston.

FESTINGER, LEON   1953b   "Group attraction and membership." Pp. 92–101 in D. Cartwright and A. Zander (eds.), Group Dynamics: Research and Theory. Evanston, Illinois: Row, Peterson.

FESTINGER, LEON   1954   "A theory of social comparison processes." Human Relations 7: 117–140.

FESTINGER, LEON et al.   1952   "The influence process in the presence of extreme deviates." Human Relations 5: 327–346.

FESTINGER, LEON, A. PEPITONE, and T. NEWCOMB   1952   "Some consequences of de-individuation in a group." Journal of Abnormal and Social Psychology 47: 382–389.

FESTINGER, LEON, HENRY W. RIECKEN, and STANLEY SCHACHTER   1956   When Prophecy Fails. Minneapolis: University of Minnesota Press.

FESTINGER, LEON, STANLEY SCHACHTER, and KURT BACK   1950   Social Pressures in Informal Groups. New York: Harper.

FIEDLER, FRED E.   1954   "Assumed similarity measures as predictors of team effectiveness." Journal of Abnormal and Social Psychology 49: 381–388.

FIEDLER, FRED E. 1960 "The leader's psychological distance and group effectiveness." Pp. 586–606 in D. Cartwright and A. Zander (eds.), Group Dynamics: Research and Theory. Evanston, Illinois: Row, Peterson.

FIEDLER, FRED E. 1964 "A contingency model of leadership effectiveness." Pp. 149–190 in L. Berkowitz (ed.), Advances in Experimental Social Psychology, Vol. 1. New York: Academic Press.

FIEDLER, FRED E. 1967 A Theory of Leadership Effectiveness. New York: McGraw-Hill.

FIEDLER, FRED E. 1971 Leadership. Morristown, New Jersey: General Learning Press.

FISEK, M. HAMIT and RICHARD OFSHE 1970 "The process of status evolution." Sociometry 33: 327–346.

FLEISHMAN, JOHN and GERALD MARWELL 1977 "Status congruence and associativeness: A test of Galtung's theory." Sociometry 40: 1–11.

FRANK, FREDERIC and LYNN R. ANDERSON 1971 "Effects of task and group size upon group productivity and member satisfaction." Sociometry 34: 135–149.

FREEDMAN, J. L., S. WALLINGTON, and E. BLESS 1967 "Compliance without pressure: The effect of guilt." Journal of Personality and Social Psychology 7: 117–124.

FREESE, LEE 1969 The Generalization of Specific Performance Expectations. Unpublished Ph.D. Thesis, Stanford University.

FREESE, LEE 1974 "Conditions for status equality in informal task groups." Sociometry 37: 174–188.

FREESE, LEE 1976 "The generalization of specific performance expectations." Sociometry 39: 194–200.

FREESE, LEE and BERNARD P. COHEN 1973 "Eliminating status generalization." Sociometry 36: 177–193.

FRENCH, J. R. P., JR. 1941 "The disruption and cohesion of groups." Journal of Abnormal and Social Psychology 36: 361–377.

FRENCH, JOHN R. P., JR. 1953 "Experiments in field settings." Pp. 98–135 in L. Festinger and D. Katz (eds.), Research Methods in the Behavioral Sciences. New York: Holt, Rinehart, and Winston.

FRENCH, JOHN R. P., JR. and BERTRAM RAVEN 1959 "The bases of social power." Pp. 150–167 in D. Cartwright (ed.), Studies in Social Power. Ann Arbor, Michigan: University of Michigan.

FRIEDMAN, A. and P. GOODMAN 1967 "Wage inequity, self-qualifications, and productivity." Organizational Behavior and Human Performance 2: 406–417.

GALLAGHER, JAMES and PETER J. BURKE 1974 "Scapegoating and leader behavior." Social Forces 52: 481–488.

GALTUNG, JOHAN 1966 "Rank and social integration: a multidimensional approach." Ch. 7 in J. Berger, M. Zelditch, Jr., and B. Anderson (eds.), Vol. 1. Sociological Theories in Progress. Boston: Houghton-Mifflin.

GAMSON, WILLIAM A. 1961 "A theory of coalition formation." American Sociological Review 26: 373–382.

GAMSON, WILLIAM A. 1964 "Experimental studies of coalition formation." Pp. 81–110 in L. Berkowitz (ed.), Advances in Experimental Social Psychology, Vol. 1. New York: Academic Press.

GAMSON, WILLIAM A. 1968 Power and Discontent. Homewood, Illinois: Dorsey.

GEKOSKI, NORMAN 1952 "Predicting group productivity." Personnel Psychology 5: 281–292.

GERARD, HAROLD B. 1954 "The anchorage of opinions in face-to-face groups." Human Relations 7: 313–325.

GERSON, LOWELL W. 1967 "Punishment and position: The sanctioning of deviants in small groups." Case Western Reserve Journal of Sociology 1: 54–62.

GESCHWENDER, JAMES A. 1967 "Continuities in theories of status consistency and cognitive dissonance." Social Forces 46: 160–171.

GIBB, CECIL A. 1954 "Leadership." Pp. 877–920 in G. Lindzey (ed.), Handbook of Social Psychology, Vol. 2. Cambridge, Massachusetts: Addison-Wesley.

GIBBS, J. P. and W. T. MARTIN 1958 "A theory of status integration and its relationship to suicide." American Sociological Review 23: 140–147.

GOFFMAN, IRWIN W. 1957 "Status consistency and preference for change in power distribution." American Sociological Review 22: 275–281.

GOLEMBIEWSKI, ROBERT T. 1962 The Small Group: An Analysis of Research Concepts and Operations. Chicago: The University of Chicago Press.

GOLEMBIEWSKI, ROBERT T. and ARTHUR BLUMBERG (eds.) 1970 Sensitivity Training and The Laboratory Approach: Readings About Concepts and Applications. Itasca, Illinois: Peacock.

GOODACRE, DANIEL M. III 1951 "The use of a sociometric test as a predictor of combat unit effectiveness." Sociometry 14: 148–152.

GORDON, MILTON M. 1958 Social Class in American Sociology. Durham, North Carolina: Duke University Press.

GOULDNER, ALVIN W. 1965 Wildcat Strike. New York: Harper and Row.

GOULDNER, ALVIN W. 1971 The Coming Crisis of Western Sociology. New York: Avon-Equinox.

GROSS, EDWARD 1954 "Primary functions of the small group." American Journal of Sociology 60: 24–30.

GROSS, NEAL and WILLIAM E. MARTIN 1952 "On group cohesiveness." American Journal of Sociology 57: 546–554.

GULLAHORN, J. 1952 "Distance and friendship as factors in the gross interaction matrix." Sociometry 15: 123–134.

GUNDLACH, R. H. 1956 "Effects of on-the-job experiences with Negroes upon racial attitudes of white workers in union shops." Psychological Reports 2: 67–77.

HAAS, J. EUGENE and THOMAS E. DRABEK 1973 Complex Organizations: A Sociological Perspective. New York: Macmillan.

HALL, ARTHUR D. and R. E. FAGEN 1956 "Definition of a system." General Systems 1: 18–28.

HAMBLIN, ROBERT L. 1958 "Leadership and crises." Sociometry 21: 322–335.

HARE, A. PAUL   1962   Handbook of Small Group Research. New York: Free Press.

HARE, A. PAUL   1973   "Group decisions by consensus: Reaching unity in the Society of Friends." Sociological Inquiry 43: 75–84.

HARE, A. PAUL   1976   Handbook of Small Group Research, 2nd ed. New York: Free Press. (Reprinted with permission of Macmillan Co., Inc. Copyright 1962, 1976 by The Free Press, a Division of Macmillan.)

HARVEY, O. J.   1953   "An experimental approach to the study of status relations in informal groups." American Sociological Review 18: 357–367.

HARTLEY, EUGENE L. and RUTH E. HARTLEY   1952   Fundamentals of Social Psychology. New York: Knopf.

HEBER, RICK F. and MARY E. HEBER   1957   "The effect of group failure and success on social status." Journal of Educational Psychology 48: 129–134.

HEINICKE, CHRISTOPH M. and ROBERT F. BALES   1953   "Developmental trends in the structure of small groups." Sociometry 16: 7–38.

HEMPHILL, JOHN K.   1961   "Why people attempt to lead." Pp. 201–215 in L. Petrullo and B. M. Bass (eds.), Leadership and Interpersonal Behavior. New York: Holt, Rinehart, and Winston.

HEMPHILL, JOHN K. and L. SECHREST   1952   "A comparison of three criteria of air crew effectiveness in combat over Korea." American Psychologist 7: 391.

HOFFER, ERIC   1958   The True Believer. New York: New American Library.

HOFFMAN, L. W.   1972   "Early childhood experiences and women's achievement motives." Journal of Social Issues 28: 129–155.

HOLLANDER, EDWIN P.   1958   "Conformity, status, and idiosyncrasy credit." Psychological Review 65: 117–127.

HOLLANDER, EDWIN P.   1976   Principles and Methods of Social Psychology. New York: Oxford University.

HOLLANDER, EDWIN P., B. J. FALLON, and M. T. EDWARDS   1974   "The influence and acceptability of appointed and elected leaders under conditions of group success or failure." Paper presented at the Eastern Psychological Association Convention.

HOLLANDER, EDWIN P. and JAMES W. JULIAN   1970   "Studies in leader legitimacy, influence, and innovation." Pp. 33–69 in L. Berkowitiz (ed.), Advances in Experimental Social Psychology, Vol. 5. New York: Academic Press.

HOLLANDER, EDWIN P. and RICHARD H. WILLIS   1967   "Some current issues in the psychology of conformity and nonconformity." Psychological Bulletin 68: 62–76.

HOMANS, GEORGE C.   1950   The Human Group. New York: Harcourt, Brace, Jovanovich, Inc. (Excerpted and adapted and reprinted with their permission.)

HOMANS, GEORGE C.   1953   "Status among clerical workers." Human Organization 12: 5–10.

HOMANS, GEORGE C.   1954   "The cash posters; A study of a group of working girls." American Sociological Review 19: 724–733.

HOMANS, GEORGE C.   1961   Social Behavior: Its Elementary Forms. New York: Harcourt, Brace, Jovanovich, Inc.

HOMANS, GEORGE C. 1974 Social Behavior: Its Elementary Forms. rev. ed. New York: Harcourt, Brace, Jovanovich, Inc. (Excerpted, abridged and adapted and reprinted by permission.)

HOPKINS, TERENCE K. 1964 The Exercise of Influence in Small Groups. Totowa, New Jersey: Bedminster.

HOROWITZ, MILTON W. and HOWARD V. PERLMUTTER 1955 "The discussion group and democratic behavior." Journal of Social Psychology 41: 231–246.

HUGHES, EVERETT C. 1945 "Dilemmas and contradictions of status." American Journal of Sociology 50: 353–359.

HUGHES, EVERETT C. 1946 "The knitting of racial groups in industry." American Sociological Review 11: 512–519.

HURLOCK, ELIZABETH 1949 Adolescent Development. New York: McGraw Hill.

HURWITZ, JACOB I., ALVIN ZANDER, and BERNARD HYMOVITCH 1953 "Some effects of power on the relations among group members." Pp. 483–492 in D. Cartwright and A. Zander (eds.), Group Dynamics: Research and Theory. Evanston, Illinois: Row, Peterson.

HUSBAND, R. W. 1940 "Cooperative versus solitary problem solution." Journal of Social Psychology 11: 405–409.

HUXLEY, ALDOUS 1958 Brave New World. New York: Bantam.

HYMAN, HERBERT J. 1942 "The psychology of status." Archives of Psychology 269: 5–94.

ISRAEL, JOACHIM 1956 Self-Evaluation and Rejection in Groups: Three Experimental Studies and a Conceptual Outline. Stockholm: Almqvist and Wiksell.

JACKSON, ELTON F. 1962 "Status consistency and symptoms of stress." American Sociological Review 27: 469–480.

JACKSON, ELTON F. and RICHARD F. CURTIS 1972 "Effects of vertical mobility and status inconsistency: A body of negative evidence." American Sociological Review 37: 701–713.

JACOBSON, WALLY D. 1972 Power and Interpersonal Relations. Belmont, California: Wadsworth.

JAFFEE, CABOT L. and RICHARD L. LUCAS 1969 "Effects of rates of talking and correctness of decisions on leader choice in small groups." Journal of Social Psychology 79: 247–254.

JANIS, IRVING L. 1963 "Group identification under conditions of external danger." British Journal of Medical Psychology 36: 227–238.

JANIS, IRVING L. 1972 Victims of Groupthink. Boston: Houghton-Mifflin.

JANIS, IRVING L. 1976 "Groupthink." Pp. 108–111 in I. Robertson (ed.), Readings in Sociology: Contemporary Perspectives. New York: Harper and Row.

JENNINGS, HELEN HALL (ed.) 1950 Leadership and Isolation, rev. ed. New York: Longman, Green.

JOHNSON, MICHAEL P. and WILLIAM L. EWENS 1971 "Power relations and affective style as determinants of confidence in impression formation in a game situation." Journal of Experimental Social Psychology 7: 98–110.

KAHN, ROBERT L. and DANIEL KATZ 1953 "Leadership practices in relation to productivity and morale." Pp. 612–628 in D. Cartwright and A. Zander (eds.), Group Dynamics: Research and Theory. Evanston, Illinois: Row, Peterson.

KASL, STANISLAV V. and SIDNEY COBB 1967 "Effect of parental status incongruence and discrepancy on physical and mental health of adult off-spring." Journal of Personality and Social Psychology 7: 1–15.

KATZ, ELIHU et al. 1957 "Leadership stability and social change: An experiment with small groups." Sociometry 20: 36–50.

KATZ, ELIHU and PAUL F. LAZARSFELD 1955 Personal Influence: The Part Played by People in the Flow of Mass Communications. Glencoe, Illinois: Free Press.

KATZ, IRWIN and LAWRENCE BENJAMIN 1960 "Effects of white authoritarianism in biracial work groups." Journal of Abnormal and Social Psychology 61: 448–456.

KATZ, IRWIN and MELVIN COHEN 1962 "The effects of training Negroes upon cooperative problem solving in biracial teams." Journal of Abnormal and Social Psychology 64: 319–325.

KATZ, IRWIN, E. G. EPPS, and A. J. AXELSON 1964 "Effect upon Negro digit-symbol performance of anticipated comparison with Whites and with other Negroes." Journal of Abnormal and Social Psychology 69: 77–83.

KATZ, IRWIN, JUDITH GOLDSTON, and LAWRENCE BENJAMIN 1958 "Behavior and productivity in biracial work groups." Human Relations 11: 123–141.

KIMBERLY, JAMES C. 1962 An Experimental Test of a Theory of Status Equilibration. Unpublished Ph.D. Thesis, Duke University.

KIMBERLY, JAMES C. 1966 "A theory of status equilibration." Chapter 9 in J. Berger, M. Zelditch, Jr., and B. Anderson (eds.), Sociological Theories in Progress, Vol. 1. Boston: Houghton-Mifflin.

KIMBERLY, JAMES C. 1967 "Status inconsistency: A reformulation of a theoretical problem." Human Relations 20: 171–179.

KIMBERLY, JAMES C. 1970 "The emergence and stabilization of stratification in simple and complex social systems." Sociological Inquiry 40: 73–101.

KIMBERLY, JAMES C. and PAUL V. CROSBIE 1967 "An experimental test of a reward-cost formulation of status inconsistency." Journal of Experimental Social Psychology 3: 399–415.

KIPNIS, DOROTHY M. 1957 "Interaction between members of bomber crews as a determinant of sociometric choice." Human Relations 10: 263–270.

KLEIN, MICHAEL and GERD CHRISTIANSEN 1969 "Group composition, group structure and group effectiveness of basketball teams." Pp. 397–408 in J. W. Loy, Jr. and G. S. Kenyon (eds.), Sport, Culture, and Society: A Reader on the Sociology of Sport. London: Collier-Macmillan.

KNUTSON, ANDIE L. 1960 "Quiet and vocal groups." Sociometry 23: 36–49.

KUHN, THOMAS S. 1970 The Structure of Scientific Revolutions, rev. ed. Chicago: The University of Chicago Press.

KURTH, S. B. 1970 "Friendships and friendly relations." Pp. 136–170 in G. J. McCall et al. (eds.), Social Relationships. Chicago: Aldine.

LAKIN, MARTIN 1972 Experimential Groups: The Uses of Interpersonal Encounter, Psychotherapy Groups, and Sensitivity Training. Morristown, New Jersey: General Learning Press.

LANDECKER, WERNER S. 1970 "Status congruence, class crystallization, and social cleavage." Sociology and Social Research 54: 343–355.

LANDERS, DANIEL M. and THOMAS F. CRUM 1971 "The effects of team success and formal structure on inter-personal relations and cohesiveness of baseball teams." International Journal of Sport Psychology 2: 88–96.

LANDERS, DANIEL M. and GUNTHER LUSCHEN 1974 "Team performance outcome and the cohesiveness of competitive coacting groups." International Review of Sport Sociology 2(9): 57–69.

LaPIERE, R. T. 1954 A Theory of Social Control. New York: McGraw-Hill.

LARSEN, OTTO N. and RICHARD J. HILL 1958 "Social structure and interpersonal communication." American Journal of Sociology 63: 497–505.

LAUMANN, EDWARD O. and DAVID R. SEGAL 1971 "Status inconsistency and ethnoreligious group membership as determinants of social participation and political attitudes." American Journal of Sociology 77: 36–61.

LAWLER, EDWARD J. 1975 "An experimental study of factors affecting the mobilization of revolutionary coalitions." Sociometry 38: 163–179.

LAZARSFELD, PAUL F. and ROBERT K. MERTON 1954 "Friendship as a social process: A substantive and methodological analysis." Pp. 18–66 in M. Berger, T. Abel, and C. H. Page (eds.), Freedom and Control in Modern Society. Princeton, New Jersey: Van Nostrand.

LEAVITT, HAROLD J. 1951 "Some effects of certain communication patterns on group performance." Journal of Abnormal and Social Psychology 46: 38–50. Copyright 1951 American Psychological Association. Reprinted by permission.

LEIGHTON, A. H. 1945 The Governing of Men. Princeton, New Jersey: Princeton University Press.

LEIK, ROBERT K. 1963 "Instrumentality and emotionality in family interaction." Sociometry 26: 131–145.

LEIK, ROBERT K. 1972 Methods, Logic, and Research of Sociology. Indianapolis, Indiana: Bobbs-Merrill.

LENK, HANS 1969 "Top performance despite internal conflict." Pp. 393–397 in J. W. Loy, Jr. and G. S. Kenyon (eds.), Sport, Culture, and Society: A Reader on the Sociology of Sport. London: Collier-Macmillan.

LENSKI, GERHARD 1954 "Status crystallization: A non-vertical dimension of social status." American Sociological Review 19: 405–413.

LENSKI, GERHARD 1956 "Social participation and status crystallization." American Sociological Review 21: 458–464.

LEVINE, JOHN M., LEONARD SAXE, and HOBART HARRIS 1973 "Amount of initial disagreement as a determinant of reaction to a shifting attitudinal deviate." Proceedings of the 81st Annual Convention of the American Psychological Association 8: 157–158.

LEVINGER, GEORGE 1964 "Task and social behavior in marriage." Sociometry 27: 433–448.

LEVINGER, GEORGE and J. DIEDRICK SNOEK 1972 Attraction in Relationship: A New Look at Interpersonal Attraction. Morristown, New Jersey: General Learning Press.

LEWIN, KURT 1947a "Frontiers in group dynamics." Human Relations 1: 5–41.

LEWIN, KURT 1947b "Frontiers in group dynamics: 2." Human Relations 1: 143–153.

LEWIN, KURT 1951 Field Theory in Social Science: Selected Papers (of Kurt Lewin). New York: Harper and Row. Edited by D. Cartwright.

LEWIN, KURT and RONALD LIPPITT 1938 "An experimental approach to the study of autocracy and democracy: a preliminary note." Sociometry 1: 292–300.

LEWIN, KURT, RONALD LIPPITT, and RALPH K. WHITE 1939 "Patterns of aggressive behavior in experimentally created 'social climates.'" Journal of Social Psychology 10: 271–299.

LEWIS, GORDON H. 1972 "Role differentiation." American Sociological Review 37: 424–434.

LIEBERMAN, MORTON A., IRVIN D. YALOM, and MATTHEW MILES 1971 "The group experience project: A comparison of ten encounter technologies." Pp. 469–497 in L. Blank, G. Gottsegen, and M. Gottsegen (eds.), Confrontation: Encounters in Self and Interpersonal Awareness. New York: Macmillan.

LIEBERMAN, MORTON A. et al. 1973 Encounter Groups. New York: Basic Books.

LINDZEY, GARDNER and EDGAR F. BORGATTA 1954 "Sociometric measurement." Pp. 405–448 in G. Lindzey (ed.), Handbook of Social Psychology. Reading, Mass.: Addison-Wesley.

LIPPITT, RONALD 1939 "Field theory and experiment in social psychology: Autocratic and democratic group atmospheres." American Journal of Sociology 45: 26–49.

LIPPITT, RONALD 1940 "An experimental study of the effect of democratic and authoritarian group atmospheres." University of Iowa Studies in Child Welfare 16: 43–195.

LIPPITT, RONALD and RALPH K. WHITE 1952 "An experimental study of leadership and group life." Pp. 340–355 in G. E. Swanson, T. M. Newcomb, and E. L. Hartley (eds.), Readings in Social Psychology, rev. ed. New York: Holt, Rinehart, and Winston.

LIPSET, SEYMOUR MARTIN 1960 Political Man. New York: Doubleday.

LIPSET, SEYMOUR MARTIN, MARTIN A. TROW, and JAMES S. COLEMAN 1956 Union Democracy: The Internal Politics of the International Typographical Union. Glencoe, Illinois: Free Press.

LOTT, ALBERT J. and BERNICE E. LOTT 1961 "Group cohesiveness, communication level, and conformity." Journal of Abnormal and Social Psychology 62: 408–412.

LOTT, ALBERT J. and BERNICE E. LOTT 1965 "Group cohesiveness as interpersonal attraction: A review of relationships with antecedent and consequent variables." Psychological Bulletin 64: 259–309.

LOY, JOHN W., JR. 1969 "Reaction to Luschen paper (concerning 'Small group research and the group in sport')." Pp. 67–69 in G. S. Kenyon (ed.), Aspects of Contemporary Sport Sociology. Chicago: Athletic Institute.

MacIVER, ROBERT M. 1947 The Web of Government. New York: Macmillan.

MacNEIL, M. K., L. E. DAVIS, and D. J. PACE 1975 "Group status displacement under stress: A serendipitous finding." Sociometry 38: 293–307.

MADRON, THOMAS WILLIAM 1969 Small Group Methods and The Study of Politics. Evanston, Illinois: Northwestern University Press.

MALEWSKI, ANDRZEJ 1966 "The degree of status incongruence and its effects." Pp. 303–308 in R. Bendix and S. M. Lipset (eds.), Class, Status and Power, 2nd ed. New York: Free Press.

MALIVER, BRUCE L. 1972 The Encounter Game. New York: Stein and Day.

MALIVER, BRUCE L. 1974 "Human potential movement." P. 130 in Encyclopedia of Sociology. Guilford, Connecticut: Dushkin.

MANN, JOHN H. 1959 "The effect of inter-racial contact on sociometric choice and perceptions." Journal of Social Psychology 50: 143–152.

MANN, RICHARD D. 1961 "Dimensions of individual performance in small groups under task and social-emotional conditions." Journal of Abnormal and Social Psychology 62: 674–682.

MARQUIS, DONALD G., HAROLD GUETZKOW, and R. W. HEYNS 1951 "A social psychological study of the decision-making conference." Pp. 55–67 in H. Guetzkow (ed.), Groups, Leadership and Men. Pittsburgh: Carnegie Press.

MARTENS, RAINER and JAMES A. PETERSON 1971 "Group cohesiveness as a determinant of success and member satisfaction in team performance." International Review of Sport Sociology 6: 49–59.

MAYER, THOMAS 1975 Mathematical Models of Group Structure. Indianapolis, Indiana: Bobbs-Merrill.

MAYO, ELTON 1933 The Human Problems of an Industrial Civilization. New York: Macmillan.

McCLINTOCK, CHARLES G. 1963 "Group support and behavior of leaders and nonleaders." Journal of Abnormal and Social Psychology 67: 105–113.

McCRANIE, EDWARD W. and JAMES C. KIMBERLY 1973 "Rank inconsistency, conflicting expectations and injustice." Sociometry 36: 152–176.

McGRATH, JOSEPH E. 1962 "The influence of positive interpersonal relations on adjustment and effectiveness in rifle teams." Journal of Abnormal and Social Psychology 65: 365–375.

McINTYRE, THOMAS D. 1970 A Field Experimental Study of Attitude Change in Four Biracial Small Groups. Unpublished Doctoral Thesis, Pennsylvania State University.

McKEACHIE, W. J. 1954 "Student centered versus instructor centered instruction." Journal of Educational Psychology 45: 143–150.

MELNICK, MERRILL J. and MARTIN M. CHEMERS 1974 "Effects of group social structure on the success of basketball teams." Research Quarterly 45: 1–8.

MEREI, FERENC 1958 "Group leadership and institutionalization." Pp.

522–532 in E. E. Maccoby, T. M. Newcomb, and E. L. Hartley (eds.), Readings in Social Psychology, 3rd ed. New York: Holt, Rinehart, and Winston.

MERTON, ROBERT K. 1961 "Epilogue: Social problems and sociological theory." In R. K. Merton and R. A. Nisbet (eds.), Contemporary Social Problems. New York: Harcourt, Brace, and Jovanovich.

MICHELINI, RONALD L. and LAWRENCE A. MESSÉ 1974 "Reactions to threat as a function of equity." Sociometry 37: 432–439.

MICHENER, H. ANDREW and MORGAN LYONS 1972 "Perceived support and upward mobility as determinants of revolutionary coalition behavior." Journal of Experimental Social Psychology 8: 180–195.

MILGRAM, STANLEY 1963 "Behavioral study of obedience." Journal of Abnormal and Social Psychology 67: 371–378.

MILGRAM, STANLEY 1964 "Group pressure and action against a person." Journal of Abnormal and Social Psychology 69: 137–143.

MILGRAM, STANLEY 1965 "Some conditions of obedience and disobedience to authority." Human Relations 18: 57–75.

MILGRAM, STANLEY 1973 Obedience to Authority: An Experimental View. New York: Harper and Row.

MILLER, JAMES G. 1955 "Toward a general theory for the behavioral sciences." American Psychologist 10: 513–531.

MILLER, NEAL E. and RICHARD BUGELSKI 1948 "Minor studies in aggression: The influence of frustrations imposed by the in-group on attitudes expressed toward out-groups." Journal of Psychology 25: 437–442.

MILLS, C. WRIGHT 1959 The Sociological Imagination. New York: Oxford University Press.

MILLS, THEODORE 1962 "A sleeper variable in small group research: The experimenter." Pacific Sociological Review 5: 21–28.

MILLS, THEODORE M. 1967 The Sociology of Small Groups. Englewood Cliffs, New Jersey: Prentice-Hall.

MILLS, THEODORE M. et al. 1970 "Group structure and the newcomer." Pp. 149–164 in T. M. Mills (ed.), Readings on the Sociology of Small Groups. Englewood Cliffs, New Jersey: Prentice-Hall.

MOORE, JAMES C., JR. 1968 "Status and influence in small group interaction." Sociometry 31: 47–63.

MORENO, JACOB L. 1934 Who Shall Survive? Washington, D.C.: Nervous and Mental Disease Publishing Co.

MORENO, JACOB L. 1943 "Sociometry and the cultural order." Sociometry 6: 299–344.

MORRIS, CHARLES G. and J. RICHARD HACKMAN 1969 "Behavioral correlates of perceived leadership." Journal of Personality and Social Psychology 13: 350–361.

MULDER, MAUK et al. 1965 "Non-instrumental liking tendencies toward powerful group members." Acta Psychologica 22: 367–386.

MYERS, ALBERT E. 1962 "Team competition, success, and the adjustment of group members." Journal of Abnormal and Social Psychology 65: 325–332.

NEMETH, CHARLAN, JEFFREY ENDICOTT, and JOEL WACHTLER 1976 "From the '50s to the '70s: Women in jury deliberations." Sociometry 39: 293–304.

NISBET, ROBERT A. 1953 The Quest for Community. New York: Oxford University Press.

NIXON, HOWARD L. II 1974 "An axiomatic theory of team success." Sport Sociology Bulletin 3: 1–12.

NIXON, HOWARD L. II 1976a Sport and Social Organization. Indianapolis, Indiana: Bobbs-Merrill.

NIXON, HOWARD L. II 1976b "Team orientations, interpersonal relations, and team success." Research Quarterly 47: 429–435.

NIXON, HOWARD L. II 1977a "'Cohesiveness' and team success: A theoretical reformulation." Review of Sport and Leisure 2: 36–57.

NIXON, HOWARD L. II 1977b "Reinforcement effects of sports team success on cohesiveness-related factors." International Review of Sport Sociology. 4(12): 17–38.

OFSHE, RICHARD J. (ed.) 1973 Interpersonal Behavior in Small Groups. Englewood Cliffs, New Jersey: Prentice-Hall.

OFSHE, RICHARD J. and S. LYNN OFSHE 1970 "Choice behavior in coalition games." Behavioral Science 15: 337–349.

OLMSTED, MICHAEL S. 1959 The Small Group. New York: Random House.

OLSEN, MARVIN E. 1968 The Process of Social Organization. New York: Holt, Rinehart, and Winston.

OLSEN, MARVIN E. and JUDY CORDER TULLY 1972 "Socioeconomic-ethnic status inconsistency and preference for political change." American Sociological Review 37: 560–574.

OROMANER, M. J. 1968 "The most cited sociologists: An analysis of introductory text citations." American Sociologist 3: 124–126.

ORWELL, GEORGE 1949 1984. New York: Harcourt, Brace, Jovanovich.

PALMORE, E. B. 1955 "The introduction of Negroes into white departments." Human Organization 14: 27–28.

PARK, ROBERT 1928 "Bases of race prejudice." The Annals 140: 11–20.

PARSONS, TALCOTT 1951 The Social System. New York: Free Press.

PARSONS, TALCOTT 1959 "General theory in sociology." Pp. 3–38 in R. K. Merton, L. Broom, and L. S. Cottrell (eds.), Sociology Today: Problems and Prospects. New York: Basic Books.

PARSONS, TALCOTT 1963 "On the concept of influence." Public Opinion Quarterly 27: 37–62.

PARSONS, TALCOTT, ROBERT F. BALES, and EDWARD A. SHILS (eds.) 1953 Working Papers in the Theory of Action. New York: Free Press.

PARSONS, TALCOTT and EDWARD SHILS (eds.) 1951 Toward a General Theory of Action. Cambridge, Massachusetts: Harvard University Press.

PEARLIN, LEONARD I. 1975 "Status inequality and stress in marriage." American Sociological Review 40: 344–357.

PENNOCK, GEORGE A. 1930 "Industrial research at Hawthorne." Personnel Journal 8: 296–313.

PETERSON, JAMES A. and RAINER MARTENS 1973 "Success and residential affiliation as determinants of team cohesiveness." Research Quarterly 43: 62–76.

RAMUZ-NIENHUIS, WILHELMINA and ANNIE VAN BERGEN 1960 "Relations between some components of attraction-to-group: A replication." Human Relations 13: 271–277.

READ, PETER B. 1974 "Source of authority and the legitimation of leadership in small groups." Sociometry 37: 189–204.

RIECKEN, HENRY W. 1958 "The effect of talkativeness on ability to influence group solutions of problems." Sociometry 21: 309–321.

RIEDESEL, PAUL L. 1974 "Bales reconsidered: A critical analysis of popularity and leadership differentiation." Sociometry 37: 557–564.

RIESMAN, DAVID, NATHAN GLAZER, and REUEL DENNEY 1950 The Lonely Crowd. New Haven, Connecticut: Yale University Press.

RIKER, WILLIAM H. 1962 The Theory of Political Coalitions. New Haven, Connecticut: Yale University Press.

ROETHLISBERGER, FRITZ J. 1941 Management and Morale. Cambridge, Massachusetts: Harvard University Press.

ROETHLISBERGER, FRITZ J. and WILLIAM J. DICKSON 1939 Management and the Worker. Cambridge, Massachusetts: Harvard University Press.

ROETHLISBERGER, FRITZ J. and WILLIAM J. DICKSON 1975 "A fair day's work." Pp. 85–94 in P. V. Crosbie (ed.), Interaction in Small Groups. New York: Macmillan.

ROTTER, GEORGE S. 1967 "An experimental evaluation of group attractiveness as a determinant of conformity." Human Relations 20: 273–282.

ROY, DONALD F. 1954 "Efficiency and 'the fix': Informal intergroup relations in a piecework machine shop." American Journal of Sociology 60: 255–266.

ROY, DONALD F. 1959-60 "'Banana time'—job satisfaction and informal interaction." Human Organization 18: 158–168.

SAMPSON, EDWARD E. 1963 "Status congruence and cognitive consistency." Sociometry 26: 146–162.

SAMPSON, EDWARD E. 1969 "Studies in status incongruence." Pp. 225–270 in L. Berkowitz (ed.), Advances in Experimental Social Psychology, Vol. 4. New York: Academic Press.

SCHACHTER, STANLEY 1951 "Deviation, rejection, and communication." Journal of Abnormal and Social Psychology 46: 190–207.

SCHACHTER, STANLEY et al. 1951 "An experimental study of cohesiveness and productivity." Human Relations 4: 229–238.

SCHACHTER, STANLEY et al. 1954 "Cross-cultural experiments on threat and rejection." Human Relations 7: 403–439.

SCHEIN, E. H. and WARREN G. BENNIS 1965 Personal and Organizational Change through Group Methods: A Laboratory Approach. New York: Wiley.

SCHLENKER, BARRY R. et al. 1970 "Compliance to threats as a function of the wording of the threat and the exploitativeness of the threatener." Sociometry 33: 394–408.

SCHLENKER, BARRY R. *et al.* 1976 "Reactions to coercive and reward power: The effects of switching influence modes on target compliance." Sociometry 39: 316–323.

SCHULMAN, GARY I. 1967 "Asch conformity studies: Conformity to the experimenter and/or to the groups?" Sociometry 30: 26–40.

SCHUTZ, WILLIAM C. 1958 FIRO: A Three-Dimensional Theory of Interpersonal Behavior. New York: Rinehart.

SCHUTZ, WILLIAM C. 1961 "The ego, FIRO theory and the leader as a completer." Pp. 48–65 in L. Petrullo and B. M. Bass (eds.), Leadership and Interpersonal Behavior. New York: Holt, Rinehart, and Winston.

SCHWARTZ, SHALOM H. 1968 "Awareness of the consequences and the influence of moral norms on interpersonal behavior." Sociometry 31: 355–369.

SCOTT, JACK 1971 The Athletic Revolution. New York: Free Press.

SEASHORE, STANLEY E. 1954 Group Cohesiveness in the Industrial Work Group. Ann Arbor, Michigan: Survey Research Center.

SHAW, MARVIN E. 1964 "Communication networks." Pp. 111–147 in L. Berkowitz (ed.), Advances in Experimental Social Psychology, Vol. 1. New York: Academic Press.

SHAW, MARVIN E. 1976 Group Dynamics: The Psychology of Small Group Behavior, 2nd ed. New York: McGraw-Hill. (Used by permission of McGraw-Hill.)

SHAW, MARVIN E. and LILLY M. SHAW 1962 "Some effects of sociometric grouping upon learning in a second grade classroom." Journal of Social Psychology 57: 453–458.

SHEPARD, JON M. 1971 "On Alex Carey's radical criticism of the Hawthorne studies." Academy of Management Journal 14: 23–32.

SHEPHERD, CLOVIS R. 1964 Small Groups: Some Sociological Perspectives. San Francisco: Chandler.

SHERIF, MUZAFER 1936 The Psychology of Social Norms. New York: Harper and Row.

SHERIF, MUZAFER 1954 "Integrating field work and laboratory in small group research." American Sociological Review 19: 759–771.

SHERIF, MUZAFER 1956 "Experiments in group conflict." Scientific American 195 (5): 54–58.

SHERIF, MUZAFER and CAROLYN W. SHERIF 1953 Groups in Harmony and Tension: An Introduction of Studies in Intergroup Relations. New York: Harper and Row.

SHERIF, MUZAFER and CAROLYN W. SHERIF 1964 Exploration into Conformity and Deviation of Adolescents. New York: Harper and Row.

SHERIF, MUZAFER and CAROLYN W. SHERIF 1967 "Group processes and collective interaction in delinquent activities." Journal of Research in Crime and Delinquency 4: 43–62.

SHERIF, MUZAFER and CAROLYN W. SHERIF 1969 Social Psychology. New York: Harper and Row.

SHERIF, MUZAFER, B. JACK WHITE, and O. J. HARVEY 1955 "Status in experimentally produced groups." American Journal of Sociology 60: 370–379.

SHILS, EDWARD A. 1950 "Primary groups in the American Army." Pp. 16–25 in R. K. Merton and P. F. Lazarsfeld (eds.), Continuities in Social Research. Glencoe, Illinois: Free Press.

SHILS, EDWARD A. 1951 "The study of the primary group." Pp. 44–69 in D. Lerner and H. Lasswell (eds.), The Policy Sciences. Stanford, California: Stanford University Press.

SHILS, EDWARD A. and MORRIS JANOWITZ 1948 "Cohesion and disintegration of the Wehrmacht in World War II." Public Opinion Quarterly 12: 260–315.

SHIROM, ARIE 1976 "On some correlates of combat performance." Administrative Science Quarterly 21: 419–432.

SHORT, JAMES F., JR. and FRED L. STRODTBECK 1963 "The response of gang leaders to status threats: An observation on group process and delinquent behavior." American Journal of Sociology 68: 571–579.

SHURE, GERALD H., ROBERT J. MEEKER, and EARLE A. HANSFORD 1965 "The effectiveness of pacifist strategies in bargaining games." Journal of Conflict Resolution 9: 106–117.

SIITER, ROLAND 1974 "Encounter group." Pp. 97–98 in Encyclopedia of Sociology. Guilford, Connecticut: Dushkin.

SIMMEL, GEORG 1908 Soziologie, Untersuchungen Uber die Formen der Vergeselschaftung. Leipzig: Verlag van Duncker und Humboldt.

SIMMEL, GEORG 1950 Sociology of Georg Simmel trans. by K. H. Wolff. Glenco, Illinois: Free Press. (Reprinted with permission of Macmillan Publishing Co., Inc. Copyright 1950, renewed 1978 by The Free Press, a division of Macmillan.)

SIMON, JULIAN 1969 Basic Research Methods in Social Science. New York: Random House.

SIMPSON, R. L. 1959 "Vertical and horizontal communication in formal organizations." Administrative Science Quarterly 4: 188–196.

SINGER, JEROME E., LENORE S. RADLOFF, and DAVID M. WARK 1963 "Renegades, heretics, and changes in sentiment." Sociometry 26: 178–189.

SKINNER, B. F. 1938 The Behavior of Organisms. Englewood Cliffs, New Jersey: Prentice-Hall.

SKINNER, B. F. 1953 Science and Human Behavior. New York: Macmillan.

SLATER, PHILIP E. 1955 "Role differentiation in small groups." American Sociological Review 20: 300–310.

SNOW, C. E. 1927 "Research on industrial illumination: A discussion of the relation of illumination intensity to productive efficiency." The Tech Engineering News (November).

STEIN, DAVID D., JANE ALLYN HARDYCK, and M. BREWSTER SMITH 1965: "Race and belief: An open and shut case." Journal of Personality and Social Psychology 1: 281–289.

STEIN, MAURICE 1960 The Eclipse of Community. Princeton, New Jersey: Princeton University Press.

STEINER, IVAN D. 1972 Group Process and Productivity. New York: Academic Press.

STEINER, IVAN D. 1974 Task-Performing Groups. Morristown, New Jersey: General Learning Press.

STOGDILL, RALPH M. 1959 Individual Behavior and Group Achievement. New York: Oxford University Press.

STOGDILL, RALPH M. 1963 Team Achievement Under High Motivation. Business Research Monograph, Ohio State University.

STOGDILL, RALPH M. 1974 Handbook of Leadership: A Survey of Theory and Research. New York: Free Press. (Reprinted with permission of Macmillan Publishing Co., Inc. Copyright 1974 by The Free Press, a Division of Macmillan.)

STREET, DAVID 1965 "The inmate group in custodial and treatment settings." American Sociological Review 30: 40–55.

STRODTBECK, FRED L. 1951 "Husband-wife interaction over revealed differences." American Sociological Review 16: 468–473.

STRODTBECK, FRED L., RITA M. JAMES, and CHARLES HAWKINS 1957 "Social status in jury deliberations." American Sociological Review 22: 713–719.

STRUPP, H. H. and H. J. HAUSMAN 1953 "Some correlates of group productivity." American Psychologist 8: 443–444.

TAYLOR, FREDERICK W. 1903 "Group management." Transactions of the American Society of Mechanical Engineers 24: 1337–1480.

TAYLOR, FREDERICK W. 1911 The Principles of Scientific Management. New York: Harper and Row.

THIBAUT, JOHN W. and HAROLD H. KELLEY 1959 The Social Psychology of Groups. New York: Wiley.

THOMAS, EDWIN J. 1957 "Effects of facilitative role interdependence on group functioning." Human Relations 10: 347–366.

TOENNIES, FERDINAND 1961 "Gemeinschaft and Gesellschaft." Pp. 191–201 in T. Parsons et al. (eds.), Theories of Society. New York: Free Press.

TORRANCE, E. PAUL 1954 "Some consequences of power differences on decision making in permanent and temporary three-man groups." Research Studies, State College of Washington 22: 130–140.

TREIMAN, DONALD J. 1966 "Status discrepancy and prejudice." American Journal of Sociology 71: 651–664.

TREIMAN, DONALD J. 1970 "Reply to Geschwender." American Journal of Sociology 76: 162–167.

TROW, W. CLARK et al. 1950 "Psychology of group behavior: The class as a group." Journal of Educational Psychology 41: 322–338.

TUMIN, MELVIN 1967 Social Stratification. Englewood Cliffs, New Jersey: Prentice-Hall.

TURNER, C. E. 1933 "Test room studies in employee effectiveness." American Journal of Public Health 23: 577–584.

TURNER, RALPH H. 1973 "Unresponsiveness as a social sanction." Sociometry 36: 1–19

UESUGI, THOMAS K. and W. EDGAR VINACKE 1963 "Strategy in a feminine game." Sociometry 26: 75–88.

UNDERWOOD, JOHN 1969 "Three-part series on the desperate coach." Pp. 66–76; 20–27; 28–40 in Sports Illustrated (August 25, September 1, 8).

VAN ZELST, RAYMOND H. 1952 "Validation of a sociometric regrouping procedure." Journal of Abnormal and Social Psychology 47: 299–301.

VEIT, HANS 1970 "Some remarks upon the elementary interpersonal relations within ball game teams." Pp. 355–362 in G. S. Kenyon (ed.), Contemporary Psychology of Sport. Chicago: Athletic Institute.

VERBA, SIDNEY 1961 Small Groups and Political Behavior: A Study of Leadership. Princeton, New Jersey: Princeton University Press (Princeton Paperback 1972) pp. 155–209. (Reprinted by permission of Princeton University Press.)

VIDICH, ARTHUR J. and JOSEPH BENSMAN 1960 Small Town in Mass Society. New York: Doubleday.

VINACKE, W. EDGAR 1959 "Sex roles in a three-person game." Sociometry 22: 343–360.

VITELES, MORRIS S. 1954 Motivation and Morale in Industry. London: Staples.

VOGEL, EZRA F. and NORMAN W. BELL 1960 "The emotionally disturbed child as the family scapegoat." Pp. 382–397 in N. W. Bell and E. F. Vogel (eds.), The Family. New York: Free Press.

VOS, KOOS and WIM BRINKMAN 1967 "Success and cohesion in sports groups." Sociologische Gids 14: 30–40.

WAHRMAN, RALPH 1970 "High status, deviance, and sanctions." Sociometry 33: 485–504.

WEBER, MAX 1946 From Max Weber: Essays in Sociology. New York: Oxford University Press. Translated by Hans H. Gerth and C. Wright Mills.

WEBER, MAX 1947 The Theory of Social and Economic Organization. Glencoe, Illinois: Free Press. Translated by Talcott Parsons.

WEBB, EUGENE J. et al. 1966 Unobtrusive Measures: Nonreactive Research in the Social Sciences. Chicago: Rand McNally.

WHEATON, BLAIR 1974 "Interpersonal conflict and cohesiveness in dyadic relationships." Sociometry 37: 328–348.

WHITE, RALPH K. and RONALD LIPPITT 1960 Autocracy and Democracy. New York: Harper and Row.

WHITEHEAD, THOMAS N. 1938 The Industrial Worker. Cambridge, Massachusetts: Harvard University Press.

WHYTE, WILLIAM F. 1943 Street Corner Society. Chicago: The University of Chicago Press.

WHYTE, WILLIAM F. 1949 "The social structure of the restaurant." American Journal of Sociology 54: 302–310.

WHYTE, WILLIAM F. 1951 "Small groups and large organizations." Pp. 297–312 in J. R. Rohrer and M. Sherif (eds.), Social Psychology at the Crossroads. New York: Harper and Row.

WHYTE, WILLIAM F. 1955 Street Corner Society, 2nd ed. Chicago: The University of Chicago Press.

WILLERMAN, BEN and L. SWANSON 1952 "An ecological determinant of differential amounts of sociometric choices within college sororities." Sociometry 15: 326–329.

WILLIS, RICHARD H. 1965 "Conformity, independence, and anti-conformity." Human Relations 18: 373–388.

WILSON, EVERETT K. 1971 Sociology: Rules, Roles, and Relationships, rev. ed. Homewood, Illinois: Dorsey.

WOLFE, DONALD M. 1959 "Power and authority in the family." Pp. 99–107 in D. Cartwright (ed.), Studies in Social Power. Ann Arbor, Michigan: Institute for Social Research.

WRONG, DENNIS H. 1968 "Some problems in defining social power." American Journal of Sociology 73: 673–681.

WYER, ROBERT S., JR. 1966 "Effects of incentive to perform well, group attraction, and group acceptance on conformity in a judgmental task." Journal of Personality and Social Psychology 4: 21–26.

ZALEZNIK, ABRAHAM, C. R. CHRISTENSEN, and F. J. ROETHLISBERGER 1958 The Motivation, Productivity, and Satisfaction of Workers. Cambridge, Massachusetts: Harvard University Press.

ZANDER, ALVIN 1974 "Productivity and group success: team spirit vs. the individual achiever." Psychology Today (November): 64–68.

ZANDER, ALVIN 1977 Groups at Work. San Francisco: Jossey-Bass.

ZANDER, ALVIN and A. R. COHEN 1955 "Attributed social power and group acceptance: a classroom experimental demonstration." Journal of Abnormal and Social Psychology 51: 490–492.

ZANDER, ALVIN and ARNOLD HAVELIN 1960 "Social comparison and interpersonal attraction." Human Relations 13: 21–32.

ZELDITCH, MORRIS, Jr. *et al.* 1970 "Equitable comparisons." Pacific Sociological Review 13: 19–26.

ZELDITCH MORRIS, JR. and BO ANDERSON 1966 "On the balance of a set of ranks." Ch. 11 in J. Berger, M. Zelditch, Jr., and B. Anderson (eds.), Sociological Theories in Progress, Vol. 1. Boston: Houghton-Mifflin.

ZILLER, ROBERT C. 1957 "Group size: A determinant of the quality and stability of group decisions." Sociometry 20: 165–173.

ZILLER, ROBERT C. and RALPH V. EXLINE 1958 "Some consequences of age heterogeneity in decision-making groups." Sociometry 21: 198–211.

Index